Financial Globalization

Financial Globalization

Growth, Integration, Innovation and Crisis

Dilip K. Das

First published 2010 by
PALGRAVE MACMILLAN

Palgrave Macmillan in the UK is an imprint of Macmillan Publishers Limited, registered in England, company number 785998, of Houndmills, Basingstoke, Hampshire RG21 6XS.

Palgrave Macmillan in the US is a division of St Martin's Press LLC, 175 Fifth Avenue, New York, NY 10010.

Palgrave Macmillan is the global academic imprint of the above companies and has companies and representatives throughout the world.

Palgrave® and Macmillan® are registered trademarks in the United States, the United Kingdom, Europe and other countries.

ISBN-13: 978–0–230–27860–8 hardback

This book is printed on paper suitable for recycling and made from fully managed and sustained forest sources. Logging, pulping and manufacturing processes are expected to conform to the environmental regulations of the country of origin.

A catalogue record for this book is available from the British Library.

A catalog record for this book is available from the Library of Congress.

10   9   8   7   6   5   4   3   2   1
19   18   17   16   15   14   13   12   11   10

Printed and bound in Great Britain by
CPI Antony Rowe, Chippenham and Eastbourne

To Vasanti,
who taught me that only in the mysterious equations of
love are logic and reason found.

Contents

List of Tables and Figure

Tables

Figure

Preface

Globalization, which encompasses financial globalization, is an ancient concept and phenomenon. Its history extends through the periods of Babylonian and Persian empires in Mesopotamia and subsequently through ancient Greece and the imperial Roman empire. It is particularly well chronicled since the Renaissance period. Over this extended stretch of time, globalization has had its periods of expansion and decline, growth and disintegration. A little over a century ago, the global economy witnessed a period characterized by the freest trans-border flows of merchandise and capital. It facilitated rising living standards in Western Europe and North America. The twentieth century then entered a period of abrupt disruptions and prolonged deglobalization. Since then, an unprecedented revival of global economic and financial integration has taken place.

Bolstered by technological advancements and the adoption of a cooperative stance in international economic policies, another phase of globalization began in the post-World War II era. It was supported by a reduction in barriers to cross-border trade and financial flows. It succeeded in accelerating the growth rate of world output and improving living standards in a much wider part of the globe than the first globalization epoch, which occurred over a century ago. New countries and country groups came forth to integrate into the global economy. They were able to reduce abject poverty and expanded the size of their middle classes. Little wonder that globalization, including financial globalization, became one of the defining academic issues of our period, one having a great deal of policy relevance as well.

The significance of financial globalization abruptly increased as a result of the current global financial crisis and so-called Great Recession, which was sparked by the sub-prime mortgage debacle in the United Kingdom (UK) and United States (US). The crisis erupted in the autumn of 2007. Following the failure of Northern Rock in September 2007, the world economy experienced what is arguably its most serious financial crisis since the Great Depression, a crisis that brusquely stopped three decades of expansion in the international capital markets. The crisis, and a nascent recovery in late 2009 and early 2010, altered the economic and financial landscape in numerous fundamental ways. This was the period when the global economy was passing through a period of profound transformation.

Progressively increasing cross-border trade in financial assets gives rise to what is called financial globalization. This is the phenomenon of rising trans-border financial flows through various channels, in effect integrating the financial markets into a global whole. Global financial integration can lead to several macroeconomic benefits, which fragmented capital markets cannot possibly reap. One measure of a country's financial integration is its gross external assets and liabilities relative to its GDP. This measure of global financial integration portends to the fact that it has increased dramatically over the past three decades. A new phase of limited or partial financial globalization began during the early post-World War-II period. As distinct from that, the contemporary wave of financial globalization got started in the 1980s and accelerated in the 1990s – albeit there is disagreement over the exact time point.

One idiosyncratic feature of the contemporary phase of financial globalization is that it made maximum progress in the advanced industrial economies, with the emerging-market and developing economies experiencing relatively more moderate increases in their external stock positions. That said, the emerging-market economies were way ahead of the other developing economies in this regard. These diverging trends were essentially caused by differences in capital control regimes, financial openness, degrees of institutional quality and domestic financial market developments. The other persistent factors included political, geographical and historical linkages that helped explain the degree of financial openness among countries.

The importance of financial globalization as a pragmatic macroeconomic policy measure has been high. This issue has generated protracted and nuanced academic debate. Some academics support it as being a magic bullet for spurring growth, while others decry it as a redundant unmanageable risk. The intensity of academic and policy discussions and deliberations on financial globalization testifies to its importance. It is the focus of comprehensive research efforts in the world of higher education, with numerous research centers zeroing in on the examination and analysis of financial globalization as well as the other associated and supplementary issues. Consequently, there has been an explosion of erudite research in this area. Various research programs have taken disparate paths, with their conclusions frequently at odds with each other. Merely stating that financial globalization is good or bad is simplistic. It is both. While it has been a benign and welfare-enhancing force under certain sets of circumstances, it is a widely acknowledged fact that financial globalization has an economically and socially detrimental downside. Therefore it warrants a more nuanced perspective. Researchers and analysts are known to hold starkly opposite views on financial globalization. Positions espoused by noted scholars like Larry Summers and Stanley Fischer are diametrically opposite to those held by Joseph Stiglitz and Dani Rodrik. The debates on financial globalization were, and continue to be, starkly polarized.

Past episodes of financial globalization were all success stories for a while, contributing to financial stability and supporting high rates of economic growth in the globalizing economies as well as the global economy. Yet after going full throttle for a few years, they all sputtered into crises. Did something like that not occur during the current period and to the present episode of financial globalization? With some interruptions, the global economy enjoyed almost three decades of financial integration, rapid growth and multilateral trade expansion. By the third quarter of 2008, the effect of the sub-prime mortgage debacle in the US began to unfurl into other financial markets and drove the global economy to the brink of a severe financial crisis. The gravity of the impact of the crisis on the global economy can be calculated from the fact that out of 182 reporting countries to the International Monetary Fund (IMF), 78 were projected to record negative growth rate in 2009.

Contagions and crises are the infamous stumbling blocks engendered by financial globalization. The macroeconomic, currency and financial crises of 1982 and those of the 1990s testify to the fact that financial globalization is not a win-win game. It can potentially lead to volatility, serious economic and financial disorder and high cost in terms of bank failures, corporate bankruptcies, stock market turbulence, depletion of foreign exchange reserves, currency depreciations and increased fiscal burden. A unique characteristic of globalized financial market is "sudden stop", or even reversal, of capital flows when market perception regarding the creditworthiness of the borrowing economy changes. The crises of the 1990s established this fact beyond doubt. Therefore, one needs to realize that if integrated global financial markets have virtues, they also have flaws. In a generalized sense this argument can be restated: if free markets provide the advantages of efficient resource allocation, they also have their limitations. What is interesting in this regard is that some of the most recent research has concluded that more volatility tends to deepen domestic financial markets and eventually underpins growth rate in the recipient economy.[1]

Recent experience shows that an agonizing aspect of financial globalization is that large cross-border capital inflows in an economy can turn into large capital outflows without any major mishap. In July 1997 in Thailand, no major financial or economic unforeseen event had occurred to validate the precipitation of a serious crisis. Second, in the recent past contagions were seen spreading to economies that were unrelated. Third, financial crises were found to have caused recessions that were so serious that it was difficult to say that the system was functioning.

Undoubtedly, financial globalization also has a welfare-enhancing munificent facet. One advantage of financial globalization for a country that has been recording high return to domestic investment is that it is able to borrow from the global capital market and supplement its rate of investment. The emerging-market economies (EMEs) succeeded in doing so. They were able to finance their investment more cheaply compared to domestic savings. Second, the advanced industrial economies which make a lot of global investment can earn higher rates of return and diversify risk by investing in the EMEs, which results in tangibly higher wealth effect. Third, allowing foreign financial institutions to operate in domestic markets improves the level of efficiency of domestic financial institutions. Often overregulated and inefficient domestic banks learn the value of conducting disciplined operations and perform in a more professional manner. Fourthly, governments learn the value of market discipline and know that there is cost to policy mistakes and lack of macroeconomic policy discipline.

A relatively newer development in financial globalization was the large and persistent current account deficits in the US. To finance this deficit, the US has been gobbling down massive savings from the economies that had capital account surpluses. These borrowing grew in volume from the late 1990s. The cumulative borrowings of the US took on colossal proportions. At the end of the first quarter of 2009, the official national debt figure for the US had crossed $11 trillion, which was close to the US GDP of $14.2 trillion. This was a period of rapid financial globalization, with surplus and deficit countries both investing a record fraction of their savings abroad. The US economy has been borrowing more than 80 percent of the external financing provided by countries having surplus saving. The downside of these capital flows was progressively increasing financial and payments imbalances in the global economy, which were regarded as potentially destabilizing. The IMF repeatedly forewarned about their possible disastrous effect in its flagship publication on the global economy, *World Economic Outlook*. Also, financial dealings of new actors like the sovereign-wealth funds (SWFs) became increasingly important. Such new events and actors are covered in the chapters that follow.

This book essentially dwells on escalating financial globalization during the contemporary period by way of trans-border financial flows, its current trends, the activities of the new financial players in the global capital markets and the global financial crisis of 2007–09. It also examines contemporary financial integration influencing growth and other macroeconomic variables. It does not leave out the recent financial innovations, like securitization, which are now being blamed for sparking the crisis and the recession. That said, this book does not propound a defined philosophy or support a certain thematic message regarding financial globalization.

Economic and financial forces have been the principal drivers of contemporary global financial integration, even if politics has also played an important role. In the process of presenting a complete picture of the contemporary phase of financial globalization, throughout this book I try to examine under what circumstances financial globalization can be welfare-enhancing and lead to rapid economic growth. That is, I try to address the issue of policy structure needed for a positive impact of financial globalization to overwhelm its negative ramifications. The current financial crisis terminated the post-1980 benign environment in the global financial markets and the so-called Great Moderation. I study the current financial crisis and its implications from various angles.

The book takes an objective view and delves into the constructive and favorable side as well as adverse and unfavorable side of the process of financial globalization. The deficiencies and imperfections have not been overlooked. It covers the global financial markets and economy through various channels of multilateral financial flows and includes the newly emerging trends, like the so-called "up-hill" flow of capital, from the low-income non-industrialized to the high-income industrialized countries.

My aspiration is to provide students, business leaders and policy mandarins around the world with a fact base to better comprehend one of the most important transformations shaping the contours of the global economy. I also aspire to bring out that, notwithstanding the current financial crisis and recession, the contemporary phase of financial globalization is a major systemic economic phenomenon. While disruptive in the short term for some economies, it is,on balance, a benevolent and positive force of historic dimension.

Dilip K. Das
Toronto

Acknowledgements

I take this opportunity to thank my son, Siddharth, for providing prompt and efficient research assistance and three anonymous referees for providing detailed comments on the manuscript. They were as helpful as they were constructive. I am grateful to Lisa von Fircks, Senior Commissioning Editor of Palgrave Macmillan Ltd, for handling the publication and production process of this book in an exceedingly efficient manner. I have been in the business of researching, writing and publishing for over three decades now. I found her level of efficiency an absolutely rare commodity in the publishing industry. I owe profound thanks to Renee Takken for the care and attention she poured into editing this book. Joel Jones is another person who deserves my grateful thanks. Hélène Côté provided first-rate assistance in research; her humor was as supportive as her library research endeavors. To nurture excellence in any area of human endeavor, credit should be given where it is deserved. One neither needs a sword nor a gun to kill excellence in any society. Ignore and it will wilt away.

Indubitably, the largest debt I owe is to my wife, Vasanti, for managing the life around me and leaving me to do the researching and writing. Dawn-to-dusk days of non-stop working would not have been feasible without her indefatigable support. She also meticulously read the first drafts and ruthlessly hunted down faulty syntax and mixed metaphors.

About the Author

Professor Dilip K. Das has been associated with several prestigious business schools around the globe, including the European Institute of Business Administration (INSEAD), Fontainebleau, France; the ESSEC, Paris; the Graduate School of Business, University of Sydney; the Australian National University, Canberra; and the Webster University, Geneva. He also was Professor and Area Chairman at the Indian Institute of Management, Lucknow, India, and EXIM Bank Distinguished Chair Professor in the International Management Institute, New Delhi. The areas of his expertise include international finance and banking, international trade and WTO-related issues, international business and strategy and the Asian economy, including the Chinese and Japanese economies. His most recent interest is globalization and the global business environment.

Professor Das has worked as a consultant for several international organizations, such as USAID, the World Bank, and the World Commission on Development and Environment in Geneva. He has organized 13 large international conferences over the last ten years. He is presently a Toronto-based consultant to international organizations.

He has an immense appetite for research. He has written extensively and published widely. He is an author or editor of 27 books. The last two books he authored were entitled *The Doha Round of Multilateral Trade Negotiations: Arduous Issues and Strategic Responses* (Palgrave Macmillan, 2005) and *The Chinese Economic Renaissance: Apocalypse or Cornucopia* (Palgrave Macmillan, 2008). The latter has been translated into Mandarin for the Chinese market. He has contributed over 90 articles to professional journals of international repute, 89 of his papers have appeared in prestigious research and working paper series and 22 of them have also been posted on well-regarded websites of business schools and universities.

He was educated at St John's College, Agra, India, where he took his BA and MA (Economics) degrees. He went on to study at the Institut Universitaire de Hautes Etudes Internationales, the University of Geneva, Switzerland, where he did his M.Phil. and Ph.D. in international economics. He is fluent in French. His language skills include basic Mandarin and Japanese.

Note

1. See papers presented during the conference organized by the International Monetary Fund, Washington. DC, on *The New Perspectives on Financial Globalization* on Friday, 27 April 2007. Presentation made by Kristin Forbes was particularly relevant.

1
The Evolution and Unfolding of Financial Globalization

1. Economic and financial globalization

The objective of this chapter is to elucidate the evolution, spread and unfolding of global integration, in particular financial globalization, since the mid-nineteenth century. While the primary focus is financial globalization, this cannot be totally separated from economic globalization. This chapter provides a preamble to the debate and essentially delves into the principal characteristic features of financial integration and related global economic developments. Unquestionably, global economic integration, in particular financial globalization, made impressive strides during the pre-World War I period and it has been extensively covered in the globalization literature. However, economic and financial globalization in the contemporary period for the most part surpassed that in the preceding periods by a sizeable margin.

Neither the concept nor the phenomenon of economic or financial globalization can be considered as novel.[1] The history of the evolution and globalization of finance stretches back over an extended period, ranging from its recorded origin in the villages of Mesopotamia 5,000 years ago to sparkling numbers on foreign exchange screens in the financial markets of today.[2] The global economy has undergone several waves of rapid and sluggish globalization as well as deglobalization. As for the contemporary phase of globalization, many economic historians believe that it kicked off around 1980, although Mundell (2000) disagreed.

Progressively increasing cross-border trade in financial assets gives rise to what is called financial globalization. It is the phenomenon of rising trans-border financial flows through various channels, that in effect integrates the financial markets into a global whole. During the 1990s the concept of globalization acquired a great deal of currency, relevance, acceptance and emotive force. Globalization became a defining economic mega-trend. With that financial globalization consolidated, strengthened and became more innovative. Taken as a whole, financial globalization also accelerated in the post-1990 period and proliferated in the global economy. The structure of global financial markets underwent marked transformation in the post-1990 era.

A salient characteristic of the current phase of financial globalization is the internationalization of financial services. In addition, financial transactions and securitization became increasingly innovative, affecting both domestic financial markets and the global. New financial innovations of this period, which essentially took place in the US, helped accelerate financial globalization. Digitalization and computerization of the global financial sector went a long way in disseminating these innovations. They were subsequently excoriated for being instrumental in setting off the global financial crisis of 2007–09, the severity of which was frequently compared to that of the Great Depression.[3] In the first half of 2009 the global economy was in recession and many systemically important economies had their banking and financial systems in utter disarray. Financial assets prices crashed and in many countries real asset prices also collapsed (Highfill, 2009). The crisis and recession were responsible for the current trend in financial deglobalization. Crises of this dimension are vigorous and authoritative events and have momentous impact over the global economy and finance. The current one is shifting financial tectonic plates in the global economy. The crisis and nascent recovery that began in later 2009 altered the economic and financial landscape of the global economy in numerous ways.

From an economic point of view, globalization represents a process of increasing international division of labor on the one hand and growing functional integration of national economies through trade in goods and services, cross-border corporate investment and capital flows on the other. Experiences of the post-World War II period demonstrate that there is serendipity in globalization. Notable in this regard is the performance of the emerging-market economies (EMEs).[4] This group of economies discernibly and measurably benefited from globalization during the preceding three decades (Chapter 4). The ascent of East Asian and the four BRIC (Brazil, Russia, India, China) economies was a prominent global economic event of the contemporary period.[5] In particular, China's globalization and vertiginous growth – and move to the center of the global economic stage – are developments of enormous relevance and consequence (Das, 2008a). During the early phase of the

2007–09 financial crisis expectations were that China and the other three BRIC economies would function as a locomotive of global growth and pick up the slack. Subsequently, as the crisis grew more severe, these expectations were belied.

Globalization did result in economic and financial convergence. Evidence of a certain number of cases of convergence exists for the late nineteenth century and the latter half of twentieth century (Williamson, 1996).[6] However, none of the periods of globalization resulted in universal convergence. Interesting parallels between the financial globalization of the late nineteenth and the late twentieth centuries are easy to recognize. Over the 1850–1914 period the erstwhile developed economies, like Britain, France and Germany, were financing infrastructure as well as extractive industries and plantation sectors in the underdeveloped world and in the so-called New World economies (Section 2.4). This group of economies included Australia, Argentina, Brazil, Canada and the US. In comparison, since 1990 the East Asian economies, in particular China, were busy financing consumption in the high-income industrial economies like the US. The other three high-borrowing debtor countries were Britain, Ireland and Spain (Section 6.1).

1.1 Global capital flows and their implications

Economic theory posits that net capital flows should be from the high-income industrial economies to the have-not economies. Within the neoclassical paradigm, capital flows from where it is to any place where it is not and therefore its marginal product is higher. This results in more efficient allocation of capital. The outcome of such a free flow of capital across national borders would be higher global welfare. Economic theory stipulates that financial globalization confers a number of potential benefits. As trans-border capital flows through various channels increase, economies tend to progressively integrate globally. They operate as a means of financial globalization. The financial structures of both capital exporting and those of host economies as well as the world of capital and finance markets *pari passu* tend to change. One of the most significant implications of financial globalization is the extremely rapid expansion of international liquidity. There has been an enormous increase in liquid assets available to participants in the global capital markets.

A few decades ago, when the contemporary phase of financial globalization was in its formative phase, a businessperson was restricted to borrowing from her domestic market. For the most part, domestic financial markets were where economic agents went for their financial transactions. This is no longer the case. If she operates in an EME, which by definition is relatively more liberal to capital movements and has access to the private global capital markets, her business firm can exploit and benefit from financial globalization. Several options are presently open to her. For instance, she can choose between issuing stocks and bonds in the domestic or foreign financial markets. She can reduce her cost of capital if foreign currency loans are available on more attractive terms than domestic loans.

A likely option for this entrepreneur could be selling equity at foreign bourses, which are far more liquid than the domestic ones. A new liquid channel for capital is not the only advantage of financial globalization. The loans can be hedged by using a variety of formerly unknown financial products. The global financial markets are vastly more accessible today than they were two decades ago. In addition, global financial markets offer much superior risk management opportunities now than they did in the recent past.

Financial globalization leads to several primary and beneficial macroeconomic and microeconomic outcomes. On the macroeconomic side, a creditworthy developing economy that has access to the private global capital markets can improve its investment level and allocation of funds to potentially productive projects, in the process increasing its total factor productivity (TFP), and thereby underpin (gross domestic product) GDP growth. One of the direct effects of financial globalization is imposing discipline over the developing country governments, making them upgrade and fine-tune macroeconomic policymaking, and adopt pro-growth reforms and promote a market-friendly business ambiance. This would not only advance income, enhancing prospects across the board, but also alleviate poverty. Thus, financial globalization can potentially lead to pro-poor growth. On the microeconomic side, it strengthens corporate governance in the financial institutions. The decision makers compete for the most efficient and productive utilization of financial resources that they are managing.

Although some of the above-mentioned benefits did materialize, they did not do so universally. In addition, perceptive and forward thinking requires that the downside of financial globalization not be ignored. It has frequently been found culpable of creating serious crisis situations in countries and regions as well as globally. Financial globalization put a serious question mark over the market mechanism. The sub-prime mortgage crisis in the US, that was triggered by a dramatic rise in mortgage defaulting in 2006 and 2007, in a short time span developed into the first global financial crisis of the twenty-first century, leading to a global recession (Felton and Reinhart, 2008).[7]

1.2 A matter of definition

Although the term globalization has gained currency recently, it is an ancient phenomenon and concept. It has inspired different kinds of analyses and research in the academe. They have traversed in different directions and engendered a rich mosaic of concepts, diagnoses and theories. Recent literature on globalization is by any measure enormous. Academics from different disciplines focus on different kinds of globalizations. In this multifaceted concept, economic and financial globalizations are two of the most important elements.[8] Put plainly, globalization unleashes market forces and facilitates Adam Smith's invisible hand to operate globally. It eradicates market barriers, eliminates countervailing pressures from governments and unleashes competitive forces.

A functional definition of financial globalization is the integration of the domestic financial system of an economy with the global financial markets and institutions. It entails increasing global linkages through trans-border financial flows. It implies liberalization of international transactions in financial instruments by a large number of integrating economies. Enabling the framework of financial globalization essentially entails the liberalization and deregulation of the domestic financial and banking sector as well as the liberalization of the capital account, which implies a free flow of funds in and out of a country's economy.

Financial integration occurs when liberalized economies experience an increase in cross-border capital movement and make widespread use of international financial intermediaries. This process strengthens an individual country's links to global capital markets. In a globalized financial environment domestic lenders and borrowers participate in the global markets and utilize global financial intermediaries for borrowing and lending. The resulting trans-border capital flows tend to integrate the domestic and global financial markets, institutions and systems.[9]

The advanced industrial economies are the most active participants in the global financial markets and also the most financially globalized. This is due to the fact that, first, participation of some groups of developing economies has grown and became substantial.

Secondly, one of the most significant aspects of financial globalization is rapid growth of international liquidity. There has been an enormous increase in liquid assets available to global market participants. Thirdly, a notable feature is the recent transformation in the borrowing and lending groups of countries. Some large borrowers of the past have turned into the new lenders of massive amounts of capital. An overarching feature is the flow of capital from the have-not, low-income countries to the high-income industrial countries. Fourthly, new players, like the sovereign-wealth funds (SWF), mutual funds and hedge funds have emerged onto the global financial stage. These institutions are awash with liquid resources and are the new financial heavyweights that are changing the structure and character of global capital and financial markets as well as capital movements (Das, 2008b; MGI, 2008).

1.3 Measures of financial globalization

Stock and flow measures of external assets can provide a good quantitative idea of the degree of financial globalization or financial integration. That is, the size of gross stocks (assets plus liabilities) of external finance can be one kind of measure, while the second can be the potential for net (assets minus liabilities) flows, or the difference in saving and investment flows. Thus, the first concept is the measure of stocks while the second is of flows. Enhancing financial globalization or financial integration should logically lead to the absence of arbitrage opportunities between returns on assets in different countries, so this can provide a third measure of financial globalization. The measures based on these premises can be divided into three broad categories:

(i) Quantity-based measure: It is the most widely applicable and accepted measure. It is a gross measure, therefore, the sum of external assets and liabilities, expressed as a proportion of the GDP (Lane and Milesi-Ferretti, 2007).

(ii) Saving-investment correlation: In an autarky, investment must equal domestic savings, but the two can differ in an economy with access to global capital markets. Therefore, saving-investment correlations have been utilized to measure the extent of financial globalization. The measure of the size of net financial flow is also closely related to this. The current account surplus is the difference between saving and investment. However, this measure has a drawback. The Feldstein and Horioka puzzle posited that saving and investment are highly correlated even for groups of countries that have access to global capital markets.

(iii) Price-based indices: In a financially integrated global economy no unexploited opportunities of arbitrage should be available in trade and financial markets. Therefore, prospective returns on financial instruments in different countries should be 'a natural gauge of the extent of international financial integration' (IMF, 2008a, p. 5). A good example of these financial instruments is covered or uncovered interest rate parities. There are several problems hampering the measurement and utilization of price-based indices. Cross-country differences in risk and liquidity premia is one of the principal problematic issues.

2. Financial globalization: The preceding periods

Economic globalization has continued since ancient times. Although scholarly academic research in this area is plentifully available, I shall briefly mention the historical developments of the ancient periods.

2.1 Ancient periods

Several erudite accounts of financial globalization over the nineteenth and twentieth centuries are available in literature,[10] however, it is essential and relevant to present a succinct account of it here. The Arab conquests of the seventh and early eighth centuries united the Mediterranean world of Rome and its ancient empire with Mesopotamia and Iran. They also united the Byzantine possessions of Egypt, Syria, Palestine and North Africa (Elliott and Lemert, 2009). This was the Islamic golden age and an example of ancient globalizm, when traders successfully established a rudimentary form of global economy. Trade in goods and migration of people took place freely. Exchanges of both ideas and knowledge were also common.

Two-way flows of ideas and knowledge took place between the east and west 'in one vast integrated space united by Islam and Arabic language' (Findlay and O'Rourke, 2007, p. 48). The Islamic golden age reached its peak during the Mongol Empire of Genghis Khan and Kublai Khan. This epoch witnessed globalization of crops, commerce, knowledge and technology. The Mongol Empire, one of the largest continuous empires in history, was responsible for a strong wave of economic globalization.[11] Marco Polo (1254–1324), the most famous traveler of the Silk Road, was a veritable trading entrepreneur. He was the most famous traveler and trader of his period. He found new products and developed markets for them, became a confidant of Kublai Khan and provided detailed accounts of the economy of the Mongol Empire, which, by his account, was prosperous.

The Ming Dynasty (1368–1644 AD) of China, the last dynasty ruled by ethnic Hans, played an important role in economic globalization. It was not only neighboring countries that had trade and tribute-paying relations with China during this period. Distant European countries like Portugal, Spain and Holland had active commercial ties. Abu-Lughod (1989) provided comprehensive accounts of the voyages of the Ming Dynasty admiral Cheng Ho (or Zheng He) until the early decades of the fifteenth century. The two voyages of discovery by Christopher Columbus and Vasco da Gama, at the end of the fifteenth century, expanded trade and economic ties over large distances. These voyages were made possible by advances in European ship-building technology and in the science of navigation. They have an eminent place in the history of globalization.

2.2 Contemporary period: The first era of globalization

Beginning around mid-nineteenth century – until the outbreak of World War I – economic and financial integration of the global economy took place at an unprecedented pace. Economic historians regard it as the 'first era of globalization' (Aizenman et al., 2007, p. 657). The years between 1870–1914 represented 'the high water mark of the 19th century globalization' (Daudin et al., 2008, p. 2). This period is known for an unparalleled free flow of goods, capital, technology and ideas across international borders. It is known particularly for large scale global migration. Global economy operated during this period under the gold standard monetary regime, which is discussed below (Section 2.3). Integration of the global capital market made impressive progress during the first era of globalization (Section 2.4).[12] Financial globalization of this era was impressive by any measure. There were few restrictions on cross-border financial flows. More than 60 governments raised capital by floating bonds in London, Paris and Berlin. Shares of business firms from almost all continents and sectors were listed on European exchanges. London was the largest and leading financial center.

The intellectual, philosophical and political climate of this period supported the creation of an overarching liberal world order. This change in the global policy mindset was more significant than the adoption of the gold standard *per se*. There was little government intervention in the markets of the principal economies of this period. Private financial and commercial activities operated more or less unhindered and both skilled and unskilled labor moved around the globe almost uninterrupted. Although this can be regarded as an era of economic *laissez-faire*, some tariff barriers and inconsequential regulations on migration did exist. The pervasive economic freedom and liberalization of the late nineteenth and early twentieth centuries seems remarkable from the perspective of twenty-first century achievements.

2.3 Gold standard monetary regime

Under the gold standard monetary regime countries voluntarily backed their money with gold at a fixed rate of exchange. The 1870s were the formative period of this classical gold standard. During the 1880s a good number of countries adopted gold standard. In 1890, this number was very high. World War I had destroyed the global financial system. Governments radically altered exchange rates and price levels and also imposed exchange controls. European countries tried to re-peg their currencies to gold. After 1925, a fleeting gold-exchange standard was established. However, this monetary regime began disintegrating in 1931 (Section 2.6).

The classical gold standard monetary regime made a momentous contribution to the economic and financial globalization of this period. Under this monetary regime the value of a national currency was determined in a fixed weight of gold. To all appearances this was a simple act. It had broad and far-reaching implications for the domestic and global economy. The fixed exchange rate provided a stable and credible monetary regime. It proved to be a functional and disciplining device. By adopting gold standard countries gave their tacit approval to playing by 'the rule of the game', which gave gold (the basic monetary asset) unrestricted movement. Furthermore, currency notes were freely convertible into specie and vice versa.

The large trading nations of this period swiftly adopted the gold standard and its orbit expanded to become near universal. This was the era of *Pax Britannica*. Near universal acceptance of the gold standard was made possible due to British leadership. The gold standard supplanted the silver and bimetallic standards that had operated before the dawning of the gold standard. It is widely acknowledged that during the pre-1914 period, 'gold standard orthodoxy conferred credibility and was a *sine qua non* for access to global capital markets on favorable terms' (Obstfeld and Taylor, 2003, p. 241).

The Bank of England played a crucial role in promoting the gold standard. Its credible commitment to convertibility gave investors confidence to move funds globally rather than worry about gold movements. Financial crises during the gold standard era had a different effect on economies than the ones today. During a crisis gold inflows increased in the crisis-stricken country. Although a crisis would lead to a fall in the prices of the domestic assets, market participants expected both exchange rate and asset prices to eventually return to the pre-crisis levels. It was reasonable because of governments' commitment to the gold standard. This caused a boost in the inward movement of gold (Steil, 2006).

The years 1880–1913 were the classical gold standard period, when a global fixed exchange rate system reigned. The resulting low exchange rate volatility made business more fluid and less costly for traders and financiers who operated globally. At the turn of the twentieth century this gold standard monetary regime was functioning smoothly and facilitated expansion of trade, payments and capital movements. The classical gold standard contributed to the smooth equilibrium of balances-of-payments in the global economy. They were kept in equilibrium at fixed exchange rates by an adjustment mechanism that functioned with 'a high degree of automaticity' (Mundell, 2000, p. 328). This was a period of economic liberalizm and little regulation. Consequently, the first global marketplace in goods and capital came into being. Obstfeld and Taylor (2005, p. 123) called it 'an era of undisputed liberalism and virtual *laissez-faire*'. Although global capital markets were established at this point, participation in them was far from global.

The gold standard conferred a 'seal of approval'[13] in the sovereign bond market. Conversely, the gold standard of the interwar era was somewhat less reliable than that of the pre-1914 period. How much less reliable remains a contentious point. By comparing bond spreads during the pre-1914 and interwar periods, Bordo et al. (1999b) concluded that the gold standard still remained a 'seal of approval' when a country returned to its pre-war exchange parity with gold. This return to the gold standard resulted in a lowering of bond spreads for this country. During the late nineteenth and early twentieth century, the gold standard linked every country in the world to a common and stable monetary order. This indisputably contributed to the global economic and financial integration of this period.

The gold standard was established with relative ease. By 1910, all the important economies had accepted it. Driven by increasing returns, this institutional device was readily adopted by a growing number of countries during the 1890s and early 1900s. How this capital market developed 'and the convergence by many different nations on a single monetary standard is well known, and it exhibits all of the "networked externality" properties' (Frieden, 2007, p. 126). Global capital markets came into being, with London developing as the most important financial center of this era (Section 2.2). Amsterdam, Berlin, Paris and New York also developed into significant financial centers. Berlin and Paris rivaled London's position in sovereign loans. In addition, Buenos Aires, Melbourne, Mexico City and Rio de Janeiro developed as smaller financial centers. In this liberal global policy atmosphere, the capital market operated in an unfettered manner. There were no transaction fees nor any restrictions on trans-border movements of financial assets (Schularick, 2006).

Large global movements of capital occurred during this era. The so-called 'open economy trilemma'[14] (dealt with in Section 2.5) was resolved in the gold standard era by opting for a fixed exchange rate and free capital mobility, often at the expense of domestic macroeconomic health. Contrary to what we observe now, short-term capital movements during this period of financial globalization played a highly stabilizing role. Economies financed their trade deficits through short-term capital inflows stimulated by modest rises in short-term interest rates. Britain became the largest capital exporter, exporting almost half of its total domestic savings by 1914. At this point, capital outflows from Britain reached 9 percent of GDP. France, Germany and the Netherlands also exported a high percentage of their capital – almost as much as Britain. Capital importing countries of the so-called New World had large current account deficits, which hovered around 10 percent of their GDP.

2.4 Proliferation of financial globalization

Global capital markets during the nineteenth century – until 1914 – were considered essentially benign and capital market integration advanced in an impressive manner. As stated above (Section 1.1), in keeping with the classical economic principles, the role of the governments was restricted to facilitating their operations and to that end providing an infrastructural framework. Governments did not believe that regulating and controlling financial market operations was their métier. There was little in the way of supranational institutional structure. The principal systemic features that governments did implement were limited to the gold standard monetary regime and the national central banking authorities.

Maritime transport innovations of this period, namely steel hull ships, steam propulsion and screw propellers, had ushered in a flourishing transport revolution. As these ships replaced the earlier wooden ones, the cost of transporting goods plummeted markedly, speed increased several times over and safety in travel improved remarkably. Also, risk in trans-Atlantic travel reduced substantially. These improvements in the transport technology continued into the twentieth century.[15]

This steady decline in the cost of transportation took place alongside another important development, declining tariff rates. Consequently both international trade and the number and variety of traded products expanded enormously in a short time span. Toward the end of the nineteenth century, multilateral trade expanded at a rapid rate – 3.5 percent annually. This was significantly higher than the growth rate of world output that was 2.7 percent per annum. Exports, as a proportion of world output, peaked in 1913; this level was not surpassed until 1970. Also, the pace of migration during this period was high. Decadal outward migration rate during the 1880s, 1890s and 1990s was estimated at between 5 and 7 percent of the population in several European economies. Inward migration ranged from 4 to 9 percent of the population in the US. The proportion of inward migration was higher in other New World countries (Masson, 2001).

The European economies that had made notable progress in post-industrial-revolution industrialization were the prosperous economies of this period. They turned into the bankers of the world during the latter half of the nineteenth century and the early twentieth century. The New World economies had easy access to European capital and they prospered with its inflows. Also, there was smaller but significant flow of European capital to the economies of South, Central and Eastern Europe. Edelstein (2004) estimated that in 1913, 32.1 percent of the net national wealth of Britain was held in countries where it made investments. Similar statistical data for France and Germany is not available but they also invested substantively large amounts of capital. During 1870–1913, Britain was responsible for 41.8 percent of total global foreign investment. For France and Germany, the corresponding proportion was 19.8 percent and 12.8 percent, respectively (Maddison, 1995).

In the mid-nineteenth and the early twentieth centuries, an important feature of financial globalization was the activities of the transnational corporations (TNCs). Toward the end of the nineteenth century and during the period before World War I, TNCs were globally active players responsible for the spread of market-driven economic and financial globalization. The book value of foreign direct investments made by the TNCs, as a proportion of world GDP, was computed by Obstfeld and Taylor (2004). The global stock of foreign direct investment (FDI) in current dollars was $14 million in 1914. Likewise, foreign portfolio investment also increased rapidly until World War I. Obstfeld and Taylor (2004) put the value of foreign portfolio investment at a low of 6.7 percent of the world GDP in 1870. It rose to 18.6 percent by 1900 and remained at 17.5 percent in 1914.

An obvious division of labor was reflected in the world trade of this period. The so-called New World economies had a comparative advantage in exporting food grains because of their abundant arable land. In turn, the industrialized economies of Europe exported manufactured products to these and other countries. By this time, the Industrial Revolution had made a great deal of progress and the industrially advanced economies of Europe had a massive demand for the import of bulky raw materials like bauxite, coal, nitrates, oil and rubber. The expansion of manufacture and trade in textiles had also created a large demand for cotton, silk and wool.[16]

Capital market integration was never a linear, ever-increasing, continuous process. It was subjected to many distinct reversals. The Baring crisis of 1891 was responsible for stopping financial globalization in its tracks. One of the most conspicuous periods in this regard is the interwar period. During the deglobalization period that followed World War I, global investment declined dramatically. Foreign assets declined to 8 percent of the world GDP in 1930 and 5 percent in 1945. They did not begin recovering immediately after World War II ended and were a measly 6 percent of the world GDP in 1960. This state of affairs began to change in the 1970s and in 1980 they soared to 25 percent of the world GDP. Trans-border capital flows steadily climbed after this point; foreign assets soared to 25 percent in 1980 and to 49 percent in 1990. The decade of the 1990s proved to be one of high growth of financial globalization. Foreign assets climbed further to the high perch of 92 percent in 2000 (Obstfeld and Taylor, 2004). Going by these statistics, the pre-1914 level of global financial integration was not reached until sometime in the 1970s.

Using another measure of financial globalization, this U-shaped trend was confirmed by Feldstein and Horioka (1980). In a closed economy, both domestic saving and investment are closely linked. This link is broken by trans-border capital movements. That is, domestic savings can be invested abroad, while domestic investment can be augmented by external savings. Therefore, the weaker the relationship between domestic savings and domestic investment, the higher are global capital movements and the stronger is financial globalization, and vice versa.

2.5 Utilization of financial resources

An interesting comparison between the past and the present can be drawn here. The directions of both portfolio investment and FDI at the beginning of the twentieth century and at the end were completely different. In the pre-World War I era, major borrowing sectors were transportation, infrastructure and government. Industry and financial sectors were minor borrowers. In contrast, during the 1990s finance was a major borrowing sector from the global capital markets in the EMEs, whereas infrastructure and transport were minor. One plausible reason behind this change in direction is that the twin problems of asymmetric information and contract enforcement were markedly reduced during the later period compared to the pre-World War I era.

In comparison to the extent of financial globalization during the present period, during the pre-World War I era this was somewhat narrow. Only a small number of countries and sectors participated in financial globalization. This era is known for large immigration. Capital flows for the most part followed the migratory trend. Also, capital flows were generally directed toward trade flows. Long-term bonds were the most popular instrument. Furthermore, large international investments were made by a small number of freestanding companies and the TNCs. These characteristic features of financial globalization at the beginning of the twentieth century make it reasonably different and less comprehensive than during the contemporary period. That being said, the extent of capital mobility was comparable to that of today.

A well-known textbook argument is that open economies face a macroeconomic policy trilemma (Section 2.3). Of the three policy objectives, namely independence in monetary policy, stability in exchange rate and free movement of capital, only two can be achieved simultaneously. This has immense policy implications. Policy makers in an economy choose the two objectives they value most and let the third be determined based on the value of the two that are being controlled.[17] Early in the twentieth century, independence of monetary policy was eschewed by the governments of industrial economies. This was due to the fact that the politicians did not have control over the level of domestic economic activity and they did not care much for the votes of the working classes. However, during the crisis decade of the 1930s (discussed below in Section 2.6) following an independent monetary policy became an all-important policy objective for these very economies.

2.6 Melancholy period of deglobalization

Although the twentieth century had begun with a 'highly efficient international monetary system' and busy capital markets, they were destroyed by World War I. Mundell (2000, p. 329) believed that the 'bungled recreation' of the gold standard in the interwar period 'brought on the Great depression, Hitler and World War II'. Also, the prevailing attitude toward the liberalization of the global economy as well as the belief in the role of the market forces and the *laissez-faire* philosophy (alluded to in Section 2.2) ended at the beginning of World War I. This was an important moment in modern economic history. Global economic and financial integration catastrophically reversed at this point.

However, whether the outbreak of a major war that involved the largest economies of the period was the cause of this reversal in global integration – including financial globalization – cannot be determined with certainty. History does not spell out whether the disintegration of the global economy was driven by this cataclysm, or whether it was influenced by lesser events as well. It remains an unanswered question whether democratic policies, and actions of legislatures, can interrupt globalization and set it back. One factor contributing to and exacerbating the disintegration of the global economy was the inability of the erstwhile global geopolitical and economic power, Britain, to exert its leadership in economic affairs. The US was the rising economic power and had surpassed Britain in absolute economic size in 1870, as an exporter in 1915 and as an international creditor in 1917, but it was unwilling to exert its leadership (Eichengreen, 2008).

During the interwar period, stringent capital controls became rampant. This change in the mindset of the public policy professionals marked the termination of the first era of globalization. The gold standard system of fixed exchange rates was abandoned and a flexible or floating exchange rate regime was adopted. This regime did not function efficiently and resulted in a great deal of disorder and confusion in the global economy. Exchange rate devaluations became the order of the day. Countries did not shy away from the beggar-thy-neighbor kind of devaluations. If anything, they took it to an outrageous extreme. A good deal of culpability for confusion and inefficiency during the interwar period was due to the restoration of the gold standard in the

1920s, which was 'mismanaged' (Mundell, 1960, p. 327). This period of economic history was uniquely crammed with problems for individual industrial economies as well as collectively for the global economy. It was also blighted by non-cooperation among the systemically important economies, to the detriment of the entire global economic system.[18]

Britain, a leading economy of this era, stopped using the gold standard in early 1931. Speculative runs on the pound sterling were so frequent that it became difficult to remain on the fixed exchange rate regime. Soon other countries began emulating Britain; 13 of them abandoned the gold parities of their currencies in 1931. The US did not abandon the gold standard until 1933. Bearing in mind their domestic-economy-related objectives, many of these economies actually caused a depreciation in their currencies. They espoused policy measures that commonly accompany such a policy regime. These measures included rigorous trade and capital controls. Throughout the 1930s, independent management of exchange rates and domestic policies were high priorities for the large economies. The two principal channels of global integration, trade and finance, were throttled and the global economy moved toward an autarky.

A melancholy, if not downright depressed, period of deglobalization ensued. It is variously described as a period of reverse globalization, disintegration or divergence. The Wall Street crash of 29 October 1929, soon turned into a global economic cataclysm. This ignominious day went down in history as Black Tuesday. The Great Depression (1929–39) hugely exacerbated the trend toward the disintegration of the global economy. Multilateral trade contracted by more than a half, almost by two-thirds. There were widespread and massive increases in tariffs and other protectionist barriers during this period. Governments erroneously believed that raising tariff barriers was an effective defense against the global economic slump, and that by limiting trade they could protect their domestic economies and citizens from an economic downturn. Instead, increasing protectionism resulted in declining domestic output, increasing unemployment and worsening of the downturn. The retreat into protectionism included, and was inspired by, two large increases in tariff barriers by the US. Of these two, the Smoot-Hawley Act of 1930 is regarded as particularly infamous. Economies of cities around the world were adversely affected, particularly those that had large manufacturing industries. In many countries construction activity came to a standstill. As the crop prices declined by nearly 60 percent, rural areas also plunged into sharp economic depression. The devastating effect of Great Depression was felt in virtually every country, rich or poor. Household incomes, government revenues, profits of firms and prices of goods and services all declined precipitously.

The causes of the Great Depression were 'catastrophic errors in American monetary policy, which provoked a huge aggregate demand shock that reduced both output and prices. They declined first domestically and then, through secondary effects, in the rest of the world' (Crafts, 2000, p. 31). The other causal factors were stickiness of wages, fragility of the banking system and malfunctioning of the modified gold standard, which was reconstituted in 1925. The floating exchange rate system of the 1930s also did not serve the global economy well. This period is known for significant bank failures in industrial economies, the drying up of bank loans and firms switching to using liquid cash instead of bank credits. The most striking and widespread bank failures took place in the US. They were caused by excessive risk-taking by the poorly regulated banking system that preceded the Great Depression – something that is jarringly comparable to the financial crisis of 2008 in the US. The credit supply to the real economy was critically interrupted in the early 1930s, which created and soon aggravated the deflationary pressure. This was the period of negative money supply shock. The drying up of bank credit at this time was the worst development that could take place. During the troubled interwar period, investment and production by TNCs was severely constrained. Interest in portfolio investment also sharply declined.

2.7 The Bretton Woods system and the Eurodollar market

Two World Wars and the Great Depression proved to be destructive to the global economy as well as to global economic and financial integration. This period is known for not only non-cooperation among the large economies but also for unreserved adoption of nationalistic policies by policy makers. At the end of World War II, attempts were made to rejuvenate economic and financial cooperation among the large economies. Resolute attempts were made to put the global economic system on an even keel. The objective was to pick up integrating where it was left off in 1914. The largest economies launched a concerted and collaborative endeavor to formulate a new global monetary regime.

The regime that was invented after World War II became known as the Bretton Woods system, named after the spa in New Hampshire where its negotiations were finalized in July 1944. Twin institutions, namely the International Monetary Fund (IMF) and the World Bank, were conceived. In all, 44 allied nations and Argentina, a neutral country, participated in this conference. Essential conference negotiations took place around two rival plans developed and supported by Harry Dexter White of the US and John Maynard Keynes of Britain. The final compromise that emerged was closer to the US plan than to that put forth by Keynes.

The Bretton Woods system was history's first fully negotiated global monetary order; its objective was to govern financial relations, in particular currency relations, among sovereign states. The novelty of this regime was the legal obligation of the member countries that were determined by multilateral negotiations conducted in a supranational institution, the IMF. However, the IMF had only a limited supranational authority. In this monetary regime, the US was the most powerful member country in a pivotal role. Its preferences and policies significantly influenced the development and operation of the Bretton Woods regime. This new regime replaced the gold standard with a dollar standard; the dollar was theoretically linked to bullion. The flexible exchange rate regime of the Bretton Woods period depended more on the dollar policies of the Federal Reserve System than on the discipline of the gold standard. The US had, therefore, a large role in the ultimate demise of this system.

One of the imperative lessons of the disorder of the interwar period was that unrestrained flexibility of exchange rates suffers from fundamental disadvantages and leads to instability in the world monetary regime. The floating exchange rate regime had effectively discouraged trade and investment. It was also given to encouraging destabilizing bouts of currency speculation and competitive depreciations, which frequently had a debilitating effect over the global monetary regime. However, this was a period of activist economic policy and most governments were disinterested in returning to a fixed exchange rate regime, modeled on the classical gold standard.

Therefore, as an intelligent compromise, the Bretton Woods system (1946–73) adopted a pegged exchange rate regime. The peg was movable or adjustable, that is, there was provision for the devaluation of a currency. The IMF members were required to establish a parity of their national currencies in terms of gold and maintain exchange rates within plus or minus 1 percent of parity by intervening in their foreign exchange markets, by the buying or selling of foreign exchange. Capital was not allowed to flow freely because of the challenging experiences during the interwar period. The pre-World War II controls on its movements were continued. This was a legacy of the chaotic interwar period.

Capital controls were also used as instruments to control demand in domestic economies. Capital markets remained caged during the 1950s and a good part of the 1960s. This was an inward-looking era and capital markets were controlled for both domestic and foreign transaction purposes. Also, both capital and current account transactions were stringently controlled in most economies. Capital controls were so rigorous that even in industrial countries like Britain people were only allowed to carry meager sums when they traveled abroad. Notwithstanding these restrictions, sporadic cases of financial crisis did take place during the Bretton Woods period but their effect tended to be entirely localized.

The IMF accepted the concept of capital controls as a means to prevent currency crises and runs. This thoughtful justification for capital controls and control-ridden capital markets was a practical measure adopted to cope with the economic reality. It helped in the organization and institutionalization of the global monetary regime of the post-war period and its survival. Capital controls allowed member governments a degree of autonomy by providing them with the power to follow activist monetary policies.

Major European economies achieved current account convertibility in 1959, although the obligations of IMF's Article III (Article III deals with current account convertibility) were not formally accepted until 1961. Capital controls applied under the Bretton Woods regime were not impermeable (Rajan and Zingales, 2003).[19] Breaches occurred commonly. There were cracks for capital to move in and out and there was pressure on the Bretton Woods regime to yield to international capital mobility. The naissance of the Eurodollar market was one outcome of this pressure. These were dollar deposits in banks outside the US, mostly in London and other European capitals, and therefore not under the jurisdiction of the Federal Reserve Board (FED). This market was free of government controls and regulations. The Eurodollar market was created in 1957 when the British government restricted capital mobility to avert a currency crisis. It was an attempt to protect the value of the pound sterling.

Several geopolitical events – one of them was the Cuban crisis – provided impetus to the growth of the Eurodollar market. The Eurodollar market grew at a rapid rate and large sums in Eurodollars began moving globally. It contributed substantially to the wearing away of the capital controls and deterioration of the Bretton Woods regime. In the mid-1960s currencies of the countries following policies inconsistent with the maintenance of their parities were subject to frequent speculative attacks. In these countries traders and financial operators had devised ways to routinely circumvent capital controls. With the passage of time the Bretton Woods regime became increasingly fragile and the US gold reserves were threatened because of growing balance-of-payments deficits. In 1965, the US imposed restrictions on capital outflows. This proved to be the largest growth impetus to the Eurodollar markets. Like the British banks before them, the US banks became increasingly interested in the Eurodollar market in order to circumvent the controls of their own government.

The Bretton Woods system served the global economy well for over two decades. The post-World War II economic boom sustained and supported it. In particular, post-war recovery in Germany and Japan – both of which began their recovery with undervalued currencies – provided helpful support. The Bretton Woods system withered away between 1971 and 1973. The US, still the leading member of the system, was instrumental in its collapse. It refused to pay the domestic price for bearing the system's weight. During this period, the balance-of-payments situation in the US had deteriorated, causing the emergence of strong protectionist sentiment in the US Congress.

In August 1971, Richard Nixon suspended the convertibility of the dollar into gold, thus freeing the dollar to find its market value in the currency markets. Destabilizing currency speculation took on epidemic proportion. Waves of currency speculation against the realigned structure of the par values negotiated in 1971 continued. Finally, in February 1973, the major currencies had to be set free to float independently. At the time of the failure of the Bretton Woods, it was not obvious what would replace it. Many European economies strongly favored a return to a fixed exchange rate regime. However, floating exchange rates eventually prevailed, largely because the three major currencies, the dollar, deutsche mark and yen, favored it.

2.8 The great moderation: The post-Bretton Woods era

The floating exchange rate system of the post-1973 era, after some experimenting, was adopted by all the industrial economies. It had two variations, namely free and managed floats. During this period, independence of monetary policy was regarded as an important policy instrument (Eichengreen, 1999). Thus, in the post-Bretton Woods period, the market forces, to all appearances, set exchange rates. Capital controls were not needed. Once the capital flows were freed, it was assumed that ill-disciplined governments could be punished by higher bond yields. With the abandoning of capital controls in the post-Bretton Woods era, capital was set free to flow from where it was to where it was needed, and to yield the highest marginal returns.

In this period, central banks were given greater powers. Many of them set explicit inflation targets. Until the early 2000s, the post-Bretton Woods system served the global economy well by engendering a fairly long period of low macroeconomic volatility. Reduction in macroeconomic variability improved the functioning of markets as well as rendered economic and financial planning easier. Blanchard and Simon (2001) documented that the variability of quarterly growth in real output, as measured by the standard deviation, had declined by half since 1983, at the same time that the variability of quarterly inflation declined by about two-thirds. Summers (2005) corroborated these results. He found that for a group of industrial economies the standard deviation of the quarterly growth rate of real GDP during 1985–2004 was half the standard deviation during 1960–84.

Most of the advanced industrial world enjoyed an era of unprecedented economic stability between 1983 and 2004. This trend has been well documented. This phenomenon gave rise to a new approach to modeling business cycles. At its core is the belief that the structure of industrial economies has changed significantly (Spehar, 2009). Although the business cycle has not been abolished, it has certainly been stretched. This trend was stronger in the Anglo-Saxon countries than in the other industrial economies. Large fluctuations in employment, output and interest rates were considerably reduced. Output volatility also declined in both the EMEs and the developing economies. During this period, the peaks of inflation were lower and the troughs of outputs shallower. This period of remarkable decline in the variability of output and inflation as well as in the other principal macroeconomic variables was christened the era of Great Moderation. Thus, monetary policy helped to stabilize inflation.

The fact that output volatility declined in tandem with inflation volatility suggests that monetary policy may have had an impact on moderating variability of output as well (Bernanke, 2004). Although there is a good-luck theory propounded by Ahmad et al. (2002), improvement in monetary policy has probably been one of the important foundations for the Great Moderation. The era of Great Moderation in relation to macroeconomic volatility provided a favorable and nurturing atmosphere for financial globalization. Great Moderation contributed to improvement in market sentiment. Investors' risk tolerance grew and alternative asset classes began getting larger liquidity. High-risk credit products saw their prices rise considerably. Capital flows to and from the EMEs also began to surge (Wellink, 2008).

3. Engendering partial convergence

The theory of convergence deals with long-term economic growth. The term convergence implies diminishing differences in per capita income, economic development levels, productivity levels and manufacturing performance, and eventually in living standards. In his seminal paper Williamson (1996, p. 277) concluded that 'globalization played *the* critical role in contributing to convergence'. Theoretically, financial globalization and free flows of global capital should result in substantial macroeconomic benefits for both the country exporting capital and the recipients. It is logical to expect these to positively influence global trend productivity and employment. They did result in doing so in countries that integrated swiftly with the global economy (including the private global financial markets).

Globalization failed to produce global convergence. While it did provide a stimulus to the convergence process, convergence in the global economy occurred in a partial, patchy and irregular manner. It took place in only certain periods of history and its application was geographically limited. Two of the most remarkable instances of convergence are: Firstly, after World War II convergence occurred in the Western European economies along with Australia, Canada and the US, the economies of European settlement. Together they are counted as the Organization for Economic Cooperation and Development (OECD) economies. Secondly, the locus of the convergence club shifted to East Asia. Following the much-vaunted Asian miracle, the dynamic East Asian economies began to converge after 1960. This group established itself as the fastest growing group economy ever. In the short span of two generations, it achieved what the North Atlantic industrial economies took much longer to achieve. In his seminal paper Williamson (1996, p. 277) concluded that 'globalization played *the* critical role in contributing to convergence'.

These two groups of economies demonstrated rapid growth in real income and productivity, rapid adoption and adaptation of core industrial technologies, and corresponding transformation in economic structure. A recent comparable case of similar characteristic changes in an economy and resulting rapid growth is that of China and India. They are two populous (2.4 billion) economies accounting for more than a third (37.49 percent) of the global population. They are increasingly being perceived as two up-and-coming economic powers that could one day become consequential players on the global economic stage (Das, 2006a). Nonetheless, it is *au point* to conclude that instances of successful convergence led by global integration have been more the exception than the rule (Dowrick and DeLong, 2005).

Convergence is regarded as a club or group phenomenon. That is, from time to time a limited number of countries in groups succeeded in generating and honing the economic forces that led to convergence. In the groups of economies that succeeded in converging, these economic forces became strong enough to counter adverse pressures. Apparently, economic and financial globalization did not succeed in spreading these forces universally.

4. Latter half of the twentieth century

One view regarding the onset of the current phase of globalization puts it in the early 1950s. Neoclassical economists deem the initial period of the latter half of the twentieth century as the beginning of a new economic era that focused on supporting and encouraging interdependence, collaboration and mutual support among the important world economies. This concerted increase in economic interdependence is regarded by them as the resumption of economic and financial globalization.

When the World War II ended, the major European countries and Japan were war-ravaged. Economies in Britain, France, Germany and Italy were in shambles and, if anything, Japan's was worse. Industrial infrastructures in several large industrial economies were destroyed. Significant financial and economic plans were drawn up by world leaders for the reparation and recovery of war-torn economies. Neoclassical economists regard these economic collaborative endeavors, together with the Bretton Woods conference, as the commencement of the post-World War II phase of globalization. Supranational institutions, namely the IMF (charged with overseeing the global financial system) and the World Bank (with a mandate for reconstruction and development) were established in 1944. These supranational institutions evolved into two principal instruments of global economic governance. Recovery from the ravages of war steadily progressed. In 1947, the General Agreement on Tariffs and Trade (GATT) was created with a mandate to eliminate trade barriers and promote multilateral trade. It provided a forum and developed procedures for the formulation of multilateral trade law from agreements between states. It played an effective role in the massive expansion of world trade in the latter half of the twentieth century.

At this point in time, the US economy, with its holding of 70 percent of world's gold and foreign exchange reserves, held a high position in the global economy. It was by far the largest global economy, accounting for 40 percent of the world's total industrial output (Peters, 2004). Through the Marshall Plan, the US provided $12 billion to war-torn economies in grants and low-interest loans. The 1950s and 1960s turned out to be a halcyon period of economic growth for Japan and Western Europe. Led by the supranational institutions, focus of the new global leadership next turned to the impoverished developing economies. During these decades, a large proportion of them were colonies that were getting their formal independence and becoming sovereign states. However, an overwhelming majority of them were low-income, resource-poor economies. They were yet to achieve economic independence.

By the 1960s, global commitment to growth and development in these impoverished and underdeveloped economies increased. The Bretton Woods twins and national economic aid organizations set up by large and small industrial economies turned their attention to supporting growth and development in these countries. The aid organizations created by Nordic countries made a name for themselves by providing soft loans and grants to a large number of developing countries. Measured as percentage of GDP this country group became the largest donor of developmental assistance (Das, 2009a). In terms of sheer volume, Japan and the US were also large supporters of growth and development. Development economics as a subject matter developed at a rapid rate. Innovative approaches to growth and development were developed by some of the best intellects in the profession. Respected economists like Hollis B. Chenery were cherry picked from the academe by the World Bank to head research in development economics.

FDI flows have been a major instrument of global economic and financial integration. Other than aiding global integration, FDI benefits the recipient country as it is a stable source of finance for expanding investment, regarded as more stable than other kinds of global capital flows. FDI usually moves in package deals. It is packaged with technology, managerial know-how and marketing linkages. After initial slow growth, the global stock FDI expanded discernibly during the latter half of the twentieth century. In current dollars it was $14 million in 1914. It soared to $60 million in 1960 and to $2.46 billion in 1995. In constant (1990) dollars the value of FDI stock soared from $153 million in 1914, to $362 million in 1960 and to $2.05 billion in 1995. As a proportion of the world GDP, the FDI level had plummeted to 4.9 percent in 1945. However, FDI by the TNCs began gradually rising again in the 1950s and reached 6.4 percent of the world GDP in 1960. The decades of 1970s and 1980s turned out to be good for the global FDI expansion from the TNCs and it reached 17.7 percent of the world GDP in 1980 and 56.8 percent in 1995. During these decades the TNCs' role in transferring technology had increased significantly and the new trends of vertically integrated production and networked production had proliferated in the global economy (Obstfeld and Taylor, 2004). The conclusion is that FDI flows, unlike bank liabilities, are not crisis-prone (Joyce, 2009).

The other channels of capital flows were bank and portfolio finance. During the early post-war period, the volume of this kind of financial flows were slow. In many countries, capital account restrictions not only persisted but were stringent. Subsequently, these restrictions began to be phased out. With that, capital flows from banks and portfolio finance markedly increased. As a generalization it can be stated that countries with more open capital accounts tended to grow faster.

4.1 Asymmetric initiation

As stated in the preceding section, the trend toward global economic integration gradually developed from global economic collaboration and interdependence. During the latter half of the twentieth century, the world economy enjoyed a remarkable era of prosperity. There was a striking general improvement in health and education indicators. Although the spread of prosperity and social services was fairly broad, it was far from uniform. Not everybody benefited from the spread of global prosperity. It was utterly uneven in terms of spread among economies as well as among individual population groups within the globalizing economies. This asymmetry was an idiosyncratic feature of the post-World War II period of globalization.

Some country groups did exceedingly well and prospered, while others continued to stagnate. The better-performing economies that benefited from global integration have been named in the preceding section. The dynamic country groups that were the first to benefit from global integration of this period (and thus benefited the most) were the industrial economies of Western Europe and Japan, followed by those that adopted outer-oriented or export-led growth policies. Adoption of macroeconomic and structural reforms was a necessary condition so that institutions of good governance could be developed. These important policy measures were indispensable as they created the required economic resilience and flexibility. Conversely, the country groups that followed inward-oriented or import-substituting and *dirigist* growth policies remained cloistered and excluded themselves from the benefits of globalization. With strong GDP growth performance, the former country groups recorded the largest increases in per capita incomes during the post-war phase of globalization. Strong growth provided them with resources to improve living standards and alleviate poverty. The latter country groups putatively failed to achieve either of these two goals.

4.2 Proliferation of prosperity

Notwithstanding the unevenness of its distribution, the latter half of the twentieth century is fairly well acclaimed for its spread of prosperity. Prosperity burgeoned in several parts of the global economy. Global economic growth in the latter half of the twentieth century was so much better and qualitatively different from any earlier periods in history that a 'new perspective of the world economy was needed to comprehend it' (Lucas, 2000, p. 159). Over this period, world GDP growth, both in the developing and industrial countries averaged more than 4 percent in real terms. A noteworthy point is that both developing and industrial economies[20] grew by and large at the same pace. A direct consequence of this was improvement in living standards, as measured by improvement in real per capita income. In the brief span of half a century, living standards improved discernibly. This rapid global growth led to average global per capita income nearly tripling in the second half of the last century (Kohler, 2002).[21] Maddison (2003) firmly corroborated this fact.[22]

According to one calculation, real per capita GDP between 1950 and 2000 increased from $5,236 to $20, 213 in Western Europe; from $6,847 to $19,704 in Australia and Canada; from $9,573 to $27,272 in the US; from $765 to $4,359 in Asia; from $2,487 to $5,495 in Latin America and from $830 to $1,311 in Africa. Real per capita GDP for the world rose from $2,138 to $5,998 over this period.[23] Two outstanding cases in this regard were China and Japan. In case of China this increase was from $614 to $6,283, while in case of Japan it was from $1,873 to $20,616.[24] Broadly speaking, country groups that benefited more from economic and financial globalization included the industrial economies and the East Asian economies, while those that were slow gainers included Africa, South Asia and Latin America. Gains recorded by China and Japan were the highest.

The rate of growth of multilateral trade in goods and services was double the rate of the global GDP growth over this period, implying integration of the global economy through trade. Multilateral trade (exports plus imports) volume expanded sizably during this period. It was a puny one-tenth of the world GDP in 1950. This proportion soared to one-third in 2000. As noted above, the two principal contributing factors to rapid multilateral trade expansion were: firstly, institutional improvements that reflected in the rolling back of the tariffs and other trade barriers and, secondly, dramatic decline in transport and communication costs.

The global integration that began with increasing economic interdependence in the early 1950s, learned from the mistakes of the interwar period. Under the auspices of the GATT, tariffs and trade barriers were progressively reduced and multilateral trade was brought under the rules of law laid down by the trading countries. Trade barriers created by governments were dramatically negotiated down during eight rounds of multilateral trade negotiations (MTNs) conducted under the egis of the GATT. In addition, barriers to trans-border capital flows were also lowered. As in the first era of globalization, decline in transport cost continued during this era. Container shipping that was invented in 1956 made the world smaller and changed the shipping industry for ever. In 1950, an average commercial vessel carried 10,000 tons at a speed of 16 knots. In 2000, an average vessel could carry 6,600 20-foot containers (77,000 tons of cargo) at a speed of 24.8 knots. Containerization sharply reduced freight costs and totally transformed global trade, particularly in manufacture.

Speedy advances in information and communication technology (ICT) took place toward the end of this period. Telecommunications, computer and the Internet became crucial change agents and promoters of economic and financial globalization. They were responsible for the precipitous decline in communication costs of voice, text and data. Although falling communication costs were ignored by international trade theory and the contribution of modern ICT to trade is often disregarded, they have had enormous implications for the modern trade expansion. Vertically integrated production and global production networks of this era could not function without ICT advances. Also, trading procedures and practices call for a great deal of communication between potential buyers and sellers, an array of middlemen and facilitations like transporting and insuring firms. Together these developments became the key globalization-enablers of the last quarter of the twentieth century. They coalesced to promote and support spread of economic and financial globalization during this era.

4.3 Global economic integration through upgradation of policies and institutions

The above-mentioned group of dynamic economies (Section 4.1) benefited from globalization by the successful exploitation of market-led outer-oriented development strategy, and by climbing the ladder of development by first producing and exporting labor-intensive goods and then by capital- and technology-intensive goods. Assisted by their adherence to the outer-oriented economic strategy, they integrated first regionally and then globally, particularly with the mature industrial economies. After a time lag, India also joined this country group. It climbed the same ladder by exploiting the information and technology-enabled services (ITeS) sector. Freeing market forces and enhancing their legitimacy in the economic system rendered these economies more efficient, which in turn led to their rapid GDP growth and material advancement.

In the process of espousing globalization, several economies improved their domestic macroeconomic policy structures and institutions. Other than the industrial economies, this observation applies to some middle- and low-income developing economies as well as to the EMEs. Many of these developing economies were essentially exporters of commodities, while the EMEs largely exported manufactured goods and services. The EMEs pursued external liberalization by dismantling trade barriers, both tariffs and non-tariffs. They also took policy measures to avoid having overvalued currencies and to liberalize current account transactions as well as preliminary measures to liberalize capital account. That is not to say that all trade restrictions and those on FDI and other financial flows were completely dismantled, although they were significantly broken down. These economies also put in place economic reform programs and markedly improved their macroeconomic policies. Instances of large fiscal deficits and current account deficits dropped to a small number. A discernible improvement in the general quality of economic institutions was noticed while the depth in their financial markets increased. As globalization has proved to be an important driver of growth in these developing economies and EMEs, some demonstration effect in adopting internal and external policy liberalization among economies cannot be denied.

Developing economies and EMEs that open to the presence of foreign financial institutions and trade in financial services are known to benefit from this. Cross-country evidence indicates that economic liberalization along these lines ushers in significant increases in both economic stability and efficiency in the domestic financial markets. In particular, the entry of foreign banks into a country tends to increase diversification of domestic risks, enhance competition and efficiency, and at the same time lower moral hazard (Litan et al., 2001; Mishkin, 2001). A large econometric exercise undertaken by the IMF analyzed data for a broad sample of 80 countries over a long period (1970–2005), to examine several aspects of global economic integration (IMF, 2008b). The econometric framework essentially consisted of cross-sectional and panel regressions. It came up with several valuable inferences. In brief, export volumes as a proportion of GDP grew for the sample countries by an average of 30 percent between 1980 and 2005. Improvement in institutional and financial frameworks accounted for as much as 25 percent of this increase. Another 25 percent of this increase was accounted for by reduced macroeconomic policy distortions. They included the relaxing of exchange restrictions, the dismantling of tariff barriers and the reduction in currency overvaluation. Thus, with progress in globalization, policy and institutional environment and economic performance has been undergoing marked improvement in a large number of economies.

The BRIC concept has proved to be an enduring one. The recent rise of these economies is credited to the launching of macroeconomic reforms and adoption of restructuring policies in these economies. At different points in time they adopted a market-oriented liberal policy framework, which in turn was instrumental in the closer integration of this sub-set of economies with the global economy.[25] Their significance in the world of finance went on increasing. In 2008, their combined GDP was $8.6 trillion and they accounted for 14 percent of global output. Together they held 42 percent of the world's currency reserves and 33 percent of the US Treasury debt in 2009. The BRIC economies met in Yekaterinburg, Russia, in June 2009, for an inaugural group summit. The objective of the summit was to deepen strategic relations and explore a range of issues including the continuing global economic recession (EIU, 2009).

This same policy framework is considered responsible for the growing salience of around 30 EMEs on the global economic stage. Sub-groups of developing economies and EMEs that benefited during the contemporary phase of globalization are customarily divided into several overlapping country groups. For instance, other than the four BRIC economies, the seven largest EMEs (China, India, Brazil, the Russian Federation, Indonesia, Mexico and Turkey) are one such group, while the EMEs that are the non-Group-of-Seven (G-7)[26] members of the Group-of-Twenty (G-20),[27] are another such group. In a globalizing world economy, the last named sub-group of economies is regarded as systemically significant countries that account for close to 85 percent of the global economic production. These countries have a significant control over global resources and account for two-thirds of the world's population. The non-G-7 members of G-20 have lately begun to play a meaningful role in global economic policy making and governance.

Disintegration of the Soviet Union into 15 independent countries and the abandoning of the non-market economic dogma contributed to global integration. Some of these economies, along with East European ones which were satellites of the Soviet economy, transformed into market economies and democracies. Many of them also made valiant attempts to turn into EMEs and integrate with the global economy.

These developments of the latter half of the twentieth century, particularly of the last three decades (analyzed in Section 5 below), not only bolstered globalization but also markedly changed the economic geography of the world economy. The economies that emerged as winners of globalization signify that it is a benign and productive force. How does globalization work as a welfare-enhancing, munificent mechanism? Economists' response is uncomplicated and direct: globalization enhances the economic opportunities of a country by allowing it to sell its goods and services in a much larger market, have access to a much bigger capital market to finance its growth and development process, and also have a larger opportunity to import technology and knowledge, which eventually enhances TFP. Thus viewed, the direct consequence of increased economic opportunities is tangible economic benefits and enhanced well-being for the globalizing economy.

According to classical economists like David Recardo, the basis of these welfare gains is the theory of comparative advantage based on differences in factors of production and technology. Exploitation of comparative advantage allows production of more goods and services with the same resources because firms are able to produce at lower opportunity costs. While the modern theory of international trade attributes the welfare gains to economies of scale, they also occur due to mobility of factors of production, which makes them far more efficient and productive than when they were static.

5. Shifting gears of globalization: The second era of globalization

Mundell (2000) posited that the genesis of the contemporary era of globalization was the oil shock of 1973 and the collapse of the

Bretton Woods system. Both of these global economic developments were momentous and were responsible for getting the global economy ready for the financial globalization that followed. The large current account surpluses of the Organization of Petroleum Exporting Countries (OPEC) were recycled to the developing economies through the so-called money-center banks. These banks suddenly came upon massive liquid resources to invest. The recycled petro-dollars went to those developing countries that were regarded as creditworthy and had access to capital markets. A large majority of petro-dollar loans were either sovereign loans or were guaranteed by the governments. For the most part sovereign loans were made as syndicated loans by the large money center banks. The Bretton Woods system of adjustable-peg exchange rate regime had disintegrated. Therefore, the borrowing economies could open to greater capital mobility while preserving the autonomy of their monetary policies (Das, 2003b).

There is another established view regarding the initiation of the present phase of globalization. Some economic historians concur that 1980 was the real beginning of what they call the 'second era of globalization' (Aizenman et al., 2007, p. 657). Supported by technological advancements, economic and financial globalization developed a compelling economic momentum of its own. This period distinguished itself from the first era of globalization by involving not only traded goods, services and capital but also a long inventory of services that were regarded non-tradable before the Internet revolution. In addition, during this period global integration was far more multidimensional than in the first period. It took place through multiple channels, namely, trade, finance, communications, intellectual property, knowledge and technology transfer, and the trans-border entrepreneurial activity of the TNCs. This multidimensionality made it far more comprehensive, vigorous and far-reaching than ever before. In addition, scale, pace and intensity of global economic and financial integration in the present era was unarguably without equal. Consequently, economic and financial globalization in this era surpassed all the previous eras by a large margin.

The volume of merchandise trade, which was 20 percent of global GDP in 2006, is one element that proves this fact. The corresponding proportion was barely 8 percent in 1913 (although by 1990 it had soared to 15 percent). Global financial flows expanded more rapidly than multilateral trade during the modern phase of globalization. Financial markets are far more mature at present than those during the earlier era of global integration and investors use a much larger array of instruments, equities and derivatives. Financial integration of the earlier era, albeit significantly expanded in volume terms, was relatively limited in comparison to the pervasive integration of the current period (Bernanke, 2006). It benefited from the institutional innovations of the current period (a great deal of institutional improvements and innovations had occurred during the recent decades and financial integration was facilitated, encouraged and promoted by it). However, in one dimension, namely mass migration, the pre-World War I period outperformed the current period of globalization. Dowrick and DeLong (2005, p. 191) concluded that except 'in mass migration in which we today are less "globalized" than our predecessors at the end of World War I'.

5.1 Neo-Liberal policy environment

The reasons why the contemporary phase of globalization is believed to have commenced around 1980 include the fact that the global political and policy climate changed in favor of neo-liberal economic strategies around this time. I use the term neo-liberal to convey the fact that globalization necessitates the adoption of free-market policies and the eradication of barriers to the operation of market forces. A series of neo-liberal policy measures that advanced global integration were taken in systemically important countries around this period. To name some of the most important ones, many medium- and large-sized developing economies made a big push toward trade and financial integration and a sub-group of them, called the EMEs, energetically came into being. This development is exemplified by China, that launched its much-vaunted *gai ge kai fang*,[28] or reform and opening up, program in late 1978. In the early 1980s, China was busy converting its non-market, or command economy, system into a market-oriented economic system.[29] Its objective was to turn away from Maoism and toward the exploitation of market forces.

A large array of neo-liberal policy measures of global significance took place around this time. For instance, Margaret Thatcher came to power in Britain (1979) and Ronald Regan came to power in the US (1980). Neo-liberal economic policies were implemented, and deregulation and tax cuts were promoted in both economies, giving a substantial boost to pro-market ideology. To all appearances, this was the launch of a new era of liberal macroeconomic and financial policy. The deregulation unleashed during this period brought about a far-reaching transformation of financial systems in the advanced industrial economies.[30]

In addition, in the mid-1980s, the European Union (EU) made a well-publicized commitment to create a single market. With the collapse of the Berlin wall in 1989 and subsequent disintegration of the Soviet Union, a large number of East European economies and the newly created countries after the break-up of the Soviet Union launched into the onerous task of turning their centrally planned economies into market economies, so that they could eventually integrate into the global economy and financial system (Section 4.3). Furthermore, the Uruguay Round of MTNs, launched in 1986, promoted global thinking in the area of multilateral trade. After eight marathon years of negotiations between 117 contracting parties (CPs) of the GATT, and after numerous challenging roadblocks it eventually came to an agreement in 1994. Its mandate was the creation of a broader international trade organization on the foundation of the GATT (Das, 2001). The World Trade Organization was founded in 1995. Each one of these developments was a consequential and influential global economic event and their cumulative effect was nothing short of seismic.

In addition to the developments enumerated in the preceding paragraph, protectionist strategies in the Latin American economies fell out of favor during the early 1980s. Also, under pressure from a major macroeconomic crisis India decided to give up its socialist-statist economic structure and launched a major macroeconomic restructure in 1991. The brisk development of China and India began to change the global economic contours in an overwhelming manner.[31] Inspired by the striking success of East Asian economies with outer-oriented development strategy during the 1970s and 1980s, a good number of developing economies began their economic turnaround during the 1980s by adopting economic liberalization and outer-oriented growth strategy. In the process, many developing economies incessantly improved various aspects of their external sector policies. Most-favored-nation (MFN) tariff rates in the developing economies on average declined from 14.1 percent during 1995–9 to 11.7 percent during 2000–04 and to 9.4 percent in 2007. This was a total decline of 33 percent, a sizeable fall in the barriers to trade (WTI, 2008). In addition, a significant proportion of world trade began to be conducted at zero MFN tariffs, or under various preferential tariff arrangements (PTAs) and free trade agreements (FTAs). Consequently, several industrial and developing economies, and especially EMEs, began a steady process of integration into the global economy. This mindset among policy makers favorably influenced the different channels of global economic integration. Policy mandarins began utilizing them in a creative manner.

5.2 Principal drivers of financial globalization

An inventory of factors promoting and powering international financial integration during this period includes enhanced activities of the following three entities: governments and policy mandarins, market players (borrowers and lenders) and financial institutions. International financial integration was powered particularly by an increasing number of countries adopting financial and trade liberalization measures, domestic financial reforms, macroeconomic restructuring and relaxation of capital account restrictions, as well as the integration of the European Union and creation of the Euro and the stepped-up activities of offshore financial centers (Lane and Milesi-Ferretti, 2008; Schmukler, 2008). While the advanced industrial economies are the most financially integrated, the EMEs played a prominent supportive role in advancing global financial integration.

The three entities named above, individually and in collaboration played an imperative role in helping countries, and country groups, become financially more integrated than in the past. In the early post-World War II period extensive controls on domestic financial markets were endemic. Credit allocation in the economy was controlled and channeled according the priorities determined by the governments. Market forces had nothing to do with the credit allocation and financial markets were frequently repressed. Restrictions were far more stringent and extensive on foreign exchange transactions. Again it was government fiat that determined which foreign exchange transactions could take place and which could not. The same applied to derivative transactions, lending and borrowing activities by banks and business corporations, the participation of foreign investors in the domestic financial markets and that of domestic investors in the global financial markets.

An economy cannot possibly financially globalize without initiatives taken by the government to dismantle these restrictions and controls. Liberalizing restrictions on the domestic financial markets and the capital account of balance-of-payments are two indispensable conditions, without the realization of which financial globalization cannot start. Thus, liberalization and deregulation and opening up of the capital account are the two imperative drivers of financial globalization. The developments of the preceding three decades demonstrated that some governments took these two necessary measures at an early stage, and financially integrated with the global economy swiftly, while others did not. As a generalization it is correct to state that there was a gradual lifting of restrictions in many countries, in some it was swift while in others it was slow. However, periods of reversals are not unknown, when the restrictions were re-imposed. Maximum reversals took place following the debt crisis in the post-1982 period. Many occurred in the mid-1990s and after the Argentine crisis in Latin America.

The development of a domestic financial system in the developing economies, particularly the EMEs, was another consequential promoter of financial integration. In many cases, it was spurred on by the gradual increase in investment from the international capital markets. This helped in the creation of domestic financial products, which in turn facilitated foreign demand and domestic liabilities. Thus, systemic development in the domestic financial sector smoothes the progress of financial globalization. A positive correlation between domestic financial sector development and financial globalization was established by Martin and Rey (2004).[32]

Market players, which include households and business firms, are also among the principal drivers of financial globalization. By borrowing or lending abroad they can make use of relaxed financial constraints to smooth out consumption and investment variations. An important objective of investing abroad is the diversification of cross-country risk. When business corporations raise capital in the global capital market directly through bonds and equity issues, they expand their financing alternatives and lower the cost of capital. This allows them to augment their investment and increase liquidity in the system.

Financial institutions are a force to reckon with in the arena of financial globalization. They are justly regarded as compelling drivers of global financial integration. Internationalization of financial services directly enhanced their role in financial globalization. The ICT revolution, which shrunk the globe, is responsible for geographical distances losing their importance. Due to modern ICT inventions and devices, the reach of large financial institutions increased enormously. They can serve markets in different parts of the globe from one location (or a small number of locations). Intensifying competition in the advanced industrial economies forced the large financial institutions to look for other markets and new lines of financial businesses. As the ICT advances reduced costs of trans-border financial transactions and an increasing number of governments adopted liberalization and deregulated their financial sector, more and more international financial institutions began participating in the local markets of other countries. This provided a substantial impetus to the proliferation of financial globalization.

A forceful factor promoting financial integration was the pace of financial innovation during this period. Acceleration in its pace stepped up financial globalization. Particularly important were securitization and increased activities of hedge funds and widespread use of offshore special-purpose vehicles by both financial and non-financial institutions.

Turning to the demand side, improved macroeconomic policy structures, stronger economic fundamentals and a steady improvement in business environment in several EMEs and middle-income developing countries ensured an attractive business climate for the international financial institutions that were determined to expand their business activities globally. The EMEs *en masse* played a prominent role in the contemporary wave of financial globalization. Since the early 1990s, the external balance sheet of these countries transformed and several of them improved their net external position extraordinarily (Lane and Milesi-Ferretti, 2008).

5.3 Impact on financial integration

If 1950–80 were the years of featherweight global interdependence and integration, the three decades following 1980 were a period of relatively more intensive integration of the global economy and financial markets. Global integration shifted into a higher gear and became a vigorous driver of epoch-making structural changes in the national, regional and global economies. Over these three decades, globalization also succeeded in alleviating poverty to an impressive extent and integrating global economy by production networks, which rendered far-reaching benefits to the global economy. One idiosyncratic tendency of global financial integration is to weaken the regulatory forces. Its progress debilitates the regulatory framework. Technological advancements in collusion with deregulation reinforced a self-reinforcing mechanism pushing strongly in the direction of the global integration of financial markets. Central banking authorities assumed that this would promote self-regulating tendencies in the integrating financial markets. However, these expectations were subsequently belied.

Post-1980 was a halcyon period for global finance, which enabled capital to spread widely in the global economy. New instruments and markets evolved and a stupendous array of new business ventures were financed in various parts of the global economy. Access of ordinary business firms to capital improved phenomenally. Its overall impact over businesses and economies was constructive, favorable and welfare-enhancing. The interruption of this golden era of global finance was marked by the bursting of housing bubble in the US in 2007. Mortgage delinquencies soared and securities backed with sub-prime mortgage lost most of their value. This led to a large decline in the capital of many US and European banks. Massive de-leveraging in the financial markets began in September 2008, when Lehman Brothers filed for bankruptcy. Subsequently, the financial crisis became global and turned into the severe recession discussed in Chapter 2 (Section 12). Its consequence was a sharp contraction of global trade and financial flows. Financial globalization had stalled.

6. Global capital movement and trade in financial services

A rational conceptual vision of an integrated global financial market entails the savings and surplus financial resources of the entire world economy coming into one financial market and competitively being priced by the forces of global demand. In this abstract visualization of a global financial market a range of financial assets would carry the same risk-adjusted expected returns and would be traded globally. During the era overtures toward this theoretical vision of an integrated global financial market were seen in the post-1973 period and 1980s. This was the beginning of a new era of financial globalization. Quadrupling of oil prices triggered capital movements of huge amounts in petro-dollars through the Eurodollar market. That is, these capital movements could bypass official capital controls.

Since the early 1980s, the world's financial system, in particular capital markets, has seen a great deal of transformation. This is clearly reflected by the following three indicators: financial depth, diversity and globalization. In particular, the present period saw impressive advances in the internationalization of financial services. This across-the-board transformation of global finance, particularly capital markets, progressed methodically, albeit not in a linear manner. It was not merely confined to advanced industrial economies and the large financial centers, although undoubtedly that is where it has occurred for the most part. Wide proliferation of financial integration is established by the fact that since 1990, 70 percent of the world economies succeeded in increasing their gross external positions (IMF, 2009a). That being said, a word of caution is necessary here. Notwithstanding the widespread progress in financial globalization, international financial markets are at present far from being perfectly integrated. Plentiful evidence of the unrelenting segmentation of capital markets, both across and within countries, is readily available (Grinblatt and Keloharju, 2001).

A notable development in this regard is that a significant amount of transformation and globalization also took place in developing economies. Many of them successfully deepened their securities markets by initiating major financial reforms, which continued well into the 1990s. These developing economies adopted all the appropriate policy measures, like liberalizing their financial systems, improving investment climate, developing new supervisory frameworks and institutions as well as improving basic infrastructure for capital market operations. These countries became conscious of the fact that macroeconomic stabilization measures were necessary for financial stability. Improvement in business environment was another necessary link for having a smoothly running financial system. To strengthen their capital markets, many developing countries also undertook comprehensive reforms, including pension reforms.

The reform measures undertaken by the developing economies had an uneven impact. The intensity of reforms in many countries was not matched by the final results, which was puzzling. The developing economies of Latin America espoused 'financial globalization more vigorously than have Asian countries, but have lagged considerably behind Asia in terms of deepening their domestic securities markets' (de la Torre and Schmukler, 2005, p. 47). To strengthen their capital markets the developing economies also quickened the pace of privatization of their state-owned enterprises (SOEs). It made FDI and portfolio investment in the EMEs attractive for firms and households in advanced industrial economies. Little wonder that an investment boom occurred in the EMEs during the decade of the 1990s.

Empirical evidence is available to show that global financial markets made discernible progress in interacting and integrating during the 1980s. Mussa and Goldstein (1993) found linkages between national financial markets during this decade and evidence of growth in these linkages. They were particularly strong among the high-grade financial instruments, which were energetically traded between the wholesale markets of major financial centers of the world. These linkages were not limited to the major industrial economies and their financial markets with the rest of the world. Capital markets in large and middle-income developing economies also interacted and participated with the markets in the rest of the world, albeit that they progressed far less in terms of integrating than those in the industrial economies.

Over the decade of the 1980s, the concept of an integrated global financial market was still an abstraction. The possibility of this abstraction turning into a reality could only be conceived for a future period.

The reality was that in most domestic financial markets threats of government intermediation when financial stress of any kind surfaced were omnipresent. Currency risk and simple preference for consuming domestic goods and investing in the domestic markets generally discouraged economic agents from turning global. They restricted their movement out of the domestic capital markets. However, from time to time the attraction of stronger arbitrage of expected returns did overtake the mindset of financial players. When the perception of individual and institutional players that had enormous financial prowess changed, regarding the risk-return outlook for a particular security or currency, temptation to trans-border for financial gains grew strong.

6.1 Prominent attributes of financial globalization

During the 1980s, international diversification of financial assets was in its early phase. Its growth was being negatively affected by the cost of gathering, processing and transmitting information. For the same reason the cost of executing financial transactions was also high. The expectation was that as advances in the ICT occurred, with the passage of time (Section 7.3) these costs would decline. Besides, financial liberalization, which promoted trans-border ownership of assets, was steadily growing in advanced industrial countries.

An important contribution to financial globalization during this period was made by evolution and growth in professionally managed pool of savings. With growth in pension funds, management of savings changed structurally. Private saving schemes supplanted the public ones. Mutual funds began managing much larger volumes of savings than banks. Hedge funds that used advanced investment strategies and aggressively managed portfolio of investments also joined the global financial market operations.

Financial reforms of this period that upgraded payments and settlement systems worked toward reducing systemic risk and encouraged legions of individual investors to participate in global financial markets. Financial reforms also improved the private sector's capacity to change the currency of composition of its assets and liabilities at a short notice. Thus viewed, the 1980s were marked by the mounting importance and agility of the private sector market players. Their operations provided an initial impetus to financial globalization.

There was little evidence of private capital markets making mistakes in important issues like choice of securities and currencies. However, market discipline during this period had a lot to be desired. It could be improved in two ways. Firstly, there was a pressing need for streamlining and strengthening the information flow regarding the debtors' obligations and debt-servicing capability. When there were quality problems with the information, lenders were only able to imperfectly separate good credit risks from bad ones. The likely effect of this could be a contagion effect in the future. Comprehensive reporting of data and transparency in revealing the obligations of borrowers go a long way to improving market discipline. Secondly, the moment it becomes obvious that the participant will be bailed out in case of a default, market discipline is effectively blighted. This knowledge gives rise to unruly and disorderly market behavior. Decision-making processes go totally haywire. Under these circumstances, the interest rate is determined on the basis of the status and stance of the guarantor, not the creditworthiness of the borrower. Also, the errant conduct of the borrower becomes of little concern to the lenders. Properly monitoring loans becomes a redundant exercise for the lenders.

With the onset of the 1990s, the general phenomenon of economic and financial globalization picked up momentum. The concept and phenomenon of globalization became more widespread as well as emotive (Das, 2009a). In accordance with this development, integration of financial transactions and markets also grew more energetic. In particular, wholesale markets of high-grade instruments witnessed closer global financial integration than they did during the 1980s. These wholesale markets of industrial economies integrated far more than those in other economies. At this point, another group that became an active participant in financial market integration was the EMEs. Other large developing economies also attempted to consciously integrate. Their pace of integration was much slower than that of the industrial economies.

In quantitative terms, global capital flows fluctuated from around 2 percent of world GDP in the 1980s to 6 percent in 1995 (IMF, 2008c). A distinguishing feature of the global capital market activity in the 1990s was remarkable growth in international bank lending to these two country groups, namely, the developing economies and the EMEs. That the latter became increasingly financially integrated with the global economy as well as into the global capital markets was dramatically demonstrated when they suffered a string of economic crises during the 1990s.

Formation of the economic and monetary union (EMU) in Europe was a supportive event. The Delors Report of 1989 set out to enunciate and introduce the concept of the EMU.[33] It prepared a three-stage process of integration involving the 16 European Union (EU) member states, culminating with the adoption of the Euro. The plan included the creation of institutions like the European System of Central Banks (ESCB), which was to become responsible for formulating and implementing monetary policy. In July 1990, exchange controls were abolished, which in turn liberalized capital movements in the EU. The Treaty of Maastricht, which came into force in November 1993, further strengthened the EMU by setting a number of economic convergence criteria. The EMU helped in global financial integration by eliminating exchange rate fluctuations among the 11 EMU member countries. Although the formal creation of the Euro Zone took place later, the concept and preparation were being worked on during the 1990s. The creation of a monetary union led to integration of money and credit markets across the member countries.

The euro was adopted as the currency of 11, out of the 16, European countries in January 1999.[34] This was a momentous development and eliminated currency risk among the member countries. It was responsible for a higher degree of substitutability between domestic and foreign securities, which contributed to a substantial reduction in home bias within the Euro Zone. It also stimulated trade in financial services and increased depth and liquidity of a single area-wide financial market. A large volume of the euro-denominated financial trade began to take place in the UK, which paradoxically is still not a member of the EMU. Creation of the euro marked the beginning of the third and final stage of the EMU. By 2009, the membership of the Euro Zone had increased to 16; Slovakia became the 16th member in January 2009.

The EMEs that suffered crises in the 1990s had successfully integrated into the global financial markets. Following the Tequila Crisis of 1994–95 in Mexico, a string of economic and financial crises broke out in the EMEs. The largest and most notable was the Asian financial and currency crisis of 1997–98, which began in Thailand and which engulfed four more Asian economies. It adversely affected the entire regional economy that had cultivated the image of being the most rapidly growing region in the world. They had earned global accolade for being 'miracle' economies over the preceding three decades (Das, 2000). Financial globalization was roundly excoriated for destabilizing this sub-group of economies. The other financial crises of the 1990s included those in Russia, Brazil and Turkey. Argentina suffered a crisis in 2001–02.

The industrial countries suffered from the Long-Term Capital Management (LTCM) debacle in the US in 1999. The reason for this crisis was

Russia's default on its government obligations. With so many financial crises precipitating in such a short time span, it began to be acknowledged that global capital movements can have a strong negative influence over the recipient, lending, regional or global economies. It began to be pointed out that capital market integration could cause contagion effects between national financial markets and that one country's irresponsible policies can spread easily to another country, no matter how responsible and vigilant the latter were. Evidence of a contagion effect was apparent in the Asian crisis. It swelled into a crisis with global repercussions on stock markets. The IMF led the supranational organizations in preparing a strategic response. Large economies like China, the EU, Japan and the US joined in this endeavor. The US Federal Reserve, that had launched a monetary contraction in the third quarter of 1997, pushed it back for fear of destabilizing the global markets further.

The 1990s were a period of boom in the capital markets of advanced industrial economies. Business firms raised more capital in bonds and equity markets than ever before. This boom was accompanied by an increase in financial integration in this group of economies (Eichengreen and Sussman, 2000). The demand side to developments also provided a boost to this boom. Both retail and institutional investors turned toward holding securities rather than bank deposits. This was a new mode of diversifying their portfolios, therefore they increased their participation in the capital markets. In the early and mid-1990s, the EMEs of Asia were the major importers of capital from the global capital markets. They were among the most rapidly growing creditworthy economies in the world and external capital helped them finance their brisk GDP growth. After 1995, world capital markets experienced a dramatic increase. By 2006, global capital flows increased to 14.6 percent of the world GDP. At this point, they totaled $7.2 trillion, which was three times their level in 1995 (de la Torre and Schmukler, 2007; IMF, 2008c).

As explained below (Section 8.2), recurrence of financial crises failed to slow financial globalization down. Its most rapid increase was recorded in the advanced industrial economies, but the EMEs and large developing economies were also becoming increasingly financially integrated. Many of these economies had reformed and strengthened their capital markets. These reform measures made them attractive destinations for global capital inflows, which in turn increased their rate of domestic investment. It helped in creating a broader entrepreneural class in these countries, which allocated imported capital efficiently and fostered economic growth. From the perspective of the global capital markets, this process facilitated international risk sharing.

After the grave 1997–8 financial crisis, the startled Asian EMEs became much less venturesome in the global capital market. They began taking defensive measures by amassing huge war chests of foreign assets. This snowballed into a saving glut. Once they emerged from the crisis, the Asian EMEs turned into huge exporters of capital to the rest of the world. Consequently, the global capital markets were awash with low-interest capital. A large proportion of these capital exports went to the US, which had a just image of a safe haven for investors due to its deep and sophisticated financial markets. Krugman (2009) looked at the sophistication of the US financial markets in a negative light. He noted that the post-Regan era deregulation of the US financial system had prepared American bankers for 'finding sophisticated ways [...] of hiding risk and fooling investors' (Krugman, 2009, p. 16). Large borrowings from China, Japan and the Asian EMEs went on ballooning the US current account deficits year after year. The borrowings topped 6 percent of GDP in 2006. The seeming ease with which the US current account deficit was funded led to the hypothesis that the deficit reflected the underlying strengths of the US economy in terms of productivity and financial market structure. Surging Asian savings also affected a number of European economies, like Britain, Ireland and Spain. Like the US, these economies were also poorly regulated. Also, the debt-fueled housing bubbles popped up in Britain, Spain and the US.

6.2 Learning from the emerging trends

To a perceptive analyst, the financial integration that took place during the 1980s and 1990s yielded plentiful policy lessons. In several EMEs (Brazil, Malaysia, Mexico, Korea, Russian Federation, Thailand) the twin strategy of a pegged exchange rate regime and openness to the global capital market proved unsustainable. All of these economies fell into financial crises at one point or other. However, this observation cannot be generalized. Not all economies become destabilized after integrating with the global capital markets. There were EMEs that supported their pegged exchange rate policy regimes with a strong commitment to following consistent monetary policies. Argentina and Hong Kong SAR came in this category of EMEs. These economies also had a proper regulatory system for their banking system and were careful about keeping banks well-capitalized. Therefore, they faced financial stress better and weathered their stormy periods without collapsing into crises.

Financial crises did not precipitate in the EMEs that maintained a flexible exchange rate regime in place of a pegged one. Singapore, Taiwan, South Africa and post-1995 Mexico came under this category. Therefore, Mussa (2000, p. 38) concluded that economies that maintain 'rigidly pegged exchange rates and free capital mobility' could only do so if other key macroeconomic policies, in particular monetary policies, 'are subordinated to the goal of financial integration'. Another lesson that emerged from the experiences of this period is that economies that had weak banking and financial systems needed to be cautious. It seems desirable for them to maintain controls over their capital inflows from the global capital market. The positive effect of maintaining restrictions over inflows and slowing down their rate of financial integration would be the stability of their currency regime, which is a desirable policy objective indeed.

Statistical data relating to capital flows over this period has been presented in Section 3. Capital flows from the global financial markets to the developing economies contributed to growth by stimulating investment and promoting financial development. Although capital flows to developing economies were subject to volatility, FDI inflows exhibited the steadiest sustained growth. The growing role of FDI in capital flows to EMEs during this era was judged favorably by both academic researchers and financial analysts. In particular, FDI flows expanded considerably during the 1990s and dominated capital flows to EMEs. There was justified confidence in the future growth of FDI to the EMEs. During the financial crises of the 1990s, FDI flows demonstrated stability. Conversely, portfolio investment in EMEs was marked by volatility, particularly during periods of financial crises. Positive assessment of growth in portfolio investment in the EMEs and of the resilience of the international financial system in dealing with any related problems proved to be somewhat exaggerated.

The crises of the 1990s demonstrated that global capital flows exposed the weaknesses of the domestic financial systems in the borrowing economies. As capital accounts were liberalized, banks and corporations became free to borrow from the global financial market. Currency and maturity mismatches occurred due to inadvertence in the borrowing economies, eventually leading to crises. These errors were common in borrowing economies in which corporate governance was weak, regulatory infrastructure was underdeveloped and supervision was poor. They were also common in environments where governments were ready to provide unconditional financial safety nets. These weaknesses coalesced to create a setting ideally suited for the precipitation of a financial crisis.

6.3 Information technology and financial markets

Advances in ICT, the newest sinew of globalization, are responsible for a sea change in the global economy. ICT is a general purpose technology, or meta-technology, that has a pervasive impact on an economy, or a sector thereof.[35] The last decades of the twentieth century are known for a rapid rate of advance in ICT. Satellite television, cellular phone, the Internet and broadband connectivity created a veritable information and communication revolution. It was responsible for *inter alia* sharply reducing the costs of processing and communicating all forms of information and giving a lift to TFP. ICT advances caused it to become a major supporter and promoter of financial globalization. Its contribution to reduction in costs of transactions in financial businesses extended to both the domestic and global markets. Its role in financial globalization cannot be overemphasized.

ICT advances made it possible to do financial business at two different geographical locations with ease, as if the transaction is being conducted locally. The same could be said about financial businesses accessing different financial sectors and services. Precipitous decline in the cost of financial transactions facilitated a sharp increase in global capital flows. However, there was a downside of declining cost and increase in the pace of financial transactions. If the inward capital flows accelerated, the same happened to the outward flows. Any economic stress situation or financial pressures in the recipient economy led to a rapid withdrawal of certain categories of capital, frequently exposing it to economic and financial instability.

As elucidated in Section 8.1, global capital flowed to the developing economies and the EMEs expanded at an unprecedented pace during the 1990s. Economies and firms increasingly began to finance their operations from the global capital markets. As the cost of financial transactions covering a larger geographical area declined, financial institutions were reoriented. They were restructured for the purpose of covering larger geographical areas as well as having greater functional range than they did in the past. This trend is discernible in the ICT-enabled restructuring of banking and other financial institutions and the resulting global integration of their operations.

7. Innovation through securitization

The post-1980 benign environment in the global financial markets and the Great Moderation (Section 2.8) coalesced to contribute to the birth of a new trend in financial innovation. A novel banking strategy was adopted in the capital markets of the advanced industrial economies. It was christened the originate-to-distribute model. Its main instrument was securitization, which was a structured finance process designed to distribute risk to those who were better able to bear it, that is, investors with deep pockets. This inventive strategy allowed banks to originate loans, pool credit risks and sell them to investors. Securitization allowed loans that were held on bank balance sheets to be repackaged into securities that could be sold to investors around the globe. Thus, securitization played a pivotal role in providing an impetus to the globalization of finance (Brender and Pisani, 2009). The credit risk transfer allows lenders to shift default risk to other investors, even though they keep the loans on their books. In a market-based financial system that is built on securitization, both the banking system and capital markets become closely intertwined. With the rapid digitalization and computerization of global finances, the new financial instruments were introduced at a rapid pace and their use proliferated globally at an equally brisk pace.

It must be stated that while they offered benefits, the structured products were complicated. The potential benefits that were offered by securitization made it look like a win-win game. Borrowers were provided with greater access to credit markets at lower costs and investors given more investment options. The latter also saw greater opportunity to manage their risk exposure. Securitization encouraged lenders to lend, which in turn resulted in a borrowing binge. When its use began, securitization was regarded as a pragmatic financial instrument that would promote financial stability because it transferred risk widely. It was spread among those who were able and willing to bear it.

The housing and real estate boom in the US began in the mid-1990s. It was fuelled by this financial innovation, that is, securitization of loans. The calculation was that credit risk could be swiftly transferred through securitization and therefore larger amounts could be loaned for housing. This new innovation offered more. It allowed the lending banks the possibility of having to finance the loan only provisionally and relieving themselves of not only credit risk but also interest-rate risk and liquidity risk. This overly optimistic expectation did not materialize.

Two quasi government-sponsored lending institutions, Fannie Mae and Freddie Mac, were created to support home ownership in the US. They played a critical role in implementing the securitization process. They were the second and the third largest lending institutions in the US, respectively, having combined assets of over $5.4 trillion. They controlled almost half of the US housing mortgage market by being the originator or buyer of home-based loans. They also insured and guaranteed home-based loans. In the early 1980s, Fannie Mae and Freddie Mac devised an ingenious way of accelerating their funding capacity. They bundled their mortgages into large pools. The next step was issuing bonds that gave investors a claim on income flows from the underlying loan pools. These mortgage-backed securities (MBSs) offered relatively attractive yields. Therefore, a large number of investors quickly picked them up. Commercial banks, who had watched the securitization process carefully, also soon entered the loan securitization business. From the perspective of the commercial banks, repackaging of mortgage loans into marketable securities was a lucrative concept. They could provide new intermediation services for high fees. Aided by securitization, the housing and real estate boom soon became a self-perpetuating bubble (Guttmann, 2009).

In the housing loan market, the banks making sub-prime mortgage loans in the US profusely utilized the new model of originate-to-distribute by securitization of these loans.[36] The sub-prime loans expanded and their stock reached $1,300 billion in 2006, compared with a mere $100 billion in 1998. This expansion of sub-prime loans began in the mid-2000s, when the prudential standards applied by those distributing these loans were markedly and continuously relaxed (Wellink, 2008). The result was a steady deterioration in the quality of sub-prime loans. When defaults began mounting in the sub-prime housing loan markets, the problem spread rapidly across the US borders to the other mature financial markets where the credit risk was transferred. Financial distress was not exclusively limited to these markets and spread further.

The sub-prime mortgages were not only granted to borrowers with unfavorable financial history but these borrowers were also allowed to take out a second loan to cover their down payments. Thus, homes were bought entirely on debt. Borrowers paid higher interest rates for 'Alt-A' mortgages because they failed to meet the normal standards of income, wealth and credit-history. The two credit-rating agencies, Moody's and Standard & Poor's, became consultants to the banks, advising them on how to compose loan pools. As consultants they were earning lucrative fees from the lending banks. In their new role as consultant, a conflict of interest was evident. Moody's and Standard & Poor's high ratings of securitization transactions based on sub-prime mortgage loans were apparently not based on objective assessment. Culpability for the sub-prime mortgage muddle, to a great extent, goes to the credit-rating agencies and the dual, if not unscrupulous, role they played (Lucchetti and Ng, 2007). Every issue of MBSs contained sub-prime mortgages, which carried high ratings along with the rest of the pool. The credit-rating agencies consciously downplayed the risk. Investors were deceived by the high ratings and by the credit-rating agencies, which were apparently misleading, if not completely deceitful. They were lulled into believing that the securities that they were buying were safe.

In the new system of MBSs, the payment streams on the pools of mortgages were 'passed through' to investors. As financial markets grew more innovative, the securitization process became progressively more complex. The next stage was to repackage these pass-through securities into other types of instruments called the collateralized mortgage obligations (CMOs). The pass-through income streams for the investors in the CMOs were carved up into different tranches. Bondholders were not provided with pro-rata disbursement of cash flows. Instead CMOs were categorized on the basis of returns on principal by tranche holders. The intricacy of this process went on increasing and soon reached an uneasy and inscrutable level (UBS, 2009). Lloyd Blankfein, CEO of Goldman Sachs, admitted that in the run-up to the current financial crisis banks had lost control of the exotic products they sold. He remarked, 'The industry let the growth and complexity in new instruments outstrip their economic and social utility as well as the operational capacity to manage them' (FT, 2009).[37] He argued strongly in favor of complex, customized derivatives having more rigorous capital requirements.

The trigger for the problems in the US financial markets was the mounting defaults in the sub-prime mortgage market, which became a source of generalized uncertainty due to valuation losses of securitized products. The decade-long US housing boom ended in mid-2006. Credit-rating agencies were justly blamed for playing down the risk involved in MBS. These agencies were more interested in earning their consultancy fee from the banks than honestly assessing risk.

The securitization process had a profound effect over traditional default and interest-rate risks. It transformed the two risks into a hard-to-comprehend counterparty risk. It also made it exceedingly hard to monitor the two risks. It created a chain of incentive conflicts that led private and government supervisors to neglect their commonsense moral obligation to understand and control these risks. Kane (2009, p. 406) reasonably noted, 'At every stage of the securitization process, incentive conflicts tempted private and government supervisors to short-cut and outsource duties of due diligence that they owed not only to one another, but to customers, investors and taxpayers.'

As set out in Chapter 2 (Section 12), in a financially globalized economy, an overspill of financial distress swiftly reached other financial markets and institutions. Financial sector stress proliferated. It first spread to other financial markets and then began to adversely affect the real sector of these economies. Global economic growth was the direct victim. The recession put an end to the halcyon period of global finance. As the soundness of financial institutions varied in different economies before the onset of the financial crisis, they were affected to a differing degree by it. Financial institutions in Asia, including Japan, as well as in Australia and Canada had much less exposure to complicated structured products, compared with those in the EU and the US. This worked to their advantage as crisis spread into the global economy (Shirakawa, 2009).

8. Destabilizing impact of financial globalization

The contemporary phase of economic and financial globalization, on balance, produced enormous aggregate benefits for the global economy as well as for several individual national economies (Sections 4.2). It has had a measurable constructive impact over global living standards (Section 5). The impact of this phase of globalization, in aggregate terms, has been positive and beneficial. Its impact on many segments of global economy has been prosperity-enhancing and, overall, highly desirable (Das, 2008c). This inference is beyond question.[38] However, this is not to refute the negative features and contradict the downsides of financial globalization.

Although standard economic theory denotes that financial globalization helps spread risk and enhances international economic and financial stability, there is a surfeit of evidence to show that a large degree of instability is associated with capital movements. Every crisis uncovers new channels of propagation of instability with sharp currency movement. The 2007–09 global financial crisis has led to a re-evaluation of the relationship between financial globalization, financial stability and crises. A pernicious feedback loop between the financial and real sectors took a large toll on global output and trade. Both began plummeting sharply in the last months of 2008. Asset values fell precipitously both across the advanced industrial economies and the EMEs, dramatically attenuating household wealth and thereby putting downward pressure on consumer demand.

Other than creating volatility in financial and economic sectors of the economy, financial globalization is also believed to have led to inequality both between and within countries. These are indubitably legitimate concerns. Volatility in particular took on a menacing dimension from time to time. Plenteous examples of this are available during both the earlier era of financial globalization and the present one (Das, 2006b).

It has been a subject of frequent observation that the exposure of economies to the global financial markets caused financial, currency and banking crises. Each one of these had high economic, social and human costs. Financial crises tended to submerge entire economies, inflicting massive economic and financial losses on firms and households. Losses were not limited to the domestic economy; trading partners also become vulnerable. Crises not only debilitated the financial and banking sectors of economies but also dealt crippling blows to the real economy. These crises often created an impression that the costs of financial integration are higher than the benefits. Therefore, merits of global financial integration came under recurrent forceful attacks. The turn of the twenty-first century was one such time. Many critics of globalization regard financial globalization as the dark side of globalization. In some quarters a firm belief that financial globalization is the Achilles heel of globalization has taken hold.

If so, should one abandon financial globalization? Do crises and their frequency justify calling off global financial integration? A considerate and perceptive response will have to be in the negative. The nexus between financial 'integration and crisis vulnerability is neither direct nor a rigid one' (Krugman, 2000, p. 76).

8.1 Financial crises then

Crises and setbacks in the financial market are not a new phenomenon particular to current period. A glance at history suggests that periodic currency and financial crises wreaked havoc on economies during various periods of globalization. Financial historians identified setbacks and stresses in the financial markets since the first era of globalization, and long before that. Notable research in this regard was done by Kindleberger (2000), who provided a detailed list of financial crises dating back to the Tulip Mania of 1636 in Holland. This was the first financial crisis noted and analyzed by a financial historian. The decade of the 1890s was important in this context. A series of serious financial crises occurred, some of which threatened to turn into systemic crises. The financial market in London, the largest of this period, played a stabilizing role. It provided much-needed liquidity to assuage market volatility. This was the gold standard era. The roles played by the fixed exchange rate regime, global financial mobility and financial regulations, and their relationship with the crises during this period have been exhaustively studied (Bordo and Eichengreen, 1999; Neal and Weidenmier, 2005).

During the first era of globalization financial crises were in general relatively short-lived and of a milder nature compared to those during the current era of globalization. However, Eichengreen and Bordo (2002) disagreed and established that the currency crises of the former period were of longer duration, albeit that recovery from banking crises was relatively more rapid than during the present period of financial globalization. In addition, banking crises of the pre-1914 period were less prone to undermine confidence in the currency. The result was that they were relatively easier to resolve because of the operating gold standard.

8.2 Financial crises now

Both the financial crises of the 1990s as well as the 2007–09 financial crisis and recession provide clear evidence of the fact that financial globalization under certain circumstances can lead to a crisis, at times a severe one. These crises adversely affected individual, regional and even global economies. Given the high costs of these crises, policy errors causing them need be cautiously eschewed. Each crisis is *sui generis* and is precipitated due to its own special circumstances. The past and present crises came to pass because *inter alia* financial globalization put pressure on the governments to relax the regulations and restrictions that govern the financial markets, which in turn rendered the financial markets vulnerable. Regulatory failure is usually regarded as one of the principal rationales behind many of these crises. Therefore, there is an imperious need for financial globalization to be handled in a pragmatic, clairvoyant and sagacious manner. Having sound knowledge about various direct and indirect linkages of global integration is imperative. Otherwise its negative effects can seriously destabilize national and/or global economies and overwhelm the positive ones.

In the modern period, financial crises that can take domestic, regional and global dimensions, have gone on becoming increasingly complex. The global financial markets have undergone a substantial transformation since the debt crisis of 1982, which broke out in Mexico, spread all over Latin America and then affected the rest of the financial world.[39] During this crisis large lending banks could coordinate with the small ones and other financial intermediaries could be contacted and handled by the IMF. As a unique supranational institution of high integrity, the IMF could make them see their collective interest and persuade them to take an agreed route out of the crisis. However, the same could not be said of the next financial crisis that broke out in Mexico in 1994–5. By this time, the securitization process had expanded enormously and the investor base had not only become much larger but also utterly heterogeneous. At this point, identifying, communicating and convincing this large and heterogeneous group of investors of their collective interest had become an exceedingly challenging task. The IMF faced an additional dilemma in restructuring and ameliorating the crisis in the latter case. This is called the moral hazard. That is, how to convince individual investors to stay in because their collective interest lay in that, although their individual interest evidently lay in getting out at an early point. In such a case, moral hazard assumed a large dimension (Eichengreen and James, 2005).

An uncomfortable assertion is frequently made that a serious disadvantage of global financial integration is that it leads to periodic crises and that its absence can certainly result in tranquility in the world of finance. If so, the upshot of the multiple financial crises of the 1990s and early 2000s should have been deceleration of financial globalization. Paradoxically, they neither unfavorably affected the policy makers' decision process in the capital-importing EMEs and the developing economies, nor adversely affected the confidence and perspective of the global investors. This was proved by the growth in mobility of international investment capital as well as the determination of investors to globally diversify their securities portfolios. This confirmed that the recurrent financial crises were not a barrier for the progress of financial globalization, as may be rationally expected.

When a crisis does occur, oftentimes the burden of culpability is instantly put at the door of financial globalization. Hastily blaming financial globalization is neither understandable nor logical. For instance, while discussing the 2007–09 financial crisis, the lethal confluence of exceedingly low levels of interest rates[40] and unprecedented levels of liquidity that preceded the onset of the crisis are often ignored. Conventional wisdom attributed the 2007–09 crisis entirely to the subprime mortgage market and the collapse of housing-market bubble in the UK and US.[41] They are believed to have led to the credit crunch, which in turn mushroomed and spread to other advanced industrial economies. After a short time lag, financial turmoil engulfed the global financial markets. Such direct causal associations generally do not focus on the correct underlying factors and are usually untenable and flawed.

Originating in the US, the current financial and banking crisis soon spread to Europe and inflicted itself on the rest of the global economy

(*The Economist*, 2009b). After Lehman Brothers, a giant Wall Street investment bank, declared bankruptcy in September 2008, the crisis had a serious turn for the worse and became a full-blown and widespread global crisis. Financial turmoil affected the real economy exceedingly badly and reinforced the cyclical downturn of the global economy. The GDP growth rate in the global economy, particularly in the advanced industrial economies, spiraled down and the unemployment rate rose sharply. The GDP growth rate of the fourth quarter of 2008 was the lowest in a long time in all the major economies, including China, Germany, India, Japan and the US. In three of these economies – the high-income industrial ones – the GDP suffered a wrenching contraction, which continued into 2009. Indubitably, China, India and the other large EMEs suffered much less than the large advanced industrial economies.

This financial crisis altered the perception and expectations of financial globalization. This was not only because of its depth but also because of its global extension. It demonstrated to the world the consequences of globalizing financially without putting in place a commensurate regulatory structure. It also exposed the structural weaknesses in the international financial architecture, which is overdue for earnest refurbishment. While the global financial landscape underwent a far-reaching transformation during the preceding two decades (Chapter 2), the financial regulatory structure and financial architecture failed to adapt to it.

The acute problems of the banking sector and global credit freeze of 2008 were reflected in the shriveling multilateral trade in goods and services. In early 2009, a global recession of severity not seen since the 1930s was in its initial phase. The continuing global financial crisis not only poses a fundamental challenge to globalization in general and financial globalization in particular, but also threatens to retard globalization and transform its character. The preceding three decades of global economic and financial integration and their widely spreading consequences had made the proponents of globalization euphoric. In early 2009, the same proponents of globalization saw the negative effects of it and for the first time felt began questioning it and its benefits (James, 2009). For them, the financial meltdown rendered it difficult to defend the existing levels of financial globalization. The question whether mainstream international economists had been myopic, even ignorant, was seriously debated in the policy and economic conclaves. They were accused of being Panglossian about determining the consequences of financial globalization.

9. Contemporary global integration and expanding middle-class

Conclusive evidence is available to demonstrate that economic and financial globalization during the post-1980s period has had a remarkable and discernable impact on the global economy (Das, 2008c). Like the post-war era for North America, Western Europe and Japan, this period was one of unmatched prosperity (Section 4.2). Subsequently, East Asian economies followed this group of advanced industrial economies (Section 3). Real income growth, in particular, in the industrial economies during this period was unprecedented compared with real income growth in all other economies during previous periods. In the post-1950s period, the resurgence of Japan and subsequently the other East Asian economies demonstrated that a significant degree of catch-up with the matured high-income industrial economies was feasible. It also became evident that the onward march of globalization could facilitate it. China's adoption of the *gai ge kai fang* strategy (Section 5), and its rapid real GDP growth also credibly and noticeably demonstrated the same (Das, 2007).

Proponents of globalization, a group that includes the author, consider economic and financial integration as one of the most powerful transformative forces in the global economy. As seen above, several countries and country-group cases exemplify the fact that globalization influenced not only their economic evolution but had a far-reaching economic impact on them. A much-vaunted and oft-cited recent case is that of the East Asian economies. Economic and financial globalization enabled this group of developing economies to achieve what is known as 'income convergence' (see also Section 3). Without denying the challenges and policy constraints that globalization imposed, it is just to say that economic globalization has been a source of dynamic change and has a myriad of positive, innovative and dynamic traits. Although some of these positive effects are reflected in the increasing volume and value of international trade in goods and services relative to world output and expansion in short- and long-term capital flows, globalization has achieved much more than that.

The global middle-class is a new term that is being bandied about. During the second era of globalization 'an explosion of the world middle class' took place (O'Neill, 2008, p. 16). This expansion was a direct and valuable consequence of the ongoing wave of globalization. It is altering the global economic contours and has become a clearly identifiable structural theme of the present period. It has influenced the global distribution of income and is spreading economic power widely. If the middle-class is defined as households falling between incomes of $6,000 and $30,000 (or €3,800 and €19,000) in terms of purchasing power parity (PPP), some 70 million people have been globally entering this income group each year. This expansion is set to continue over the next two decades and is 'likely to be critical to how the world is changing' (Wilson and Dragusanu, 2008, p. 3). This novel trend is reminiscent of the formation of the middle classes in the today's high-income industrial economies during the latter half of the nineteenth century.

This emergence of a large middle class has been heralded as 'a silent revolution in human affairs' (*The Economist*, 2009a, p. 18). Its beneficiaries have been quietly transforming societies while enjoying their fruits of enterprise, industriousness and assiduousness. Their success was propped up by macroeconomic growth, which in turn was bolstered by global economic and financial integration.

An estimate of the expansion of the middle class was made by the World Bank (2007), which concluded that globalization would lead to the convergence of a large number of developing economies, in the process enhancing the size of the global middle class.[42] In 2000, 7.6 percent of the world's population came into the category of the global middle class. By 2030, this proportion is likely to increase to 16.1 percent. That is, in 2030 over a billion people in the developing countries will have improved living standards which will change their consumption pattern of goods and services, as indicated in Section 3. In 2005, only 400 million people in the developing world had access to such high living standards. These projections are, however, based on the assumption that the globalization-led income convergence will progress at a moderate pace.

In developing economies, globalization has perceptibly helped increase the size of the middle class. Ravallion (2009) defined the middle class in a more appropriate, applicable and defensible manner than in the past. A person with a per capita consumption level of between $2 and $13 a day at 2005 purchasing power parity (PPP) was defined to be in the middle class. According to this new definition the size of the middle class increased from 33 percent of the total population in 1990 to 49 percent in 2005. Therefore, according to this estimate, the size of the middle class increased to a staggering degree between 1990 and 2005, from 1.4 billion to 2.6 billion. An additional 1.2 billion people joined the middle class over the period under consideration. A positive conclusion indeed!

Ravallion's (2009) re-estimates suggest that East Asian economies contributed the most to the expansion of the global middle class during the 1990–2005 period. The size of their middle classes soared from 315.5 million in 1990 to 1,117.1 million in 2005. High growth rates in China and India also played a decisive role in creating the middle-income bulge. In China there was a five-fold increase in the middle class, while that in India doubled. This large expansion in the middle class in the developing economies, particularly the EMEs, reflects global distributional shifts that have entailed greater poverty reduction than was possible under a distribution-neutral growth process. The mean income has risen, while the modal income level has changed little.

According to two widely acclaimed Goldman Sachs studies (2003, 2005), going forward the four BRIC economies and six members of the GCC (Gulf Cooperation Council) will be much larger in terms of GDP than they are at present. By 2030, all four members of BRIC will be among the seven largest economies in the global economy. Several members of the N-11 group – in particular Egypt, the Philippines, Indonesia, Iran, Mexico and Vietnam – will also have much larger GDP sizes. These economies are likely to become those with considerable sized middle classes and therefore substantial consumer demand.

There will be two apparent consequences of this structural shift in the global economy. The first will be a shift in the spending power toward middle-income economies and away from the richest economies. As the large population countries come to have large middle classes, they will dominate global spending power. The second shift will be the transfer in spending power toward middle-income households. This shift in spending power was evident since 2000. The pace of expansion of spending power of the middle-income households is likely to pick up further. It is unlikely to peak before 2020. Wilson and Dragusanu (2008) estimated that by 2030 the size of the middle class will have grown to 2 billion. In a select group of countries a large middle class was created during the first era of globalization that lasted from the mid-nineteenth century to World War I. However, this new rise will dwarf the middle-class expansion that took place during the first era by a large margin.

10. Summary and conclusions

The concept of economic or financial globalization is not new. If anything, it is a several-millennia-old phenomenon. This chapter essentially provides a backdrop to the more recent periods of globalization, which essentially covers the period since the mid-nineteenth century.

Although its emphasis is financial globalization, it has not ignored the economic aspect. It is because the two are intricately and thoroughly intertwined. A functional definition of financial globalization can be the integration of the domestic financial system of an economy with the global financial markets and institutions. Although the beginning of economic and financial globalization can be regarded as an ancient phenomenon, we focus on the post-nineteenth century developments.

Until World War I, economic and financial globalization progressed at an unprecedented rate. This period is known for an unparalleled free flow of goods and capital across international borders. Economic historians regard it as the first era of globalization. During this era the gold standard monetary regime made a momentous contribution to globalization. Consequently, the early twentieth century saw the efficient operation of financial globalization. The large trading nations of this period swiftly adopted the gold standard. Another idiosyncratic feature of this period was steady decline in the cost of transportation as well as declining tariffs. As a result, both international trade and the number and variety of traded products expanded enormously. The industrialized economies of Europe exported manufactured products to other countries. By this time, the Industrial Revolution had made a great deal of progress and the industrially advanced economies of Europe had a massive demand for the import of bulky raw materials, like bauxite, coal, nitrates, oil and rubber. The so-called New World economies played an active role by exporting agricultural products and raw materials.

With the breakout of World War I, the first era of globalization ended. The interwar period is known for deglobalization or reverse-globalization. The gold standard system of fixed exchange rates was abandoned and the floating exchange rate regime was adopted. Stringent capital controls were widely imposed to guard against currency crises and to protect domestic gold reserves. However, the floating exchange rate regime did not function efficiently, resulting in a great deal of global economic disorder and confusion. Exchange rate devaluations became the order of the day. Under the floating exchange rate regime, countries did not shy away from the begger-thy-neighbor kind of devaluations. Also, monetary policy was used to achieve domestic political objectives, like financing wartime deficits. In a short time the global economic environment moved from practically *laissez-faire* to autarkic.[43]

The Bretton Woods system was adopted after World War II. In all 44 allied nations and Argentina, a neutral country, participated in the

Bretton Woods conference. Negotiations concerned two rival plans, presented by Britain and the US.

One view regarding the onset of the present phase of globalization puts it in the early 1950s. The new economic era that focused on supporting and encouraging interdependence, collaboration and mutual support among the important world economies is regarded as a new phase of contemporary globalization. It is believed to be resumption of economic and financial globalization. The world economy enjoyed a remarkable era of prosperity during the latter half of the twentieth century. Although the spread of prosperity and social services was fairly broad, it was far from uniform. Not everybody benefited from the spread of global prosperity. It was utterly uneven in terms of spread among economies as well as among individual population groups within the globalizing economies.

There is another established view regarding the initiation of the contemporary phase of globalization. Some economic historians regard 1980 as the real beginning of what they call the second era of globalization. This period distinguishes itself from the first era of globalization by involving not only traded goods, services and capital but also a long inventory of services that were regarded non-tradable, before the Internet revolution. The contemporary phase of globalization is thought to have commenced around 1980 also because the global political and policy climate changed in favor of neo-liberal economic strategies around this time. The contours of the global economy began to change. EMEs became active participants in financial and economic globalization. Also, a striking emergence of a global middle class occurred during this period.

The decade of the 1990s is known for several economic and financial crises, which had high economic and social costs. Among them, the Asian crisis of 1997–8 was the major one. Economic and financial globalization of this period yielded plentiful policy lessons. This chapter briefly discusses them.

ICT advances became a major promoter and supporter of financial globalization. They contributed a great deal to the reduction in costs of transaction in financial businesses, both in the domestic and global markets. Their role in supporting financial globalization cannot be overemphasized. Although the impact of the contemporary phase of globalization, in aggregate terms, has been positive and beneficial, this is not to refute the negative features and contradict the downsides of globalization. Global integration did lead to economic and financial vulnerabilities and has raised legitimate concerns. Two of the principal areas of justifiable concern are: inequality both between and within countries, and volatility in financial and economic activities. The latter in particular took on a menacing dimension from time to time. Periodic currency and financial crises wreaked havoc on economies.

Notes

1. The two expressions 'financial integration' and 'financial globalization' are being used interchangeably here. Both of them are aggregate concepts implying progressive integration of individual economies with global markets.
2. Chapter 1 in Das (2009a) provides a succinct historical account. See also Ferguson (2008).
3. The global financial crisis of 2007–09 is referred to in the financial media as the crash of 2008.
4. The term emerging-market economy (EME) was coined in 1981 by Antoine W. van Agtmael of the International Finance Corporation, the private sector arm of the World Bank. The developing countries in this category are far from homogeneous and vary from small to large, even very large. They are characterized as emerging because they have adopted market-friendly economic reform programs, resulting in sounder macroeconomic policy structures. China is the largest and most important EME, along with several smaller economies like Tunisia. The common strand between these two economies is that both of them embarked on reform programs and consequently recorded rapid GDP growth. Both of them have liberalized their markets and are in the process of emerging onto the global economic stage. Sustained rapid GDP growth is the first indispensable characteristic of an EME. Many of them are in the process of making a transition from a command economy framework to an open market economy, building accountability within the system. The Russian Federation and the East European economies that were part of the Soviet bloc in the past fall under this category. Secondly, other than the adoption of an economic reform program, an EME builds a transparent and efficient domestic capital market. Thirdly, it reforms its exchange rate regime because a stable currency creates confidence in the economy and investors in the global capital markets regard it as fit for investment. Fourthly, a crucial feature of an EME is its ability to integrate with the global capital markets and attract significant amount of foreign investment, both portfolio and direct. Growing investment – foreign and domestic – implies rising confidence level in the domestic economy. Global capital flows into an EME add volume to its stock market and long-term investment into its infrastructure. For the global investing community the EMEs present an opportunity to diversify their investment portfolios. Investing in EMEs gradually became a standard practice among global investors who wished to diversify, although they added some risk to their portfolios.
5. The acronym BRIC stands for Brazil, the Russian Federation, India and China. It came in use in 2001 for the emerging economic powerhouses.

6. See Section 3.
7. The origin of this crisis was the bursting of the housing bubble in the US. The US housing market peaked in 2006. The global economic and financial crisis that followed was the most severe since the Great Depression. In an interview on the CNN on 4 May 2009, Waren Buffet called it the 'economic Pearl Harbor'.
8. Das (2009a) provides a detailed discussion on various facets of the definition of globalization.
9. See Das (2003a) for more details.
10. For instance see Crafts (2000), Obstfeld and Taylor (1998 and 2003), Bordo et al. (1999a), Mussa (2000) and Frieden (2007).
11. After Kublai Khan's conquest of southern China in 1279, the Mongol empire extended from the coasts of southern Siberia, Manchuria, Korea and China down to Amman in the east, to Hungary and Belarus in the west. It covered India, Indochina, the Persian Gulf and Turkey.
12. A classic account of financial globalization during the nineteenth century has been provided by Herbert Feis (1930). Das (1986) also analyzes it in Chapter 1. A recent scholarly work that addresses this issue is Mauro et al. (2006).
13. An expression first used by Obstfeld and Taylor (2003, p. 241).
14. This expression was first used by Obstfeld and Taylor (1998).
15. Discussing the real beginning of global integration, O'Rourke and Williamson (2002) argue that this was the time when globalization really began. It was essentially triggered by a dramatic reduction in freight and transportation costs. They found evidence for this conclusion by analyzing and making connections between factor prizes, commodity prizes and endowments worldwide.
16. Both Bairoch (1989) and Williamson (2002) provide a detailed analysis of the trading pattern of this period.
17. See Chapter 22 in Krugman and Obstfeld (2008).
18. See also Mundell (1960).
19. For a detailed account, see Chapter 11 in Rajan and Zingales (2003).
20. The term industrial economy or country has become a misnomer, because some of the emerging-market economies, like China, have become extensively industrialized. The contribution of the industrial sector to their GDP is larger than that in the high-income countries of the developed world, whose economies are overwhelmingly dominated by the services sector. These countries have increasingly become large exporters of manufactured products as well.
21. Horst Kohler, Managing Director, International Monetary Fund, 'Strengthening the Framework for the Global Economy', a speech given on the occasion of the Award Ceremony of the Konrad Adenauer Foundation, Berlin, 15 November 2002. Available on the Internet at http://www.imf.org/external/np/speeches/2002/111502.htm.
22. See Table 8-B, Maddison (2003).
23. See Mussa (2000), Table 1.
24. Ibid.
25. See Goldman Sachs (2003, 2005).

26. The Group-of-Seven (G-7) comprises the seven largest mature industrial economies, namely, the US, Japan, Germany, France, the UK, Italy and Canada. In 1976, Canada was the last to join the G-7.
27. The inaugural meeting of the Group-of-Twenty (G-20) took place in Berlin on 15–16 December 1999. It was jointly hosted by the German finance minister Hans Eichel and chaired by the Canadian finance minister Paul Martin. The G-20 had been set up on the recommendation of the G-7 finance ministers (in their report to the economic summit in Cologne on strengthening the international financial architecture) and was confirmed by them and the central bank governors in their joint communiqué in September 1999. The members of the G-20 are the finance ministries and central banks of 19 countries: Argentina, Australia, Brazil, Canada, China, France, Germany, India, Indonesia, Italy, Japan, Korea, Mexico, Russia, Saudi-Arabia, South Africa, Turkey, the UK and the US. The twentieth member is the European Union, represented by the Council presidency and the European Central Bank. To ensure that the G-20's activities are closely aligned with those of the Bretton-Woods institutions, the managing director of the IMF and the president of the World Bank, plus the chairpersons of the International Monetary and Financial Committee and Development Committee of the IMF and World Bank, also participate in the talks as ex-officio members.
28. Literally translated it means 'change the system, open the door'.
29. Several detailed and well-researched accounts of this process are available. For instance, see Lardy (2002, 2006) and Das (2008d).
30. See Brender and Pisani (2009), Chapter 1, for the relationship between deregulation and financial globalization.
31. This issue has been intensively studied in Winters and Yusuf (2007) and Das (2006b).
32. See also Mishkin (2003).
33. Jacque Delors was the president of the European Commission. He chaired a committee which proposed a three-stage plan to reach full economic union.
34. At the time of the launch of the Euro, only 11 EU member-states had met the convergence criteria. Therefore the official launch of the Euro included only these members. Greece qualified in 2000 and was admitted to the Euro Zone in 2001.
35. See Das (2009a), Chapter 1, for a detailed discussion on the significance of the role that ICT played in the contemporary phase of globalization.
36. These loans were called sub-prime because they did not meet the standards set by Fannie Mae and Freddie Mac for the 'prime' loans guaranteed by these institutions.
37. Cited in *The Financial Times*, 9 September 2009. These observations were made during a speech delivered to the Handelsblatt banking conference in Frankfurt.
38. See Das (2003a) for a comprehensive account of financial globalization during the pre-2000 period.
39. Argentina, Brazil and Mexico had borrowed large sums from international creditors for industrialization and infrastructure programs, which they could not repay. Mexico declared moratorium in August 1982.

40. In the wake of the 11 September 2001 attack on the World Trade Center, the US Federal Reserve Board lowered interest to 1 percent and kept it there for almost three years, until mid-2004.
41. Meltdown in securitization instruments in the US and UK began in the summer of 2007. Demirguc-Kunt and Serven (2009) provide an incisive account of the dynamics of the crisis.
42. See Chapter 3, the World Bank (2007).
43. James (2001) provides an in-depth treatment of the breakdown of globalization.

References

Abu-Lughod, J. 1989. *Before European Hegemony: The World System A.D. 1250–1350*. New York. Oxford University Press.
Ahmad, S., A. Levin and A. Wilson. 2002. "Recent US Macroeconomic Stability: Good Policies, Good Practices or Good Luck?" Washington. DC. The Board of Governors of the Federal Reserve System. International Finance Discussion Paper 2002-730. July.
Aizenman, J., J.R. Lothian and B. Pinto. 2007. "Overview of Conference Volume: Financial and Commercial Integrations". *Journal of International Money and Finance*. Vol. 26. No. 7. pp. 657–672.
Bairoch, P. 1989. "European Trade Policy, 1815–1914" in P. Mathias and S. Pollard (eds) *The Cambridge Economic History of Europe*. Vol. VIII. pp. 1–160.
Bernanke, B.S. 2006. "Global Economic Integration: What's New and What's Not?" in *The New Economic Geography: Effects and Policy Implications*, Kansas City. KA. The Federal Reserve Bank of Kansas City. August. pp. 1–14.
Bernanke, B.S. 2004. "Remarks by Governor Ben Bernanke" at the meeting of the Eastern Economic Association, in Washington. DC, on 20 February.
Blanchard, O. and J. Simon. 2001. "The Long and Large Decline in US Output Volatility". *The Brookings Papers on Economic Activity*. Vol. 1. pp. 135–164.
Bordo, M.D. and B.J. Eichengreen. 1999. "Is Our Current International Economic Environment Unusually Crisis Prone?" in D. Gruen and L. Gower (eds) *Capital Flows and International Financial System*. Sydney. The Reserve Bank of Australia. pp. 18–75.
Bordo, M.D., B.S. Eichengreen and D.A. Irwin. 1999a. "Is Globalization Today Really Different than Globalization a Hundred Years Ago?" Cambridge. MA. National Bureau of Economic Research. Working Paper. No. 7185. April.
Bordo, M.D., M. Edelstein and H. Rockoff. 1999b. "Was Adherence to the Gold Standard a 'Good Housekeeping Seal of Approval' During the Interwar Period?" Cambridge. MA. National Bureau of Economic Research. Working Paper No. 7186. June.
Brender, A. and F. Pisani. 2009. *Globalized Finance and its Collapse*. Brussels. Belgium. Dexia Asset Management.
Crafts, N. 2000. "Globalization and Growth in the Twentieth Century". Washington. DC. International Monetary Fund. Working Paper No. WP/00/44. March.
Das, Dilip K. 2009a. *The Two Faces of Globalization: Munificent and Malevolent*. Northampton. MA. USA and Cheltenham. Glos. UK. Edward Elgar Publishing, Inc.

Das, Dilip K. 2008a. "Repositioning the Chinese Economy on the Global Economic Stage". *International Review of Economics*. Vol. 55. No. 4. September 2008. pp. 4–417.

Das, Dilip K. 2008b. "Sovereign-Wealth Funds: A New Role for the Emerging Market Economies in the World of Global Finance". *International Journal of Development Issues*. Sydney. Vol. 7. No. 2. pp. 80–96.

Das, Dilip K. 2008c. *Winners of Globalization*. University of Warwick, UK, Center for the Study of Globalization and Regionalization, CSGR Working Paper No. 249/08. Also available on the Internet at http://www2.warwick.ac.uk/fac/soc/csgr/research/workingpapers/2008/24908.pdf. August 2008.

Das, Dilip K. 2008d. *The Chinese Economic Renaissance: Apocalypse or Cornucopia*. Houndmills. Hampshire. UK. Palgrave Macmillan Ltd.

Das, Dilip K. 2007. "The East is Rich: China's Inexorable Climb to Economic Dominance". Sydney. Macquarie University. Center for Japanese Economic Studies. Research Paper No. 2007-4. December.

Das, Dilip K. 2006a. *China and India: A Tale of Two Economies*. London and New York. Routledge.

Das, Dilip K. 2006b. "Globalization in the World of Finance: An Analytical History". *Global Economic Journal*. Vol. 6. No. 1. Article 2. Berkeley. CA. The Berkeley Electronic Press. Available on the Internet at http://www.bepress.com/cgi/viewcontent.cgi?article=1115&contex=gej. 10 October 2009.

Das, Dilip K. 2004. *Financial Globalization and the Emerging-Market Economies*. London and New York. Routledge.

Das, Dilip K. 2003a. "Globalization in the World of Finance" in Dilip K. Das (ed.) *An International Finance Reader*. London and New York. Routledge. pp. 12–26.

Das, Dilip K. 2003b. "Financial Flows and Global Integration". Coventry. UK. University of Warwick. Center for the Study of Globalization and Regionalization. CSGR Working Paper No. 132/04. June.

Das, Dilip K. 2001. *The Global Trading System at Crossroads: A Post-Seattle Perspective*. London and New York. Routledge.

Das, Dilip K. 2000. *Asian Crisis: Distilling Critical Lessons*. Geneva. United Nations Conference on Trade and Development (UNCTAD). Discussion Paper No. 152. December.

Das, Dilip K. 1986. *Migration of Financial Resources to Developing Countries*. London. The Macmillan Press Ltd and New York. St. Martin's Press, Inc.

Daudin, G., M. Morys and K.H. O'Kourke. 2008. "Globalization 1870–1914". Dublin. Ireland. Trinity College. IIIS Discussion Paper No. 250. May.

de la Torre, A. and S.L. Schmukler. 2007. *Emerging Capital Markets and Globalization*. Palo Alto. CA. Stanford University Press.

de la Torre, A. and S.L. Schmukler. 2005. "Small Fish, Big Pond". *Finance and Development*. Vol. 42. No. 2. pp. 47–49.

Demirguc-Kunt, A. and L. Serven. 2009. "Are All the Sacred Cows Dead?" The World Bank. Policy Research Working Paper No. 4807. January.

Dowrick, S. and J.B. DeLong. 2005. "Globalization and Convergence" in M.D. Bordo, A.M. Taylor and J.G. Williamson (eds) *Globalization in Historical Perspective*. Chicago. The University of Chicago Press. pp. 191–205.

The Economic Intelligene Unit (EIU). 2009. "World Economy: BRIC, but No Bloc". Available on the Internet at http://viewswire.eiu.com/index.asp?layout=VWPrintVW3&article_id=734586458&printer=printer. Posted on June 16.

The Economist. 2009a. "Two Billion More Bourgeois". 14 February. p. 18.

The Economist. 2009b. "Whom Can They Rely on?" 6 May. p. 61.

Edelstein, M. 2004. "Foreign Investment, Accumulation and Empire 1860–1940" in R. Floud and P. Johnson (eds) *The Cambridge Economic History of Modern Britain.* Cambridge. Cambridge University Press.

Eichengreen, B.J. 2008. "The Global Credit Crisis as History". Paper presented at Bank of Thailand International Symposium on *Financial Globalization and Emerging Market Economies* at Dusit Thani Hotel, Bangkok, during November 7–8.

Eichengreen, B.J. 1999. *Globalizing Capital: A History of the International Monetary System.* Princeton. NJ. Princeton University Press.

Eichengreen, B.J. and H. James. 2005. "Monetary and Financial Reforms in Two Eras of Globalization" in M.D. Bordo, A.M. Taylor and J.G. Williamson (eds) *Globalization in Historical Perspective.* Chicago. The University of Chicago Press. pp. 515–548.

Eichengreen, B.J. and M.D. Bordo. 2002. "Cries Then and Now: What Lessons from the Last Era of Globalization". Cambridge. MA. National Bureau of Economic Research. NBER Working Paper 8716. January.

Eichengreen, B.J. and N. Sussman. 2000. "The International Monetary System in the Very Long Run" in *World Economic Outlook Supporting Studies.* Washington. DC. International Monetary Fund. pp. 52–85.

Elliott, A. and C. Lemert. 2009. *Globalization.* London and New York. Routledge.

Feis, H. 1930. *Europe the World's Banker, 1870–1914.* New Haven. CT. Yale University Press.

Feldstein, M. and C. Horioka. 1980. "Domestic Savings and International Capital Flows". *The Economic Journal.* Vol. 90. No. 2. pp. 314–329.

Felton, F. and C. Reinhart. 2008. *The First Financial Crisis of the 21st Century.* London. Center for Economic Policy Research.

Ferguson, N. 2008. *The Ascent of Money.* New York. The Penguin Press.

The Financial Times (FT). 2009. "Goldman Chief Admits Banks Lost Control". London. 9 September. Available on the Internet at http://www.ft.com/cms/s/0/ffb670be-9d33–11de-9f4a-00144feabdc0.html?catid=20&SID=google. 10 October 2009.

Findlay, R. and K.H. O'Rourke. 2007. *Power and Plenty.* Princeton. Princeton University Press.

Frieden, J.A. 2007. *Global Capitalism, Its Fall and Rise in the Twentieth Century.* New York. W.W. Norton & Co.

Goldman Sachs. 2005. "How Solid are the BRICs?" New York. Global Economics Paper No: 134. December.

Goldman Sachs. 2003. "Dreaming With BRICs: The Path to 2050" New York. Global Economics Paper No: 99. October.

Grinblatt, M. and M. Keloharju. 2001. "How Distance, Language and Culture Influence Stockholdings and Trades". *Journal of Finance.* Vol. 56. No. 3. pp. 1053–1074.

Guttmann, R. 2009. "The Collapse of Securitization: From Subprime to Global Credit Crunch". Laurentian University, Ontario. International Economic Policy Institute. Canada. Working Paper 2009-05. June.

Highfill, J. 2009. "The Economic Crisis as of December 2008". *Global Economy Journal.* Vol. 8. No. 4. pp. 1–5.

The International Monetary Fund (IMF). 2009a. *World Economic Outlook.* Washington. DC. April.

The International Monetary Fund (IMF). 2008a. "Reaping Benefits of Financial Globalization". Washington. DC. Occasional Paper 264. December.

The International Monetary Fund (IMF). 2008b. *World Economic Outlook.* Washington. DC. April.

The International Monetary Fund (IMF). 2008c. "Globalization: A Brief Overview". *Issues Brief.* No. 02/08. Washington. DC. May.

James, H. 2009. "The Making of a Mess". *Foreign Affairs.* January/February. Vol. 80. No. 1. pp. 48–59.

James, H. 2001. *The End of Globalization: Lessons from the Great Depression.* Cambridge. MA. Harvard University Press.

Joyce, J.P. 2009. "Financial Globalization and Banking Crises in Emerging Markets". Wellesley. MA. Wellesley College. Department of Economics. Working Paper. January.

Kane, E.J. 2009. "Incentive Roots of the Securitization Crisis and Its Early Mismanagement". *The Yale Journal on Regulation.* Vol. 26. No. 2. pp. 405–416.

Kindleberger, C.P. 2000. *Manias, Panics and Crashes.* New York. Wiley & Sons.

Kohler, H. 2002. "Strengthening the Framework for the Global Economy". A speech given on the occasion of the Award Ceremony of the Konrad Adenauer Foundation, Berlin, Germany. 15 November 2002. Available on the Internet at http://www.imf.org/external/np/speeches/2002/111502.htm. 15 October 2009.

Krugman, P.R. 2009. "Revenge of the Glut". *The New York Times.* March 2. p. 16.

Krugman, P.R. 2000. "Crises: A Price of Globalization?" in *Global Economic Integration: Opportunities and Challenges.* Kansas City. KA. The Federal Reserve Bank of Kansas City. pp. 75–109. August.

Krugman, P.R. and M. Obstfeld. 2008. *International Economics: Theory and Policy.* 8th edition. Boston. Pearson Addison Wesley.

Lane, P.R. and G.M. Milesi-Ferretti. 2008. "The Drivers of Financial Globalization". *American Economic Review.* Vol. 98. No. 2. pp. 327–332.

Lane, P.R. and G.M. Milesi-Ferretti. 2007. "The External Wealth of Nations Mark II". *Journal of International Economics.* Vol. 73. No. 2. pp. 223–250.

Lardy, N.R. 2006. "China's Interaction with the Global Economy" in R. Garnaut and L. Song (eds) *The Turning Point in China's Economic Development.* Canberra. Australia. The Asia Pacific Press. Australian National University. pp. 76–86.

Lardy, N.R. 2002. *Integrating China into the Global Economy.* Washington. DC. The Brookings Institutions.

Litan, R., P. Masson and M. Pomerleano. 2001. *Open Doors: Foreign Participation in Financial Systems in Developing Countries.* Washington. DC. The Prookings Institution.

Lucas, R.E. 2000. "Some Macroeconomics for the 21st Century". *Journal of Economic Perspectives.* Vol. 14. No. 1. pp. 159–168.

Lucchetti, A. and S. Ng. 2007. "Credit and Blame: How Rating Firms' Calls Fueled Subprime Mess". *Wall Street Journal.* 15 August. p. A1.

Maddison, A. 2003. *The World Economy: Historical Statistics.* Paris. The Development Center. Organization for Economic Cooperation and Development.

Maddison, A. 1995. *Monitoring the World Economy 1920–1992.* Paris. Organization for Economic Cooperation and Development.

Martin, P. and H. Rey. 2004. "Financial Super-Markets: Size Matters for Asset Trade". *Journal of International Economics*. Vol. 64. No. 2. pp. 335–361.

Masson, P. 2001. "Globalization: Facts and Figures". Washington. DC. International Monetary Fund. Policy Discussion Working Paper. October.

Mauro, P., N. Sussman and Y. Yafeh. 2006. *Emerging Markets, Sovereign Debts and International Financial Integration*. New York. Oxford University Press.

McKinsey Global Institute (MGI). 2008. "The New Power Brokers: Gaining Clout in Turbulent Markets". San Francisco. July.

Mishkin, F.S. 2003. "Financial Policies and the Prevention of Financial Crises in Emerging Markets" in M. Feldstein (ed.) *Economic and Financial Crisis in Emerging Markets*. Chicago. University of Chicago Press. pp. 130–147.

Mishkin, F.S. 2001. "Financial Policies and Prevention of Financial Crises in Emerging Market Economies". Cambridge. MA. National Bureau of Economic Research. Working Paper. No. 8087. April.

Mundell, R.A. 2000. "A Reconsideration of the Twentieth Century". *American Economic Review*. Vol. 90. No. 3. pp. 327–340.

Mundell, R.A. 1960. "The Monetary Dynamics of International Adjustment under Fixed and Flexible Exchange Rates". *Quarterly Journal of Economics*. Vol. 84. No. 2. pp. 227–257.

Mussa, M. 2000. "Factors Driving Global Economic Integration" in *Global Economic Integration: Opportunities and Challenges*. Kansas City. Missouri. The Federal Reserve Bank of Kansas City. pp. 8–56. August.

Mussa, M. and M. Goldstein. 1993. "The Integration of World Capital Markets" in *Changing Capital Markets: Implications for Monetary Policy*. Kansas City. Missouri. The Federal Reserve Bank of Kansas City. pp. 55–93. August.

Neal, L. 1990. *The Rise of Financial Capitalism: International Capital Markets in the Age of Reason*. Cambridge. Cambridge University press.

Neal, L. and M. Weidenmier. 2005. "Crises in the Global Economy from Tulip to Today" in M.D. Bordo, A.M. Taylor and J.G. Williamson (eds) *Globalization in Historical Perspective*. Chicago. The University of Chicago Press. pp. 473–513.

Obstfeld, M and A.M. Taylor. 2005. "Globalization in Historical Perspective" in M.D. Bordo, A.M. Taylor and J.G. Williamson (eds) *Globalization in Historical Perspective*. Chicago. The University of Chicago Press. pp. 121–183.

Obstfeld, M and A.M. Taylor. 2004. *Global Capital Markets: Integration, Crisis and Growth*. Cambridge. Cambridge University Press.

Obstfeld, M and A.M. Taylor. 2003. "Sovereign Risk, Credibility and the Gold Standard: 1870–1913 Versus 1925–31". *The Economic Journal*. Vol. 113. April. pp. 241–275.

Obstfeld, M and A.M. Taylor. 1998. "The Great Depression as a Watershed: International Capital Mobility over the Long Run" in M.D. Bordo, D.G. Claudia and E.N. Eugene (eds) *The Defining Moment: The Great Depression and the American Economy*. Chicago. The University of Chicago Press. pp. 353–402.

O'Neill, J. 2008. "Boom Time for the Global Bourgeoisie". *The Financial Times*. July 15. p. 16.

O'Rourke, K. and J.G. Williamson. 2002. "When Did Globalization Really Begin?" Cambridge. MA. National Bureau of Economic Research. Working Paper. No. 7632. April.

Peters, R.T. 2004. *The Ethics of Globalization*. New York. Continuum International Publishing.

Rajan, R.G. and L. Zingales. 2003. *Saving Capitalism from the Capitalists*. New York. Crown Business Division of Random House.

Ravallion, M. 2009. "The Developing World's Bulging (but Vulnerable) Middle Class". Washington. DC. The World Bank. Policy Research Working Paper 4816. January.

Schmukler, S.L. 2008. "Benefits and Risks of Financial Globalization" in J. Ocampro and J.E. Stiglitz (eds) *Capital Market Liberalization*. Oxford. UK. Oxford University Press. pp. 48–73.

Schularick, M. 2006. "A Tale of Two Globalizations". *International Journal of Finance and Economics*. Vol. 11. No. 4. pp. 339–354.

Shirakawa, M. 2009. "International Policy Response to Financial Crisis". Paper presented at the Federal Reserve Bank of Kansas City's *Annual Economic Symposium on Financial Stability and Macroeconomic Stability* at Jackson Hole, Wyoming, on 21–22 August.

Spehar, A.O. 2009. "The Great Moderation and the New Business Cycle". Munich. Munich Personal RePEc Archive. MPRA Paper No. 12274. February. Available on line at http://mpra.ub.uni-muenchen.de/12274/. 5 November 2009.

Steil, B. 2006. "The Developing World Should Abandon Parochial Currencies". *The Financial Times*. 16 January. p. 16.

Summers, P.M. 2005. "What Caused the Great Moderation? Some Cross-Country Evidence". Available on the Internet at http://www.kc.Frb.org/Publicat/Econrev/PDF/3q05summ.pdf. 5 November 2009.

Union Bank of Switzerland (UBS). 2009. *Financial Crisis and Its Aftermath*. Zurich. Switzerland.

Wellink, N. 2008. "Financial Globalization, Growth and Asset Prices". Paper presented at a conference on *Globalization, Inflation and Monetary Policy* organized by the Bank of France, in Paris, on 7 March.

Williamson, J.G. 2002. "Winners and Losers over Two Centuries of Globalization". Cambridge. MA. National Bureau of Economic Research. NBER Working Paper 9161. September.

Williamson, J.G. 1996. "Globalization, Convergence and History". *Journal of Economic History*. Vol. 56. No. 2. pp. 277–310.

Wilson, D. and R. Dragusanu. 2008. "The Expanding Middle: The Exploding World Middle Class". New York. Goldman Sachs. July.

Winters, L.A. and S. Yusuf. 2007. *Dancing with Giants*. Washington. DC. The World Bank.

The World Bank(WB). 2007. *Global Economic Outlook*. Washington. DC.

World Trade Indicators (WTI). 2008. Washington. DC. The World Bank.

2
Financial Globalization and the Shifting Sands in Contemporary Financial Markets

1. Introduction

The focus of this chapter is the financial globalization in the contemporary period. It begins with the impact of several momentous developments in the post-World War II era, which helped shape the contours of the contemporary era of financial globalization. It traces the emergence of the financial and capital markets and delineates the shifting trends during the post-2000 period. Thus, it covers the global financial canvas of a large time span. It examines, *inter alia*, the resumption of financial globalization after the deglobalization period of the 1930s and World War II, and looks at its principal drivers.

Modern history of financial globalization starts from the Renaissance, when Italian banks financed trade and governments in Europe and around the Mediterranean. The Medici family of Venice was among the wealthiest in Europe.[1] They was among the first to venture successfully into international banking. Italian banks developed instruments to methodically finance trade. The Medici bank was one of the most prosperous and respected European financial institutions of this period. Although it could be regarded as the precursor of financial globalization, its geographical scope was limited. As European trade expanded, financial innovations spread northward through letters of credit. They were invented at the Champagne Fair in France and became a widely accepted financial instrument (Obstfeld and Taylor, 2005). International banking spread north from Italy. Banks in northern ports like Bruges and Antwerp also used financial instruments developed by the Italian banks as well as letters of credit. Amsterdam and London were next to develop as hubs of international finance, with their currencies playing key international roles.[2] Financial instruments developed and used in these two centers were considered credible and valuable by the market players of this period.

This chapter begins with the widely acknowledged fact that global economic and financial integration can and did go into a reverse gear. Following a breakdown during the interwar period, the global financial system and capital markets began their reconstruction and rejuvenation task in the post-World War II period. The reconstruction efforts of the immediate post-World War II era are the first focus of this chapter. During the decades immediately after World War II, particularly in 1973, several developments took place that had momentous global economic and financial implications. They made a contribution to the rejuvenation of international financial architecture and global capital markets. Also at this juncture, in a small group of the advanced industrial economies, a spurt in global capital market flows occurred. A large global market for cross-border syndicated loans developed in post-1973. This market had a wide geographical spread.

Adoption of macroeconomic reforms, and restructuring and dismantling controls and restrictions were the preconditions of financial globalization. Other than these, adoption of privatization and ushering in the necessary innovations in their financial markets were other strategies which could help. Several factors like liberalization and deregulation adopted by the advanced industrial economies, and emergence of a strong institutional and retail demand for financial assets supported the onward march of financial globalization. As elaborated at length in this chapter, spurred by deregulation and financial innovation securities markets in the advanced industrial economies also began to develop much faster than ever before. Consequently, rapid transformations in the global financial landscape began to take place. The decades of the 1990s and 2000s were of particular significance in this regard. The pace of financial globalization had accelerated. Over these decades the rate of increase of global cross-border investment was twice that of the rate of growth of multilateral trade in goods and services, which in turn exceeded the rate of global GDP growth (Lane and Milesi-Ferretti, 2007). Also, the average daily turnover of the foreign exchange market more than doubled in one decade. It was $1.5 trillion in April 1998 but increased to $3.2 trillion in 2007 (BIS, 2007).

The advanced industrial economies were the first to financially globalize, while the emerging-market economies (EMEs) and the other large developing economies followed suit later. The latter two types of economies were influenced by the structural changes that were occurring in the financial and capital markets in advanced industrial economies, and began to unilaterally liberalize and restructure their own macroeconomic policy framework and usher in identical policy transformations in their financial sector. The growth of financial globalization picked up momentum. Rapid progress in financial globalization turned the decade of the 1990s into one of unparalleled boom. In particular, the mid-1990s are regarded as an invigorating period of growth and financial globalization.

International financial integration during the contemporary period is of substantially higher intensity than in the past. Gross world assets divided by global GDP is a good measure of capital market integration. Its volume is roughly 100 percent of the global GDP at present, compared to approximately 20 percent in 1913, the last year of the previous era of financial globalization (Schularick, 2006). Similar numbers were computed by Obstfeld and Taylor (2004). This increase in global financial integration is largely due to much closer financial ties between the advanced industrial economies. The present period of financial globalization has been characterized as a 'rich-rich affair' (Obstfeld and Taylor, 2003, p. 254).

Although financial globalization progressed with increasing market capitalization and liquidity in a small number of large financial centers, its idiosyncratic feature was that financial activity was essentially concentrated in the large financial centers of the advanced industrial economies, namely, Germany, Japan, the UK and the US. Financial markets in Frankfurt, London, New York and Tokyo overwhelmingly dominated global financial market activity. This period of rapid progress of financial globalization was interrupted by the fallout from some serious crises. The Asian financial crisis (1997–8) unfavorably affected it. The Asian crisis was followed by the Russian or Ruble crisis (1998), which obviously had a negative impact on global investors' psychology. Although the interruption caused by these crises and the bursting of the information technology (IT) bubble was acute, the world economy continued to grow more integrated in terms of accelerated movements of goods, services and capital, which made the 1990s and 2000s even more momentous than the preceding decade (Das, 2009a).

Notwithstanding the 1997–8 financial crises, financial flows and integration among the advanced industrial economies continued to surge at an even pace. They were uninfluenced by the meltdown of 1998. A much broader global impact was made by the end of the so-called IT boom, or bursting of the dot-com bubble, in early 2001. The advanced industrial economies and their financial markets were adversely affected by the short recession caused by it. Notwithstanding this blip, between 1995 and 2006 global capital flows soared from 6 percent of the world's GDP to 14.8 percent. In 2008, their value was $7.2 trillion, more than triple their value in 1995 (IMF, 2008c).

Although a major part of this increase in global capital flows took place in the advanced industrial economies, the developing economies did not remain as rank outsiders. Many of them participated fairly actively. Debt and equity finances to the developing countries increased during the 1990s and the post-2000 period. This increase was far from monotonic. Cross-border syndicated bank lending to developing countries, international bond market flows and those in the form of equity (foreign direct investment and equity) investment soared dramatically after 2004. The sub-prime crisis, leading to global financial turbulence in the fall of 2007, did not affect these financial flows to the developing economies adversely. Although proliferation of financial globalization was far from uniform in the global economy, rapid advances in financial globalization began progressively changing the nature of capitalism in the world economy.

2. Resumption of financial globalization

Deglobalization or reverse globalization has happened on several occasions in the past and it is happening again in the present. In the last quarter of 2008, the global crisis that originated in the financial sector spilled into the real economy. Supranational institutions produced a flurry of projections in 2008 for sharp decline in industrial production, steep demand-driven contractions in multilateral trade and trans-border financial flows in 2009. In early 2009, they revised those projections downwards. Until the first quarter of 2009, little progress was made in addressing distressed assets in the advanced industrial economies and credit conditions remained severely impaired. Financial deglobalization hit different groups of global economies in a variety of ways in 2009. Whether this crisis began in the financial markets or the real economy is a contentious issue. A global saving glut in East Asia, in particular China, Japan and Germany, and in the Gulf Cooperation Council (GCC)[3] economies was the same as the consumption glut in the destination counties, particularly the US (Mizen, 2008).

One oft-cited example of reversal of financial integration is that of the interwar period; although financial integration did come to a standstill during the Baring crisis in 1891 as well. As World War II ended, endeavors were made to reconstruct and rebuild the war-ravaged economies.

Economic growth in the war-ravaged countries and multilateral trade picked up gradually first and then began to flourish at a more rapid pace, leading to the advent of a unique era of rapid trade and GDP growth performance. However, this trade and the GDP growth expansion of the early post-war era was unevenly spread over the global economy.

Immediately after World War II, capital markets around the world were in a moribund state and needed time to rejuvenate and become operative. The early post-war development of international capital markets was exceedingly slow. Their medium-term growth was far from linear. They did not smoothly evolve as ever-more-perfectly functioning markets with ever-falling transaction costs and constantly expanding scope. Their progress took place in fits and start. Vicissitudes in the volume of financial flows were more common than uncommon. Despite rapid GDP growth and multilateral trade liberalization and expansion, capital was not fluently mobile during the initial post-war decades. Several global factors constrained cross-border capital flows during this period.

As it was a source of serious destability and economic and financial disarray during the interwar period, cross-border capital movement was initially regarded by policy mandarins as an anathema. These experiences of the interwar period could not be disregarded by policy makers. They had caused a strong reaction against the operation of market forces and created an anti-market environment. A belief took hold that, left to their own devices, free markets malfunctioned. This observation applied to both domestic and international markets, particularly the financial markets. Consequently, the Bretton Woods regime (1946–73) adopted capital immobility as one of its principal policy pillars. Capital controls were also used as an instrument to control domestic demand. The International Monetary Fund (IMF) approved of the concept of capital controls for the member countries as a mechanism of preventing currency crises and disastrous speculative runs on currencies, common during the interwar period. This was a significant policy decision that also provided IMF member countries autonomy to follow much-needed activist monetary policies at home.

2.1 Reviving the global capital markets

With good reason, economic history regards the interwar period as one of severe economic and financial deterioration and disruption; at time when the disintegrated global economy reached a critical point. Fragmented financial markets could not possibly reap the benefits of financial globalization. As World War II ended, the process of its reconstruction started in earnest. In the following decades, private global capital markets re-evolved. This section sets out how the process of slow recreation worked, how private global capital markets were affected by trilemma-related strategic decisions and in what shape they finally re-emerged. In the immediate aftermath of the war, global capital markets remained by and large dormant. Their depressed and sluggish state continued during a good part of the 1950s. In this inward-looking period they were essentially controlled markets; the controls applied both domestically and for foreign transaction purposes. Also, both capital and current account transactions were stringently controlled in the majority of the industrial economies and the developing ones (Chapter 1, Section 2.7).

The positive effect of virtual inaction in the capital markets during this period was that it provided them with an opportunity to slowly recover structurally and, over time, arrive at an operational state. By the late 1960s, the so-called Eurodollar markets were active in trans-border transactions and capital flows. In addition, in major industrial countries traders and financial operators devised ways to circumvent capital controls. Consequently, the compromise that was sustaining the adjustable pegged exchange rate regime of this period broke down. Market forces preferred and worked for capital mobility. This could no longer be held back by capital controls and resumed in a meaningful manner. With that, speculative runs on currencies began again.

The IMF was founded in December 1945, when the 29 founding member countries signed its Articles of Agreement.[4] It began operations in March 1947. Its statutory purpose was to promote global economic growth through international trade and financial stability, and secure international monetary cooperation to stabilize exchange rates and expand international liquidity. After the founding of the IMF, the movable peg exchange rate regime was accepted by the members and began functioning as the new global financial architecture (Section 2.3). The official classification of the exchange rate regime was agreed to by the member countries of the IMF and recorded in the *Annual Report on Exchange Rate Arrangements and Exchange Rate Restrictions*.

However, the official agreement of the member countries needs to be taken with a pinch of salt. Only the over-credulous can believe them. Based on an extensive new monthly data set spanning 153 countries and focusing on the period 1946–2001 Reinhart and Rogoff (2004a) found that the officially declared positions of countries were in most cases different to how they really functioned. Availability of new statistical data facilitated a nuanced distinction between what countries declared as their *de jure* exchange rate regimes and their actual *de facto* exchange rate practices. Reinhart and Rogoff (2004a) concluded that dual or multiple rate markets and parallel or black markets prevailed far more frequently than was commonly acknowledged, or revealed by the *de jure* declarations by the member governments. In 1950, 45 percent of the countries in the sample were found to have dual or multiple rates and many more had flourishing parallel or black markets in foreign currency. This reality had no relationship with the *de jure* movable peg regime. Among the industrial economies, dual or multiple rates were an accepted norm during the latter half of the 1940s and the 1950s. In many of them dual rates lasted for much longer. In the developing countries these practices continued until the 1980s, on occasions even longer.

The dual or parallel rates were essentially market-determined. When market-determined behavior of exchange rates is taken into account, the post-World War II history of exchange rates begins to differ from the official pronouncements and records. It becomes evident that *de facto* floating was a common practice during the Bretton Woods era of pegged exchange rates. This shows that merely accepting the *de jure* arrangements publicized by governments equips us with a foggy, if not an illusory, perspective of history. Knowledge of the *de facto* situation concealed behind the *de jure* situation is essential to correct our vision regarding the reality of operational exchange rate regimes.

2.2 Trilemma leading to conflicting policy stance

One of the reasons why the post-war re-evolutionary process of global capital markets progressed at a snail's pace was the so-called trilemma in the macroeconomic policy making (Chapter 1, Section 2.3).[5] It is also known as 'open economy trilemma' or 'the inconsistent trinity proposition'. An open and liberalized capital market limits the macroeconomic policy options of a country's government. A country cannot simultaneously maintain (i) a fixed exchange rate, (ii) an open capital market, while at the same time pursuing (iii) a monetary policy toward domestic economic goals. At a given point in time, only two of the above policy measures can be simultaneously used.

First, if a government decides to use monetary policy instruments to determine interest rates and target domestic macroeconomic objectives, it must either abandon its commitment to free capital mobility or allow the exchange rate to float. Only one of the two can be chosen.

Second, if a government decides that it wishes to target the exchange rate and liberalize capital mobility, it cannot use monetary policy to achieve domestic policy objectives. Simultaneous targeting of domestic objectives and the exchange rate is only possible if controls on capital mobility are imposed. Thus, trilemma can clearly create conflict in significant policy areas. It relates to crucial areas of domestic and external macroeconomic policy and makes it difficult for governments to choose the appropriate policy stance. Also, in adopting a policy in this area most governments try to first cautiously watch the policy stance of the principal trading partners and large economies. They have a decisive influence over the choice of policy stance.

A good case in point is the classical gold standard era which began during the 1870s (Chapter 1, Section 2.3). Rapid capital mobility had prevailed during this period because there was widespread political support in the major economies for an exchange rate policy subordinating the monetary policy. All of the systemically important economies of this period fixed the price of their currencies in gold, which signified that every major currency had a fixed rate of exchange vis-à-vis every other. During this period the trilemma was resolved by adopting a fixed exchange rate and rapid capital mobility. Domestic macroeconomic strategy was assigned a lower priority by the policy mandarins. There were periods when it resulted in domestic macroeconomic cost to some individual economies. In the early 1930s, all systemically important economies jettisoned the fixed exchange rate regime and open capital markets that the gold standard provided. High priority was instead given to domestic macroeconomic policy objectives and floating exchange rates.

Another example of the trilemma influencing the policy stance of countries is the post-1973 era of progressively increasing capital mobility. During this period monetary policy was geared toward domestic objectives and the stability of exchange rate regime was accepted as the cost of such a policy stance. Thus, as alluded to above, the policy stance countries settle for is rationally influenced by the choices of other governments. This is not to suggest that the domestic circumstances of economies are regarded as less significant and are therefore discounted. They have indeed a great bearing on the final choice. However, many countries vie for the middle ground when they attempt to achieve the twin goals of an exchange rate target and domestic policy objectives. This policy stance cannot be achieved without either rigid exchange controls or restrictions on international transactions and capital flows.[6]

2.3 Dormant capital markets in the Bretton Woods era

As elucidated in the preceding chapter (Chapter 1, Section 2.7), the Bretton Woods system adopted the compromise of a movable peg exchange rate regime. Taking a lesson from the challenges posed by the disorder of the interwar period, this regime did not allow capital to flow freely. The pre-World War II controls on capital movements were continued so that monetary policy autonomy could be regained. Capital markets and flows remained nearly dormant during the 1950s and depressed during a good part of the 1960s. As stated above, in Section 2.1, in this inward-looking era capital markets were controlled both domestically and for foreign transaction purposes. Also, both capital and current account transactions were stringently controlled in the majority of the large economies. Notwithstanding these restrictions, sporadic cases of financial crisis did take place during the Bretton Woods period but their effect tended to be small and entirely localized.

The newly established supranational institution, the IMF, accepted the concept of capital controls as a means of preventing currency crises and speculative runs.[7] The Articles of Agreement of the IMF empowered member countries to enforce capital controls. This was a pragmatic measure adopted to cope with the economic reality. There was a pressing need to eschew the challenging global economic scenario of the interwar period. Capital controls allowed member governments a degree of autonomy by providing them with the power to follow activist monetary policies. These controls were instrumental in the dormancy of the capital markets over the 1950s. However, in the mid-1960s currencies of the countries that were following policies inconsistent with the maintenance of their parities were subject to speculative attacks.

Frequent speculative runs began against the major currencies. Although repeated attempts were made to quell speculation, the Bretton Woods regime began wilting away in 1971. The collapse of the regime began in August 1971. By February 1973, the major currencies had to be set free to float independently. Country after country shifted to the floating exchange rate regime. The major currencies of the large industrial economies switched to floating exchange rates. Soon the new regime of the post-1973 era was adopted by all the advanced industrial economies. Consequently, global economic architecture underwent a methodical transformation. After a time lag, the large developing economies adapted their exchange rate regimes to the changing global financial architecture. The floating exchange rates had two basic variations, namely the free floats and the managed floats. The notion of a complete free float is an abstraction. The developing economies showed a clear preference for the managed floats. In reality, the degree of exchange-rate flexibility lies on a continuum. In today's policy atmosphere it can take varying forms like exchange-rate target zones, crawling pegs, crawling zones and managed floats of various kinds.

During early 1973, independence of monetary policy was regarded as an important policy instrument, while capital controls were abandoned freeing capital to flow from where it was to where it yielded the highest rates of returns. It should be pointed out that when the floating exchange rate regime was adopted it was regarded as a temporary emergency measure to tide countries over a period of uncertainty and transition. Apparently it became a permanent one. At this juncture, major systemic economies like Germany and the US were unwilling to accept the ramifications of a fixed exchange rate regime. They found the notion of loss of control over domestic monetary policy particularly unappealing and thought it could be costly. Their apprehension was that it could result in slower GDP growth or higher inflation. Besides, tentative attempts to create a fixed dollar exchange rate regime were made but even the limited capital mobility that had began in the late 1960s and early 1970s had led to speculative attacks on the major currencies. Some countries were furious at these attacks so, for them, this made retreating to floating exchange rates the last available option.

Having adopted the floating exchange rate regime in 1973, the large industrial economies became freed from the demands of maintaining a fixed exchange rate – one of the three elements of the trilemma. Public policy professionals were able to get their hands on the monetary policy lever and move it in pursuit of national macroeconomic policy objectives, and free their capital markets. Besides, adoption of floating rates 'helped reconcile the social demand for domestic macroeconomic stabilization with the interest of the business community for open markets in goods and assets' (Obstfeld and Taylor, 2005, p. 173). This amounted to creating a mechanism for restoration of the global capital markets. It led to the beginning of financial integration in the contemporary period of globalization.

2.4 Floating exchange rate regime and capital mobility

The floating rate regime was fully compatible with free cross-border capital movements. It lubricated the progress of capital mobility (see also Chapter 1, Section 7). The 1973 quadrupling of oil prices proved to be a seismic economic event that affected the global economy and financial markets. Because of this, the so-called money center banks in the major industrialized countries began accumulating large sums in petro-dollars from the Organization of the Petroleum Exporting Countries (OPEC).[8] This started large global capital movements through the Eurodollar market. This movement accelerated, particularly during the 1979–81 period (Chapter 1, Section 2.7). As offshore markets controlled these capital movements, they could bypass official domestic regulations and controls. The new scenario that emerged was as follows: The global financial architecture and market mechanism were aptly suitable for global capital movements and there were large sums of petro-dollars available for global investment. This marked the beginning of a new era of financial globalization.

Regarding the floating exchange rate regime adopted after the breakdown of the Bretton Woods regime, Reinhart and Rogoff (2004a) reached different conclusions. They asserted that officially proclaimed exchange rate arrangements were profoundly misleading. The found that *de jure* pegs could be *de facto* floats. The reverse was equally true. They inferred that 'the most popular exchange rate regime over modern history has been the crawling peg, which accounted for over 26 percent of the observations. During 1990–2001, this was the most common type of arrangement in emerging Asia and western hemisphere (excluding Canada and the US), making up for about 36 and 42 percent of the observations, respectively' (Reinhart and Rogoff, 2004a, p. 3). They invented a new category called 'free falling'. This was intended for currencies where the economies recorded annual inflation rates of 40 percent. In their sample, 12.5 percent of the observations occurred in the free falling category. This made the free falling exchange rate more frequently occurring than free floating, which accounted for only 4.5 percent of the total observations. In *de jure* classification free floating represented over 30 percent of the observations, which was far from the *de facto* situation. Another classification issue was associated with what became popularly known as the 'managed float'. When there was a *de facto* peg or crawling peg, it was named the managed float. About 53 percent of the observations fell under this category.

During the immediate post-1973 period and the 1980s, capital markets in advanced industrial economies geared up for global capital mobility and increased their steady resumption toward financial globalization. At the beginning, this resumption was essentially concentrated in this group of economies and the financial centers located within them. As the volume of capital flows between these economies increased, global financial integration received such an impetus that it could not continue at a steady and stable rate. Increase in trans-border capital flows was neither evenly paced nor monotonic. It also did not affect all the economies in a similar way. Uneven geographical spread was its obvious characteristic.

As elaborated below, during the 1980s, several EMEs and medium-sized developing economies began implementing macroeconomic reform measures and restructured their economies. Many of them also earnestly began liberalizing and reforming their capital markets (Section 3). Policy mandarins in these economies were influenced by the popularity of the neo-liberal policy environment that was developing and gaining force in the 1980s. Deregulation and tax reduction were increasingly being adopted first in the large high-income industrial economies and then by the other country groups in different parts of the global economy. No doubt these measures and reforms reduced transaction costs and risks to long- and short-term foreign investment in the EMEs. Consequently, this group of economies also started to participate in the global capital markets and receive gradual flows of international capital. The number of economies participating in the global capital markets increased and trans-border capital flows gained markedly strong momentum during the 1990s.[9]

3. Gearing up for financial globalization

For the developing economies, several strategic policy measures were an essential precondition for financial globalization. They included adoption of macroeconomic reforms and restructuring, as well as dismantling controls and restrictions on their markets, particularly financial markets. Adoption of privatization, deregulation and the ushering in of the necessary innovations in their financial markets were the other strategies which were needed for preparing a conducive policy environment for financial globalization. 'Waves of liberalization and deregulation' that took place in this country group provided an unquestionable stimulus to financial globalization (Lane and Milesi-Ferretti, 2008a, p. 328).

3.1 Macroeconomic reforms

A good number of lower- and upper-middle income developing economies broke from their tradition of following erroneous and unproductive economic strategies. They committed to improving the macroeconomic and financial climate in their economies by carrying out macroeconomic reforms and restructuring. A series of long-term pol-icy measures were required for economic macroeconomic restructuring. This was done, *inter alia*, with an objective to make their economies more attractive for global capital inflows, which in turn helped them integrate with the global financial markets. The indispensable policy measures to achieve this objective were: pursuing macroeconomic sta-bilization, improving business environment and aiming for stronger economic fundamentals.

These vital policy objectives were by and large ignored in the past. For the first time, a good number of lower- and upper-middle income developing economies began paying attention to these strategies. Many of them achieved a sufficient degree of success as well. Broad policy objectives like adoption of outer-oriented policies in trade and financial sectors and inflation control began to be given closer policy considera-tion in these economies. The direct result of this policy transformation was that for the first time these developing economies prevailed over their history of poor macroeconomic policies, which had resulted in apathetic growth and inadequate financial sector development. The adoption of much-needed and long-awaited policy measures and steady policy transformation eventually geared them up for global financial integration (IMF, 2008a).

3.2 Elimination of controls and regulations

The application of an array of controls and restrictions in the domestic financial sector was an endemic story in the 1970s. The financial sector has had a tradition of being controlled and restricted by governments, both domestically and externally. Mature industrialized economies were not devoid of controls, although these were far more stringent and endemic in the developing economies. The latter group of countries had to systemically prepare themselves for financially globalizing by removing controls and restrictions and implementing a much-needed liberalization of the domestic economy, deregulation and financial reforms. One area that needed particular attention was the controls over financial markets. They were widespread and had existed for a long time. The controlled economic and financial landscape in many developing economies called for serious reforms in several areas. The commonest being (i) credit and interest rate controls and regulations, (ii) entry barriers and controls on banking industry, (iii) banks oper-ating on guidelines laid down by governments, (iv) dominance of state-owned banks, (v) controls on capital account and on trans-border movements of capital, (vi) restrictions of securities markets and foreign direct investment (FDI) inflows and (vii) restrictions on foreign exchange. Liberalization of the financial sector entails liberalization on some, or preferably all, of these fronts.

Many developing economies undertook a sympathetic string of reform and liberalization measures simply to promote development of their financial and securities markets in order to attract private capital from the global capital markets. That being said, countries and regions took to financial liberalization in an uneven manner. The only uniformity in terms of liberalization strategy that could be found was among the advanced industrial economies where a discernible degree of policy convergence took place. When developing economies began adopting liberalization and reform measures, these were essentially along the lines of the reform, restructuring and deregulation measures of the advanced industrial economies. These measures entailed *de jure* policy initiatives like removing restrictions on trans-border capital movements, fully or partially opening the capital account and removing restrictions on foreign exchange transactions. Financial globalization was the critical objective behind such reforms. Over time, a sizable group of lower- and upper-middle income developing economies adopted financial market reforms and liberalization. This was a vitally important development and caused the terrain of global capital markets to transform. However, many developing countries steered clear of financial sector liberalization and have ignored it thus far.

Financial sector liberalization, both domestic and external, is a far-reaching policy issue. Theoretically, financial liberalization, which facilitates free allocation of global capital, can potentially generate benefits for both the capital-exporting countries and the recipients. Therefore, academic debate on this issue is age-old. In this context the acclaimed seminal writings of McKinnon (1973) and Shaw (1973) are frequently and universally referred to. They are known to have influenced the thinking of academics and policy makers in this regard. These two scholars planted the seeds of the concept of financial repression and established how economic stagnation and economic crises have close ties with economic repression (Fry, 1995).[10] Conventional wisdom has stated that financial sector liberalization and financial sector development are essential ingredients of economic growth. The premise that there is a finance-growth nexus is widely accepted. A large literature emerged around this nexus.[11]

The basic line of logic supporting the finance-growth nexus is that deregulation in the capital and financial markets results in higher savings and greater saving mobilization as well as methodical and efficient resource allocation; all of which contribute to superior growth performance. King and Levine (1993) emphasized the information-processing role of financial institutions and capital markets and added to the broad approach that was taken by McKinnon (1973) and Shaw (1973). They refined the McKinnon-Shaw hypothesis by redefining finance-growth nexus in the light of this new role played by the financial institutions and capital markets. As these institutions and markets select innovative projects with high creditworthiness and therefore profitability, they buttress productivity in the economy. This was regarded by King and Levine (1993) as the better-developed capital markets' fundamental input to economic growth. When capital markets are regulated, repressed, control-ridden or weak, economic growth performance of the country remains mediocre or worse.[12] In addition, when the trend toward financial globalization began to take hold, it put pressure on governments to reconsider financial market controls. Restriction on the financial sector began to be slowly lifted, beginning with the liberalization of the domestic banking sector, which started with the deregulation of the domestic interest rates.

3.3 Liberalization and deregulation

Predictably, the advanced industrial economies were ahead of the developing ones in their liberalization and deregulation endeavors. In advanced industrial economies, financial sector reforms and liberalization picked up momentum in the late 1970s. As more and more countries liberalized their capital markets, the global financial scenario began transforming. Financial globalization could not possibly make headway without a critical amount of liberalization and deregulation taking place. For the policy mandarins in developing economies, the first step toward attracting private investors and drawing private capital from the liquidity-rich global capital markets was to liberalize their economies and financial markets. It was their gateway to global financial integration. The focus of the first episode of liberalization was essentially the domestic financial sector and the capital account. When the capital account is liberalized, capital is allowed to move freely in and out of the economy. Securities markets remained untouched during this phase and were not opened for foreign investment. However, the debt crisis of 1982 brought these liberalization endeavors to a standstill.

After a hiatus they restarted. The second episode of financial sector liberalization began in the late 1980s, with focus on the deregulation of both the domestic financial sector and the securities markets. In this context the recommendations of the United Nations – World Institute for Development Economic Research (UN-WIDER) (1990) group study, led by an eminent banker, Sir Kenneth Berrill, are particularly relevant.[13] This group emphatically argued that developing countries should liberalize their financial markets in order to attract foreign equity investment. Their line of reasoning was perfectly logical. It advocated that there was a massive amount of financial capital available in the financial markets of advanced industrial economies that was searching for profitable opportunities. These potential investors were pension funds, mutual funds and similar investment funds that were enormously liquidity-rich. The developing economies could attract this capital provided they liberalized their markets externally and developed their stock markets internally. Liberalization was an imperative measure.

Around this period, in the late 1980s, a large number of lower- and upper-middle income developing economies started the process of liberalization of the financial system.[14] The developing economies *mutatis mutandis* followed the lead of the advanced industrial economies in this regard. Some of them delayed their liberalization and began in the early 1990s. Supranational institutions, like the IMF, were instrumental in catalyzing this wave of liberalization in the developing economies. Far-reaching financial market reforms were being undertaken as a part of the structural adjustment programs devised by the IMF and the World Bank. Many of the developing economies partially or fully opened their capital accounts. The advanced industrial economies and some developing ones had deregulated virtually all the sectors of the financial system by the early 1990s (Kaminsky and Schmukler, 2008). While financial market reforms and liberalization had an enormous welfare-enhancing effect, there was a downside. They exposed the liberalizing economies to potential risk and to the volatility of the global financial markets (Stiglitz and Ocampo, 2008).

Traditionally, developing economies labored under rigid regulations that thwarted market forces at every step. In most cases the liberalization and deregulation process in the developing economies started from a low level. After liberalization succeeded in reaching a critical level, business firms and governments began raising capital in the global capital markets. Breaking away from their past, the developing economies granted foreign investors access to their domestic markets, including domestic stock markets. Facilitated by systemic liberalization and deregulation, financial institutions from the advanced industrial economies moved into developing economies that demonstrated reasonably high economic promise. They established their local presence by setting up branches, subsidiaries and joint-ventures, and by acquiring local banks.

In the context of financial globalization, capital account liberalization takes on a special meaning. A theoretical approach that became popular in the mid-1990s was in keeping with the neoclassical tenets. It robustly prescribed complete liberalization of the capital account, freeing capital to move across borders. The assumption was that this would facilitate efficient allocation of resources and therefore result in global welfare enhancement. It was expected to benefit both the lenders and the borrowers. Some prominent economists (Fischer, 1997, 2003) were absolutely convinced that the risks associated with global capital flows were more than offset by the potential benefits. This moment in time was considered the appropriate one for developing economies to embrace capital account liberalization. In late 1997, the governing body of the IMF decided to make liberalization of capital movements one of the *raison d'etre* of the IMF. The plan was to amend the Articles of Agreement of the IMF and extend the jurisdiction of the IMF to cover it (IMF, 1997). The Asian crisis of 1997–8 ignominiously terminated this plan.

However, there were strong opponents of this logically purist stance of liberalizing the capital account. The alternative was the Theory of the Second Best. It opposed capital account liberalization on the premise of impracticality. That is, it argued that removing one economic distortion while numerous others still existed may not necessarily enhance welfare (Newbery and Stiglitz, 1984; Stiglitz, 2008). This alternative view gained relevance after the myriad financial crises of the 1990s, particularly the Asian crisis. The crises clearly exhibited how incomplete and poorly functioning domestic financial markets in recipient countries on the one hand, and poor risk management in capital-exporting countries on the other, could undermine the case for capital account liberalization. The macroeconomic and growth implications of capital account liberalization have been fervently debated in the profession, resulting in a large empirical literature.[15]

3.4 Espousing privatization

Privatization was another strategy that could and did help the developing economies to make progress toward financial globalization. Adoption of the strategy of selling off publicly owned enterprises to global investors and operators proved to be a productive channel to financially globalizing. For the developing countries, selling state-owned assets to private operators internationally served twin objectives: first, creating liquidity for the governments and, second, unloading expensive and unsustainable assets. It was a win-win situation. Since the 1980s, privatization of public sector enterprises became one of the favorite instruments of developing economies for attracting global capital. Privatization began in the UK, with the Thatcher government creating a prototype for privatization by privatizing British Telecom in 1984. Such privatization programs were regarded as an important policy event. Large state-owned enterprises were privatized with the help of tranches. A tranch was a large block of shares allocated to underwriters, which they sold in countries in their designated geographical area. Initially tranches were allocated to foreign investors along with sale to domestic investors.

These privatization practices soon spread to the other countries, including lower- and upper-middle income developing economies. Putting state-owned firms, particularly utility companies, on the market and selling them with the help of foreign tranches developed into an accepted market practice. Developing countries in Latin America made far greater use of this channel of financial globalization than others. In this part of the world, Chile pioneered privatization as a mode of drawing in global capital. According to de la Torre and Schmukler (2007), privatization revenues in the developing economies were a paltry $3 billion in 1988, but reached $67 billion in 1997. Over the 1988–2003 period, the cumulative amount of privatization revenue was $413 billion. The usual manner of conducting the sale of privatization-related assets was through public offerings on the domestic stock exchanges. Thus privatization indirectly bolstered the growth of capital market capitalization in developing economies. Rapid increases in trans-border equity investment and FDI were partly due to acquisitions of public sector enterprises by global investors.

3.5 Financial innovation

The increasing capital mobility of the post-Bretton Woods era intensified pressure on countries to liberalize and deregulate their financial sector. When liberalization and deregulation measures were taken, they stimulated rapid growth of security markets, which in turn cleared the way for financial innovation. Thus a virtual circle was established with an increase in cross-border capital mobility being followed by more deregulation, which in turn stimulated innovation, thus leading to further growth in cross-border capital mobility. Striking progress in financial innovations is regarded as an idiosyncratic feature of the post-1973 era. It was continually being made, giving the appearance of one set of innovations following the other. Every new set of innovations was based on and supported by the previous onset, creating an image of a spiral of financial innovation in operation. Thus, a wave of financial innovation swept the financial markets in the advanced industrial economies. The financial sectors in the developing economies and the EMEs, while they followed those in the advanced industrial economies, did not innovate to the same degree.

Rapid and continuous innovations transformed the global securities markets. One immediate benefit of novel and innovative financial products was that they satisfied previously unmet market demand and generated demand for further innovations. Furthermore, innovative financial instruments allowed investors to diversify their portfolio and at the same time manage risk better by utilizing advanced hedging practices. Thus, the overall outcome of financial innovation was a marked improvement in portfolio diversification and risk management. The newly adopted financial practices involved enhanced use of derivatives, which are financial instruments created for reducing risk. Using these is known as hedging and their values depend on the value of other underlying financial instruments. Futures, forwards, options and swaps are the principal kinds of derivatives.[16] Futures are forwards traded outside a regular exchange. Options are the rights to buy or sell something at a specific date and price. Swaps are contracts involving an exchange of assets or payments. According to the estimates made by the Bank for International Settlements (BIS, 2009), the face value of all derivative contracts in the global financial markets soared from $106 trillion in 2002 to $680 trillion in December 2008. As the prevalence and complexity of derivatives ballooned, they created new kinds of risk. Derivatives stoked uncertainty and actually spread risk amid doubts about how firms valued them. They played a major role in the meltdown of the global financial system.

An important innovation of this period was structured finance. This broad term refers to a sector of finance that was created to help transfer risk. Structured financial products allow the investor to benefit from the investments in the equity markets without facing the usual risk. The direct impact of this was the enlargement of the securities markets. An upsurge in mortgage and consumer lending in the 1990s in the advanced industrial economies was facilitated by structured financial instruments. It contributed to increased financial intermediation. The other side of structured finance is that it contributed to the degradation in underwriting standards for financial assets, which gave rise to the credit bubble of the mid-2000s. Part of the blame for the 2007–09 financial crisis was justly laid at the door of the structured financial instruments. The process of securitization was a major causal factor behind the sub-prime mortgage crisis. Added to that was the absence of transparency regarding the characteristics of the underlying assets that the multiple layers of financial intermediation fostered (Gallegati et al., 2008).

Technological advances provided a considerable lift to financial innovation. They further stimulated and reinforced the expansion of international securities markets and enhanced financial globalization. Rapid advances in information and communication technology (ICT) took place after 1980. This was nothing short of a revolution. The advances in ICT were instrumental in the efficient transmission of financial information. In addition, the sharply declining costs of communications proved to be a veritable stimulus to financial globalization. The progress made in ICT was an essential element in revolutionizing financial globalization. By eliminating the information gap and rendering geographical distances inconsequential they underpinned financial globalization. Application of ICT technology and innovations as well as widespread exploitation of information technology enabled services (ITeS) changed trading practices on bourses out of recognition. Trading shifted from the floor to electronic trading systems. Likewise, ICT also made custody, clearing and settlement practices efficient. Real-time performance of these practices was not possible without application of ICT innovations. Thus, ICT advances proved to be a major causal factor behind transformation of the global financial landscape. They not only lowered transaction costs but also improved liquidity in the securities markets and provided 'tools for around-the-globe and around-the-clock trading' (de la Torre and Schmukler, 2007, p. 29).

The role played by demand side-factors in the advanced industrial economies cannot be underestimated. They played a decisive role in ushering in a securities market expansion and boom. Robust and strengthening market demand was an essential factor behind the fervent growth in above-mentioned twin factors, namely, financial innovations and ICT advances. In an environment of slack market demand, their growth would have taken place only at a slow pace. The demand side-factors were, first, strengthened by increasing household wealth during the decades under consideration. This transformed both the saving and investment behavior of households as well as their risk-taking tendencies. Searches for higher returns on financial assets shifted household investors' preference from banks to security markets. Second, this period is also known for the emergence of privately managed pension funds. These funds created a large demand for securities. Third, this demand was supplemented by demand from the rapidly growing mutual fund industry in advanced industrial countries. Consequently, a broad base of retail investors began participating in the international securities markets leading to a strong demand for securities.

In a space of a few decades, a confluence of the events enumerated above transformed the financial and capital markets in advanced industrial economies. The focus of these financial activities was no doubt the advanced industrial economies, where capital markets attracted the largest share of global capital flows. In comparison to the 1970s, the volume of capital flows was dramatically higher in the 1990s. Investors' interest in international securities was steadily on the rise, in lockstep with that expansion of financial services took place globally. Subsequently, financial markets in the EMEs and the large developing economies followed many of the trends in the advanced industrial economies.

Financial intermediaries in the advanced industrial economies began expanding their operations as well as physical presence in the EMEs and the large developing economies. Mergers and acquisitions (M&A) was employed by them as a frequently used tool of expansion. Large banks and financial houses created an international network of branches and subsidiaries. One direct impact of this was the integration of capital markets in the advanced industrial economies, followed by their integration in the EMEs and developing economies. Tangible proof of financial globalization on these lines was a spectacular increase in foreign holdings of US securities. In 2004, 30 percent of US treasury bonds, 20 percent of corporate bonds and 10 percent of stocks were owned by global investors (de la Torre and Schmukler, 2007). Supported by the developments noted above, during the 1990s, stock market capitalization in the G-7 countries increased swiftly. In one decade it doubled in value. It peaked in 1999.

4. Drivers of financial globalization in the contemporary era

What factors were, and can be, responsible for the rapidity of financial integration is a valid query. As discussed above (Section 3.5), ICT is an enabling technology that played a crucial role in advancing financial globalization. Recent advances in ICT shrank the globe and made national boundaries less significant. What is particularly relevant for the purpose of financial globalization is that they proved to be a resilient and momentous driver of it. They played a key role in advancing financial innovation in the capital markets. They facilitated efficient transmission of financial information and caused a sharp decline in the costs of communication and transactions, which in turn proved to be a veritable stimulus to financial globalization. Advances in ICT and computer-based technologies increased the computing power of financial institutions and individuals alike. They facilitated the collection and processing of financial information for the market participants and for monetary and regulatory authorities. They made it possible to measure, monitor and manage financial risk for the market participants. Without computers, the pricing and trading of complex new financial instruments was not feasible. Managing large and rapid transactions, and then managing the books for these transactions, which are usually spread across continents, could not be accomplished without the support of ICT. The overall impact of ICT was thus a dramatic expansion of cross-border financial flows.

In advanced industrial economies, recent growth in financial globalization was primarily stimulated by early waves of liberalization of capital account and financial deregulation. Recent cross-border financial integration in this group of economies was *a fortiori* driven by the rapid pace of financial innovation (Section 3.5). Sectoral developments like securitization, rise in the activities of hedge funds and increased use of offshore special-purpose vehicles by financial and non-financial corporations has also led to rapid growth in cross-border financial holdings among advanced industrial economies. The influence of rapid financial innovation on financial globalization in this group of economies has been greater than generally visualized. It has been observed in recent years that financial innovation in one advanced industrial economy raised demand by foreign investors in the other. These investors rationally wished to access and profit from the new asset class that had just come into being.

The pattern of merchandise trade is another consequential variable in this context. As stated below, cross-country FDI and portfolio equities flows are driven by the underlying patterns of merchandise trade between the investing and the recipient countries (Section 7.3). It is possible that the level of trade may be a proxy for bilateral information flows. Other factors that influence cross-country investment flows are the links through common language and common legal systems. In addition, the impact of the recent emergence of a highly successful group of exporting economies on contemporary financial globalization was enormous. This group includes both exporters of manufacturers and services as well as those who export commodities. The four BRIC economies and the East Asian economies come under the first category, while the GCC countries come under the second (Section 7.4).

Hedge funds and private equity firms are the other active groups that have a growing impact on global financial markets. They have been termed 'the new power brokers' by McKinsey Global Institute (MGI, 2008, p. 5). The emergence of these four institutions in the global financial market represents a dispersion of financial power away from the traditional institutions in the advanced industrial economies. The new players and other parts of the world rather than the advanced industrial economies have the financial clout. The wealth and influence of the new power brokers has grown in the recent years. According to estimates made by the MGI (2008, 2009), the combined financial assets of the Asian central banks, GCC, hedge funds and private equity firms were $11.5 trillion in 2007 and $12 trillion at the end of 2008.

The first half of 2008 was not very bad for the Asian economies, whose current account surpluses persisted. The petro-profits of the members of the GCC also continued to grow. The sub-prime mortgage crisis that began the global financial turbulence in the fall of 2007 initially did not affect the private equity firms very much. They survived the turbulence in a reasonably good shape. Conversely, hedge funds have been hit hard ever since the beginning of the global financial turbulence. There is no denying that the financial crisis and recession abruptly halted the power brokers' rapid ascent. In 2008, both hedge funds and private equity firms were hit hard when the credit markets seized up, depriving them of the leverage that amplified their influence in the global financial markets. They were further battered by the decline in global equities, which erased much of their investors' wealth. In 2009 both of these industries had grown smaller and were still shrinking. Their future will be different from their past. They will need to adapt to the new climate of tight credit and stringent regulation (MGI, 2009).

Financial globalization can be potentially driven by financial development in the domestic economy. As the depth of the domestic financial system increases, it tends to become increasingly globalized. The GCC economies are a case in point. There can be a direct link between financial development and financial globalization. Also, the development of the domestic sector can be promoted by foreign investment and the entry of foreign banks. Yet another relevant variable is the level of economic development in the domestic economy.

Better-developed economies generally make a concerted drive toward financial globalization. The level of economic development influences the propensity of the domestic economic agents to engage in cross-border asset trade. Higher international financial integration is commonly seen in well-off economies. Switzerland, one of the highest-income economies in the industrial world, has also been a long-standing prosperous and efficient center of trade in global financial assets.

5. Transformations in global financial landscape

The collapse of the Bretton Woods regime was a momentous event for the world of global finance. It was followed by a surge in capital flows from the private global capital markets. With the largest industrial economies of the world abandoning the concept of capital control and with an increasing amount of financial activity taking place in the Eurodollar markets, other countries had little choice but to open their financial sectors as well. The 1973 quadrupling of oil prices affected the global financial markets in a significant manner. It had both an immediate and long-term impact. Driven by the gush of liquidity from the OPEC, impressive systemic growth in the financial and capital markets began. By the mid-1980s, the majority of the advanced industrialized economies were open to cross-border capital flows.

A large amount of financial capital accumulated in the OPEC economies, which could not invest them domestically in the short-term. Increased financial intermediation of these resources began, first through financial institutions and then through the securities markets. Their operations expanded at a remarkable pace. The depth in the financial markets of the advanced industrial economies increased sharply. Participation of these countries in global financial markets also expanded beyond that of the high-income industrial economies. The range of financial services and financial instruments *pari passu* expanded enormously to reach unprecedented dimensions. For the private global financial markets, these developments marked the initiation of a period of major structural and qualitative transformation. They not only kicked off but also catalyzed the contemporary globalization of financial and capital markets.

After a good deal of experimentation, the Brady initiative – named after Nicholas Brady, the US treasury secretary – was launched in the late 1980s (Section 4.2). It had a significant objective; its express purpose was to resolve the Mexican debt crisis. It facilitated the process of bringing the developing economies of Latin America back into the fold of the global financial market. Under this plan the distressed or non-performing bank loans were repackaged into the so-called Brady bonds. The Brady plan allowed debt-ridden economies to restructure their debt by converting existing bank loans into collateralized bonds at a significant discount, or at below-market interest rates. The principal was collateralized by the US treasury in 1989. These were 30-year zero-coupon bonds were purchased by the debtor country using financial resources from the IMF, the World Bank and the foreign exchange reserves of the purchasing country. The Brady bonds created under this plan were more liquid and therefore more tradable. This innovation allowed commercial banks to exchange their claims on the indebted developing economies of Latin America for tradable instruments. This measure helped them eliminate large debt volumes, or impaired assets, from their balance sheets. These dollar-denominated bonds were traded on the international bond markets (Das, 1989).

One of the immediate consequences of the creation of Brady bond market was the creation of a deep market for sovereign bonds in a short time span. It proved to be a thoughtful and successful initiative, resulting in a gradual return of investor confidence in developing countries. The Brady initiative had the desired impact of clearing the way for the crisis-affected developing countries of Latin America to re-enter the booming international capital markets. It influenced the private global financial markets and their operation during the decade of the 1990s, proving to be a strong impetus to them.

5.1 Dawn of the cross-border syndicated bank loan market

Among the different genre of financial markets, the syndicated loan market was the first international financial market to develop. These loans were the recycled petro-dollars of the OPEC. The large post-1973 surpluses of the OPEC were channeled through the Eurodollar markets to the developing countries of Africa, Asia, the Middle East and, particularly, Latin America. An immediate consequence of this was that the financial markets in the advanced industrial economies developed, deepened and in the process transformed dramatically. The developing economies of Latin America emerged as large borrowers of syndicated loans during the 1970s. These loans were made by the money center banks of the large industrial economies in the European Union (EU), Japan and the US.

Syndicated lending expanded at a rapid pace, peaking in 1982 at $57 billion. Mexico defaulted on its sovereign loans in August 1982, setting off the Latin American debt crisis. This crisis revealed that the Latin American economies had over-borrowed and that the money center banks over-lent. The ensuing financial crisis was a major one and drove global financial markets to the brink of a veritable debacle. In the early stage, this crisis was designated as a liquidity issue, which could be resolved easily with time. However, it was eventually realized that there was a question mark over the sovereign solvency of the borrowing countries. Protracted endeavors were needed in terms of internationally agreed-upon debt-reduction protocol. Syndicated lending to the Latin American economies came to an abrupt halt. For good reasons, these and many other developing economies were ostracized from the global financial markets. Their participation was not reconsidered until the late 1980s.

In the mid-1980s, European economies began their journey toward formation of the economic and monetary union (EMU). They liberalized their financial markets and began participating increasingly in global bonds and equity markets. The capital raised by them increased from a paltry $6 billion in 1980 to $72 billion in 1989. This contributed to further globalization of the financial markets (Lane and Milesi-Ferretti, 2008a).

5.2 Contribution of Brady bonds to financial integration and globalization

The Brady bond initiative helped restore investor confidence in the developing economies. Soon the developing countries' governments began issuing debt outside the Brady market. This mitigated the negative impact of the Latin American debt crisis and financial globalization once again began to flourish. The Brady bonds turned out to be a catalyst for the development of the EMEs bond markets in the 1990s. Private firms from large developing economies followed their governments and began raising capital in the global bond markets. Bond issuance activity soon picked up momentum and EME bond issuance began to rise. In stages, the demand for developing country bonds began to rise in global capital markets. The developing countries of Latin America, which were being ignored by global capital markets, benefited particularly from the international bond issuance. Their bond issuance soared from $1.5 billion in 1990 to $58 billion in 1997. The compelling trend in global financial integration during the 1990s was provided with an impetus by the lifting of capital account restrictions in many countries. Other barriers to overseas investment were also dismantled. The level of activity in global financial markets picked up markedly during this period, which in turn enhanced global financial integration.

In 1990 the EME bond issuance was a mere $4 billion, but before the Asian crisis in 1997 it reached $99 billion. The Asian and Russian crises understandably dampened issuance activity. However, it soon recovered and reached $183 billion in 2005. From decade to decade, there was a continual rise in the volume of capital flows to developing economies. Capital flows were far higher in the 1990s than in the 1980s. In constant (2000) dollars they peaked at $158 billion in the 1980s, against $353 billion in the 1990s. After a crisis-driven decline in 1997, capital flows to the developing economies picked up again to reach a new peak in 2004 of $379 billion (de la Torre and Schmukler, 2007).

The easing of market sentiment in global capital markets by the Brady initiative provided incentive to the syndicated loans market as well. As the monetary conditions in the early 1990s in advanced industrial economies were relaxed, syndicated lending to the developing economies rose at a brisk pace. It peaked in 1997 at $190 billion, which was close to four times its level in the early 1980s. One major difference from the early 1980s was that during the 1990s the largest beneficiary country group was not the economies of Latin America but those of Asia. The borrowings of the economies of Asia added up to almost $100 billion in 1997. The nationality of lending banks also changed. In the early 1980s, syndicated lending was dominated by US banks. During the 1990s, European and Japanese banks led global syndicated lending business. During the boom of the 1990s, large business corporations from advanced industrial economies emerged as the other large borrowing entity. By 2004, global syndicated bank lending touched $2.5 trillion. A major part of these financial resources, $1.8 trillion, went to the advanced industrial economies (Cipriani and Kaminsky, 2006).

One remarkable development in the arena of global finance during the 1990s was the accelerated growth of the international equity market. It experienced a boom during this decade. Business corporations around the world not only started raising capital from the unregulated international bond and syndicated loan markets but also began participating in the regulated equity markets of the large and liquid financial centers. Most notable in this regard was the highly liquid US capital market which began attracting global equity issuers as well as investors in the early 1990s. Instruments like the American Depository Receipts (ADRs) facilitated global issuers' task of raising capital on the US stock market. In place of foreign stocks, ADRs were traded on the US stock market with ease. Likewise, other important stock markets around the world also attracted global issuers. As global financial integration progressed, business firms around the globe were able to simultaneously issue equity underwritten and distributed in multiple foreign equity markets as well as in their domestic markets. This was termed the Euroequity market. Generally, an international syndicate issued Euroequity, which entailed an initial public offering (IPO) occurring simultaneously on more than one national stock market.

With an increase in the volume of capital flows to developing economies, a great deal of transformation took place in the composition of capital flows. In this regard, the 1990s were an era of demarcation. Before this time, external capital flows to developing economies predominantly comprised of official development assistance (ODA) and syndicated lending by the commercial banks. After the 1990s, this structure of capital flows changed due, *inter alia*, to a sharp decline in ODA. Loans from commercial banks were supplanted by capital raised in the global stock and bond markets. Also, FDI in the developing economies increased during the latter period. FDI expansion was partly stimulated by large scale privatization in many large- and middle-income developing countries. Since the early and mid-2000s, the shift toward FDI and equity-related capital flows strengthened further. Popularity of Euroequity increased and the EMEs in Asia and Latin America began attracting growing amounts of global capital in the form of equity investment.

A high degree of concentration in global private capital flows to developing economies and instability are two of the negative characteristics of contemporary financial globalization. No doubt that, while the recent wave of financial globalization has accelerated flows of private global capital to developing economies, it has not gone to all developing economies. Not all of them have access to global capital markets. In addition, the distribution of private global capital demonstrates extreme unevenness. The ten largest recipients of private capital siphon off more than 65 percent of the total. The next significant group of recipients is the middle-income developing countries. Unlike these two country groups, the low-income ones are at the other extreme. They receive only marginal amounts, if any. Besides, a high degree of instability in these flows was caused by impulsive and unexpected shifts in investor sentiment toward the EMEs. The Asian and Russian crises demonstrated that sudden stoppage or reversal in global capital flows were real threats. Their macroeconomic implications were painful for the recipient economies.

5.3 Financial integration and the developing economies

The advanced industrial economies and their financial markets took the lead and forged the way forward in the arena of financial globalization. They were and continue to be the principal players in this arena. Although not directly involved, developing economies could not remain impervious for long to the transformations in the financial markets of advanced industrial economies and in the global financial market. In a rapidly globalizing world economy, external economic and financial environments had changed profoundly. Developing economies' domestic financial and capital markets reacted to the forces of change in industrial countries as well as to ongoing financial globalization and innovation. These forces had a demonstrative learning effect on the developing economies (Section 3). They decisively influenced and shaped the financial markets in the developing countries. Many developing economies unilaterally pursued extensive reform agenda to harmonize with the changes and advancements in the capital markets of advanced industrial economies. Consequently, after some time capital markets in many developing economies, albeit much smaller, began to look similar to those in the advanced industrial economies.

The steady growth of global financial markets enhanced global financial integration as well as led to boom conditions in the 1990s. This was a defining moment and reshaped the global financial landscape. At this juncture, the pace of financial intermediation expanded at a remarkable pace. This is clearly exemplified by the cross-border flows of gross financial assets and liability. At the end of the 1990s, the sum of cross-border financial assets and liabilities (in gross terms) exceeded the nominal GDP of advanced industrial economies by 200 percent. During the 1980s, the corresponding figure was equal to the GDP of this country group (de la Torre and Schmukler, 2007). This is convincing proof of the vigorous expansion of global cross-border financial flows. Similarly, Cipriani and Kaminsky (2006) reported an explosive increase in the international bond, equity and syndicated loan markets. While the international bond and equity markets recorded a 100-fold increase in gross issuance between 1984 and 2004, the syndicated loan markets increased 30 times over the same period. The total amount raised by firms in securities markets outside their home countries grew more than four-fold since 1990; it reached $1 trillion in 2005 (Gozzi et al., 2008). Increasing global financial integration has essentially altered the framework for interpreting and responding to major economic events (Greenspan, 2007).

Both financial institutions and securities markets participated in global financial intermediation operations. High-income industrial countries led the financial globalization. According to one estimate, the financial markets in the Group-of-Seven (G-7) countries were so active that the outstanding sum of credit from the banks, stock market capitalization and private bonds averaged 260 percent of the GDP in 2004. In 1975 the corresponding figure was 100 percent (de la Torre and Schmukler, 2007). These statistics clearly show the exhilarating rate of expansion of the global financial markets and their rapid integration.

Statistical data series on capital flows and investment positions for individual economies are not easily available. The financial flow data for large developing economies are available from the 1980s. The IMF began to compile more comprehensive data on investment positions of individual countries since 1997. The data available for advanced industrial economies indicates, as stated in the preceding paragraph, an unmistakable slant in global financial integration during the contemporary period. This essentially takes the form of asset swapping among the economies of advanced industrial economies. In contrast, asset swapping between advanced industrial economies and developing ones was on a much smaller scale (Lane and Milesi-Ferrtti, 2003; Obstfeld, 2007; Obstfeld and Taylor, 2004).

The principal factors driving the strong performance of securities markets in the main financial centers in advanced industrial economies were: First, financial liberalization and deregulation progressed at a steady pace in the advanced industrial countries. Second, in the financial markets, pioneering technological and financial innovation took place during these decades (Section 3.5). Third, a large dedicated investor base developed and grew rapidly in the high-income industrial economies. This included both institutional and retail investors. These were important developments. The developing economies watched these developments, learned these practices and after a time lag implemented them in their own economies. These factors coalesced to have an enormous effect over financial globalization and the integration of a group of dynamic developing economies into the global financial market.

5.4 Transformation in the financial markets of the developing countries

How and to what extent the developing countries brought about changes in their financial markets is a valid query. Most developing economies had traditionally adhered to strict capital controls. The

Bretton Woods period reinforced and extended that tradition. Stringent controls were continued in the EMEs, both domestically and on international transactions. As elaborated above, the course of financial globalization and progress that occurred over the preceding few decades in the advanced industrial economies had an influence on the developing economies. They swayed the financial sector and capital market development in this group of economies. These developments generated an inclination for much-needed transformation in their capital markets.

In addition, until the early 1990s, domestic financial markets in the developing economies were dominated by the banking sector. Diminutive securities markets were the long-standing weakness of the developing economies. In many of them securities markets were nonexistent. Government intervention in the financial sector was almost omnipresent. In many developing countries government controls were so excessive that market forces had little role left to play. Governments regulated both interest rates and credit disbursement by banks. Financial repression was rampant. The direction of bank credit flows were often maneuvered by the ministries of finance in these countries and government interventions in the operations of financial institutions were endemic. The central banks played an energetic role in influencing the operations of the domestic banks. In many of the developing countries, the largest banks were in the public sector. However, this state of affairs began to change in the early 1990s.

5.5 Financial deepening in the contemporary period

The contemporary period of financial globalization is different from that around the turn of the twentieth century, which was overwhelmingly dominated by a select group of economies, namely the Western European economies and the so-called economies of the New World. The low-income developing economies of that era played a peripheral role. Conversely, in the present era, capital mobility was far more broadly based in terms of the economies involved and the financial instruments used. The current phase of financial globalization has entailed the participation of a good number of developing economies.

Recent decades saw a striking transformation in the global financial system. As the costs of gathering and processing information fell, and as sophisticated modeling techniques came into use in finance and competitive pressure intensified, more and more economies began to move away from the traditional bank-based system of financial intermediation to a more market-based system. Rapid growth of the financial market was the natural consequence. The growth rate of financial markets has been much faster than that of the global GDP. Consequently, financial depth, which is measured as the ratio of a country's financial assets to GDP, has been steadily rising. It has happened not only in individual countries but also in all the regions of the global economy.

As financial markets grow deeper they come to have greater liquidity, something which directly benefits entrepreneurs. Another direct benefit of a deeper financial market is that it prices assets more efficiently and provides more opportunities to spread risk. That individual financial markets are far deeper at present than ever before and many more countries have deeper financial markets is proved by the following statistics. In 1990 only 33 countries had financial assets of larger value than their respective GDPs. By 2006, this number more than doubled to 72. The four BRIC economies, namely, Brazil, the Russian Federation, India and China stand out as countries with financial assets far larger than their GDPs. In 1990, only two countries had financial depth exceeding 300 percent. This number at present is 26 (Farrell et al., 2008).

Increasing depth and advances in financial globalization favorably affected capital flows to developing economies, in particular to EMEs, in two distinct ways: First, the volume and composition of the capital flows to them were evidently influenced. Second, financial services were progressively internationalized, which favorably affected capital flows to developing economies. As financial globalization progressed, liquidity in international capital markets increased, which resulted in the growth in capital flows to EMEs. Increasing expansion in trans-border capital flows during the current century completely eroded the boundaries that existed between the national capital markets during the early post-World War II era. A single global capital market gradually emerged (Crockett, 2009).

5.6 Impact of financial crises and setbacks

This period of rapid progress of financial globalization was interrupted by the fallout from some serious crises. The Asian financial crisis (1997–8) unfavorably affected it. Although several economy-specific crises, like the Tequila Crisis of 1994, had occurred in the interim, the Asian crisis was the first major setback to the global economy since the Latin American debt crisis of 1982. The Asian crisis not only mangled the so-called miracle economies of Asia and the regional economy, it also affected global capital and stock markets adversely. It was intensively analyzed by the economic profession and a large crisis-related analytical literature came into being. One tangible result of this research was the development of policy tools to comprehend and manage such financial and currency crises.[17]

During this period, many developing economies, particularly EMEs, were still on one kind of fixed exchange rate regime or the other. The fragility of these economies was brought home by the Asian crisis. In contrast, some of the large EMEs, like Brazil, Chile and Mexico, had switched to exchange rate flexibility coupled with inflation targeting. The continuing economic and financial globalization picked up a good deal of momentum during the mid-1990s. The Asian crisis was followed by the Russian or Ruble crisis (1998), which also impacted global investors' psychology. Ensuing these two crises, global capital flows to the developing economies dwindled and commodity markets went into a sharp decline. This was followed by the end of the so-called ICT boom, or bursting of the dot-com bubble, in early 2001.

Notwithstanding the 1997–8 financial crises, financial flows and integration among advanced industrial economies continued to surge at an even pace. They were uninfluenced by the meltdown of 1998. The large current account deficits of the US continued to be financed by the industrial and developing countries that were running surpluses. This implies that divergent trends in financial integration among the industrial and the developing economies had materialized. While the former were integrating at a progressive rate, the latter group of economies was lagging. A strong increase in corporate bond issuance – both domestic and international – took place during the 1990s in the bond markets in advanced industrial economies. While equity issuance slackened after 2000, corporate bond issuance – both domestic and international – continued as an active alternate source of raising finance.

6. Benefits of enhanced access to global capital markets

Adoption of economic reforms and liberalization of financial and capital markets help provide access to private global capital markets for a developing economy. A myriad of benefits accrue from this. First, improved access provides entrepreneurs in the developing economies with a rich source of capital at a lower cost than that available domestically. The availability of financial resources is no longer limited to domestic resources. Without access to the private global financial markets, a low-saving economy would be forced to truncate its investment plans and keep them confined to all but most lucrative business projects. Access to the deep private global financial markets increases the funding possibilities of potentially productive and creditworthy projects, often at lower borrowing costs than that at home.

Large availability of the advanced industrial economies' liquid financial resources can finance much-needed investment in the resource-poor developing economies. The result is an increase in the rate of return on capital for the former group of countries and economic growth in the latter. This theoretical argument was the mainstay of the strategy of capital account liberalization in many parts of the developing world during the 1990s. First, as developing countries liberalized their securities markets, they benefited from both, global capital inflows and the declining cost of investments. The direct impact of this was general expansion of private business firms and their activities. As liquidity of domestic security markets in developing economies grew, they become capable of providing long-term financing to business firms and had a favorable impact on GDP growth.

Second, several developing economies had emerged as high-savers and therefore high investors in the global capital markets over the preceding three decades. Their ability to access the global capital markets provided the domestic savers – both public and private – in these economies an opportunity to earn greater returns on their savings than those available domestically. Their savings funded high-return projects in low-savings economies (which be either developing or advanced industrial economies), which had enormous welfare-enhancing implications for the global economy. The high-savers in the developing economies were also able to find a channel of improved risk management by diversifying their investment in the global capital markets.

Third, borrowing from the private global capital markets proved to be helpful to low-saving developing economies. It tided them over financially stressful periods so it was no longer necessary to sharply cut down consumption in severe recessionary periods. The ability to access international financial markets therefore facilitates consumption smoothing. Fourth, as the resource-rich financial intermediaries from the advanced industrial economies began to operate in the financial markets of the developing economies, they raised the standards of efficiency and corporate management in the domestic financial institutions in these countries. This happened because financial intermediaries in the developing economies are forced to compete with the subsidiaries and branches of financial institutions from advanced industrial economies. Enhanced competition with more sophisticated and resourceful institutions renders the developing countries' domestic financial sector more efficacious. In addition, the very presence of financial intermediaries from the advanced industrial economies helped inculcate greater market and financial discipline in the host developing economies.

7. Surge in global private financial flows to the developing economies

Although the 1990s saw several small financial and economic crises, the two crises of 1997 and 1998 had done considerable harm to global investors' confidence in the developing economies, and to the developing economies' own aptitude and ability for macroeconomic and financial management, and overall creditworthiness. Global investors began considering them to be unsafe economies for investment. The private global financial flows reversed their direction and began moving out of this country group. However, by 2002 market confidence in this group of economies was restored and capital market flows began to recover. This was the beginning of a new trend in global private capital flows. Rise in capital flows materialized despite lingering uncertainty about the impact of higher oil prices, rising global interest rates and growing global financial and payments imbalances. Net private capital flows, which included debt and equity, were down to $187 billion in 2000. They increased to $274.1 billion in 2003. Bond issuance, bank lending, FDI and portfolio equity – all components of global private capital – recorded an increase in 2003.

There was a noticeable surge after this point, with most of the flows going to a few large developing economies. Total debt and equity flows in 2004 amounted to $412.5 billion and in 2005, $551.4 billion. This strong surge continued unabated and in 2006 the amount increased to $760.3 billion. In the latter half of 2007, global capital markets became volatile as the crisis in the US sub-prime mortgage market spilled over into equity, currency and bond markets worldwide. Still the level of flows to developing economies at the end of the year was $1,025 billion. Notwithstanding the appreciable deterioration in the global financial conditions in the latter part of 2007, private flows to developing countries reached a record level. However, the majority of developing economies still depended heavily on concessionary loans and grants from official sources.[18]

7.1 Syndicated private bank lending

Syndicated private bank finances have been an important component of global private financial market flows to developing economies. The net cross-border syndicated private bank lending flows are defined as the gross lending by syndicated banks minus principal repayments. They were negative during the early years of the decade but began rising in 2003. The net flows soared precipitously after 2004, when they were

Table 2.1 Cross-border syndicated bank lending to developing countries (in billions of $)

Year	Gross Lending	Principal Repayments	Net Lending
2000	116.5	120.4	−3.9
2001	137.6	139.6	−2.0
2002	146.0	147.8	−1.7
2003	175.3	160.1	15.2
2004	235.2	184.7	50.4
2005	285.5	200.1	85.3
2006	397.0	31.3	172.4
2007	454.7	240.0	214.7

Source: The World Bank. 2008. *Global Development Finance 2008*. Washington. DC. Data gleaned from Table 2.2, Chapter 2, p. 39.

$50.4 billion. Syndicated bank lending in 2005 was dominated by the Russian Federation, China and India. The credit rating of many large developing countries improved during 2005. Net syndicated bank lending more than doubled the next year, to $172.4 billion. It recorded a further dramatic rise in 2007, to $214.7 billion (Table 2.1).

At present, cross-border syndicated bank lending is overwhelmingly dominated by private corporate sector loans by business firms in the BRIC and other large developing countries. Although sovereign governments could also avail themselves of this facility, over the past few years they accounted for a mere 3 percent of the total syndicated bank lending. This scenario is strikingly different from the early 1990s, when sovereign governments were substantive borrowers and accounted for approximately 15 percent of all syndicated bank lending. The proportion of the corporate sector has been rising and it presently attracts over 70 percent of the total syndicated loans. A noteworthy development of 2007 is a dramatic increase in the proportion of bank lending denominated in domestic currency. It was less than 5 percent during 2005 and 2006 but spurted to 11 percent in 2007. Leading borrowers of domestic currency loans were South Africa, China, Brazil and India, in that order.

7.2 Bond issuance in the international bond markets

Bond issuance in the international bond markets grew slowly over the past decades. In the early 2000s, it became a popular instrument of raising capital by the developing countries in global private capital. Net bond flows, which implies bond issuance minus principal repayments, hovered around $20 billion in 2003 but began to soar thereafter

Table 2.2 International bond market flows to developing countries (in billions of $)

Year	Bond Issuance	Principal Repayments	Net Bond Flows
2000	69.4	49.9	19.5
2001	54.6	44.4	10.2
2002	49.2	40.8	8.8
2003	68.2	48.6	19.6
2004	102.8	61.7	41.1
2005	115.1	62.5	52.6
2006	105.1	80.6	25.3
2007	142.2	62.9	79.3

Source: The World Bank. 2008. *Global Development Finance 2008*. Washington. DC. Data gleaned from Table 2.5, Chapter 2, p. 41.

(Table 2.2). In 2006, bond issuances by developing economies declined. However, the very next year it rebounded to $142.2 billion; the net bond flows rose to $79.3 billion in 2007. The rebound had occurred due to both higher bond issuance and lower principal repayments.

Both private and public corporations from the developing economies traditionally dominated bond issuance in the international bond markets. This tradition has continued thus far. The sovereign bond issuance has had a waning trend. After peaking in 2000 at 75 percent of all developing country bonds, the share of sovereign bonds fell below 24 percent in 2007. Conversely, the share of bonds issued by private corporations steadily soared. It was less than 20 percent of the total in 2000. In 2007, it rose to more than 50 percent.

A common characteristic of cross-border syndicated bank lending and bond issuance was that they remained highly concentrated in a few large developing economies. Other than the BRIC economies, principal borrowers in these two markets included Mexico, Turkey, Kazakhstan, South Africa, Malaysia and Venezuela. In 2007, the top five borrowers in the syndicated bank market accounted for 57.6 percent of the total and in the international bond issuance, 51 percent. The same trend of concentration is confirmed by the borrowings of the top ten borrowers. In the syndicated bank lending market they accounted for 76.7 percent of the total and in the international bond issuance, 72.5 percent.

Likewise, the international bond issuance activity traditionally remained concentrated. Its past trend did not show any tendency toward a decline in concentration. In the 2003–07 period, five large developing economies accounted for two-thirds of issuance by private corporations and three-quarters of issuance by public corporations. Thus viewed, bond issuance activity was, and continues to be, dominated by business corporations from a few large developing economies. Three in five developing countries have never accessed the international bond market. Until recently, India was the only low-income country to issue bonds in the international bond market on a frequent basis – almost annually. However, the nature of the international bond market is gradually changing. Countries that are first time issuers, and are also low-income, are for the first time being well received by the international bond market. The 2007 bond issuance by Belarus, Ghana, Georgia, Mongolia, Nigeria, Serbia, Sri Lanka and Vietnam are cases in point. Access to the international bond market is geographically broadening. Therefore, it can be expected that bond issuance activity may not remain as concentrated in the future as it was in the past.

7.3 FDI and portfolio equities

Equities inflows comprise FDI and portfolio investment. They are two increasingly important channels through which cross-border global private capital flows to developing economies. Over the last two decades, cross-border equity capital flows were boosted by the significant implementation of capital market reforms in both developing and advanced industrial economies. These reforms included stock market liberalization, improvement in securities clearance and settlement systems, and the development of a regulatory and supervisory framework. Aided by macroeconomic restructuring, they propped up domestic financial development. Capital market reforms also fostered and promoted domestic market development through stock market internationalization (Levine and Schmukler, 2006).

Traditionally, equity flows were heavily biased in favor of FDI. However, recently, portfolio flows have begun playing a prominent role. These flows recorded strong gains over the three-year period between 2005 and 2007. They reached a high point of $615.9 billion in 2007 (Table 2.3). As a proportion of the GDP of developing economies, FDI and portfolio equity investment was 4.2 percent in 2006. It reached 2.5 percent in 2007, the highest level ever reached by capital flows through these channels. The trend in portfolio equity flows was different from that of FDI. They were a tiny proportion of the total equity flows at the turn of the twentieth century. Gradually they increased and accounted for 20 percent of total equity flows between 2005 and 2007 (Table 2.3).

Table 2.3   Net equity inflows to developing economies (in billions of $)

Year	Net (FDI and Portfolio) Equity Investment	Net FDI Investment	Net Portfolio Equity Inflows
2000	179.0	165.5	13.5
2001	178.7	173.0	5.7
2002	166.0	160.7	5.3
2003	185.9	161.9	24.0
2004	265.9	225.5	40.4
2005	357.4	288.5	68.9
2006	472.3	367.5	104.8
2007	615.9	470.8	145.1

Source: The World Bank. 2008. *Global Development Finance 2008*. Washington. DC. Data gleaned from Table 2.10, Chapter 2, p. 46.

The largest increase in cross-border equity investments during 2005–07 took place in Latin America and the Caribbean. This was reversal of the past trend. Notwithstanding the reversal, these regions' share in global equity stock continues to remain low – almost half of what it was a decade ago. Other regions' share recorded strong increases. In particular, Europe, Central Asia and South Asia recorded substantive increases in equity inflows.

The global FDI flows to developing economies recorded a sharp increase in 2004. The reasons for a rise included a marked improvement in the investment climate of many developing countries. Corporate earning in these countries had improved and foreign ownership rules were liberalized. This improvement was reinforced by strong global recovery from the 2001 recession. As a consequence, FDI flows to developing economies increased to $225.5 billion in 2004.

The subsequent period was that of strong gains in global FDI. The surge in global FDI continued and it reached a record level of $1.7 trillion in 2007, over a quarter of which went to the developing economies. Net FDI flows to the developing economies increased to $470.8 billion, which was 3.4 percent of their GDP. This was marginally higher than their 2006 proportion of 3.25 percent. The increase of $103 billion in 2007 was more or less evenly distributed across different geographical regions. The Russian Federations and Brazil were the strongest gainers in 2007. China has continued to be the most attractive destination for FDI in the developing world for over two decades, albeit its share has been on a decline in the recent years (Das, 2008b). Brazil and Turkey recorded strong gains in FDI flows in recent years, both in absolute and relative terms. The Russian Federation also recorded a rise in FDI in 2007, which was unexpected because the investment climate had not improved there. If anything, unfavorable regulations had increased. Nevertheless, global investors were drawn by the potential of high returns in extractive industries.

Over the 2005–07 period, FDI flows to China in dollar terms did not record a large variance. However, its share in total developing-country FDI declined from 30 percent in 2002–03 to 18 percent in 2007. FDI accounted for 15 percent of total investment in China in the mid-1990s, this proportion steadily declined to 8 percent in 2006–07. The old strategy of a comprehensive welcome of FDI had changed. The Chinese government has become increasingly selective in allowing FDI inflows. The FDI proposals are rigorously scrutinized *inter alia* for their technology content and environmental impact. Proposals that show promise of significant technology transfer are approved without much delay. Projects that are to be located in the interior of the country, away from the Eastern and Southern coastal provinces, are preferred. The new strategy is sure to slow FDI inflows in the manufacturing sector, but at the time of accession to the World Trade Organization (WTO) in 2001, China had committed to substantially opening its services sectors to FDI. Foreign banks have been positioning themselves in China. As they open their insurance and other financial services to FDI, net FDI inflows will pick up momentum again.

After a slow start, since 2004 portfolio equity flows to developing economies began recording discernibly large increases. In 2006, they increased by $36 billion and in 2007 they jumped again by $40 billion (Table 2.3). This increase in dollar terms did not affect the percentage share of portfolio equity flows in the GDP of the recipient countries. They continued to remain 0.9 percent of the GDP. Portfolio equity flows remained heavily concentrated in a small group of large developing economies, the BRIC economies. Of these, Brazil and India have been recording strong increases in recent years, while China a decline. However, this decline was more than offset by the large gains in the portfolio equity investment in Brazil and India. The BRIC and other large developing economies have begun playing an increasingly prominent role in global equity markets. The issuance of equity in these markets 'is on par with that of the high-income countries' (WB, 2008, p. 47). When ranked by the value of cross-border initial public offerings (IPOs) in 2007, China, Brazil and Russian Federation, in that order, ranked immediately after the US. The BRIC economies are regarded as the largest issuance countries. In 2007, companies located in each one of the four BRICs launched at least one IPO valued at $2 billion or more. Returns on cross-border portfolio investment in the stock markets of BRIC economies tend to be high. While the stock markets in BRICs and other large developing economies are more volatile than those in advanced industrial economies, returns on equity investment in these markets have continued to outperform those in the advanced industrial markets. This has become an established trend.

Claessens and Schmukler (2007) studied data from 39,517 firms in 111 countries to conclude that global financial integration by trading equities and/or cross-listing in major capital markets has increased over time. They found that relatively few countries and firms actively participated and that firms more likely to participate in global equities transactions were from larger and more open economies. Cross-country portfolio investment pattern is influenced by several factors. With the help of a stylized theoretical model, Lane and Milesi-Ferretti (2008b) demonstrated that bilateral equity investment is strongly correlated with the underlying patterns of merchandise trade. This variable was found to be robustly significant in their empirical exercise. It is plausible that the level of trade may be a proxy for bilateral information flows. In addition, international linkages by way of common language and common legal systems are also influential factors. A common language factor alone increased equity holdings by approximately 40 percent. The level of development and the depth of the financial markets are the other factors that affect cross-country portfolio investment. High-income countries with a well-developed equity culture tend to hold larger gross foreign equity positions.

Although the above statistical data show the spurt in capital flows to developing economies, they do not reveal a striking transformation in the status of these economies. In the recent past, the external balance sheet of developing and emerging-market economies has undergone a dramatic change. The net external position of this group of economies has improved significantly. So much so that there has been a reversal in the historical pattern of global financial flows. Advanced industrial economies have slowly become a net issuer of liabilities to the developing world. The old principle of capital flowing from the rich economies of the industrialized world to the have-not economies of the developing world has been turned around. The external liabilities of developing and emerging-market economies have declined. This applies particularly to the debt category. The reason was deleveraging in several large developing economies as a reaction to the Asian crisis.[19]

Another important recent transformation is that equity instruments, particularly FDI, now account for a much larger proportion of external liabilities than before. This implies that the external investors in developing economies share production risk to a much greater degree. Besides, owing to the accumulation of large official reserves, external asset holdings of the developing and emerging-market economies have markedly expanded. This has meant, in an unprecedented change, that the monetary authorities in these countries are now mostly foreign investors and managers of large funds in hard currencies (Lane and Milesi-Ferretti, 2007). Many GCC and developing economies have established large sovereign-wealth funds (SWFs).

8. International banks and the developing economies

Both the liaison and business association between the international banking world and the developing economies are undergoing a transformation. This changing relationship is influencing the financial health of both sides. On the one hand the structure of the international banking industry is changing and on the other numerous developing economies have liberalized their economies and taken to high-growth trajectory. This has created a new locus of mutual interest and a different dynamic of engagement from the past. The traditional role of the international banks was seen as suppliers of trade credit and providers of sovereign loans to developing countries in financial distress. This role is now in the past.

Internal lending activity per se of the international banks, as measured by the foreign assets of these banks, has expanded at an exceedingly fast pace since the late 1980s. The causal factors were expanding world trade, rapid increase in the activities of the transnational corporations (TNCs) and growth in financing global financial and payments imbalances. After the fall of the Berlin Wall, the transition economies became part of the global banking system, which further expanded the lending operations of international banks. Total international bank assets were a paltry $100 billion in 1970. They soared to $6.3 trillion in 1990 and to 31.8 trillion in mid-2007 (WB, 2008).

The presence of international banks in the developing world was sparse in the past. It is no longer so. They have expanded through a large network of local agencies, branches and subsidiaries. By 2007, they had 2,027 local offices and branches in 127 developing countries (WB, 2008). Their operating infrastructure in the developing economies is much larger than that in the past and modern advances in ICT have made their operations widespread. Cross-border syndicated lending was one of their old activities. Large volume lending operations presently enable international banks to play an increasingly important role in the financial systems of the developing countries. In some of them, international banks even dominate the financial markets. According to the Bank for International Settlements (BIS) data, foreign claims on developing country residents held by major international banks stood at $3.1 trillion in mid-2007. They were only $1.1 trillion in 2002. The deposits of the residents of developing countries with international banks were $917 billion. In 2002, the deposits were less than a third of this amount (BIS, 2005).

Changes in legislation in the home countries of the foreign banks facilitated their recent expansion in the developing economies. As the presence of foreign banks, and banks with majority ownership by foreign banks, increased in the developing economies, the lending operations of foreign banks and foreign-owned banks began to account for a particularly high proportion of local bank assets. This applies particularly to the developing economies in Eastern Europe and Latin America, where foreign banks own 70 percent and 40 percent of local banking asset, respectively. Increased presence of foreign banks in developing economies engendered substantial economic and financial benefits. Major areas in which they contributed included greater availability of capital as well as the provision of sophisticated financial services. In addition, they encouraged efficiency gains in the domestic banking systems and provided expertise in dealing with ailing banking and financial institutions. Usually foreign banks outperform domestic banks when competitiveness in the host developing country's banking industry is low. Also, foreign banks that are familiar with the domestic business environment and culture of the host countries perform better than distant foreign banks that are unfamiliar with the business and culture of the host country (Claessens and van Horen, 2009).

9. Pro-cyclicality in global capital flows

An appropriate time for borrowing from the global private capital markets can vary. It can be both pro- and counter-cyclical. The property of cyclicality in global capital flows can take three forms: First, capital inflows are called counter-cyclical when the correlation between the net capital inflows and domestic output is negative. That is, an economy borrows from the global capital markets during periods of tepid economic performance, while it lends or repays during buoyant growth periods. Second, capital inflows are pro-cyclical when the correlation between the net capital inflows and domestic output is positive. That is, an economy borrows from the global capital markets during periods of brisk economic performance and lends or repays during lean periods, or during crisis periods. There is a third possibility as well. That is, when net capital inflows and domestic output do not have a significant relationship. In this case the correlation is statistically insignificant, capital inflows are regarded as acyclical. The implication of acyclical capital flows is that the borrowing or lending propensity of an economy has no systemic relationship with the domestic business cycle.

Net private global capital flows, over the preceding four decades, demonstrated a pro-cyclical relationship with fiscal policy and monetary policy in the recipient countries. Pro-cyclical capital inflows was found to be a broad characteristic among the capital recipients. This characteristic was not limited merely to developing economies. The primary cause of many financial and debt crises can be traced to a strong proclivity among governments to bouts of high borrowing and profligate spending during buoyant domestic economic growth periods and when the global capital markets are exceptionally liquid (Reinhart et al., 2003). This is generalization that seems intuitively correct.

An empirical study conducted with the help of long-term (1960–2003) statistical capital flow data for 104 countries by Kaminsky et al. (2004) found strong evidence of the pro-cyclicality of fiscal policy. They analyzed countries grouped into several income levels to capture an important truth of the global capital markets, that is, while high-income countries have instantaneous access to them at any point, the ones at the other extreme of the income spectrum are shut out of them completely because of their low credit ratings. The middle income countries live in a world of uncertainty in this regard. Their access to the global capital markets is marked by unpredictability. Kaminsky et al. examined the relationship between the capital flow cycle and the business cycle and the fiscal and monetary policies in the borrowing countries. Their principle findings are summarized below:

(i) Net capital inflows from global capital markets were pro-cyclical both in the most advanced industrial economies and the developing ones.

(ii) Fiscal policy was pro-cyclical for most of the developing economies, in particular for the middle-income ones. This implies an increase in government spending in high external capital inflow periods and a fall in the low capital inflow periods.

(iii) Monetary policy was also found to be pro-cyclical for most of the developing economies, in particular for the middle-income countries. The interest rate was lowered during the high external capital inflow periods and increased in the low capital inflow periods.
(iv) There was some evidence of counter-cyclical monetary policy in some advanced industrial economies.
 (v) For the middle- to high-income developing countries, the capital inflow cycle and the macroeconomic cycles reinforced each other. This trend substantiated the so-called when-it-rains-it-pours syndrome.

Thus viewed, the objective of macroeconomic policy in advanced industrial economies was, for the most part, either stabilizing the business cycle, or remaining neutral. Conversely, the objective of macroeconomic policy in the developing economies was, for the most part, to reinforce the business cycle, which amounted to turning rainy days into those of torrential downpours. Evidently, this group of economies would have done well to switch its macroeconomic policy stance and conduct it in a neutral or stabilizing manner.

10. Asymmetrical progress in financial globalization

The current phase of financial globalization reflects a high degree of heterogeneity in international financial linkages. Although financial globalization in the contemporary era proliferated broadly, it increased unevenly across regions. What is more noteworthy is that it was never truly global or a globe-encompassing phenomenon. It still is not. The extent of integration around the globe varied from country group to country group and from region to region. All regions did not integrate financially evenly, nor did all financial crises have a comparable impact over the financial integration of different economies. According to IMF (2009a), since 1990, 70 percent of the world's economies have increased their gross external positions; this fact reflects increased global financial integration. In other countries, gross external positions have declined. Economies on the continent of Africa come under this category, largely because of debt relief. The economies that have observed large increases were the EMEs, particularly those in Europe. Gross external positions in the latter group of EMEs rose by more than 50 percent of annual GDP in just over a decade.

A precondition for global financial integration is the liberalization of the domestic financial sector and opening up of the economy for trans-border capital flows. As set out above (Section 3), these indispensable policy measures were not only taken in an asymmetric manner at different times in different countries and country groups but also the degree of adoption of these two courses of action varied widely among economies. High-income industrial economies were the first to embark on the path of liberalization, deregulation and opening up and therefore also first to financially globalize. They were the pioneers in taking the *de jure* measures of capital account opening. Although their beginning was slow, they also pioneered opening up their capital accounts. The theoretical comprehension of this course of action and their policy implications was reasonably good in the high-income industrial countries. As they were the most financially open economies, they also became the most globally integrated group of economies in financial terms. A striking degree of macroeconomic policy convergence also took place among this country group. Among the other country groups, two groups learned from them and followed them to their advantage. They were the high-income members of the GCC and high-growth and better developed economies of East Asia. Their financial integration with the global financial markets was much quicker than that of other regions.

Judged by cross-border asset and liability positions, the advanced industrial economies were far ahead of the developing and emerging-market economies. These countries were the members of the Organization for Economic Cooperation and Development (OECD) and have been the most active participants in the financial globalization process. For these advanced industrial economies the median value of cross-border asset and liability positions was well over 200 percent of GDP for the 1999–2006 period. In comparison, the median value for the developing and emerging-market economies was much smaller, 70–80 percent (Lane and Milesi-Ferretti, 2008a).

The high-growth economies of East Asia led the way for the developing economies. Among the developing countries, this group of economies took initiative in adopting *de jure* measures of capital account opening (Das, 2005). This group was atypical in the sense that, having taken the initiative in financial globalization, they reversed their course when the Asian financial crisis struck in 1997. Two fast-growing major developing economies, China and India, recently took *de jure* steps to open their capital account. While China is more financially integrated in aggregate terms with the global financial markets, India has had more experience with portfolio investment flows. In both the countries, the public sector is a large holder of international assets. China is a large net creditor economy, while India a net debtor (Das, 2006a; McCauley, 2008).

Other regional economies displayed limited policy commitment to financial sector and capital account liberalization and financial globalization. Consequently, intra-regional differences are evident in financial globalization. A significant number of developing countries neither liberalized their domestic financial sector to the required extent, nor opened up their capital account. There are numerous cases of partial opening. Therefore, these developing economies remained only peripherally integrated with the global financial markets. The South Asian economies remained among the slowest in opening up their financial markets. However, after 2000 India took several measures to liberalize and open up its financial sector. Its stock market in particular became an important EME market that characteristically attracts large investments from global institutional investors (Das, 2009b; Kose et al., 2009).[20]

Financial market integration by means of FDI reflected approximately the same scenario. The members of the GCC stood out as the principal force, followed by the advanced industrial economies and the East Asian economies. After the breakdown of the socialism, Eastern European and Central Asian economies also began to benefit from large FDI inflows. They received an impetus from the widespread privatization strategies that these country groups adopted. Three country groups that have begun benefiting lately from FDI inflows more than others are the Sub-Saharan Africa, Latin America and Caribbean economies. FDI inflows in them have been on the rise. The Sub-Saharan African countries are likely to receive an increasing amount of FDI due to investors' interest in mining and extracting industries (Nellor, 2008).

Calculations of some simple ratios can unmistakably demonstrate the heterogeneity in the spread of financial globalization. To demonstrate the differences in the degree of global integration, Lane and Milesi-Ferretti (2003) computed a volume-based measure of financial integration using the following ratio:

$$\text{IFIGDP} = \frac{(\text{FA} + \text{FL})}{\text{GDP}}$$

FA and LA refer to the stock of aggregate foreign assets and liabilities, respectively. When this ratio was computed for the industrial countries for the 1983–2001 period, it showed an increase by 250 percent. It recorded a sharp acceleration during the 1990s. However, the increase in financial integration was far from uniform across countries.

Lane and Milesi-Ferretti (2003) also computed an equity-based measure of financial integration based on the following ratio:

$$GEQGDP = \frac{(PEQA + FDIA + PEQL + FDIL)}{GDP}$$

PEQA and FDIA are stocks of portfolio assets and FDI stocks, and PEQL and FDIL are stocks of portfolio liability and FDI liabilities. GEQGDP stands for the level of equity cross-holdings, which includes both the equity and FDI. This ratio multiplied 300 percent over the 1983–2001 period. Increase in international trade affected this ratio favorably.

Cipriani and Kaminski (2006) used a Bayesian dynamic latent factor model to gauge the extent of financial integration by looking at gross issuance at four (Frankfurt, London, New York and Tokyo) financial centers and five regions (advanced industrial economies, East Asia, Latin America, the Middle East and the transition economies) in three international markets (namely, bonds, equities and cross-border syndicated loans markets) from 1980 to 2004. They used financial market data for 101 countries.

Many of their conclusions, based on this econometric exercise, were notable, revealing and confirmed casual empiricism. They found evidence for fairly well globally synchronized fluctuations in issuance in the equity markets. However, fluctuations in the bond and cross-border syndicated loan markets were less synchronized. The co-movement in fluctuations in equity issuance in the global stock markets was found to be twice as high as the co-movement in the international bond and syndicated loans markets. The average idiosyncratic component in equity market could explain merely 37 percent of the fluctuations in equity issuance. In contrast, the average idiosyncratic component across all regions for international bonds and cross-border syndicated loans markets could explain more than 60 percent of the variance of the total issuance.

As for the global international bonds and syndicated loan markets, Japan stood out as a matured economy that was less integrated with the global capital markets and its trends. Its variance in international issuance was explained more by idiosyncratic factors than by common movements across markets and regions. The variance of the idiosyncratic factors explained 84 percent of the total variance for the international bond markets and 89 percent of the total for the syndicated loan markets.

Likewise, Latin America and the Middle East were found to be relatively less integrated regions. International issuance of both the debt
instruments could be mostly explained by idiosyncratic factors; its
range varied between 80 percent and 84 percent. In contrast to this,
international bonds and syndicated loan markets in the advanced
industrial economies were well integrated and world shocks moved
them in a synchronized manner in the same direction. Only a small
share of variance in this group of economies could be explained by
idiosyncratic factors. In case of international bond issuance, 18 percent of the total variance could be explained by idiosyncratic factors,
while that for syndicated loans only 12 percent. These results demonstrated a close financial integration among the advanced industrial
economies. This group of economies integrated financially most closely,
while those of Latin America and the Middle East were at the other
extreme. The remaining groups of economies fell in between these two
extremes.

11. Financial globalization and convergence of capitalism

As financial and macroeconomic liberalization measures are adopted by
economies to financially integrate the domestic financial sector with the
global financial markets, macroeconomic performance of the domestic
economy is affected. An immediate impact is to constrain the income
redistribution policies commonly implemented by governments. As
financial globalization lays down its roots, cross-border capital mobility
progressively increases and the ability of the government to tax income
is eroded. In case a government decides to take austere measures to
tax capital, two unwanted consequences follow. First, capital exiting to
other locations where it is not taxed heavily and, second, reversal of
capital inflows. As the mobility of capital increases with deepening in
financial globalization in the domestic economy, the incidence of tax
on labor increases. It happens largely because it is an immobile factor
of production. Complaints on these lines are frequently heard in many
advanced industrial economies.

In addition, in a financially liberalized and globally integrated
economy, policy makers become more aware of the wastefulness
of unproductive macroeconomic policies that lead to overvaluation
of currencies and high rates of inflation. The costs of such policies grow higher than in an economy that has not been liberalized
as yet. These outcomes encourage macroeconomic discipline in liberalized economies and ensure that policy makers cautiously shun

reckless, risky and imprudent macroeconomic policies. Thus viewed, improvement in macroeconomic policy discipline is considered an indirect positive effect of financial globalization, which in turn is expected to sustain or strengthen the trend GDP growth rates in those economies.

As an economy globalizes financially and policy makers make concerted efforts to nurture, support and enhance it, they change the domestic economic structure by unintentionally adopting policies that favor the domestic economic class that is the owner of capital. Sound, welfare-enhancing macroeconomic policies and a lower tax burden are generally biased in favor of high-income households. They benefit this segment of the society more than the usually larger low-income class of households. Also, the policies that nurture, support and enhance financial globalization include the adoption of specific accounting rules and higher supervisory standards. The adoption of internationally accepted norms promotes inward flows of investible capital from the private global capital markets. This applies particularly to a range of global investment funds and sovereign-wealth funds, both of which control and actively make gargantuan amounts of investment globally. These cash-rich funds look for uniformity in accounting standards and supervisory norms across the globe as these ensure that their operations and decision process run smoothly. When countries adopt uniformity in accounting standards and supervisory norms to attract global capital, they indirectly and unintentionally support and make the creditors and equity-owning class better off. Two of the most telling recent examples of this are the introduction of corporate law and the legal framework of public companies in the European countries as well as in many developing economies, and the near universal adoption of prudential regulations devised under the Basel II accord.

There is another dimension to this argument. The adoption of parallel practices in several domains in various economies has created an environment in which capitalism around the globe is growing increasingly indistinguishable. As the global investing class of people or institutions prefer to make investment in countries that provide comparable rates of return to them, the economic, accounting, supervisory and legal frameworks in different countries will increasingly tend to become homogeneous around the globe. This implies a leveling of the playing field in the arena of global finance. Eventually, it could catalyze the process of convergence in the nature and practices of capitalism around the globe.

12. Summary and conclusions

The post-World War II era began with global financial markets in a moribund state. They needed time to rejuvenate and become operative. The early post-war development of international financial and capital markets was exceedingly slow and far from linear. Due to disturbing developments during the interwar period, cross-border capital movement was initially regarded by policy mandarins as an anathema. Consequently, the Bretton Woods regime (1946–73) adopted capital immobility as one of its principal policy pillars.

As the post-war process of reconstruction started, private global capital markets also began their re-evolution. Their recreation was slow and was affected by trilemma-related strategic decisions. However, in the immediate aftermath of the war, global capital markets remained by and large dormant. This depressed and sluggish state continued during a good part of the 1950s. After the founding of the IMF, the movable peg exchange rate regime was accepted by the members and began functioning as the new global financial architecture.

However, the official self-declarations by countries about the exchange rate regimes need to be taken with a pinch of salt. Only the over-credulous can believe them. The officially declared positions of countries were in most cases different from how they really functioned. The availability of new statistical data facilitated a nuanced distinction between what countries declared as their *de jure* exchange rate regimes and their actual *de facto* exchange rate practices.

In the mid-1960s currencies of the countries that were following policies inconsistent with the maintenance of their parities were subject to speculative attacks. Frequent speculative runs began against the major currencies. Although repeated attempts were made to quell speculation, the Bretton Woods regime began wilting away in 1971. The collapse of the regime began in August 1971. By February 1973, the major currencies had to be set free to float independently. During early 1973, independence of monetary policy was regarded as an important policy instrument, while capital controls were abandoned, freeing capital to flow from where it was to where it yielded the highest rates of returns.

The floating rate regime was fully compatible with free cross-border capital movements. It lubricated the progress of capital mobility. The 1973 quadrupling of oil prices occurred, which proved to be a seismic economic event that affected the global economy and financial markets. Around this period, a good number of lower- and upper-middle income developing economies broke from their tradition of following erroneous and unproductive economic strategies. They committed to improving the macroeconomic and financial climate in their economies by carrying out macroeconomic reforms and restructuring their economies. A series of long-term policy measures were required for economic macroeconomic restructuring. This was done, *inter alia*, with an objective to make their economies more attractive for global capital inflows, which in turn helped them integrate with the global financial market. The indispensable policy measures to achieve this objective were: pursuing macroeconomic stabilization, improving business environment and aiming for stronger economic fundamentals.

The collapse of the Bretton Woods regime was a defining moment for the world of global finance. It was followed by a surge in cross-border capital flows from the private global capital markets. With the largest industrial economies of the world abandoning the concept of capital control and with an increasing amount of financial activity taking place in the Eurodollar markets, other countries had little choice but to open their financial sectors as well. The 1973 quadrupling of oil prices affected the global financial markets in a significant manner. Post-1973, cross-border syndicated bank loan market began to pick up momentum.

The Brady initiative was launched in the late 1980s. Its express purpose was to resolve the Mexican debt crisis. The Brady bond initiative helped restore investor confidence in the developing economies. Soon the developing country governments began issuing debt outside the Brady market. This mitigated the negative impact of the Latin American debt crisis and financial globalization once again began to flourish.

Developing economies could not remain impervious for long to the transformations in both the financial markets of advanced industrial economies and the global financial markets. Their domestic financial and capital markets reacted to the forces of change in the advanced industrial countries as well as to the ongoing financial globalization and innovation. These forces had a demonstrative learning effect on the developing economies. The period of rapid progress of financial globalization was interrupted by the fallout from some serious crises. The Asian financial crisis (1997–8) unfavorably affected it. Although several economy-specific crises, like the Tequila Crisis of 1994, had occurred in the interim, the Asian crisis was the first major setback to the global economy since the Latin American debt crisis of 1982. The Asian crisis not only mangled the so-called miracle economies of Asia and the regional economy, it also affected the global capital and stock markets adversely.

Although financial globalization in the contemporary era proliferated broadly across the globe, it did not proliferate evenly. The extent of integration around the globe varied significantly. All regions did not integrate financially uniformly, nor did all financial crises have comparable impact over the financial integration of different economies. Due to the negative impact of the crises of 1997 and 1998 over global private capital markets and investor confidence, global investors began considering developing economies to be unsafe for investment. The private global financial flows reversed their direction and began moving out of this country group. However, by 2002 market confidence in this group of economies was restored and, with that, capital market flows began to recover. This was the beginning of a new surge in global private capital flows to the developing economies.

Notes

1. Lorenzo de Medici took Michelangelo Buonarroti under his wings when Michelangelo was still a little boy and provided the right artistic ambiance to him to nurture and hone his genius.
2. For the birth and expansion of international banking and finance and a detailed historical account of international capital flows see Cameron (1993), Das (1986) and Neal (1990).
3. The concept of the Gulf Cooperation Council (GCC) was initiated by Saudi Arabia in 1981. The other members of the GCC are Bahrain, Kuwait, Oman, Qatar and the United Arab Emirates (UAE).
4. In mid-2009, its membership was 185.
5. The term trilemma was used by Obstfeld and Taylor (1998) for the first time.
6. Obstfeld and Taylor (2004) provide a detailed treatment of this issue.
7. The IMF began its operations on 1 March 1947. That very year, France became the first borrowing member. As more and more countries became independent, its membership began to increase in the 1950s and 1960s. However, due to the cold War, most countries in the Soviet sphere of influence did not join initially.
8. The Organization of the Petroleum Exporting Countries (OPEC) is an intergovernmental organization of twelve oil-exporting developing nations that coordinates and unifies the petroleum policies of its member countries. The current (2009) membership includes Algeria, Angola, Ecuador, Iran, Iraq, Kuwait, Libya, Nigeria, Qatar, Saudi Arabia, the United Arab Emirates (UAE) and Venezuela.
9. See Das (2003).
10. See Fry (1995) for a comprehensive analysis of financial repression.
11. Comprehensive literature reviews are provided by Fry (1997) and Andersen and Tarp (2003).
12. This section draws on de la Torre and Schmukler (2007).

13. The UN-WIDER is a Helsinki-based United Nations institution. The acronym WIDER stands for World Institute for Development Economics Research.
14. The World Development Indicators 2008, published by the World Bank in July 2008, provide definitions of these terms.
15. See Henry (2007) and Reinhart and Reinhart (2008) for surveys of this literature.
16. Simply defined, derivatives are financial instruments or contracts that are used to mitigate the risk of economic loss by change in the value of the underlying assets. This practice is known as hedging. The underlying value on which a derivative is based can be the value of an asset like commodities, equities or stocks, residential mortgage, loans and bonds. It can also be an index like interest rate, exchange rate, stock market indices or consumer price index.
17. For instance, see Das (2000), Demirguc-Kunt and Detragiache (1998), Edison (2000), Edwards (1999), Eichengreen and Rose (1998), Kaminsky and Reinhart (1999), Krugman (2000), Krugman (1998) and Reinhart and Rogoff (2004b) among others.
18. The source of statistical data used in this section is *Global Development Finance 2008* published by the World Bank in December 2008, and its earlier volumes.
19. This subject has been discussed in greater detail in Chapter 4 (Section 2.2) and Chapter 5 (Section 2.5).
20. A recent example of the Indian stock market being well integrated with the global community of investors was seen in May 2009 when as soon as the Congress Party victory was announced in the general election, global institutional investors invested $209 million in a matter of hours in Indian stocks, causing the Sensex to jump by 17.3 percent in one day. The stock market had to be closed twice during one day because such a sharp rise caused the circuit breakers to be activated.

References

Andersen, T. and F. Tarp. 2003. "Financial Liberalization, Financial Development and Economic Growth in LDCs". *Journal of International Development*. Vol. 15. No. 2. pp. 189–209.

The Bank for International Settlements (BIS). 2009. "BIS Report on Derivatives". Basel. Switzerland. 19 May.

The Bank for International Settlements (BIS). 2007. *Triennial Central Bank Survey of Foreign Exchange and Derivatives Market Activity*. Basel. Switzerland. December.

The Bank for International Settlements (BIS). 2005. *74th Annual Report, 2004*. Basel. Switzerland. 28 June.

Cipriani, M. and G. Kaminski. 2006. "A New Era of International Financial Integration". George Washington. DC. The GW Center for the Study of Globalization". Occasional Paper Series.

Claessens, S. and N. van Horen. 2009. "Being a Foreigner among Domestic Banks: Asset or Liability". Available on the Internet at http://mpra.ub.uni-muenchen. de/13467/1/MPRA_paper_13467.pdf. 20 January 2009.

Claessens, S. and S.L. Schmukler. 2007. "International Financial Integration through Equity Markets." *Journal of International Money and Finance*. Vol. 26. No. 3. pp. 788–813.

Crockett, A. 2009. "Asia and the Global Financial Crisis". Paper presented at the conference on *Reforming the Global Financial Architecture* sponsored by the Federal Reserve Bank of San Francisco, Santa Barbara. California. 18–20 October.

Das, Dilip K. 2009a. *The Two Faces of Globalization: Munificent and Malevolent.* Northampton. MA. USA and Cheltenham. Glos. UK. Edward Elgar Publishing, Inc.

Das, Dilip K. 2009b. "Short- and Long-Term Prospects of Indian Economic Growth: A Dispassionate Analysis". *International Journal of Trade and Global Markets.* Vol. 20. No. 2. pp. 194–210.

Das, Dilip K. 2006a. *China and India: A Tale of Two Economies.* London and New York. Routledge.

Das, Dilip K. 2005. *Asian Economy and Finance: A Post-Crisis Perspective.* Cambridge. UK and New York. USA. Springer Publications.

Das, Dilip K. 2003. "Financial Flows and Global Integration". Coventry. UK. University of Warwick. Center for the Study of Globalization. Working Paper No. 132/04. June.

Das, Dilip K. 2000. *Asian Crisis: Distilling Critical Lessons.* United Nations Conference on Trade and Development (UNCTAD), Geneva. Discussion Paper No. 152. December.

Das, Dilip K. 1989. "Brady Plan and the International Banks: A Cautious Reception". *The Business Standard*. Bombay. 24 August. p. 8.

Das, Dilip K. 1986. *Migration of Financial Resources to Developing Countries.* London. The Macmillan Press Ltd. and New York. St. Martin's Press, Inc.

de la Torre, A. and S.L. Schmukler. 2007. *Emerging Capital Markets and Globalization.* Palo Alto. CA. Stanford University Press.

Demirguc-Kunt, A. and E. Detragiache. 1998. "The Determinants of Banking Crises in Developing and Developed Countries". *IMF Staff Papers.* Vol. 45. No. 1. pp. 81–109.

Edison, H. 2000. "Do Indicators of Financial Crises Work? An Evaluation". Washington. DC. The Board of Governers of the Federal Reserve Board. International Finance Discussion Paper No. 675. November.

Edwards, S. 1999. "How Effective are Capital Controls?" *The Journal of Economic Perspectives.* Vol. 13. No. 4. (Autumn) pp. 65–84.

Eichengreen, B.J. and A. Rose. 1998. "Staying Afloat When the Wind Shifts. External Factors and Emerging-Market Banking Crisis". Cambridge. MA. National Bureau of Economic Research. Working Paper No. 6370.

Farrell, D., C.S. Folster and S. Lund. 2008. "Long-Term Trends in the Global Capital Markets". *The McKinsey Quarterly*. February. Available on the Internet at http://www.stern.nyu.edu/eco/B012303/Backus/Writing_samples/McKinsey%20Quarterly%2008.PDF. 22 January 2009.

Fischer, S. 2003. "Globalization and its Challenges". *American Economic review.* Vol. 93. No. 2. pp. 1–30.

Fischer, S. 1997. "Capital Account Liberalization and the Role of the IMF". Lecture at the annual Meeting of the International Monetary Fund, 19 September.

Available on the Internet at http://www.imf.org/external/np/speeches.199/0 91997.htm. 29 January 2009.

Fry, M.J. 1997. "In Favor of Financial Liberalization". *Economic Journal*. Vol. 107. pp. 754–770.

Fry, M.J. 1995. *Money, Interest and Banking in Economic Development*. Baltimore. Maryland. The Johns Hopkins University Press.

Gallegati, M., B. Greenwald, M.G. Richiardi and J.E. Stiglitz. 2008. "The Asymmetric Effect of Diffusion Process: Risk Sharing and Contagion". *Global Economy Journal*. Vol. 8. No. 2. pp. 30–58.

Gozzi, J.C., R. Levine and S.L. Schmukler. 2008. "Patterns of International Capital Ratings". Washington. DC. The World Bank. Policy Research Working Paper No. 4687. August.

Greenspan, A. 2007. *The Age of Turbulence: Adventures in a New World*. New York. Penguin Press.

Henry, P.B. 2007. "Capital Account Liberalization, Theory, Evidence and Speculation". *Journal of Economic Literature*. Vol. 45. No. 4. pp. 887–935.

The International Monetary Fund (IMF). 2009a. *World Economic Outlook*. Washington. DC. April.

The International Monetary Fund (IMF). 2008a. "Reaping Benefits of Financial Globalization". Washington. DC. Occasional Paper 264. December.

The International Monetary Fund (IMF). 2008c. "Globalization: A Brief Overview". *Issues Brief*. No. 02/08. Washington. DC. May.

The International Monetary Fund (IMF). 1997. "Communiqué of the Interim Committee of the Board of Governors: The Liberalization of Capital Movements under an Amendment of the IMF's Articles". Washington. DC. Press Release No. 97/44.

Kaminsky, G. and S. Schmukler. 2008. "Short-Run Pain, Long-Run Gain: The Effects of Financial Liberalization". *Review of Finance*. Vol. 12. No. 2. pp. 253–292.

Kaminsky, G., C. Reinhart and C.A. Vegh. 2004. "When it Rains, It Pours: Procyclical Capital Flows and Macroeconomic Development". Cambridge. MA. National Bureau of Economic Research. Working Paper. No. 10780. September.

Kaminsky, G. and C. Reinhart. 1999. "The Twin Crises: The Causes of Banking and Balance-of-Payments Problems". *American Economic Review*. Vol. 89. No. 2. pp. 473–500.

King, R.G. and R. Levine. 1993. "Finance and Growth: Schumpeter Might Be Right". *Quarterly Journal of Economics*. Vol. 108. No. 3. pp. 717–38.

Kose, M.A., E.S. Prasad, K.S. Kogoff and S.J. Wei. 2009. "Financial Globalization and Economic Policies". Washington. DC. The Brookings Institution. Working Paper No. 24. April.

Krugman, P. 2000. "Crises: The Price of Globalization?" *Global Economic Integration*. Symposium Sponsored by the Federal Reserve Bank of Kansas City. pp. 75–106.

Krugman, P. 1998. "What Happened to Asia?" Available on his website at http://www.hartford-hwp.com/archives/50/010.html. 24 January 2009.

Lane, P.R. and G.M. Milesi-Ferretti. 2008a. "The Drivers of Financial Globalization". *American Economic Review*. Vol. 98. No. 2. pp. 327–332.

Lane, P.R. and G.M. Milesi-Ferretti. 2008b. "International Investment Patterns". *The Review of Economics and Statistics.* Vol. 90. No. 3. pp. 538–549.

Lane, P.R. and G.M. Milesi-Ferretti. 2007. "The External Wealth of Nations Mark II". *Journal of International Economics.* Vol. 73. No. 2. pp. 223–250.

Lane, P.R. and G.M. Milesi-Ferrtti. 2003. "International Financial Integration". *IMF Staff Papers.* Vol. 50. Special Issue. pp. 82–113.

Levine, R. and S.L. Schmukler. 2006. "Internationalization and Stock Market Liquidity". *Review of Finance.* Vol. 10. No. 1. pp. 153–187.

McCauley, R.N. 2008. "Fuller Capital Account Opening in China and India". Paper presented at the third research meeting of NIPFP-DEA Program on Capital Flows, held in New Delhi, on 30 September.

McKinnon, R.I. 1973. *Money and Capital in Economic Development.* Washington. DC. The Brookings Institution Press.

McKinsey Global Institute (MGI). 2009. "The New Power Brokers". San Francisco. July.

McKinsey Global Institute (MGI). 2008. "The New Power Brokers: Gaining Clout in Turbulent Markets". San Francisco. July.

Mizen, P. 2008. "The Credit Crunch of 2007–2008: A Discussion of the Background". *Federal Reserve Bank of St. Louis Review.* Vol. 50. No. 5. pp. 531–67.

Nellor, D.C. 2008. "The Rise of Africa's Frontier Markets". *Finance and Development.* Vol. 45. No. 3. pp. 28–32.

Newbery, D.M. and J.E. Stiglitz. 1984. "Pareto Inferior Trade". *Review of Economic Studies.* Vol. 51. No. 1. pp. 1–12.

Obstfeld, M. 2007. "International Risk Sharing and the Cost of Trade". Ohlin lectures delivered at the Stockholm School of Economics, in May.

Obstfeld, M. and A.M. Taylor. 2005. "Globalization and Capital Markets" in M.D. Bordo, A.M. Taylor and J.G. Williamson (eds) *Globalization in Historical Perspective.* Chicago. The University of Chicago Press. pp. 121–183.

Obstfeld, M. and A.M. Taylor. 2004. *Global Capital Markets: Integration, Crisis and Growth.* Cambridge. Cambridge University Press.

Obstfeld, M. and A.M. Taylor. 2003. "Sovereign Risk, Credibility and the Gold Standard: 1870–1913 versus 1925–31". *The Economic Journal.* Vol. 113. April. pp. 241–275.

Obstfeld, M. and A.M. Taylor. 1998. "The Great Depression as a Watershed: International Capital Mobility over the Long Run" in M.D. Bordo, D.G. Claudia and E.N. Eugene (eds) *The Defining Moment: The Great Depression and the American Economy.* Chicago. The University of Chicago Press. pp. 353–402.

Reinhart, C.M. and K.S. Rogoff. 2004a. "The Modern History of Exchange Rate Arrangements: A Reinterpretation". *The Quarterly Journal of Economics.* Vol. CXIX. No. 1. pp. 1–40.

Reinhart, C.M. and K.S. Rogoff. 2004b. "Serial Default and the 'Paradox' of Rich to Poor Capital Flows". *American Economic Review.* Vol. 94. No. 3. pp. 73–95.

Reinhart, C.M., K.S. Rogoff and M.A. Savastano. 2003. "Debt Intolerance" in W. Brainard and G. Perry (eds) *Brookings Papers on Economic Activity.* Vol. 1. Spring. pp. 1–73.

Schularick, M. 2006. "A Tale of Two Globalizations". *International Journal of Finance and Economics.* Vol. 11. No. 4. pp. 339–354.

Shaw, E. 1973. *Financial Deepening in Economic Development.* New York. Oxford University Press.

Stiglitz, J.E. 2008. "Capital Account Liberalization" in J.E. Stiglitz and J.A. Ocampo (eds) *Capital Market Liberalization and Development*. New York. Oxford University Press. pp. 76–100.

Stiglitz, J.E. and J.A. Ocampo. 2008. *Capital Market Liberalization and Development*. New York. Oxford University Press.

United Nations-World Institute of Development Economics Research. (UN-WIDER). 1990. *Foreign Portfolio Investment in Emerging Equity Markets*. Helsinki. Finland. Study Group Report No. 5.

The World Bank (WB). 2008. *Global Development Finance 2008*. Washington. DC.

3
Global Financial Crisis: The Great Recession and the Approaching Recovery

1. Onset of the global financial crisis and recession

This book was written over the 2007–10 period, when the present global financial crisis precipitated. This chapter focuses on essential facets of the crisis. In particular its causal factors and how it was sparked in the US and UK and then spread globally. It also delves into the fact that while apprehension of a second Great Depression persisted, it was averted by swift policy action. Although financial deglobalization did occur, signs of a moderate recovery – albeit uneven – became evident in the latter half of 2009.

The global financial crisis of 2007–09 will go down in the history indubitably as the foremost economic and financial cataclysm of the twenty-first century, a seismic economic and financial event. It also acquired the dubious distinction of being the gravest crisis since the Great Depression, adversely affecting both the financial and real sectors of the global economy. The banking and financial system in the advanced industrial economies, which was at the epicenter of this crisis, was driven close to collapse. Soon this had dismal consequences for the global economy. Crises of this dimension transpire once or twice in a century. The contemporary phase of financial globalization was progressing at a commendable pace until the crisis interrupted. According to the McKinsey Global Institute (MGI, 2009a), financial assets in the international markets, which included equities, private and public debt and bank deposits, had increased almost fourfold during the 1980–2007 period. The crisis brusquely stopped three decades of expansion in the international financial markets.

Although multiple short- and long-term factors were responsible for the financial crisis (Section 2), it was sparked by the bursting of the housing bubble in the UK and US in the fall of 2007. The US housing bubble burst in August 2007 and in the UK Northern Rock failed in September 2007. That said, the seeds of the sub-prime[1] mortgage crisis in the US were sown much earlier, in the late 1990s. Large inflows of foreign capital and low interest rates had created easy credit conditions for several years before the financial crisis essentially materialized. This financial environment not only promoted a housing market boom but also encouraged debt financed by over-consumption. Such excesses are never sustainable. History testifies that such excesses, without fail, culminate in financial crises. Sub-prime loans were the riskiest category of loans. Consequently, in 2007 a dramatic increase took place in mortgage delinquencies and foreclosures in the US, which had a severe adverse effect on banks and financial markets around the globe. The largest banks in the world like HSBC and Citigroup had begun writing down their holdings of sub-prime related mortgage-backed securities (MBS) since early 2007.

1.1 Financial crisis spills out globally

The financial crisis spilled over globally when Lehman Brothers[2] declared bankruptcy on 15 September 2008. This event traumatized financial markets, causing panic in the global financial system.[3] The failure of a reputed investment bank of long standing shocked the financial world and took a heavy toll on market confidence. Other similar catastrophic events included the near-failure of the American International Group (AIG), which occurred because it sold large amounts of credit default swaps (CDS) without properly offsetting or covering its position. As market confidence plunged, many financial giants struggled to remain on their feet. After the failure of Lehman Brothers, Merrill Lynch came under pressure and agreed to be acquired by the Bank of America. Other high-profile debacles included Washington Mutual, a prominent thrift institution, which was resolved by the Federal Deposit Insurance Corporation (FDIC). Wachovia, a large commercial bank, suffered large liquidity outflows and agreed to be sold. This list of the demise of elite financial institutions is far from exhaustive. It manifestly caused unimaginable loss of wealth.

At this point many of the world's largest banks were undercapitalized. Day by day, the global financial system was inching close to sheer disarray and disintegration. These catastrophic events proved to be a catalyst for a massive sell-off in the credit and stock markets. They set off a general flight from risk to safety in the capital markets of advanced industrial economies first, followed by the EMEs. The financial crisis went into an intensified phase and mutated into a global recession. According to the National Bureau of Economic Research (NBER, 2008), the US recession had began in December 2007. In its composition and character, this recession was a balance-sheet driven recession. It originated in the financial sector and spread into the real economy. Its tentacles spread into household budgets and the balance sheets of business firms, banks and other financial institutions.

Given the economic, financial and trade inter-linkages of the global economy, the US financial crisis briskly spilled over into the other economies. The impact on and reaction from advanced industrial economies, EMEs and developing economies varied. This essentially depended on their degree of economic and financial integration with the global economy and the macroeconomic policy responses devised individually by them. Some large and venerable European banks were driven into enormous financial distress by their exposure to the so-called toxic assets.[4] The Union Bank of Switzerland (UBS), the largest and most resourceful Swiss bank, which was reputed to be world's largest wealth manager, was among the hardest hit banks by the sub-prime crisis. After suffering disastrous losses in the US housing mortgage market, USB was forced to write down the value of billions of francs-worth of assets and retreat from its previously profitable investment banking operations.[5] Citigroup enjoyed the reputation of being the world's most sophisticated financial institution with operations around the globe; this reputation was gravely tarnished by its *de facto* nationalization. Numerous hedge funds folded. There is no gainsaying that the global financial system was driven to the brink of a collapse. So was the global economy. The worst point of the global financial crisis was in the last quarter of 2008 and the first of 2009.

Stark forewarnings of dire consequences were given by Nouriel Roubini of the Stern School of Business[6] and the Bank for International Settlements (BIS),[7] but they were ignored because the relevant macroeconomic variables reflected relatively sound economic health. Economic fundamentals justified the rapid rise in asset prices. Alan Greenspan (2005), erstwhile Federal Reserve Board (Fed) Chairman, supported the view that this was a new era of prosperity and its *causae causante* was improved productivity due to endemic use of computers, IT and other high-technology equipment. He found the pre-crisis years comparable to the periods of the advent of electricity and the automobile. Large global capital flows into the US economy and a worsening current account deficit was explained away by Greenspan by decline in home bias. To him global savers were reaching across national borders to invest in foreign assets. His logic was that the risk-adjusted expected returns in the US economy were higher, therefore, as the home bias declined, the demand for US financial assets increased globally.

1.2 Failure of the economics profession

No one foresaw the timing, extent, scale, intensity and severity of this crisis that convulsed the very foundation of the global financial system and economy. The economics profession was squarely excoriated from inside and externally for its failure to see the origins of the crisis and appreciate its worst symptoms. Trenchant criticism by Nobel Laureate Robert Lucas and Robert Barro was widely cited in the financial press.[8] Paul Krugman (2009a) wrote about 'the dark age of macroeconomics' in his *New York Times* column. A global recession of this dimension is undeniably an unmitigated economic disaster. It was the first time that a recession of this severity had occurred during the last eight decades. It is reasonable to ask to what extent it could have been foreseen. The answer is that its causes were a highly complicated and interconnected set of issues, errors and policy flaws. As seen below (Section 2), no one institution or group could therefore be blamed for it.

However, on a fundamental level, failure of the economics profession to see the possibility of a catastrophic malfunction of market economy was unquestionably much worse than its predictive failure. During the halcyon period of global growth and expansion, economists had come to the belief that markets were stable, even self-correcting. The economics profession went up the garden path because it 'mistook beauty, clad in impressive-looking mathematics, for truth' (Krugman, 2009b). For several decades they had regarded capitalism as a perfect and flawless system. They were in love with an idealized vision of an economy in which rational individuals interact in perfect markets. During the contemporary period this idealized vision was fortified with fancy mathematical equations. This romanticized vision of the economy made economists disregard all that could possibly go wrong. They remained oblivious to 'the limitations of human rationality that often led to bubbles and bursts; to the problems of institutions that run amok; to the imperfections of markets – especially financial markets – that can cause the economy's operating system to undergo sudden, unpredictable crashes; and to the dangers created when regulators don't believe in regulation' (Krugman, 2009b).

The reputation of market forces and the institution of free markets took a knock during 2007–09. The financial meltdown of 2008 particularly did considerable discredit to the mystique of free markets. The Anglo-Saxon model of liberalism and deregulation was upbraided by many, ranging from Kevin Rudd to Yukio Hatoyama. Some of the ideas of Keynes, which had held sway early during the post-World War II period, became relevant again in 2008. Keynes regarded market economies as fundamentally uncertain and markets as far from self-correcting. Large shocks like the current financial crisis were not anomalies but normal market behavior. Governments therefore needed to intervene in crises, providing a judicious and firm hand on the tiller (Keynes, 1936). However, since the adoption of the free-market ethos of Reagan and Thatcher, Keynesian ideas had been spurned.

2. Principal contributing factors

An unmitigated disaster of this magnitude characteristically does not have one or two causal factors or lapses. Therefore, identifying the elemental causal factor of the crisis is not possible. Several factors coalesced and together they were responsible for the crash of 2008. While multifarious, these causes were interrelated and in many cases they were also the causes and consequences of each other. The seeds of the crisis were planted in the past. The beginning was the financial and payments imbalances in the global economy which steadily grew (Section 8.2). Huge inflows of external capital into the US economy were responsible for low real interest rates in the US during the first half of this decade. Accommodating monetary policy and excessive liquidity were explained by these capital inflows and global payments imbalances. The so-called 'global saving glut' supported the low US interest rates. Little was done to offset the imbalances, albeit they were being constantly analyzed in the academic fora and debated in supranational institutions. Steadily worsening global financial payments imbalances proved to be tinder for the global financial crisis. The imbalances in the US economy were particularly flagrant and deteriorated from year to year (Cline, 2006). Unsound policy configuration dangerously debilitated the global financial system.

In the financial environment of low interest rates, financial markets went in search of high yields. Low interest rates were the source of easy credit conditions and cheap money that spawned a consumption binge in the US and some of the other high-income industrial economies. Excessively easy monetary policy by the Federal Reserve in the first half of the last decade helped cause a bubble in the housing prices in the US (Bernanke, 2010). In this macroeconomic environment sub-prime mortgage and risky asset markets boomed. This encouraged increased financial leverage and excessive risk-taking in the intermediation of global savings and investment across economies. Under these circumstances, a competent, well-organized and prudent regulatory and supervisory regime was sorely needed. It was conspicuous by its absence.

One consequence of easy credit conditions was that lending standards were outrageously lowered, particularly in the mortgage and corporate buy-out markets. The debt of financial firms in the US climbed from 39 percent of GDP to 111 percent in 20 years to 2008 (*The Economist*, 2009c). Easier access to housing loans, often secured with no down payments to encourage home ownership, was a noble social objective but an imprudent and hazardous financial strategy. The sub-prime borrowers in the US housing loan market characteristically had poor credit history and limited capacity to access service loans.

The other contributing factor was over two decades of deregulation and expansion in a large number of financial markets, particularly those in advanced industrial economies. This introduced a lack of market discipline and failure of supervision and regulatory systems during the period leading up to the crisis. The financial regulatory system failed in a fundamental sense, so did the prudential supervision. SaKong (2009) described the crisis as 'the greatest regulatory failure of modern history'. Both regulatory and supervising agencies poorly understood the potential risks. The erstwhile regulatory framework was inadequate, obsolete and failed to manage risk across a variety of institutions and market players. The crisis not only exposed the weaknesses in regulators' oversight of financial institutions but also exposed gaps in the architecture of financial regulations around the world (Bernanke, 2010). The global financial scenario in the twenty-first century had transformed significantly. The regulatory framework needed updating accordingly, even considerable redesigning. Furthermore, the inadequate regulatory framework was not enforced. Publicly funded supervising agencies were found to be incompetent. They slumbered through the crisis.

One lesson from the events of the last quarter century is that while the current financial system was a source of prosperity and flexibility, there have been several crises since the stock markets crashed in 1987. A financial system with over ten crises in a quarter century cannot be considered to be functional. The events of 2007 and 2008 further corroborate the observation that the present financial system is dysfunctional and the systemic architecture needs to change radically. Summers (2008) observed, 'Regulation will have to shift from its traditional focus on regulating individual institutions to focus on the stability of the entire system.' Against the backdrop of the current financial crisis this thought is realistic, germane and sagacious.

A lesson from the crises of the past is that rapid growth of novel and untested financial instruments plays an extremely destabilizing role and exacerbates a crisis. This crisis was no exception. Certain design features of sub-prime mortgage securitization and the use of market-value accounting had destabilizing results. Use of securitization grew at a rapid pace in the capital markets. Hindsight reveals that asset mangers did not fully understand the ramifications of this novel instrument. Excessive risk was built-up in the financial system over many years; this was facilitated by new complex securitization instruments that obscured debtor-creditor relations. This build-up of risk was one of the major causes of the financial crisis.

Mortgage-backed securities (MBS) bear a great deal of culpability for causing the financial crisis. The risk contained in the securitized assets was highly underestimated. Securitization and financial globalization connected the financial institutions within and across countries. In the initial stages of the crisis, the large exposure of some regional German and Swiss banks to US sub-prime loans was a topic of discussion. Finally, the financial institutions increased leverage. They financed their portfolios with less and less capital, which enabled them to increase the rate of return on capital. They did it because they underestimated risk at play. In doing so, banks were helped by regulatory weaknesses. As they were allowed to reduce their capital requirement by moving assets off their balance sheets into so-called structured investment vehicles, the off-balance-sheet assets of large banks grew rapidly and took on large dimensions, measured in trillions of dollars (Blanchard, 2009). This was a highly unstable financial situation. Sooner or later the house of cards had to come tumbling down.

Unnecessary and excessive risk taken by banks and other financial institutions was another causal factor. They are known to take risks when they know that while they can reap the benefits, any losses they incur will be passed on to taxpayers. As noted above in this section, banks and financial institutions got away with this misbehavior because regulations were inadequate and supervisors were asleep. In addition, there is universal agreement on the excesses committed and egregious errors made by large banking institutions and the other financial entities. Failures and near-collapses of several large banks and leading financial institutions are still justifiably blamed on the short-term mentality, incompetence and venality of the bankers and financiers running them. Reckless and myopic strategies were continued until several large banks and non-banking financial institutions stood at the brink of an abyss. Despite warnings of large debt and high exposure to MBS, Lehman Brothers failed to address its risky strategies and continued blissfully on its self-destructive path until the end. Smug disregard for the mounting risk eventually had a massive cost – corporate death. The corporate conduct of other large financial institutions was not much different.

The major credit-rating agencies also failed to play their intended role. They customarily assign credit ratings for issuers of certain types of debt obligations as well as debt instruments. They have been roundly criticized for severely understating the risk involved with the new complex securities that fueled the housing bubble in the US. These securities were MBS and collateralized debt obligations (CDO). The operations of credit-rating agencies are now under scrutiny. They unhesitatingly gave investment grade and 'money safe' ratings to securitization transactions based on sub-prime mortgage loans. These high ratings facilitated steady flows of global capital into MBSs and CDOs. Some regard credit-rating agencies as the principal culprits responsible for the financial crisis. They were the source of an extreme degree of deception in financial transactions (see also Chapter 1, Section 7).

Systemic mispricing of assets added to the financial confusion. Calomiris (2008) noted that that the origin of the sub-prime debacle in the US, widely regarded as the spark of the global financial crisis and recession, was essentially caused equally by accommodative monetary policies and government subsidization of risk-taking. The maximum blame for the sub-prime lending debacle needs to go to the financial institutions and institutional investors who were large purchasers of securitized loans. They deliberately allowed asset managers to under-price the risks of sub-prime loans and securities backed by these loans.

This crisis testified to the fact that the belief of the policy makers in the efficiency and self-correcting nature of financial markets, which was regarded as the rationale for the liberalization and globalization of financial markets, was highly exaggerated, if not absolutely erroneous. The term self-correcting was, and subsequently proved to be, an oxymoron. Wall Street took the efficient-market theories literally and paid academics extravagant fees to design complex financial strategies based on them. They played a significant role in leading financial markets into the catastrophe that followed. Fox (2009) recently delved into how the structure of efficient-market hypothesis was built and concluded that it was a veritable house of cards. The financial crisis is living proof that financial turmoil can occur in any economy, regardless of its size, whether it is developing, emerging or developed, whether it is macroeconomically well-managed and disciplined or poorly managed. Given the globalized nature of the world's financial, trade and payments systems, it can impart huge externalities on the rest of the world.

There are some who believed that the causes for the financial crisis and recession were much more than mere systemic shortcomings and mistakes made in the financial sector of the global economy. They call for a complete and comprehensive reform of the global economic and financial system. Stiglitz (2009) blamed the financial crisis on 'the deeper problems of the modern version of capitalism, at least of the American style'. He went on to say, 'I think we are coming to a realization that the institutions that were created sixty years ago are not up to the task, and we need to begin re-thinking these institutions. We are also realizing that some of the ideologies that prevailed over the last quarter century are greatly flawed.'

3. Liquidity crunch

In general, in a crisis situation the balance sheets of banks and other financial institutions are adversely affected. They are weakened by loan losses and therefore these institutions reduce or stop lending. The result is a sudden and prolonged evaporation of both market and funding liquidity (Borio, 2009).[9] This has a direct and debilitating effect on the stability of the financial system as well as on the performance of the real economy. Claessens et al. (2008) studied the links between macroeconomic and financial variables around business and financial cycles during the 1960–2007 period. They paid particular attention to the implications of recessions when they coincide with financial market difficulties, including credit crunches. They found that recessions frequently coincide with episodes of contraction of domestic credit and declines in asset prices. Their conclusion also demonstrated that recessions associated with credit crunches and housing-price busts tend to be deeper and longer than other recessions.

The situation during the current crisis is more complicated than described above. The recession was indeed activated by the bursting of the housing bubbles in the UK and US. However, different financial institutions were exposed to toxic assets to varying degrees. There was a serious loss of confidence in the financial system per se, which caused a liquidity crunch in, *inter alia*, the inter-bank market. In this crisis, the lending banks did not know the exposure of the borrowing bank to toxic assets. As they wanted to err on the side of caution, they stopped lending to one another. Liquidity in the financial markets dried up. Freezing of credit adversely affected the real economy. Unemployment soared, numerous business firms failed and output contracted. In addition, spreads on inter-bank loans and what banks expected pay to central banks jumped to unprecedented levels. The pall of uncertainly about the future hovered for a long time and apprehensions regarding a prolonged recession, even a depression, increased.

4. Estimates of direct and indirect losses

The crisis and its impact critically shook the confidence of investors, business corporations and households. For quite some time, the probability of this crisis turning into full-blown financial and economic catastrophe – something of a second Great Depression – seemed threateningly high, particularly during late 2008 and early 2009. This implied a sizeable welfare loss to the global economy. In a seminal paper, Reinhart and Rogoff (2009b) put forth three essential pernicious effects of the current crisis. First, they found that the asset market collapses in most large economies were deep, even profound. Second, global output and employment suffered grievous losses. Third, the budget deficits and real value of government debt tended to explode. The impact of the current global financial crisis may therefore take an increasing toll on education, health and welfare expenditures even after the global economy has stabilized.

According to the World Bank projections made in June 2009 the global economy is to shrink by almost 3 percent in 2009, the first such contraction since World War II (Table 3.1). These projections were revised subsequently by the World Bank. According to the *Global Economic Prospects*, January 2010, global economy shrank by 2.2 percent in 2009 (see WB, 2010). A moderate recovery has been projected for 2010. As firms failed and the number of bankruptcies rose, a record number of jobs was shed. An OECD annual publication on employment, called *OECD Employment Outlook*, forecasted that in most OECD countries unemployment would continue to rise.[10] This would occur despite the early signs of recovery from recession in the third quarter of 2009. The rate of unemployment had reached a post-World War II high of 8.5 percent for OECD economies, corresponding to an increase of more than 15 million in the ranks of the unemployed since the end of 2007.

In the event that recovery takes hold slowly, the OECD unemployment rate is predicted to increase further and reach a new post-war high level of 10 percent, with 57 million out of work (OECD, 2009a).

That the impact of the current financial crisis was widespread and precipitous is revealed by a fleeting examination of the database of the *World Economic Outlook* (IMF, 2009a). Out of 182 reporting countries, 78 are expected to record negative GDP growth rates in 2009. To put this in perspective, in 2006 and 2007 only three economies recorded negative GDP growth, while in 2008 this number was 12. Considered in groups, the advanced industrial economies and central and eastern European economies were projected to record the largest economic contraction in 2009. For three groups of economies growth forecasts were slashed continually in 2008 and early 2009. These groups were: the highly globalized economies, the commodity economies and the countries that were part of the former Soviet Union. All three categories shared one characteristic, a high degree of exposure to external shocks (Chandy et al., 2009, p. 3). They were far more dependent on international economic activity, international financial flows and global demand per se. During the crisis period, unemployment has proliferated globally. In addition, multilateral trade, FDI and cross-border capital flows has slumped.

The sub-prime loan defaults caused serious losses in the US banking system and capital markets. Of the $1.4 trillion exposure to the sub-prime mortgages, almost half of the loss was borne by US leveraged financial institutions, which included commercial banks, securities firms and hedge funds. In addition, a third of the loss was borne by foreign leveraged financial institutions. Greenlaw et al. (2008) remarked, 'Far from passing on the bad loans to greater fool next in the chain, the most sophisticated financial institutions amassed the largest exposures to the bad assets.' In principle, securitization was originally expected to disperse credit risk. As banks buy each other's securities with borrowed money, they weave cross-claims on each other. The end result is that one bank's liability becomes another bank's asset. Thus, the real impact of securitization was not dispersal of credit risk. Securitization ended up concentrating risk in the financial intermediary sector (Shin, 2009a). The first post-securitization financial crisis will have a definite effect on the securitization process and sector. Shin (2009b) speculated that the securities sector would emerge much smaller from the crisis. Its intermediation chain would be much shorter, maturity transformation would decline and so will its profitability. The overall consequence of innovative securitization on the banking industry in the advanced industrial economies was increased fragility, not less.

Like all such financial crises, this one also affected the stock of global wealth. Equity markets recorded enormous losses all around the world; they declined in 112 countries. Sharp decline in the values of equity and real estate wiped out $28.8 trillion in global wealth during 2008. Equity markets regained some ground during 2009, replacing $4.6 trillion in value between January and July (MGI, 2009a). Replenishing this wealth completely would require increasing saving efforts, curtailing consumption and raising investment rate. This in turn would lead to lower global GDP growth rate in the short term. The International Monetary Fund (IMF, 2009c) calculated the direct cost of the current financial crisis and recession. Banks will bear about two-thirds of the total loss as their asset values have degraded. This in turn threatened their capital adequacy and seriously discouraged them from lending. Non-bank financial institutions like insurance companies and pension funds have also been hit by the decline in asset prices, both equities and bonds. The IMF estimates show that financial institutions in the US suffered the largest losses, $2.7 trillion. European institutions needed to write down $1.2 trillion, with Japan adding another $150 billion. Thus, estimated losses add up to around $4 trillion. These estimates went on increasing because, as the crisis went on intensifying, more types of assets depreciated.

In a recession, clear links exist between the financial sector and the real economy. Claessens et al. (2008) analyzed exhaustive data covering 122 recessions over the 1960–2007 period. They provided a comprehensive empirical characterization of the linkages between key macroeconomic and financial variables around business and financial cycles. They found evidence that recessions associated with credit crunches and housing-price busts tend to be deeper and longer than other recessions. They estimated that a credit crunch episode typically lasts for two-and-a-half years, with nearly a 20 percent decline in credit. However, a housing-price bust tends to last four-and-a-half years, with a 30 percent decline in real, that is inflation-adjusted, house prices.

The crisis exacerbated poverty in the developing economies. Before the outbreak of the crisis, 1.4 billion people lived below the poverty line worldwide. Preliminary World Bank estimates show that the global downturn will be responsible for inflating this number by 53 million in 2009 (Lin, 2009). The long-run consequences of crises for developing economies may be more severe than those observed in the short-run.

The indirect cost of the crisis for the global economy was also huge, albeit difficult to compute. The financial and economic crisis in the global economy provoked a liquidation of investments, significant erosion of wealth around the world and the tightening of lending conditions. Economic uncertainly was widespread. Economic activity weakened globally and GDP growth rates slumped. Owing to flaccid trans-border capital flows, low- and middle-income developing countries came under serious financial strain. As demand weakened globally, many developing economies could not generate sufficient currency from their exports. Many of them found it difficult to borrow to cover their imports, therefore consumption suffered in these economies. One way of meeting this financing gap was drawing on the reserve assets that they had built up during their buoyant economic periods and many developing economies took that route. Thus, global welfare losses were enormous.

5. Averting the second great depression

In August 2009, Paul Krugman (2009c) declared that 'we are not going to have a second Great Depression after all'. Some semblance of a stimulus-triggered recovery did appear to be taking hold around this period. What saved the global economy? The answer is decisive, forceful and coordinated policy measures aggressively taken by the governments and central banks in all the systemically important economies of the world. They moved briskly, purposefully, resolutely and in a collaborative manner. History provides evidence of instances when the policy responses to financial crises by governments were slow, untimely and inadequate. The result was huge economic damage and large fiscal costs. However, during the current financial crisis policy makers responded with 'speed and force to arrest a rapidly deteriorating and dangerous situation' (Bernanke, 2009). Timely, innovative and effective action by governments and central banks needs to be commended. It succeeded in averting an utter collapse of the global financial system in the fall of 2008. However, the crisis was still sufficiently severe to spark a deep global recession.

Forces that ushered in a restrained recovery in the global economy included widespread and coordinated fiscal and monetary stimuli initiated in the advanced industrial economies and the EMEs. They succeeded in activating this slow economic rebound. The IMF-supported measures and enhanced lending to the developing and emerging-market economies also contributed to it. In addition, the role played by central banks in the systemically important economies was significant. They slashed interest rates, injected liquidity and propped up credit flows when they were most needed. Equally important were the financial support function of the governments, which launched sizable fiscal stimulus programs. The simultaneous impact of these public policy measures was reduced uncertainty in the financial and real sectors of the economies.

In their policy response to the financial crisis, many governments in advanced industrial economies and EMEs and their central banks intervened in a two-pronged manner: First, they took measures to stabilize the financial and banking sector, which in some cases included nationalizing crippled financial institutions. Second, they used a standard repertoire of fiscal and monetary tools to counteract the recessionary forces. These policy steps were indispensable in turning the tide of contracting global demand, spurting unemployment rates and looming deflation. If these policy measures had not been implemented in a judicious and timely manner, and if the global financial markets had continued to remain dysfunctional and frozen, most forms of global commerce would have ground to a halt.

In averting the materialization of second Great Depression, the Fed played a constructive role. As the crisis erupted, the Fed began flooding financial markets with liquidity. By keeping the federal fund rate close to zero in 2008 and encouraging lending, the Fed averted an L-shaped near-depression. Ben Bernanke, the chairman of Fed, a former academic authority on the Great Depression, did err by initially supporting the flawed policies of Alan Greenspan that had created the housing and credit bubbles. In the initial stages, he was famously wrong but he succeeded in engineering a U-turn in Fed policy that prevented the crisis from worsening. During the year spanning two springs, 2008 and 2009, Ben Bernanke's academic expertise and policy role meshed impeccably. He continued to come up with aggressive and unorthodox strategies to head off a second Great Depression.

The first dose of financial stimulus was administered in the US in February 2008. This stimulus was small at $152 billion, around 1 percent of the GDP. Therefore, it was hoped that the next one would be larger. In February 2009, President Obama signed a $787 billion stimulus package amid a global wave of stimulus spending. Bernanke also used tools that hitherto were not part of the traditional repertoire of monetary policy. Governments in many countries responded by putting in place appropriate fiscal and monetary policy measures and planned their stimulus packages. In addition, central banking authorities took aggressive policy action and were ready to do more. Massive assistance in the form of capital, loans and guarantees were provided to banks in the advanced industrial economies and several of the EMEs.

For the first time since the Great Depression, the Fed's role as the lender of last resort was extended to investment banks. The Fed was also directly involved in rescuing financial institutions like Bear Stearns and the AIG and it lent large sums to foreign central banks to ease their dollar shortages. The Fed committed to purchasing up to $1.7 trillion of treasury bonds, mortgage-backed securities (MBS) and agency debt to reduce market rates. These radical actions had never been undertaken by the Fed in the past (Roubini, 2009).

During the third quarter of 2009, it was widely being felt that the worst of the global recession was behind us. The first signs of global recovery began to appear. A lot of credit needs to be given to the sustenance and reinforcement provided by the fiscal and monetary stimulus packages of governments in the high-income industrial economies and EMEs, as well as to financial repair measures and *ad hoc* assistance programs for financial institutions. First, these measures succeeded in encouraging overly cautious banks to resume lending. A thaw set in in the credit market, although the volume has remained low. Official interventions in the form of loans to banks and monetary and fiscal stimulus, in both high-income industrial economies and developing economies, helped restore short-term liquidity (WB, 2009a).[11] Second, official initiatives effectively improved economic performance in several crisis-affected economies during the latter half of 2009. This was evident in the US economy. In May 2009, inter-bank spread began to come down both in the US and the European arena. In contrast to the EU and the US, during the third quarter of 2009, Japan and the EMEs of Asia were showing more and clearer symptoms of rebounding. Quarterly GDP growth rates and industrial production statistics in these economies recorded a strong increase (*The Economist*, 2009d). In addition, by September 2009 the interest rates at which banks lent to each other had fallen to near pre-crisis levels. Also, stock markets had stabilized and were showing a rebounding proclivity. While small banks continued to be vulnerable and were in danger of extinction, large ones were not. They had raised enough equity capital. The healthier ones among them repaid public capital, at a profit to tax payers. Capital markets were partially revived, adding to market optimism.

6. Creeping financial deglobalization

This was an idyllic climate for the onset of financial deglobalization and Cassandras began warning about the era of globalization being behind us. Globalization did tend to be fragile in the past. As set out above (Section 1), financial crisis stalled financial globalization in its tracks; it proved to be an effective trend breaker. With the onset of recession, firms, investors and financial institutions in the advanced industrial economies began a large-scale repatriation of their capital. They needed it for strengthening their own balance sheets. Global stock markets, particularly those in the EMEs, paid the price of this by slumping. Individual stock markets lost 40–60 percent of their dollar value. Also, currencies depreciated vis-à-vis the dollar globally, implying a colossal loss in global wealth. The movement toward market liberalization and deregulation stopped in its tracks, particularly in the advanced industrial economies which were hit intensively and directly by the financial crisis.

6.1 Contracting multilateral trade and plunging trans-border financial flows

Collapse in global demand brought on by the economic downturn led to a sharp contraction in multilateral trade. Non-tariff barriers began rising. A paltry 2 percent growth in world trade was recorded in 2008. This was less than half the trend growth rate expected for that year. A 9 percent decline in volume terms was projected in multilateral trade for 2009 by the World Trade Organization (WTO), the largest decline in six decades. Contraction in the advanced industrial economies was particularly severe. They were projected to record a 10 percent decline in their exports. In contrast, in the developing economies, which are more dependent on trade for growth, exports were projected to shrink by 2.5 percent (WTO, 2009a).

The global banking crisis was another causal factor behind the sharp fall in multilateral trade. It led to a rapid contraction in the availability of credit to finance trade movements. As globalization progressed, the elasticity of world trade to output had increased (Freund, 2009). Therefore, the financial crisis had a larger impact on world trade than it would have had in the past. According to early calculations made in the *Global Economic Prospects* (GEP, 2010), the fall in multilateral trade was worse than WTO projections. The volume of world trade in 2009 was 2.8 percent below its pre-crisis level and 10 percent below the level consistent with its pre-crisis trend growth rate. World trade volume declined by 14.4 percent in 2009; it was projected to increase by a weak 4.3 percent in 2011. This amplified the shock to the global economy. References to the spectre of the 1930s were not unfounded. Data analysis by Eichengreen and O'Rourke (2009) show that the 2009 decline in the world trade exceeded that of the Great Depression.

During crisis periods governments face pressure to adopt measures to restrict trade so that domestic employment can be protected. While countries did not initially resort to tit-for-tat protectionism and high intensity protectionism neither seemed imminent nor started, there was real danger of an incremental build up of restrictions that could slow down multilateral trade further. This could in effect undercut the policies to boost aggregate demand and restore global growth.

In early 2009, many WTO members appeared to have kept pressures to take protectionist measures under control, but after that point in time there was a significant slippage. Both developed and developing countries were turning inwards. Many countries that had launched stimulus packages also had tacit or open buy-domestic provision. The World Bank noted that, after committing not to increase protectionism, 17 Group-of-Twenty (G-20) members implemented 47 trade restricting measures (WTO, 2009b). In addition, the stimulus packages launched by governments were so devised that they had elements of subsidies and purchase requirements favouring domestic goods and services over imports. The WTO identified 85 such protectionist measures imposed by 23 countries the last quarter of 2008 and the first quarter of 2009 (EIU, 2009a).

The crisis affected trans-border financial flows adversely in a striking manner. Taken together, global FDI flows, sale of foreign equities and debt securities, and cross-border lending and deposits fell from $10.5 trillion in 2007 to $1.9 trillion in 2008, a decline of 82 percent (MGI, 2009b). Such a massive short-fall in trans-border credit flows resulted in serious destabilization in the global banking system, causing severe liquidity crises. Investors, banks, non-banking financial institutions and corporations hastily sold their foreign assets and brought their finances home where they were badly needed. Borrowers who relied on foreign borrowings were stranded. In addition, such a serious disruption of international capital flows resulted in a spike in short-term exchange rate volatility. For instance, the Korean won and Mexican peso depreciated by 20 percent in the short span of a week.

Against this backdrop of widespread financial turmoil, it could not be overlooked that countries that had not totally liberalized their financial sector and capital account transactions, like China, India, Indonesia and some EMEs, suffered the least direct damage from the current crisis and recession. Although their GDP growth rates distinctly suffered, they remained in the positive quadrant. A rare achievement indeed! A new era of protectionism, re-regulation and market intervention had begun. Financial globalization, that had made impressive progressive over the preceding three decades went into a reversal. The philosophy of a globalized economy being a win-win game for all the participants began to appear irrelevant. Benefits from economic insulation and nationalism began to appear real.

6.2 Plummeting global FDI flows

Deglobalization intensely disturbed the global FDI flows. The global financial crisis gravely dampened their momentum. After an uninterrupted period of growth over 2003–07, they peaked in 2007 at $1,979 billion. They recorded a decline of 14 percent in 2008 at $1,679 billion (WIR, 2009). During the first half of 2009 the rate of decline accelerated. Shrinking corporate profits, plunging stock prices and the diminishing value and scope of mergers and acquisitions (M&As) were the reasons behind plummeting global FDI flows. Rapidly shriveling demand of goods and services caused business firms to cut back on their investment plans, both at home and abroad. Greenfield investment was the last to fall off. FDI into advanced industrial economies declined at a much faster rate than that into the developing ones. FDI flows to EMEs held up well and those to China and India surged. This was a rational decision by investing firms and TNCs. In troubled times, they sought footholds in resilient economies.

In the first half of 2009, FDI inflows into the advanced industrial economies recorded a dramatic decline; they were estimated to have declined between 30 and 50 percent. In contrast, FDI inflows into the developing economies proved to be resilient and recorded a rise of 44 percent in 2008 over their 2007 level. However, they went into a declining mode in late 2008. This increased their share in global FDI to 43 percent, close to the record share achieved in 2004. This also demonstrates the increasing importance of this group of economies as a host for FDI. Statistics reveal that FDI inflows into developing economies began slumping almost a year after they began to slump in the advanced industrial economies. The reason behind the time lag was the recession-caused consequent slump in demand in the advanced industrial economies, which did not move in step with the recession. These markets are very important destinations for goods produced in developing economies (WIR, 2009). If recovery from the recession is weak, any future move in FDI from advanced industrial economies to the developing ones will suffer.

6.3 Contraction in the global economy

According to the mid-2009 projections of the World Bank (Table 3.1), global economy is projected to contract by almost 3 percent during 2009. Table 3.1 below shows that the OECD economies would contract by more than 4 percent during 2009. A feeble recovery is to follow this bleak performance in the OECD economies. They are projected to grow by 1.2 percent in 2010. Likewise, after sharp contractions in 2009, the US, Euro Area and Japan, three of the largest global economies, are projected to recover slowly. The World Bank forecasts regarding the lackluster recovery, made in June 2009, are as follows:

Table 3.1   Projections of recovery from recession (2009 and 2010) (in percent)

	2009	2010
World Economy	−2.9	2.0
High-Income Economies	−4.2	1.3
Of which OECD Economies	−4.2	1.2
Euro Area	−4.5	0.5
Japan	−6.8	1.0
United States	−3.0	1.8
Developing Countries	1.2	4.4

Source: Statistics gleaned from Table 1.1, p. 9, *Global Development Finance: Charting a Global Recovery*. The World Bank, Washington. DC. June, 2009.

Due to recession and projections of a slow recovery in the large industrial economies, the developing economies that are normally dependent on market growth in them would also face a prolonged period of slow growth. Also, financial flows from the industrial economies to the developing economies have sharply plunged and will stagnate in the short-term, or be reduced to a trickle. Commodity exporters, at least in the initial stages of the recovery, will suffer due to soft prices, which will reduce their revenues.

Immigrant workers are being eased out in the labor-importing countries and being forced to return to their native lands. Japan and Spain are paying them to return. Banks have been returning from global banking to national banking, which will have a damaging effect on both efficiency and growth in the global banking sector (Norris, 2009). Taken as a whole, the concepts of free-market, *laissez-faire* as well as financial and economic globalization are in retreat. Altman's (2009) assertion that 'the Anglo-Saxon model of free-market capitalism spread across the globe' has ended does not appear to be too much of an exaggeration.

7. Sparks of an inchoate recovery from the crisis

In late 2008 and early 2009 the big question was whether recession would become depression. Global economy contracted by 6.4 percent in the first quarter of 2009.[12] EMEs of Europe and members of the Commonwealth of Independent States (CIS) were the worst affected economies. However, the developing and emerging-market economies (other than the EMEs of Europe) suffered relatively less damage. Cline (2009) observed that these two groups of economies were damaged less than they were during Latin America's debt crisis of 1982 and Asia's financial crisis of 1997–98. In general these EMEs weathered the storm better than the rest of the global economy, including the advanced industrial economies. Conversely, several fiscal challenges will confront the advanced industrial economies in the near future. They will essentially stem from the high costs of the bailouts and recessionary fiscal losses.

Some indications of a nascent recovery in the EMEs of Asia became evident in the second quarter of 2009. This sub-group of EMEs performed far better than the rest of the global economy in the second quarter of 2009 and was at the forefront of a subdued global economic recovery. At the end of the third quarter of 2009 and the beginning of the fourth, the global economy began exhibiting signs of a slow recovery and a bottoming out of the recession. Large EMEs were the first to accelerate. The EMEs of Asia were projected to return to 6 percent GDP growth in 2010, the best recovery performance by any subgroups of the global economy. The role of the Asian EMEs in underpinning the global recovery was widely acclaimed. The IMF opined that the global economy was being 'pulled up by the strong performance of the Asian economies' (IMF, 2009e, p. 1).

The signs of recovery included improved conditions in the global financial markets, which demonstrated decisive improvement. The Dow Jones index topped 10,000 on 14 October 2009, which was indicative of fairly rapid recovery in the US financial market. Also, most regional stock markets rose by approximately 50 percent from their lows around March 2009. Credit markets had improved markedly since the last quarter of 2008 and the first quarter of 2009, when the global financial system virtually froze. In addition, interest rate spreads were declining, business and consumer confidence in some advanced industrial economies were improving and inventory levels were declining. By mid-2009, anxieties of a systemic financial collapse had receded and the pall of gloom and insecurity began to lift.

That being said, even in the last quarter of 2009, high rates of unemployment in the advanced industrial economies not only persisted, but were also not showing any signs of amelioration. In addition, housing prices were still on the decline. Bank lending, necessary for growth, continued to remain anemic. Demand for credit was also weak as businesses and consumers had to be cautious. Capacity utilization rates were low globally. Most forecasters expected the pace of recovery to be sluggish. This observation applied particularly to the advanced industrial economies, where unemployment rates were projected to remain high.

The subdued recovery was developing at a characteristically uneven pace. The EMEs and large developing economies were ahead on the recovery path. The EMEs (other than those in Europe) managed financial turmoil well. These economies suffered relatively less damage than the rest of the global economies by the current financial crisis. One of the reasons for this was that in response to the previous crises of the 1990s and early 2000s, their policy framework had significantly improved, which gave them economic resilience. This proved beneficial to these EMEs during this financially stressful period. As set out in Chapter 4 (Section 8.4), the EMEs of Asia were leading the recovery. They in turn were led by China (Section 7.2).

Unevenness of recovery extended to the two principal sectors of the global economy. That is, the financial sector moved up the recovery path earlier than the real sector. This applied *a fortiori* to the advanced industrial economies, where the real sector remained sluggish and was expected to remain so in 2010. The high unemployment scenario was the result of sluggish real sector recovery in high-income industrial economies, giving rise to anxiety about the threat of a jobless recovery. In contrast, commodity prices began to recover slowly. In particular, oil prices reached $77 per barrel on 16 October 2009, the highest level in a year. They continued their rise thereafter and hovered at around $80 a barrel. In February 2009 they had fallen to $34 a barrel.

The forces driving this recovery (discussed in Section 5) were somewhat temporary in nature. For one, central banks and governments were not expected to play the roles in 2010 that they did in 2009. Although considerably improved, the financial sector in most advanced industrial economies was still far from healthy. Credit conditions were still tight and deleveraging by banks was still a possibility. If deleveraging does take place in the future, credit flows may be reined in again in the advanced industrial economies, which in turn would stall the real economy. Thus, it would be premature and unwarranted to be complacent about this recovery. The financial sector recovery that was underway in the third and the fourth quarters of 2009 could not be regarded as one on a firm and steady footing. At this point, supportive macroeconomic policies needed to be followed for the medium-term. Global economy could then recover and be on an even keel. The next important policy measure would be to begin unwinding the exceptionally high level of public intervention that occurred during 2009.

7.1 Tenuous recovery in the advanced industrial economies

In the advanced industrial economies there were some feeble signs of recovery in the second quarter of 2009. For instance, France, Germany and Sweden all recorded minuscule positive second quarter GDP growth and were tentatively edging out of recession. Japan also began to show signs of a fledgling recovery, growing non-annualized 0.9 percent in the second quarter. Furthermore, the third quarter growth performance in this group of economies was even better. The US posted 0.9 percent growth. This was their first quarterly growth after four quarters of contraction. Although the fact that the largest economy in the world was emerging out of recession was indeed a healthy development for the global economy, countering this was consumer spending in the US. It not only failed to pick up even in the third quarter but actually declined. The US recovery was *inter alia* driven by government programs like popular discounts on new motor vehicles which stimulated auto sales and production as well as an $8,000 tax credit for first-time home buyers. The Japanese economy grew by 1.2 percent during the third quarter of 2009. Japanese exports contributed to it by jumping to 6.4 percent. Also, capital spending increased by 1.6 percent. The fact that the advanced industrial economies had begun on their path of tenuous recovery was confirmed by the fact that the 30 members of the OECD grew by 0.8 percent during the third quarter.[13]

After a contraction of five consecutive quarters, the 16-country Eurozone recovered, albeit slightly, in the third quarter of 2009, with GDP expansion of non-annualized 0.4 percent. This weak rebound was supported by a strong revival in industrial production. It was also driven by stimulus packages and less aggressive de-stocking. The Eurozone rebound was powered by 0.7 percent GDP growth in Germany, the largest economy in the Eurozone. Exports and investment had supported German growth, making up for a decline in consumer demand. Italy was another large European economy that performed well by growing 0.6 percent and ending its recession. However, the French economy posted a surprisingly feeble 0.3 percent growth again. Strong industrial production had led to higher growth expectations for France (Atkins, 2009). Consumption did not grow in France at all. Austria, Belgium, the Netherlands and Portugal also emerged from recession in the third quarter. Conversely, GDP contracted in both Greece and Spain. Technically the Eurozone escaped recession in the third quarter. In contrast, GDP growth in the UK, the second largest economy in Europe, was −0.4 percent even in the third quarter of 2009 and it continued to be in recession. The financial sector in the UK was badly affected by the crisis; it did not recover from the recession until the fourth quarter, with a feeble growth of 0.1 percent. In contrast, the US economy grew by 5.7 percent in the fourth quarter, which was a convincing indication that it was out of recession.

In 2010 and 2011, recovery in the advanced industrial economies of the Eurozone and the US will be supported by the rebound in world trade which is underpinned by increasing demand from the EMEs, particularly the large ones. Stockpiling by businesses and stabilization of housing market will have the same favorable impact on these economies. Recovery in Japan will be supported by strong growth in Asia, although weak domestic demand will continue to constrain growth. Consumer prices have been falling in Japan. This was partly because the Japanese economy was loaded with excess capacity after a sharp decline in exports during the crisis. Deflation may continue to plague the economy (OECD, 2009b).

7.2 Early and strong rebound of China

China rebounded faster from the global downturn than any other large economy. It was able to lead Asia, particularly the EMEs, to a recovery. It also led the global recovery (OECD, 2009b). Estimated annualized quarter-on-quarter GDP growth plummeted to a low of 4 percent in the fourth quarter of 2008, but picked up to 8 percent in the first quarter of 2009 (Mussa, 2009). China was helped by its limited direct exposure to the global financial crisis. Additionally, it had relatively sounder economic fundamentals and prepared a powerful policy response to the great recession. It also made a meaningful contribution to preventing the global financial crisis from getting worse (Chapter 4, Section 9.3). China had launched one of the largest fiscal stimulus packages, when measured as a proportion of GDP. Its GDP growth rate picked up from 7.9 percent in the second quarter of 2009 to 8.9 percent in the third. It was well on track to hit its growth target of 8 percent for 2009. However, according to the September 2009 consensus forecast, its economy was projected to expand to 8.3 percent in 2009 and 9.4 percent in 2010, when it is projected to become the second largest global economy, not in PPP terms but at market prices.[14] This would be another notable milestone for China.

The earlier rise of the Chinese economy was supported by a massive 4 trillion renminbi yuan ($585 billion) stimulus package. It was one of the largest stimulus packages and was 4.8 percent of Chinese GDP ($3.9 trillion). A major part of China's fiscal stimulus spending was committed to infrastructure projects (Chapter 4, Section 9.1). In addition, a huge surge in government-mandated bank lending followed, which amounted to 7 trillion renminbi yuan between January and June 2009. This monetary expansion resulted in new credit expansion of a huge proportion – almost 20 percent – of the GDP. This made the Chinese economy vulnerable to overinvestment in several sectors; overcapacity reached troubling proportions in the steel, cement, glass, chemicals, coal, polysilicon and wind-power equipment sectors (Roberts, 2009).

China's GDP growth during 2009 stemmed largely from investment. In addition, there was a revival in private real estate expenditure and resilience in consumer sector. Retail sales grew by 15.1 percent in first three quarters of 2009. Thus viewed, domestic demand supported and reinforced China's recovery. During the first half of 2009, real net exports made a significant negative contribution to the rise in GDP. China made a net positive contribution to demand of goods and services produced in other countries (Mussa, 2009).

The recovery continued to broaden in the Chinese economy and it thus favorably influenced neighboring Japan and Asia, in that order. As noted above (Section 7), together the Asian EMEs proved to be a locomotive force in slowly tugging the global economy out of recession. In the fourth quarter China began implementing its exit strategy, which entailed gradual reduction in the level of stimulus, credit expansion and infrastructure spending. Rising private investment and consumption could pick the slack.

There was a spike in China's trade and current account surpluses during the 2003–07 period. This was a remarkably strong performance. As China's exports and imports suffered during the global financial crisis, with exports declining more than imports, these surpluses shrank in 2009. The exports sector performed badly even in the fourth quarter. As the pace of global recovery is projected to be slow, a swift return to the pre-2007 trade performance is not on the cards. Although exports are likely to pick up after the recovery gains momentum, a repetition of the 2003–07 trade performance may not occur even after a recovery

takes hold. Global demand is unlikely to be strong over the next quin-
quennium. Also, in the medium-term a substantial appreciation of the
renminbi yuan is inevitable. Currency appreciation will help reduce
distortions in China's domestic economy as well.

8. The Group-of-Twenty: Its role in stabilizing the global economy

It has been continually debated in academic literature whether the G-7
or G-8 had ceased to be a representative group of economies in the
present-day globalized economy. In addition, given the geography of
large payments imbalances, the role, value, helpfulness and effectiveness of the G-7 or G-8 had steadily diminished. Except for Japan and
the Russian Federation, all the countries that succeeded in accumulating
large forex surpluses were non-G-8.

Against the backdrop of the global financial crisis, three successive
summits of the Group-of-Twenty (G-20)[15] took place: in Washington DC
(November 2008), London (April 2009) and Pittsburg (September 2009).
The G-20 economies were cognizant of the need for a harmonized global
policy response to the crisis. The first G-20 summit in Washington DC
essentially focused on the fiscal stimuli, which played a crucial role in
stabilizing the global economy. The G-20 policy makers agreed to launch
concerted and coordinated fiscal stimuli. China and the US responded
in the most forceful manner.

As the present crisis was essentially that of the banking and financial systems of the advanced industrial economies, in the first two G-20
meetings the members assigned a great deal of importance to strengthening the financial regulation and supervision network. The objective
of the G-20 summit of London was to stabilize the battered financial
and banking systems in the EU and the US. At this juncture, the G-20
had achieved an unprecedented fiscal expansion as well as adoption of
appropriately relaxed monetary measures, which became the turning
point in addressing the worsening global recession. The G-20 countries
also agreed on and initiated national and international reforms in the
overview, supervision, and regulation of financial systems. They helped
initiate a process of reform of the international financial institutions
(IFI), which went a long way to restoring the IMF to its pivotal position in the global financial system and providing it with the resources it
needed to carry out this role (Bradford and Linn, 2009). The G-20 leaders
also committed $1 trillion to assist the developing economies through
the IMF. Many of these countries did not have adequate resources to

assemble fiscal stimulus packages and rescue their respective financial sectors.

A timely decision with far-reaching consequences, taken during the Pittsburg G-20 summit, was regarding the supplanting of the old G-8 by the G-20. The latter was designated the premier forum for global economic and financial cooperation; this represented a defining change in world economic order. It was an acknowledgement of the fact that global economic and financial coordination needs to be handled more broadly, by a larger group of countries than the G-7 or G-8. This decision was of historic significance and denoted the passing of the baton. During the Pittsburg summit members went further, and agreed to 'commit to sustained recovery' until a durable recovery is secured. The communiqué was substantive and emphasized the need for a regulatory system for banks and other financial institutions that could 'rein in the excesses that led to the crisis' (G-20 Communiqué, p. 1). The Pittsburg communiqué also promised to peer-review members' economic policy, which was a first in global economic cooperation. The themes deliberated on were appropriate and courageous. Some of the notable concerns were regarding the harmonization of macroeconomic policies to correct global payments imbalances (with the IMF playing a central role), a meaningful shift of voting power toward the EMEs, reform of global reserve system and capital increases for the multilateral development banks (Dervis, 2009).

There is little disagreement that the utter lack of market discipline in the large financial markets was one of the causes behind the global financial crisis. Also, national financial regulators and supervisors did not have a tradition of cooperating with one another. These limitations encouraged the G-20 members to develop recommendations for strengthening national regulatory frameworks and cooperation within them. They also took the initiative in strengthening the Financial Stability Board (FSB) and its mandate. Membership of the FSB was expanded to include all the G-20 members, which drew in the large EMEs and some Gulf Cooperation Council (GCC) members (Lombardi, 2009).

The G-20 members also instructed the Basel Committee, a club of bank regulators and supervisors, to formulate new proposals on capital and liquidity 'buffers'. Since 1988, the Basel Committee has set the global capital rules. Basel-2, the strengthened and upgraded version of the original rules, was being implemented in most European banks in 2008. Banks in the US were on track to implement it in 2011. Work on the new buffers was launched swiftly; they could be in force in the latter half of 2012. The definition of capital in the new rules is much stricter than before and risk-adjustment methods have been fundamentally revised. They have been christened Basel-3.

The G-20 is gradually establishing itself as a forum responsible for global macroeconomic as well as monetary and financial policies. China and other EMEs had an input in the Pittsburg summit and they benefited from a greater voice in the IMF. The non-G-7 members of the G-20 will be a part of the new steering committee for the global economic and financial decision-making process. In the past, creditor countries tended to set the rules of global monetary system. It is logical then to assume that the influence of creditor Asian economies, particularly that of China, will soon rise (Das, 2010).

9. Inevitable structural realignment in the global economy and financial sector

Before the global financial crisis struck, the old 'international economic order was struggling to keep up with changes (that had taken place) before the crisis' (Zoellick, 2009). A global financial crisis of this magnitude, recession and the process of recovery from the crisis are all potent, persuasive and dynamic economic events, which will decisively change the post-crisis economic and financial contour of the global economy. They will bring about discernible transformations in currency markets, international monetary policy, cross-border financial flows, multilateral trade relations, and the role played by the EMEs and the developing economies in the global economy.

One fundamental transformation that is sure to materialize is the relative shift in economic heft of countries and country groups. The country where the financial crisis originated, the US, has been hit hard by it. Economic heft will manifestly shift away from the US and toward two economic groups: first, the dynamic East Asian economies and China and, second, the Eurozone. Likewise the era of dominance of the dollar in the global currency markets as well as its favored reserve currency status will gradually come to an end (Section 8.1). The importance of the euro has been on the rise. It steadily appreciated since 2002, *a fortiori* since 2006. At the end of October 2009 it had appreciated to $1.50, an all-time high value. It is increasingly being treated as an alternative currency in which to hold international assets and conduct international business. How fast it will become a major international currency is an issue open to debate, but its importance as an international currency has been on the rise.

The post-crisis structural realignment of the global economy needs, really, to be the subject matter of a large research project. However, a cursory assessment can still be attempted. China's response to the crisis was timely and proportionate, both in terms of the size of the stimulus and its monetary policy. Increased domestic demand contributed to GDP growth, which had suffered a blow due to the collapse of external demand and declining exports. Although, between 2007 and November 2009, China's current account surplus almost halved to around 6 percent of GDP from 11 percent in 2007, China was also the first country to pick up growth momentum, which assisted its neighboring regional economies (Section 7.2). It also supported the stabilization of the global economy.

China and India together accounted for 8.5 percent of the global GDP in 2008 and are not insubstantial economies. Neither suffered a recession and they continued to grow considerably more rapidly than the advanced industrial economies and discernibly contributed to the recovery and stabilization process of the global economy. This role can be logically projected for the foreseeable future. Their economic and financial significance on the global economic state will rise. A change that China and the Asian EMEs will need to accept and get used to will be regarding their export-led growth. Their future growth will need to increasingly rely on domestic demand. If the Southeast Asian economies seize the opportunities that the crisis offered, they may come out of the crisis stronger. Indonesia and Vietnam have a sizable weight in this subgroup of economies; the two performed soundly under the economic turmoil during the crisis.

Japan suffered political disturbance in the wake of the crisis. In the post-crisis period, it is likely to deepen its cooperation with other Asia-Pacific economies, while maintaining its global role. The crisis was a real test for the new Europe, born out of the revolution of 1989. European institutions may grow stronger from it. The hardest hit group from the crisis was the central and eastern European Union members. In their hour of economic distress, they were assisted by the European Commission, the European Bank of Reconstruction and Development and the European Investment Bank as well as by the World Bank Group. The crisis has strengthened the economic ties of the members of the European Union (EU).[16]

There will also be intra-economic changes in the systemically significant economies. Profligacy of the consumers in the US is one of the first variables to be affected by the crisis. Consumer spending in the US began declining in 2008 and savings began to build up, albeit at a snail's pace. The personal saving rate in the US zoomed to 5.7 percent in the first half of 2009, the highest since 1995 (CEA, 2009). Businesses were putting cost-trimming ahead of expansion. As this trend strengthens, US imports from the rest of the world are bound to go into a decline. According to the forecasts of the Economic Intelligence Unit (EIU, 2009b) the US current account deficit will then narrow from a high of 6 percent of GDP in 2006 to 2.9 percent in 2010; it has been projected to continue to decline to 3 percent, or less, during the 2010–13 period. Correspondingly, China's merchandise trade surplus narrowed in 2008 and continued on the same path in 2009. Its current account surplus is projected to decline from 10.7 percent of GDP in 2007 to 4.3 percent 2010, and thereafter will hover around 2.3 percent until 2013. The export-oriented economies of Asia will follow the same trend. Aggregate current account surplus for the region was projected to decline from 5 percent of GDP in 2007 to 1.6 percent in 2013.

The crisis is sure to alter the current trading pattern of the high-income industrial economies, which have strong trade ties with the EMEs. They have become accustomed to importing large volumes of products and services from the EMEs. They are not likely to suspend importing forthwith, but there will be a gradual reduction over the next five years. The US and several large advanced industrial economies are likely to continue running current account deficits, and Asia, particularly China, will continue to run surpluses, but the gap between these two groups of economies will substantially narrow. In addition, in its bid to rebalance the domestic and global economies, the Chinese government has been stimulating domestic demand for some time, particularly consumption expenditure (Das, 2008d). However, a structural change of this kind cannot materialize in the short-term. A logical and plausible scenario is that global economic, financial and payments imbalances will persist but at a far narrower level than during the pre-crisis period. This has implications for the dollar which would need to weaken further to further reduce the current account deficit. Correspondingly, the renminbi yuan is likely to begin appreciating again. The economic downturn disrupted the steady appreciation of the renminbi yuan vis-à-vis the dollar since the mid-2005. In July 2008, it had stopped appreciating (Das, 2010). Concerns regarding slumping exports had pegged it to the dollar.

9.1 Descent of the dollar from its high perch

Since the end of World War II, the dollar remained the pre-eminent currency in the global economy and the bedrock of international trade and finance. It has been the principal reserve asset of the world. This was natural because US economic dominance was overwhelming during this period. Although the largest, the US economy has at present lost the kind of dominance it enjoyed in the early post-World War II era. According to the 2008 statistics, the GDP of the European Monetary Union (EMU) ($13.56 trillion) is not far below that of the US ($14.29 trillion) (WB, 2009b).[17] The current global financial crisis reignited the anxieties of policy makers about one country's currency being the anchor of the world monetary system. The financial crisis has ominously downgraded the status of the US economy, particularly that of its financial sector. The financial crisis, *inter alia*, exposed structural weaknesses in the US banking and financial system. There is no gainsaying that they were of serious order, to put it euphemistically. For the first time in the post-World War II period, dominance of the dollar is facing a serious challenge.

In international discussions about the pressing need for launching financial and monetary reforms, the role of the dollar serving as the main international reserve asset lately received renewed attention. Advanced industrial economies and BRICs have expressed their concern about the inordinately heavy debt burden and the level of deficit of the US government. Since 1991, the US has had a current account deficit, and this increased by 40 percent in 2001. It was over 6 percent of the US GDP in 2006, although it declined to $706 billion in 2008, or 5 percent of the GDP. The largest global economy cannot be regarded to be in the pink of health. That the dollar faces a secular decline has some justification. The dollar depreciated 33 percent against the other major currencies between 2002 and 2009. Its value also declined during the financial crisis. During the March–September 2009 period the dollar steadily depreciated against a group of leading international currencies. Its trade-weighted value dropped by 11.5 percent. Against the euro, it steadily eroded. As stated above (Section 8), in October 2009 it was $1.50 to a euro. There are also apprehensions of inflation because of large financial commitments to stimulus packages and spiraling deficits, which are likely to further depreciate the dollar.

Over the preceding decades, the dollar's pre-eminence has been in decline. Its position as a reserve currency has eroded considerably. Its share in global foreign exchange reserves has declined from 80 percent of the total in 1975 to around 65 percent in the first half of 2009 (Carbaugh and Hedrick, 2009). How long the dollar can continue to hold its current position as the principal reserve currency of the central banks of the world remains a moot issue. Numerous central banks have been diversifying their reserves holdings to reduce exchange rate risk in a world of financial and currency instability. The euro became an attractive option to them and it benefited from this trend. The Eurozone has a track record of relative economic stability. Between 1999 and 2009, the euro's share in global foreign exchange reserves rose from 18 percent in 1999 to 26 percent in the first half of 2009. Central banks in Europe primarily hold euros as reserves.

The current financial crisis lent urgency to the enduring debate on the future role of the dollar in the global economy. Recently, the EMEs, in particular the BRIC economies, repeatedly broached the issue of the role played by the dollar in international trade and finance in the international fora. They have asked for a reduction in the role played by the dollar and suggest this can be achieved by establishing a new currency. This demand was also made by them at the first BRIC summit on 16 June 2009, held in Yekaterinburg, Russia (Kramer, 2009). In November 2009, India changed the composition of its reserves by buying 200 tonnes of gold from the IMF.

The established practice of pricing of oil in the dollar is likely to be discontinued in the foreseeable future. In October 2009, members of the Gulf Cooperation Council (GCC),[18] China, France, Japan and the Russian Federation met to end the practice of conducting oil deals in dollars. A proposal to replace the dollar by a basket of currencies was discussed by these countries. Oil-producing countries have been uncertain about the dollar's future value.

Against the backdrop of the global financial crisis and recession, broadening the use of Special Drawing Rights (SDRs) is increasingly being regarded as a concept deserving greater deliberation and consideration from the global policy making community. SDRs are a quasi-currency issued by the IMF and are internationally tradable, albeit only among governments and central banks. They could also be used in future to settle international payments (UNCTAD, 2009). That said, assets denominated in SDRs are less liquid that those in dollar.

One country that is particularly concerned about the dollar's global status is China. Its concern is understandable because 70 percent of its $2.1 trillion foreign exchange reserves are in dollars.[19] It stands to make a significant loss if the value of the dollar abruptly declines. China needs to bring down its dollar holdings but if it does so hastily, it will cause the devaluation of the dollar that it needs to avoid. It is in China's interest to see this transition taking place gradually in, say, a decade. During and in the run-up to the Group-of-Twenty (G-20) meeting in London (in April 2009), China succeeded in injecting a frisson of excitement by emphasizing the enlarged future role of SDRs. It regarded SDRs as a viable alternative to the dollar as a global economic currency.

Given China's newly acquired prominence and clout in the global economy, the proposal was considered worthy and taken seriously by the G-20 participants. It undoubtedly had objective appeal and systemic relevance.

To all appearances, while the dollar is and will continue to be an important currency, there is a distinct possibility that this issue will be followed up by the global policy making community and that the global importance of the dollar will eventually be downgraded. Structural problems in the US economy, in particular in the banking and financial sectors, would continue the erosion of the dollar as a premier reserve currency. While the SDR – or the euro, yen or renminbi yuan – is not likely to supplant the dollar in the short-term, it is well within the realm of possibilities that the dollar will share the role of a reserve currency with another currency or currencies in the foreseeable future.

Pre-eminence of the dollar as the world currency has diminished and it is certain to leave its high perch in the global capital and currency markets, while the relative significance of the other currencies particularly that of the euro has been growing (Helleiner and Kirshner, 2009). In the future, the yen and renminbi yuan may well emerge as the other important global currencies. However, the renminbi yuan would need to become a convertible currency for this purpose.

9.2 New global equilibrium

In a financially globalized economy, financial and payments imbalances may be the consequence of financial integration among economies that are at different stages of financial market development. Under these circumstances countries with more advanced financial markets tend to accumulate foreign liabilities in a gradual and long-lasting manner (Mendoza et al., 2009). This line of logic is reflected in the global economic and payments imbalances that have developed since the late 1990s. They encompassed the mounting current account deficits in the US and large foreign assets positions in many EMEs.[20] Expanding financial globalization leading to rapid trans-border capital flows, vigorous export growth and favorable terms of trade for commodity exports enabled many developing countries to build up large foreign asset positions. This trend was reinforced by high saving rates in the Asian EMEs. This sub-group of economies was also determined to self-insure its economies against any future crises by building up large foreign exchange reserves – a lesson they had learned from the Asian crisis of 1997–8.

Gradually China became the largest creditor nation and the US largest debtor. The symbiotic relationship between the lending EMEs and developing economies and the US, the borrowing economy, had the semblance of an ephemeral equilibrium. At best it could only last for a short term because the US current account deficit could neither be a permanent feature of the largest global economy nor could it be met from external sources for a long period.

Financial globalization and trans-border capital flows were among the first victims of the outbreak of the global financial crisis. The capital-exporting EMEs forthwith turned to domestic assets. Their aversion to exporting capital during a crisis period was logical and understandable. Countries that were running trade surpluses came under financial pressure due to the sharp contraction of multilateral trade and collapse of commodity prices.

The global financial crisis evoked a prima facie unforeseen and unexpected response among the global investing community. Although the epicenter of the on-going crisis was Wall Street, during the crisis period the global investing community paradoxically perceived the dollar to be the safe-haven currency. Risk-averse global and US investors perceived US treasury securities as a safe-haven investment. Their crisis strategy was to shift to US treasury securities and ignore other investment modes like equity, corporate bonds, emerging market bonds, money market funds, bank deposits and any other kinds of assets that involved credit risk. No doubt this was a short-term reaction to the on-going crisis. As the global economy and financial markets recover and risk aversion diminishes, the global investing community is likely to turn to risky assets.

The post-crisis global equilibrium will not entail complete disappearance of the imbalances, certainly not in the short-term. The attractiveness of US assets is not likely to be evaporated nor is the dollar likely to become a currency to spurn in the global financial markets. At the same time, it is equally certain that both of them will lose their favored pre-crisis role. The global currency system will be less dollar-centric in the future and the economic imperatives of this transformation will be immense.

During the present financial crisis, the US current account deficit declined from 6.61 percent of the GDP in the last quarter of 2006 to 2.9 percent in the first quarter of 2009 and 2.8 percent in the second quarter (USDC, 2009). A wholesome turn of events indeed. A sharp decline in oil prices, slow GDP growth and falling imports were largely responsible for the decline of current account deficit. In the future, as the US economy recovers current account deficit may rise as private consumption and fiscal expansion increase. However, the probability that the deficit will quickly leap to its pre-crisis level is not strong as US borrowings from the surplus countries are sure to decline. Also, EMEs may reduce their rate of expansion of foreign exchange reserves because their utility for self-insurance purposes would decline with the establishment of the contingent credit facilities of the IMF. In addition, enhanced safety nets in the EMEs, particularly those of Asia, may reduce their domestic saving rates and their external surpluses. These developments could push the global economy closer toward equilibrium (de la Torre et al., 2009). That said, this penchant toward equilibrium need not be a permanent feature of the global economy.

9.3 Vision of a post-crisis global economic landscape

Although few estimates have been made, the size of the post-crisis global economy will surely be substantially smaller than in the first half of 2007. A stimulus-powered tentative recovery that began taking shape in the third quarter of 2009 will continue in 2010, but the landscape of the global economy and finance will fundamentally alter. Also, any return to pre-crisis growth trajectory for the global economy may well be unlikely because GDP growth will be constrained by numerous small and large factors, in particular by large debt overhangs in many systemically important economies. At the macroeconomic level, investment rates would suffer in the crisis-affected economies. At the microeconomic level, firms with weak balance sheets will continue to disregard investment opportunities in the foreseeable future.

Disruptions to production processes in many economies were large and of a crucial order. Many of production processes may be beyond restoration. Low capacity utilization during such crises often turns into a permanent loss of production capacity. Many large economies will suffer such crisis-driven losses in production capacity. The crisis critically battered the banking and financial sector in many economies, particularly in the advanced industrial economies. Weaknesses and limitations in this vitally important sector may continue during the early post-crisis period. This sector is being justly blamed for adventurism and recklessness; it would certainly emerge heavily regulated from the crisis. A good deal of effort to ensure this was being expended in international fora like the G-20, IMF and FSB (Section 8).

Well-timed fiscal and monetary stimulus plans were prepared and implemented by all the systemically significant economies. Although they were essential for setting off a recovery, there is a downside to stimulus packages. They tend to make an economy dependent on them. Once the support of the monetary and fiscal stimuli is phased out, sustainability of growth becomes questionable. As the global recovery takes hold, the stronger economies that feel secure about it will soon normalize their interest rates. Conversely, those that recovered weakly and feel insecure will not be able to restore their monetary policy. They will be forced to maintain their interest rates at a low level to revive and sustain growth.

On the demand side, consumers in countries like the US that had supported large global demand, may not play their pre-crisis period role in the near future. Hindsight reveals that they had committed excesses and were persistently given to profligacy (Section 9). The post-crisis period will be one of readjustment and debt repayment for them. The new trend may well be the reversal of the past proclivities. Consumers in the economies like the US may well emphasize redressing the over-consumption of the past and improve upon their dismal saving performance. This trend in the US economy was underway since early 2009.

10. A corporate perspective of financial crisis and approaching recovery

According a global survey conducted by *McKinsey Quarterly*, in September 2009, a hunkering down period for the corporate world was coming to an end.[21] Corporate chieftains reported during the last quarter of 2008 that they were focused intensely on slashing costs, capital investment and headcount. To cope with the financial crisis and recession, they turned into short-term oriented managers. Their planning and management horizon extended for weeks, or at most a month, never a year. Product development and long-term planning activities were completely abandoned. Their expectations were that of sharply plummeting sales and profits.

The results of the September (2009) survey were radically, even diametrically, different. More respondents expected their companies' sales and profits to rise than fall in the short-term. These expectations rose consistently in tandem with the improving performance in the global stock markets. They also manifested optimism about long-term business prospects. Corporate optimism was markedly higher in the US than in the Eurozone. For many companies, product development and long-term planning acquired the high priorities that these imperative corporate objectives merited. These respondents were expecting that the global business environment will be a 'new normal', which would be less congenial than that which existed during the pre-crisis period.

A majority of respondents recommended that their governments continue the support their respective economies received when the global financial crisis was at its worst. Only 20 percent expected a rapid recovery; a much larger proportion expected a long and slow one. A high proportion (31 percent) of them expected financial globalization to resume in the medium-term, after a disconcerting period of deglobalization. Half of them (49 percent) expected more integrated global financial markets, more extensive global operations and multilateral trade within five years. Almost a third (31 percent) foresaw significant changes in their industries and economies, in particular a larger role played by their governments. Three-quarters of them predicted that their companies would be on a stronger footing within next five years than they were during the pre-crisis period. One long-term impact of the global financial crisis, according to many, would be increased innovation and consolidation in their respective industries.

11. Summary and conclusions

Three decades of commendable progress in financial globalization was brusquely stifled by the current financial crisis and recession. Its background was partly caused by the macroeconomic, financial and payments imbalances that steadily grew in the global economy over some ten years before the outbreak of the crisis. Other contributing causal factors included the lowering of lending standards in the mortgage and corporate buy-out markets, over two decades of deregulation in a large number of financial markets, failure of regulatory bodies and supervising agencies to understand the potential risks, excessive use of novel and untested financial instruments, the short-term mentality of banks and other financial institutions – and the incompetence and venality of bankers and financers running them –, the failure of credit-rating agencies to play their intended role and thus in effect fueling the housing bubble, and the systemic mis-pricing of assets and subsidization of risk-taking by governments. Some even believed that shortcomings and mistakes in the financial system were not to be blamed for the global financial crisis but it was more of a problem of capitalism per se.

Freezing of credit flows during the crisis affected the real economy. It spread globally, causing a spike in unemployment rates and the failure of business firms. In addition, spreads on inter-bank loans and what banks expected pay to central banks jumped to unprecedented levels.

There was a general loss of confidence in the financial system. The crisis caused a sizable loss in global economic welfare. It occurred through asset market collapse and global output and employment losses. Both direct and indirect losses in the global economy were huge. Also, the budget deficits and real value of government debt tended to explode. In the medium-term, the global financial crisis may take an increasing toll on education, health and welfare expenditures even after the global economy has stabilized.

Finance ministries and central banks in the systemically important economies of the world moved briskly, purposefully, resolutely and in a collaborative manner to avert a Great Depression-like prolonged and severe crisis. Several of them designed and launched fiscal and monetary stimulus plans with alacrity. In this context, the Group-of-Twenty (G-20) summit in London on 2 April 2009 and the successive G-20 summits proved to be meaningful and fairly successful.

Financial crisis stalled financial globalization in its tracks; it proved to be an effective trend breaker. With the onset of recession, firms, investors and financial institutions in the advanced industrial economies began a large-scale repatriation of their capital. Deglobalization in the form of stalling or reversing trans-border capital flows began and multilateral trade contracted at an alarming rate. Transborder FDI flows also suffered seriously. After a contraction in 2009, the OECD economies are projected to recover at a subdued pace in 2010. This in turn would affect performance and recovery in the developing economies. The EMEs in general were showing symptoms of recovery earlier than other economies. In particular, Asian EMEs began to show inchoate signs of recovery in the second quarter of 2009. They were leading the recovery from the global financial crisis. The financial sector in the advanced industrial economies was recovering at a more rapid rate than the real sector, although unemployment continued to remain high and was persistently showing signs of worsening.

The global economy contracted in the first quarter of 2009. However, the EMEs weathered the storm better. Some indications of a nascent recovery in the EMEs of Asia became evident in the second quarter of 2009. This group of EMEs was the first to give an indication of coming out of recession and pulling the others out. At the end of the third quarter of 2009 and the beginning of the fourth, the symptoms of a subdued global recovery in 2010 became more evident than in the past. The financial crisis, recession and the process of recovery from the crisis would change the post-crisis global economic and financial scenario to a considerable extent.

Notes

1. The term sub-prime was invented and popularized by the media during the credit crunch that began in 2007.
2. It was founded in 1850 by the three Lehman brothers in Montgomery Alabama, as a cotton trading firm. In 1858, it opened its first branch office in New York city's Manhattan borough.
3. One recent scholarly book on the failure of Lehman Brothers and subsequently the financial system is by Reinhart and Rogoff (2009a), while a highly readably yarn, which rings true, on the same theme was written by McDonald and Robinson (2009).
4. This non-technical term began to be used widely since the financial crisis started in 2007. It is used to describe financial assets whose value has markedly declined and for which there is no functioning market so they cannot be resold. Toxic assets played a major role in the on-going financial crisis. When the market for toxic assets ceased to function it was termed as 'frozen'. Markets for these assets froze in 2007. It became worse in 2008, particularly in the latter half. Toxic assets poison a bank's balance sheet.
5. In August 2009, it declared a loss of SFr1.9 billion, the seventh quarterly loss in 2 years.
6. On 7 September 2006, Nouriel Roubbini told an IMF audience that a crisis was brewing. He admonished that the US was likely to face a once-in-a-lifetime housing bust, an oil shock and dramatic decline in consumer confidence followed by a severe recession. The sequence of events according to Roubini was going to be as follows: First the homeowners would default on their mortgage loans, trillions of dollars worth of mortgage-backed securities (MBS) would unravel worldwide, which would lead to financial disarray, if not a debacle, in the global financial markets. These developments in turn would cripple hedge funds, investment banks and other major financial institutions, like Fannie Mae and Freddie Mac. The moderator of the event reacted in jest by asking for stiff drink, while his audience was dismissive. (As reported in *The New York Times* by Stephen Mihn, 15 August 2008. 'Dr. Doom'.
7. See Chapter VII of the *74th Annual Report*, 2004, Bank for International Settlements, Basel, Switzerland.
8. Robert E. Lucas won the coveted Nobel Prize in 1995, while Robert Barro was one of the three finalists for it in 2003.
9. Market liquidity implies the ability to trade an asset or financial instrument at short notice without any impact on its price, while funding liquidity means the ability to raise cash via either the sale of an asset or by borrowing.
10. These forecasts were published in September 2009. Available on the OECD website at http://www.oecd.org/document/62/0,3343,en_2649_37457_43701438_1_1_1_1,00.html.
11. For a detailed account see WB (2009a), Chapter 1.
12. The source of statistics in this section is Chapter 1, IMF (2009c).
13. The quarterly growth statistics here come from media sources and various publications in which the announcements of the respective governments are reported.
14. The consensus forecast figures were cited by Wolf (2009).

15. What the Group-of-Twenty (G-20) economies are is explained in Chapter 1, Section 4.3.
16. See Zoellick (2009).
17. Although total membership of the European Union (EU) is 27, in 2009, the European Monetary Union (EMU) had 16 members.
18. The Gulf Cooperation Council (GCC) was established in 1981. Its members are Bahrain, Kuwait, Oman, Qatar, Saudi Arabia and the United Arab Emirates (UAE).
19. In the mid-1990s China's foreign exchange reserves, in absolute and relative terms, began to rise. In mid-July 2009, China's foreign exchange reserve level topped the $2.1 trillion mark, over 40 percent of GDP. It seems difficult to believe that in 2003 China's reserves were $300 billion. In early 2010 they reached $2.3 trillion.
20. The present period is not unique in this regard. The US experienced large current account deficits in the late 1960s, late 1970s and the mid-1980s.
21. This survey was based on 1,677 responses from corporate CEOs representing all the regions of the global economy and a large number of manufacturing and services sector industries. It covered business firms of varying sizes and functional specialties.

References

Altman, R.C. 2009. "Globalization in Retreat". *Foreign Affairs*. Vol. 88. No. 4. pp. 1–6.

Atkins, R. 2009. "Eurozone Escapes Recession after Five Quarters". *The Financial Times*. 13 November. p. 16.

Bernanke, B.S. 2010. "Monetary Policy and the Housing Bubble". Paper presented at the annual meeting of the American Economic Association held in Atlanta. Georgia, on 3 January.

Bernanke, B.S. 2009. "Reflections on a Year of Crisis". Paper presented at the Federal Reserve Bank of Kansas City's *Annual Economic Symposium on Financial Stability and Macroeconomic Stability* at Jackson Hole, Wyoming, on 21–22 August.

Blanchard, O. 2009. "The Perfect Storm". *Finance and Development*. Vol. 46. No. 2. pp. 37–39.

Borio, C. 2009. "Ten Propositions about Liquidity Crisis". Basel. Switzerland. Bank for International Settlements. BIS Working Paper No. 293. November.

Bradford, C. and J. Linn. 2009. "Welcome to the New Era of G-20 Global Leadership" in K. Dervis (ed.) *G-20- Summit: Recovering from the Crisis*. Washington. DC. Brookings Institution. pp. 16–18.

Calomiris, C.W. 2008. "The Sub-Prime Turmoil: What's Old, What's New" in *Maintaining Stability in a Changing Financial System*. Kansas City MO. The Federal Reserve Bank of Kansas City. pp. 19–110.

Carbaugh, R.J. and D.W. Hedrick. 2009. "Will the Dollar be Dethroned as the Main Reserve Currency?" *Global Economy Journal*. Vol. 9. No. 3. Article 1. pp. 1–14.

Chandy, L., G. Gertz and J. Linn. 2009. "Tracking the Global Financial Crisis". Washington. DC. The Brookings Institution. May.

Claessens, S., M. Ayhan Kose and M.E. Terrones. 2008. "What Happens During Recessions, Crunches and Busts?" Washington. DC. International Monetary Fund. Working Paper No. WP/08/274.

Cline, W.R. 2009. "The Global Financial Crisis and Developing Strategy for Emerging Market Economies". Paper presented at the Annual Bank Conference on Development Economics, 23 June, in Seoul, the Republic of Korea.

Cline, W. 2006. "The US External Deficits and the Developing Economies". Washington. DC. The Center for Global Development. Working Paper No. 86. March.

Council of Economic Advisers (CEA). 2009. "First Quarterly Report" Washington. DC. Executive Office of the President of the United States. 10 September.

Das, Dilip K. 2010. "The Renminbi Yuan and its Accelerating Global Clout". *Journal of Asian Business Studies*. San Francisco. Vol. 5. No. 1. Spring. (forthcoming).

Das, Dilip K. 2008d. *The Chinese Economic Renaissance: Apocalypse or Cornucopia*. Houndmills, Hampshire, UK. Palgrave Macmillan Ltd.

de la Torre, A., S. Schmukler and L. Serven. 2009. "Back to Global Imbalances?" Washington. DC. The World Bank. 13 July.

Dervis, K. 2009. "The G-20, the Istanbul Decisions and the Way Forward". Washington. DC. The Brookings Institution. 17 November. Available on the Internet at http://www.brookings.edu/opinions/2009/1008_g20_istanbul_dervis.aspx?p=1. 12 October 2009.

The Economic Intelligence Unit (EIU). 2009a. "The Risk of Trade protectionism". Available on the Internet at http://viewswire.eiu.com/index.asp?layout=VWPrintVW3&article_id=1714520356&printer=printer&rf=0. Posted on May 19.

The Economic Intelligence Unit (EIU). 2009b. "World Economy: Balancing Act". London. 31 August.

The Economist. 2009c."From Slump to Jump". 1 August. p. 16.

The Economist. 2009d. "Rearranging the Towers of Gold". 12 September. pp. 75–77.

Eichengreen, B.J. and K. O'Rourke. 2009. "A Tale of Two Depressions". Available on the Internet at http://www.voxeu.org/index.php?q=node/3421. 12 October 2009.

Fox, J. 2009. *A History of Risk, Reward and Delusion on Wall Street*. New York. Harper Collins.

Freund, C. 2009. "The Trade Response to Global Downturns: Historic Evidence". Washington. DC. The World Bank. Research Working Paper No. 5015. November.

Global Economic Prospects (GEP). 2010. Washington. DC. The World Bank. 16 January.

Greenlaw, D., J, Hatzius, A.K. Kashyap and H.S. Shin. 2008. "Leveraged Losses: Lessons from the Mortgage Market Meltdown". Chicago. University of Chicago. Graduate School of Business. Monetary Policy Forum Report No. 2.

Greenspan, A. 2005. "International Imbalances". Speech given to the Advancing Enterprise Conference, London, UK. on 2 December.

G-20 Communiqué. 2009. "Leaders' Statement: The Pittsburg Summit". Pittsburg. 15 September. Available on the Internet at http://www.pittsburghsummit.gov/documents/organization/129853.pdf. 6 November 2009.

Helleiner, E. and J. Kirshner. 2009. *The Future of the Dollar.* Ithaca. New York. Cornell University Press.

The International Monetary Fund (IMF). 2009c. *Global Financial Stability Report.* Washington. DC. April.

The International Monetary Fund (IMF). 2009e. *World Economic Outlook.* Washington DC. October.

Keynes, J.M. 1936. *The General Theory of Employment, Interest and Money.* Cambridge. UK. Cambridge University Press for Royal Economic Society.

Kramer, A.E. 2009. "Emerging Economies Meet in Russia". *The New York Times.* 17 June. p. 3.

Krugman, P. 2009a. "The Dark Age of Macroeconomics" *The New York Times.* 27 January. Available on the Internet at http://krugman.blogs.nytimes.com/2009/01/27/a-dark-age-of-macroeconomics-wonkish/. 4 February 2009.

Krugman, P. 2009b. "How Did Economists Get it So Wrong?" *The New York Times.* 6 September. p. 14.

Krugman, P. 2009c. "Averting the Worst". *The New York Times.* 9 August.

Lin, J.Y. 2009. "Learning from the Past to reinvent the Future". Opening remarks at the Annual Bank Conference on Development Economics, 23 June, in Seoul, the Republic of Korea.

Lombardi, D. 2009. "Washington Roundtable on the Global Economic Agenda". Washington. DC. The Brookings Institution. Issues Paper. October.

McDonald, L.G. and P. Robinson. 2009. *A Colossal Failure of Commonsense: The Inside Story of the Collapse of Lehman Brothers.* New York. Crown Business.

McKinsey Global Institute (MGI). 2009a. "The New Power Brokers". San Francisco. July.

McKinsey Global Institute (MGI). 2009b. *Global Capital Markets: Entering a New Era.* San Francisco. September.

McKinsey Quarterly. 2009. "The Crisis – One Year on: September 2009". Available on the Internet at http:www.mckinseyquarterly.com/article_print.aspx?L2=10&ar=2437. 29 September 2009.

Mendoza, E.G., V. Quadrini and J.V. Rios-Rull. 2009. "Financial Integration, Financial Development and Global Imbalances". *Journal of Political Economy.* Vol. 117. No. 2. pp. 60–89.

Mihn, S. 2008. "Dr. Doom". *The New York Times.* 15 August. p. 3.

Mussa, M. 2009. "Global Economic Prospects as of September 2009". Paper presented at the sixteenth semiannual meeting on Global Economic Prospects, organized by the Peterson Institute of International Economics in Washington. DC, on 17 September.

National Bureau of Economic Research (NBER). (2008). "Determination of December 2007 Peak in Economic Activity. Business Cycle dating Committee. Cambridge. MA. Available on the Internet at http://www.nber.org/dec2008.pdf. Posted on 11 December.

Norris, F. 2009. "A Retreat from Global Banking". *The New York Times.* 24 July. p. 2.

Organization for Economic Cooperation and Development (OECD). 2009a. *OECD Employment Outlook 2009.* Paris. September.

Organization for Economic Cooperation and Development (OECD). 2009b. *OECD Economic Outlook.* No. 86. Paris. 19 November.

Reinhart, C.M. and K.S. Rogoff. 2009a. *This Time is Different: Eight Centuries of Financial Folly*. Princeton. NJ. Princeton University Press.

Reinhart, C.M. and K.S. Rogoff. 2009b. "The Aftermath of Financial Crises". *American Economic Review*. Vol. 99. No. 2. pp. 466–472.

Roberts, D. 2009. "China's Third Quarter GDP 8.9%: Is it Sustainable?" *Business Week International*. 22 October. p. 86.

Roubini, N. 2009. "The Great Preventer". *The New York Times*. 26 July. p. 18.

SaKong, I. 2009. "The Global Financial Crisis: Causes and Policy". Paper presented at the Annual Bank Conference on Development Economics, on 23 June. Seoul. Republic of Korea.

Shin, H.S. 2009a. "Securitization and Financial Stability". *The Economic Journal*. No. 119. pp. 309–332. March.

Shin, H.S. 2009b. "Financial Intermediation and Post-Crisis Financial System". Paper presented at the Eight BIS Annual Conference held at Basel, Switzerland, during 25–26 June.

Stiglitz, J.E. 2009. "Explaining the Financial Crisis". Lecture given under the Emerging Thinking on Global Issues Lecture Series at the United Nations University, the UN Headquarters, New York, on 24 February. Available on the Internet at http://www.google.ca/search?hl=en&source=hp&q=joseph+stiglitz+UNU+lecture+february+2009&meta=&aq=f&oq=. 13 April 2009.

Summers, L. H. 2008. "The Future of Market Capitalism". Keynote address at the Global Business Summit, held at the Harvard Business School, Cambridge. MA, on 14 October.

United Nations Conference on Trade and Development (UNCTAD). 2009. "Trade and Development Report 2009". Geneva and New York. 7 September.

United States Department of Commerce (USDC). 2009. "US Current Account Deficit Decreases in Second Quarter 2009". Washington. DC. 16 September. Available on the Internet at http://www.bea.gov/newsreleases/international/transactions/trans_highlights.pdf. 4 June 2009.

Wolf, M. 2009. "Why China do More to Rebalance its Economy". *The Financial Times*. 22 September. p. 12.

The World Bank (WB). 2010. *Global Economic Prospects*. Washington DC. January 21.

The World Bank (WB). 2009a. *Global Development Finance: Charting a Global Recovery*. Washington. DC. 22 June.

The World Bank (WB). 2009b. *World Development Indicator*. Washington. DC. July.

World Investment Report 2009 (WIR). 2009. Geneva ad New York. United Nations Conference on Trade and Development. 17 September.

World Trade Organization (WTO). 2009a. "World Trade 2008, Prospects for 2009". Geneva. Switzerland. WTO Press Release No. 554. 23 March.

World Trade Organization (WTO). 2009b. *World Trade News*. No. 1979. Geneva. Switzerland. 22 July.

Zoellick, R.B. 2009. "After the Crisis?" Speech delivered at the Paul H. Nitze School of Advanced International Studies of the Johns Hopkins University, Washington. DC. on 28 September.

4
Financial Globalization and the Integrating Emerging-Market Economies

1. Financial integration of the emerging-market economies

The objective of this chapter is to analyze the role, participation and contribution of the emerging-market economies (EMEs) in the financially integrating world economy. The particular focus of this chapter is the contour of deepening financial globalization of EMEs *en masse*. For starters, it provides an explanation regarding what EMEs are and the challenges of preparing a universally agreed-upon country classification (Section 2). Comprehensive details regarding the qualitative and quantitative evolution of global private capital flows to EMEs have been analyzed. To render precision to the analysis, this discussion has been divided into cohesive chronological sub-periods. The temporal evolution of financial flows from the global private capital markets has been profiled in this section. It exemplifies that global integration of EMEs took place in the manner of a crescendo, reaching its qualitative climax in the post-2002 period. Quantitatively, 2007 was the high noon of financial globalization in EMEs. As analyzed in-depth in Chapter 3, the sub-prime mortgage crisis erupted in the fall of 2007, mutated into a global financial crisis, spilled into the real economy and thus put paid to the financial globalization of EMEs. The on-going financial globalization reversed abruptly in the EMEs. The transmission mechanism of financial stress from advanced industrial economies into EMEs has also been previously discussed at length.

The genesis of the EMEs as constructive participants and partners in the global economy is a development with far-reaching consequences. Their integration into the global financial markets has been growing. To be sure they are not an integral part of the financially globalized economy, but since the early 1970s they certainly have been increasingly active players in and contributors to it. In the process they have been persistently making a tangible input to the financial globalization of the world economy. This is evident from the sustained rise in gross capital inflows into EMEs and the outflows from them. They now have an exclusive niche in the global financial landscape. The participation of the EMEs has made the contemporary phase of financial globalization patently different from its earlier epochs, which were limited in terms of country participation. The economies and populations that bene-fited from financial globalization during the preceding eras were much smaller compared to the present one.

It is worthwhile and rewarding to scrutinize financial globalization in EMEs because there are important differences across country groups in the pace of financial globalization as well as in the relative importance of different types of capital inflows. EMEs are a sub-group of the much larger developing country group. It accounts for the bulk of global finan-cial integration among developing economies. After advanced industrial economies, this group of economies adopted financial globalization most successfully and benefited from it most conspicuously. Propo-nents of globalization see EMEs as conclusive evidence of the validity of their assertion that globalization is benign, growth-promoting as well as welfare-enhancing. China's vertiginous economic growth, its vault-ing over other economies to become the third-largest in the world, and its economic and financial integration with the global economy in an astonishingly short time span exemplifies this (Das, 2008d). In 2009, China's GDP ($3.86 trillion) was larger than that of Germany ($3.65 trillion).[1]

The dynamics of the rise of China, India and the other large EMEs is fraught with long-term implications for the global economy. Of par-ticular importance is China substituting as the counterpart of the US economy in place of the USSR. Unlike the aggressive geopolitical ambi-tions of the USSR, China only aimed at conquering world markets. Although China is an EME, variations in its capital markets impinge on the capital markets of the rest of the world.[2] China, India and the other EMEs created their niche as constructive economic partners for the advanced industrial world. Taken as a whole, their influence over the global economy has been quite stabilizing. China's so-called posi-tive supply shock has been endlessly focused on in the recent economic analysis (Wang et al., 2009; WB, 2009a). The majority of advanced industrial economies enjoyed economic stability for almost a quarter century before the eruption of the sub-prime mortgage crisis in the US in the fall of 2007. This trend was stronger in Anglo-Saxon countries. This quarter century was christened an era of Great Moderation (Chapter 1, Section 2.8). Thus, the rise of EMEs has been a positive and beneficial feature for the global economy.

Over the last two decades, financial globalization in EMEs picked up greater momentum and non-resident purchase of EMEs' domestic assets as well as EMEs residents' purchase of foreign assets grew appreciably, albeit not monotonically. Of late, the role of EMEs in the global banking and capital markets has expanded remarkably. One indicator of deeper integration of EMEs with the global financial markets is the financial account of the balance-of-payments of EMEs. In the 1990s gross private capital flows averaged $170 billion a year, of which $100 billion was foreign direct investment (FDI). By 2007, gross private capital flows exceeded $1,400 billion. It needs to be clarified that gross capital flows are the sum of the total inflows and total outflows. It is a better indicator of financial integration than net inflows. The reason is that it provides a less volatile and more reliable indicator of financial integration. This indicator has the advantage of capturing two-way flows. Net private capital flows are inflows minus outflows. Net flows into EMEs have also steadily risen. They exceeded $400 billion in 2007, more than four times the amount of the 1990s (Turner, 2008). Concurrently, the aggregate current account position of EMEs has shifted from deficits over the 1980s and the 1990s to wholesome surpluses during the present period (Section 2.1).

2. What are emerging-market economies?

The definition of the term EME has been explained in Chapter 1 (Section 1). This is a fuzzy concept and EMEs are somewhat loosely defined. They have several definitions, each slightly at variance to the other. The developing countries that are placed in this category are heterogeneous and vary from small to large. They share neither history nor similarities in income or resource endowment. However, an important common trait of this group of countries is superior growth performance as well as prospects of sustainable future growth. This is a widely accepted fact. Over the years, global retail and institutional investors as well as transnational corporations (TNCs) have appreciably increased their exposure to this group of economies.

China, a manufacturing powerhouse, is the largest and the most important EME. China and India, the two populous giants, and Brazil and the Russian Federation are the four largest EMEs. They accounted for almost 15 percent of the world's GDP in 2009, at current market exchange rates. According to 2009 statistical data, published by the World Bank (2009b), both Brazil ($1.61 trillion) and the Russian Federation ($1.60 trillion) have larger GDPs than Canada ($1.40 trillion). The size of India's $1.2 trillion GDP is only marginally less than that of Canada.[3] If the four BRIC[4] economies continue to invest in and welcome technology inflows, their large labor forces and expanding skill bases would certainly succeed in creating high productive potential for these economies. These EMEs could grow to become some of the world's largest economies. As alluded to in the preceding section, in 2009 China had already acquired the sought-after position of being the third largest global economy. Momentous developments like China overtaking Japan and India overtaking Canada in the short-term are well within the realm of possibilities. The brisk growth of these economies will affect not only goods and services markets but also global flows of savings and investment (Das, 2006).

If Hong Kong SAR, the Republic of Korea (hereafter Korea), Singapore and Taiwan are segregated to be categorized as newly industrialized economies (NIEs), the six largest EMEs are Brazil, China, India, Indonesia, Mexico and the Russian Federation. They are known as EME-6. Some of the other large EMEs include Argentina, Chile, Colombia, the Czech Republic, Kenya, Malaysia, Poland, South Africa, Turkey and the United Arab Emirates (UAE). These economies are regarded as being a transitional group, placed between developing countries on one side and matured industrial economies on the other. They assumed their emerging status essentially by implementing macroeconomic policy reforms, liberalizing their economies and adopting market-friendly economic and financial policies, which resulted in a sounder economic policy structure compared to other developing economies. The tenable result was discernible in more rapid growth rates for this country group. An EME deliberately builds a transparent and efficient domestic capital market. It pays copious attention to its exchange rate regime and to the development of the external sector and ensures a stable currency. The basic objective of doing so is to encourage confidence in the domestic economy, so that investors in global private capital markets regard it as suitable for investment.

Many EMEs have succeeded in alleviating poverty and improving the standard of living of their populations. The size of their middle class has been steadily growing (Das, 2009a). In addition, EMEs are growing into an important phenomenon for the business corporations of advanced industrial economies. Prahalad (2004) pointed to EMEs as a source of not only a large number of value-conscious customers but also creative entrepreneurs. Several EMEs are individually regarded as important economies and markets in their own right. EMEs, such as China, have been playing an important global role individually (Das, 2008e). Their combined impact on the global economy has progressively increased and has become increasingly noticeable through their contribution to global economic growth. Together they have become an economic entity to reckon with and are changing the contours of the global economy.

2.1 Common characteristics

EMEs are not a monolithic group of economies. Yet there are some common, albeit not universal, characteristics that can be associated with them. First, they are usually large regional economies, frequently with a significant size population. Their resource base and markets are also of substantive size. Due to this size advantage, their impact on their respective regions and sub-regions is extensive. Their rapid growth favorably impacts their neighbors' economic performance. Second, as macroeconomic reforms and restructuring have been progressing in these EMEs, their economies have been liberalizing and deregulating. Due to macroeconomic reforms and liberalization, this group of economies benefited from more rapid growth than other developing economies. There is another common characteristic of EMEs. Although EMEs are not an institutionally mature group of economies, they do show notable progress in this direction. On the premise of the logic of macroeconomic reforms, liberalization and superior institutions, their future growth prospects are widely regarded as higher than other developing economies. Although excessive booms and bursts in the economy in the short-term is the downside of financial liberalization, its long-run effect on financial markets is stability (Kaminsky and Schmukler, 2003).

Third, these economies have been contributing meaningfully to multilateral trade expansion. Being more open than other economies has allowed them to integrate better with the global economy. Fourth, during 1990–98, the EMEs ran a moderate current account deficit of 1.7 percent of GDP. Between 1999 and 2008, this deficit turned into a surplus of 2.5 percent of GDP (IMF, 2009b). Fifth, many of them believed that liquidity is the key to self-protection. Therefore, they have accumulated large foreign exchange reserves. This turned EMEs into net exporters of capital to advanced industrial economies, particularly the US, thus changing a fundamental economic tenet. The direction of capital flows in the global economy reversed and it began flowing from low-income economies to the high-income matured ones.

There are some structural factors that enable EMEs to sustain high growth rates. These countries have higher productivity growth rates due partly to large and underutilized labor forces. They also have large pent-up domestic demands. This latent demand is not limited to that of consumer goods and services. It also includes demand for infrastructure, education and health services. Together, these two factors can propel high long-term growth.

The ability to integrate with global capital markets and attract a significant amount of equity investment, both portfolio and direct, is regarded as *sine qua non* of an EME. Business firms and governments in an EME are expected to have access to private global capital markets, or the ability to attract institutional portfolio investment, or both. This access is directly related to their perceived creditworthiness in the global financial market place. Some economies like China, East Asia and the large Latin American economies presently have easy access and can count on attracting a substantial amount of global capital resources if they need them. This is because global investors have sufficient, and rising, confidence in these economies.

Increasing domestic and foreign investment in the economy is another crucial and common characteristic of EMEs. Rising rates of investment reflect increasing confidence levels in the future prospects of an economy. Increasing importance of this group of economies in the world economy has given rise to profitable investment opportunities for global investors. For foreign business firms, EMEs provide an avenue for expanding businesses and creating new manufacturing facilities. One direct result of this has been increasing employment generation. Also, there has been a qualitative improvement in the labor force while managerial skills have became more refined. The most important benefit to EMEs has been from the technology transfer. In conclusion, increase in the GDP growth rate and production level in EMEs advanced them on their path of convergence with advanced industrial economies.

2.2 Growing significance in the global financial markets

Over the past decades, essentially due to implementation of macroeconomic policy reforms and liberalization of their economies, EMEs' per capita GDP growth was superior to that of other country groups. Figure 4.1 below shows the evolution of indexes of purchasing power parity (PPP) weighted per capita GDP of EMEs in comparison

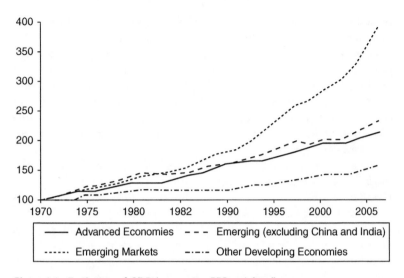

Figure 4.1   Evolution of GDP (per capita, PPP weighted)

Notes: This plot shows cumulative changes in indexes of per capita GDP for each group of countries, computed using growth rates of real GDP for each country and weighting these by a PPP adjustment factor. The indices are set to 100 in the base period. The time period of analysis is 1970–2006.

Source: Kose, et al. (2009), p. 15.

to those of advanced industrial economies and other developing economies. As a group, EMEs have recorded far higher cumulative growth since 1970. When China and India are excluded from the EMEs, the trend performance becomes a trifle less impressive, although it is still superior to that of other developing economies. EMEs not only surpassed the trend performance of other developing countries but the difference between the performances of the two groups of economies continued to grow with the passage of time. The phenomenon of sustained rapid growth for this group of economies incited a debate regarding the changing dynamics of north-south growth linkage and a possible shift in the locus of global growth. The contribution of EMEs to global growth has steadily increased, conspicuously so since the turn of the twenty-first century.

During the post-2000 period, EMEs turned in a stellar economic performance. Their performance was so much better than the other two country groups that it sparked a new conventional wisdom on decoupling. Many analysts began to believe that EMEs have decoupled from the business cycle in advanced industrial economies and that they were capable of determining their own economic rhythm and moving forward using their own momentum (Pula and Pultonen, 2009). The effect of slow US growth compared with the growth rate in most other countries was not discernible during this period. The old adage, if the US sneezes the rest of the world catches cold, seemed to lose its relevance. One explanation was that many EMEs had become much larger and more self-reliant. With the strengthening momentum of domestic demand in them, they ceased to rely on global locomotives like the US economy. The argument that developed was that, with decoupling, global growth has become more resilient than in the past and less dependant on the growth in advanced industrial economies.[5] More evidence toward this decoupling argument was provided by Kose et al. (2008), who demonstrated that business cycles were becoming increasingly synchronized among advanced industrial countries and, independently, among EMEs. There was indeed decoupling between the business cycles of these two groups of economies.

Capital flows from global private capital markets not only augment investment in an EME but also add volume to its stock market. Foreign investment flows can increase long-term investment into its muchneeded infrastructure, including its financial infrastructure. For the global investing community EMEs present an opportunity to diversify their investment portfolios. During the 1980s, EMEs used to hold an obscure niche in the global investing community. However, when their economies and financial markets developed rapidly, many of them began playing an increasingly noticeable global economic role. In the post-2000 period, more than half of global economic growth was driven by this group of economies (Prasad and Kose, 2009). In addition, in the arena of multilateral trade the significance of EMEs has been ascending. Several of them now figure in the league table of leading exporters annually published by the World Trade Organization (WTO). Although financial markets in EMEs are considered volatile, they are also known to offer some of the most spectacular returns on investment. These financial markets are still regarded as in transition so there is an element of risk involved in investing in EMEs. Over the preceding quarter century, investing in EMEs had gradually become standard practice among the global investors, hedge funds and fund managers who wished to diversify, although such investments added some risk to their portfolios.

To finance economic growth developing economies traditionally borrowed capital either from advanced industrial economies or, multilaterally, from regional and global institutional financial institutions (IFIs); thus creating a debt burden. Frequently, the borrowing countries did not manage borrowed capital resources efficiently. The resulting economic growth turned out to be of dubious quality. Due to dissatisfactory outcomes of this mode of external capital inflows, developing economies changed their strategy and began to rely on equity investment as a means of financing sustainable economic growth. To achieve this objective, EMEs needed to attract global private capital by making their economies creditworthy. As noted above, many succeeded in launching economic reforms, fostering a business-friendly investment climate and move closer to a market economy structure. This also entailed restraining unwanted government invention in the economy.

EMEs had a sense of economic and financial strength about them until the global financial crisis erupted. It originated in the sub-prime mortgage markets in the UK and the US in the fall of 2007. In the initial phase, EME policy makers believed that decoupling had materialized and EMEs would not have to suffer from the crisis-generated financial stress. Initially, their economies were not adversely affected by the sub-prime crisis. Their expectation was that its impact would remain confined to advanced industrial economies because banks in these economies had trillions of dollars-worth of toxic securitized assets on their balance sheets – assets whose value had markedly declined and for which there was no functional market. This calculation proved to be wrong. Following the Lehman Brothers bankruptcy in September 2008, the financial crisis spilled into the real economy and became a global crisis. The resulting credit crunch caused severe financial tremors (Mizen, 2008). Inter-bank accommodations and all categories of private credit dried up, which brought day-to-day economic activity to a stop. Repatriation of global capital from EMEs occurred at a swift pace, causing serious dislocation and destabilization in several EMEs.

During the Pittsburg Group-of-Twenty (G-20) summit in September 2009, the imperative decision to supplant the old G-8 with the G-20 was taken (Chapter 2, Section 5). This was a particularly consequential move from the perspective of the EMEs. Several large ones among them became a part of the foremost global economic and financial decision-making forum. Their inclusion gave this forum greater legitimacy in making global decisions. Unlike the G-8, the G-20 is a diverse group of influential countries, far more representative than the one it supplanted. The G-20 also proved to be a more active group in terms of being result-oriented than the G-8. The Washington (November 2008), London (April 2009) and Pittsburg G-20 summits were fairly successful in terms of their outcome (Bradford and Linn, 2009). Three summits took place in less than a year and addressed heavyweight issues related to the global financial crisis, recovery from it and the reforms of the IFIs. The G-20 was establishing itself as an energetic forum responsible for global macroeconomic and financial policy. It seemed to regard itself as working for a global public good and therefore asserted this stewardship from its inception. It may well emerge as a driver of long-awaited international institutional reforms. In future, the G-20 can access more resources, and judiciously and creatively add to international public good (Subramanian, 2009).

2.3 Country classification conundrum

It is difficult to present a universally, even widely, accepted list of economies that are classified as EMEs. The reason is that there is no consensus on the concept, definition and classification of EMEs (Section 2). They vary according to the institution using them. Even the Bretton Woods institutions have not put forward an agreed standardized classification in this regard. At times, one organization uses two country classifications. Esteemed supranational institutions like the IMF were found to use inconsistent definitions. Although the IMF classifies NIEs as a distinct group, in presenting statistical tables it includes them with EMEs, rendering confusion and presenting inflated and misleading statistical data. It classifies 23 countries, including the four NIES, as EMEs.[6] There is a small hint of commonality in the total number of EMEs in various classifications. It hovers around 30. *The Economist* and the Institute of International Finance (IIF) include 34 countries in their classifications, many of them common to the two classifications.

Morgan Stanley Capital International (MSCI), a leading provider of investment data to principal financial institutions, computes indices of portfolio risk for EMEs. Their list of EMEs includes the following 25 economies: Argentina, Brazil, Chile, China, Colombia, the Czech Republic, Egypt, Hungary, India, Indonesia, Kuwait, Malaysia, Mexico, Morocco, Pakistan, Peru, the Philippines, Poland, Qatar, the Russian Federation, South Africa, Taiwan, Thailand, Turkey and the United Arab Emirates. This classification was later revised in 2008.

The Financial Times and the London Stock Exchange jointly publish the FTSE indices for EMEs. The FTSE indices are extensively used by a range of investors, asset owners, investment banks and fund managers. They classify EMEs into two sub-groups. Advanced EMEs include six countries, namely, Brazil, Hungary, Mexico, Poland, South Africa and Taiwan. There are 16 secondary EMEs: Argentina, Chile, China, Colombia, the Czech Republic, Egypt, India, Indonesia,

Malaysia, Morocco, Pakistan, Peru, the Philippines, the Russian Federation, Thailand and Turkey.

3. Differentiating financial globalization in the EMEs

The extent of financial globalization in EMEs is both qualitatively and quantitatively different from other country groups, namely, the other developing economies and the advanced industrial economies (Section 4). This fact can be established with the help of *de jure* and *de facto* measures as well as the temporal evolution of capital flows to EMEs. *De jure* measures are based on the traditional measures of legal restrictions. They calibrate the degree of financial globalization with the help of the degree of controls on cross-border capital movements and those on foreign exchange transactions. These measures have several limitations and are therefore not regarded as accurate. Conversely, *de facto* measures of global integration are quantity-based and are calibrated from actual capital flows. Quantity-based measures of financial integration can also be price-based measures or those based on saving-investment correlations. This is regarded as providing relatively superior measures of a country's *de facto* integration with global financial markets.

Using both *de facto* and *de jure* indicators, Kose et al. (2009) inferred that the level of global financial integration has decidedly been highest in advanced industrial economies. This was an inescapable conclusion. Among developing economies, EMEs were found to have made maximum progress in financial globalization. Since 1990, the gross stock of assets and liabilities of EMEs rose by more than five-fold. Their magnitude has been much larger than the average of other developing countries.

Both *de jure* integration measures, which were computed from the IMF's binary capital account restrictiveness measures, and *de facto* measures of financial openness, computed from the stock of financial assets and liabilities expressed as a proportion of GDP, were compared for different country groups. Both of these indicators established beyond doubt that advanced industrial economies have become significantly integrated into the global financial markets. For EMEs, the *de jure* integration measures did not show a large change over the period under consideration. However, the *de facto* measures of financial openness showed a dramatic increase. Conversely, for other developing economies *de jure* openness rose sharply during the period under consideration, but the *de facto* measures did not change at all.[7]

4. Capital flows to the EMEs: Qualitative and quantitative dimensions

This section succinctly provides details of the global private capital flows to EMEs since the early 1970s, when the so-called oil shock struck the global economy. It had enormous significance for global financial markets. The following time period has been divided into various sub-periods, which have been analyzed independently below. Temporal evolution of capital flows to EMEs has been portrayed in this section and idiosyncratic features of different sub-periods have been identified. Both qualitative and quantitative details of the financial flows and the emerging trends during each sub-period have been analyzed. The Latin American and Asian financial crises have not been analyzed in-depth but have been alluded to in the discussion of the relevant periods.

4.1 Post-oil shock era and the Latin American debt crisis

Following the quadrupling of oil prices in 1973 many large commercial banks in the large industrial economies, called the money center banks, found themselves holding large petro-dollar deposits. During this period US banks were most active in international banking, followed by European banks and those from Japan. The money center banks recycled liquid resources to some of the better-performing, creditworthy, developing countries. It was a productive and prudent investment strategy. This liquidity was turned into sovereign loans to EMEs. These were syndicated loan arrangements on floating interest rates. Due to rising commodity prices and, with that, improving terms of trade, borrowing economies initially did not face problems in servicing their debts. Global financial flows to EMEs at this juncture were low, a paltry $28 billion, during the mid-1970s. Global private capital flows steadily increased reaching $49.8 billion in 1981 and peaking at $57.0 billion in mid-1982. Growth of the Eurodollar markets facilitated the bank lending of the late 1970s and early 1980s. A large proportion of sovereign loans had gone to the EMEs of Latin America, with capital flows to the region peaking at $44 billion in 1981. As a proportion of GDP, it was 6 percent of the GDP of this region.

During the early 1980s, the global economic environment changed radically from the 1970s in that commodity prices softened and there was a spike in the interest rates to levels not seen since 1930s. The LIBOR rate reached an unprecedented level. In addition, advanced industrial economies suffered a recession. These two factors (softening of commodity prices and spike in interest rates) coalesced to create serious debt servicing problems for the Latin American EMEs, the largest borrowing EMEs. They found themselves in dire financial straits. Beginning with Mexico in August 1982, several of them declared moratoriums on their sovereign obligations. This developed into a major financial crisis of global proportion, the first in the post-World War II era. For global financial markets, EMEs suddenly became pariahs. The Latin American debt crisis of 1982–3 caused serious deterioration in the macroeconomic performance of EMEs, particularly those in Latin America. It also made capital markets more cautious in making syndicated sovereign loans. Capital flows from the other channels also suffered a decline. Net private capital flows to EMEs were reduced to a trickle. The annual average net capital flows for the 1983–9 period plummeted to $11.6 billion. Compared to this, the average net capital flows for the 1971–9 period were $17.8 billion.[8]

EMEs, particularly those in the western hemisphere, experienced severe debt-servicing difficulties and their rate of inflation accelerated menacingly. They found themselves laboring under inordinately heavy debt-servicing burdens. The most heavily indebted EMEs had a ratio of external debt to exports in the neighborhood of 370 percent in the latter half of the 1980s. This group of EMEs was not only excluded from capital market flows but was also forced to run current account surpluses to enable it to repay its external debts (Kaminsky, 2005). Global private capital market observers, therefore, argued that it could take several years before market access for the EMEs from Latin America could be fully restored. It was reasonably expected that these economies needed several years of macroeconomic and financial restructuring and adjustment. Declining global private capital flows to EMEs during the 1980s led some observers to describe this period as the 'lost decade'. The IFIs, particularly the IMF, took up the slack. Throughout the 1980s, the IMF introduced a number of new lending facilities aimed at assisting the highly indebted economies of the western hemisphere. The US treasury took the initiative to launch the Brady Plan in 1989 to facilitate debt-ridden economies' ability to restructure their debt.

Toward the end of the 1980s, the gloomy relationship between EMEs and global capital markets began to transform. EMEs again became a favorite investment destination. However, the comeback made by EMEs was under a strikingly different set of circumstances than that from the past. As elaborated below (Section 4.2), this time capital flows to the Asian EMEs surged at a rapid clip. Global private capital flows to this group of EMEs were ten times larger in the late 1980s than their average in the early part of the decade. Also, the composition of capital flows changed. The relative significance of FDI was on the rise since the latter half of the 1980s. Bank lending was no longer the principal channel of capital transfer; it was supplanted by portfolio investment, which comprised FDI, equity and bond investment.

4.2 Transforming scenario of the 1990s

Not only did the EMEs' relationship with global capital markets transform during the late 1980s but they were also being widely extolled for their sound macroeconomic policies, superior institutional base, market-friendly and pragmatic governments, and high quality of their human resources. EMEs from Asia became the largest recipients of investment after 1993. Cumulative private capital flows to EMEs during 1990–96 added up to $1,055 billion. This was seven-fold higher than the amount this group of economies received during 1973–83. It was also nine-fold higher than the amount borrowed from official creditors – both bilateral and multilateral – by EMEs during the same period. By the mid-1990s, a veritable explosion in capital flows to EMEs occurred (Table 4.1).

FDI became an important and dependable source of finance not only for EMEs but also for several other middle-income developing countries during the 1990s. Its growth was particularly strong during this period. A good part of FDI to EMEs was in the form of mergers and acquisitions (M&As). This was a period when many EMEs and large developing economies were privatizing their public sector enterprises. EMEs and other large developing economies that were rated as creditworthy by the global capital markets succeeded in attracting FDI. In accordance with the above-mentioned transformation in the composition of capital flows to EMEs in the later part of the 1980s and early 1990s, the proportion of bank lending to the EMEs of both Asia and Latin America began plummeting. It was 70 percent of the net private capital flows during the 1970s, but declined to a mere 20 percent by the mid-1990s. The proportion of FDI and bond and equity investment in total private capital flows to EMEs soared. It accounted for 40 percent of the total in the mid-1990s (Kaminsky, 2005). An investigation of 20 EMEs over the 1976–2002 period, using measures of *de facto* and *de jure* openness revealed that an important characteristic of FDI is that it contributes to a decrease in the number of financial macroeconomic crises (Joyce, 2009).

A sanguine mainstream view developed regarding FDI. Its growth during the 1990s was regarded as a wholesome development for EMEs

Table 4.1 Net private capital flows to emerging markets (1990–2002) (in billions of $)

Year	1990	1991	1992	1993	1994	1995	1996	1997	1998	1999	2000	2001	2002
Total Net Flows	45.7	118.1	120.6	176.3	151.5	208.3	228.3	75.5	53.4	96.0	51.1	38.8	85.9
Net Foreign Direct Investment	18.8	31.5	35.3	57.9	80.6	95.0	109.5	136.0	148.8	156.8	149.0	170.5	139.2
Net Equity Investment	17.0	24.7	55.6	98.7	113.0	48.0	94.6	48.5	1.7	41.4	12.1	-38.5	-36.6
Other Net Flows	9.9	62.0	29.7	19.6	-41.9	64.6	24.2	-108.8	-97.1	-102.2	-110.1	-93.2	-16.7
Total Net Flows to													
Asia	21.4	24.8	29.0	31.8	70.3	98.4	132.2	12.0	-44.9	6.3	-18.3	-15.5	69.5
Middle East and Europe	7.0	65.7	38.8	29.1	15.7	8.2	9.5	16.9	10.2	-3.9	-18.8	-38.3	-25.3
Western Hemisphere	10.3	24.1	55.7	61.4	47.1	39.1	65.3	58.7	63.3	50.0	50.5	34.7	2.1
Economies in Transition	4.2	-9.9	3.1	19.7	4.3	51.4	20.2	-20.9	14.5	29.8	32.9	20.9	34.1

Sources: International Monetary Fund, *World Economic Outlook.* Washington. DC. October 1999, Table 2.2, p. 52. International Monetary Fund, *World Economic Outlook.* Washington. DC. September 2002, Table 1.4, p. 30. International Monetary Fund, *World Economic Outlook.* Washington. DC. April 2003, Table 1.3, p. 9.

NB. Net capital flows comprise net foreign direct investment, net portfolio investment and other long- and short-term net investment flows, including official and private borrowings from the global capital markets.

and for the global economy. This mode of global capital transfer set itself apart from other channels of private capital flows. Economic theory testifies to the fact that capital is a necessary, albeit not sufficient, condition for growth. FDI flows not only provided capital to EMEs but also overcame the pervasive investment-saving gap. What is more consequential is that it ushered modern management techniques and advanced technologies into the recipient EMEs. This provided a tangible impetus to economic growth rate, without sacrificing current consumption. Stability was another one of its favorable attributes. FDI was usually viewed as a long-term commitment by the investing TNCs. Its growth impact on EMEs was significant and it reduced external vulnerability. Large current account deficits in EMEs were considered sustainable if they were largely financed through FDI, instead of through bank lending or equity investment, both of which are characterized by a highly degree of volatility.

Bank lending to EMEs after 1990 also underwent qualitative transformations. First, as expected it was most pronounced in Asia, followed by Europe and Latin America. Conversely, it stagnated in Africa and the Middle East. Second, a large part of the increase in bank lending to Asia was in short-term claims. This trend has been attributed to several factors. These included a rapid growth in trade financing, the establishment of off-shore financial centers and the so-called 'arbitrage' opportunities offered by a combination of high local nominal interest rates on the one hand and fixed or nearly fixed exchange rates on the other. Exposure to short-term bank credits was considered easy to monitor and manage by the borrowing firms in Asia, giving it an edge. In addition, during this period the financial sector was being liberalized briskly in many EMEs. The prevailing regulatory framework also encouraged short-term capital flows from global capital markets.

Two characteristic features of global financial markets during the 1990s were: first, a remarkable growth in international bank lending and, second, large investment from non-bank financial institutions in EMEs. This latter set of institutions included mutual funds, insurance companies, pension funds and hedge funds, which were liquidity-rich. The presence of these institutions broadened the investor base of the global capital market. They found equity investment to be their favorite instrument. Table 4.1 shows that total net capital inflows soared from $45.7 billion in 1990 to $228.3 billion in 1996. Bank lending and equity investments in EMEs are known to be highly volatile. Net FDI flows soared from $18.8 billion to $109.5 billion over the same period. These are more than five-fold increases in net terms. Net global capital flows to EMEs peaked in 1996. However, net FDI flows resisted this trend and continued to increase, peaking in 2001 at $170.5 billion.

The trend in portfolio investment, particularly in capital flows through international bonds, was not so smooth. They rose from $17 billion to $113 billion between 1990 and 1994, but declined sharply to $48.8 billion in 1995. This was less than half the level of a year earlier. The currency crisis in Mexico had begun in the last quarter of 1994 and the international bond market was adversely affected by it. After dampening down, net capital flows through portfolio investment again picked up in 1996 reaching $94.6 billion, although this was again much less than the peak reached in 1994. Likewise, the category of other net flows, which included mostly bank lending, after rising sharply during the early 1990s, became negative in 1994. This implies that withdrawals or repayments were larger than fresh lending. However, 1995 again saw steep increases in net flows in this category. They reached $46.6 billion in 1996. The Mexican currency crisis had failed to affect global capital flows to the EMEs of Asia. It is worth pointing out that official capital flows – both bilateral and multilateral – during this period remained flat (Table 4.1).[9]

Two other notable financial market trends of the 1990s, which were noted above, helped stimulate private capital flows to EMEs. The first one was the globalization of markets for securities of EMEs. The second one was the broadening of investor base. To be sure, the increasing activity of liquidity-rich non-bank institutions was responsible for the latter trend. Latin American securities were being sold in the stock markets of Europe and Asia. Similarly, as the range of mainstream institutional investors grew, investing institutions in EMEs grew more diverse. The pricing process of EMEs' securities was working reasonably well; consequently, new investors from global private capital markets were attracted toward them. There was a dark side to the 1990s. It is also known for a string of financial crises (Section 5). These caused reversal of capital flows, which predictably reignited the debate on the costs and benefits of financial globalization in the economic profession and the policy making community.

4.3 On the eve of the Asian crisis

After peaking in nominal terms in 1996, net capital flows to EMEs did not recover for a while. As seen in Table 4.1, considerable tightening in emerging-market financial conditions took place after this juncture. The principal reason was obviously the recurring crises in individual EMEs and groups thereof during 1997–8 (Section 5), which led to an increased perception of risk in them in the global private capital markets. The Asian crisis (1997–8) and the Russian default (1998) in particular had a pronounced effect over global financial markets. Asian EMEs had accumulated large short-term liabilities (Section 3.2). In the latter half of 2007, large international banks rapidly moved to reduce their claims on Asian borrowers through the non-renewal of short-term loans.

The combined influence of the Asian crisis and the Russian debt moratorium was far from localized. They impeded cross-border capital flows in a definite and lasting manner. To be sure, Asian EMEs suffered most. The crisis did not cause a sudden stop of global private capital flows but a reversal. Total capital flows declined from a large inflow of $132.2 billion in 1996 to an outflow of $44.9 billion in 1998 (Table 4.1). Beginning in the second half of 1998, all EMEs except those in Africa and the Middle East, were affected by the retrenchment in international bank lending following the Russian debt moratorium. The decline in lending activity reflected both reduced willingness to lend by banks and a weak demand from borrowers, particularly from Asian firms. Asian EMEs sharply reduced their bank borrowings because, first, in the aftermath of the crisis Asian corporations were rapidly deleveraging and, second, their economies were keen to have current account surpluses and accordingly shifted their borrowing strategy. In addition, increasing inflows of equity capital made external bank borrowings redundant for them.

Portfolio investment in EMEs through stock markets peaked in real terms at $103 billion in 1996 (Das, 2004). Global non-bank or institutional investors were the principal users of this channel of investment. They found it functional and profitable. Mutual funds, insurance companies and pension funds routed significant amounts of capital through this channel into EMEs. To match this proclivity, EMEs had implemented wide-ranging financial restructures and reforms to facilitate portfolio investment from liquidity-rich financial institutions. This process suffered during the Asian crisis and private capital flows through this channel sharply declined.

As institutional investors and others began to play a greater role, the structure of global financial markets began to transform. Commercial banks and syndicated loans dominated the 1980s by traditionally providing loans to EMEs. During the 1990s, while large commercial banks continued to provide loans, their volumes were limited. The commercial banks actively turned toward originating, distributing, trading and investing emerging-market assets. Hedge funds emerged as increasingly active traders of emerging-market assets. In addition, large mutual and other funds became much more significant investors in EMEs. The large commercial banks were relegated into a secondary position by the activity of mutual and other funds (Leijonhufvud, 2007).

On the eve of the Asian financial crisis in July 1997, net flows reached their peak in real terms.[10] This was the highest level they had reached in two decades. It is well-known that the Asian and other crises had a serious deleterious impact and that, subsequently, financial flows to EMEs suffered a sharp decline. The composition of external capital flows also underwent a dramatic transformation after this juncture. Official development assistance (ODA), which was not quantitatively important, either stagnated completely or declined. Consequently, the relative significance of ODAs in cross-country capital flows declined. In place of ODA, private capital flows from the global financial markets became the major source of external finance for a good number of EMEs.

It was evident that, in the matter of financial globalization, EMEs were a distinct category. That they performed better in this matter than other developing countries had become obvious in the 1990s. Middle-income developing countries were able to attract much smaller amounts of net global capital than EMEs. In accordance with the perception of creditworthiness, the lion's share of global capital flows was attracted by the top 12 recipient countries during the 1990s.[11] All of them fell into the category of the EMEs that were relatively more financially globalized. Although EMEs were the more attractive destination for global private capital flows, an interesting feature of the 1990s was that these capital flows were far from uniform across EMEs. Five major EMEs, namely Brazil, China, Korea, Mexico and Thailand accounted for over half of total private capital inflows. If this tally is extended to a dozen EMEs, they account for almost 80 percent of total global private capital flows.

As global capital flows began accelerating toward these EMEs, the composition of the total global financial resources going to developing economies *en masse* was affected. The proportion of financial flows dedicated to low- and middle-income developing economies declined significantly toward the end of the 1990s. To all appearances, many individual economies in the EME group of rapidly financially globalizing economies were diverging from the rest of the developing economies in terms of economic performance (Das, 2003).

During the 1990s, a transformation in the external financial profile of EMEs was clearly discernible. The scale of net foreign liabilities in many EMEs declined and their foreign currency reserves went on building up, albeit slowly. They also successfully developed alternatives to foreign-currency debt financing. In this regard, the EMEs of Central and Eastern Europe were exceptions. They did not succeed in developing any of these positive characteristics and or in strengthening their fundamentals. The EMEs of the other regions had strong fundamentals at this juncture. When the 2001 Argentina crisis broke out, it did not have a contagious effect. No doubt it affected the regional economies but it failed to transmit across to other EMEs inside Latin America and drag them down into a regional crisis. Only a close neighbor of Argentina, Uruguay, was badly affected. Likewise, the 2001 crisis in Turkey failed to affect other EMEs and was largely contained in terms of its international effect (Lane, 2009).

4.4 Dawn of the twenty-first century

Global equity markets remained volatile in 2000. Particularly noteworthy was the sovereign default by Argentina and deep recession in the EMEs of the western hemisphere during 2001–02. The FDI flows to EMEs did not strengthen, but were not particularly badly affected. The Asian crisis and the individual country crises failed to dampen FDI flows significantly. In absolute terms they declined from $170.5 billion in 2001 to $139.2 billion in 2002. However, this decline was part of the general decline in FDI flows. The essential causes were unsettled investor sentiment until 2003, and falloff in the privatization activity in EMEs and in transactions involving acquisitions and mergers (A&Ms). As in the past, FDI continued to be heavily concentrated in a small number of host countries.

Weakness in the equity markets continued and equity investment in EMEs turned negative in 2001. Due to high risk perception, institutional investors in advanced industrial economies were not eager to invest in EMEs. Stock markets in EMEs continued to lose ground until 2003. Return on equity in EMEs by and large followed the trend set by matured industrial economies. The EMEs of Asia were supported by improvements in macroeconomic fundamentals. Asian business corporations had healthier balance sheets as a result of continued deleveraging since the Asian crisis. Yet Asian equity markets performed poorly in 2002, although dollar returns were slightly inflated due to regional currency movements. Only the EMEs in Europe generated positive returns in dollar terms. The worst performance in dollar terms was that of the stock markets in the western hemisphere. Sizable depreciation in the regional currencies was partly to blame. It reflected the dollar's decline vis-à-vis the euro.

Syndicated bank lending had slipped into the negative quadrant during the Asian crisis; it did not become positive soon after the recovery. Despite marginal improvement in 2002, syndicated loan volumes remained weak. Due to several high-profile bankruptcies in the corporate world in the European Union (EU) and the US and sovereign default in Argentina, banks continued to tighten their international lending standards. However, lending activities remained buoyant in the high-grade sectors and problem-free economies.

The dot-com recession affected the advanced industrial economies of Western Europe (2000–01) and the US (2002), although Australia and Canada were spared. Due to this recession, there was a sharp decline in global capital flows to EMEs of the western hemisphere during 2001–02. Risk perception in the global financial markets for the EMEs in the western hemisphere and in the Middle East had increased during the early 2000s. However, by the end of 2002 the EMEs of the western hemisphere had regained market access to global capital markets. The saving grace was that, with some exceptions, the flexible exchange rate regime facilitated a relatively smooth adjustment to the movement of funds in major currencies. As the net cross-border capital flows had maintained a low level since 2000, the prospect of a contagion spreading in the EMEs had markedly declined.

Net private capital flows to EMEs in 2002 were $85.9 billion (Table 4.1), close to the 1997 Asian crisis-year level. There was an improvement in 2003. In terms of the proportion of the net private capital flows from global capital markets, Asian EMEs overwhelmingly dominated the early 2000s period. They became so much more important for the global investing community that in 2002 they accounted for 80.9 percent of total net flows to EMEs. Real GDP growth rate in this group of EMEs, in particular China, exceeded expectations, increasing their appeal as destinations for global investors. However, there was a downside. After the burst of the so-called dot-com bubble in 2001, the information and communication technology (ICT) sector had slowed down in the ASEAN-4 (Indonesia, Malaysia, the Philippines and Thailand) economies.

During 2000–02, there was a strong trend of reversal of capital flows in the EMEs of Europe and the Middle East. The EMEs of the western hemisphere were still grappling with their problems and were not able to attract much capital from global private capital markets. They received merely 2.4 percent of the total net capital flows in 2002. Although the GDP growth rate improved in 2003, serious vulnerabilities remained in Argentina, Brazil and Uruguay. The political crisis in Venezuela continued to have economic fallout. Net capital flows to Africa were weak and grew weaker after 2000.[12]

Around the turn of the twenty-first century a noteworthy phenomenon occurred in the global financial market. The US economy, that had run current account deficits since 1989, began recording larger deficits. They reached 7 percent of GDP in 2006 and hovered around the same level in 2009. To finance this, the US needed surplus savings from economies that ran surpluses. The period of large US deficits coincided with the period of rapid financial globalization, with both surplus and deficit countries investing a large fraction of their savings abroad. The on-going financial globalization enabled the US to finance its current account deficit and worked in its favor. At the end of the first quarter in 2009, the official national debt figure for the US had crossed $11 trillion, which was close to the US GDP figure of $14.2 trillion. In the recent past the large US current account deficit absorbed over 80 percent of all the surpluses that occurred in the global economy. It was widely apprehended that if financial globalization slows down, the US will not be able to finance its current account deficit on favorable terms. The US will then need to attract a larger share of other countries' foreign investment.

5. An Extraordinary phase of financial globalization in the EMEs

The myriad crises of the 1990s and early 2000s that struck the EMEs, both individually and in groups, have been alluded to above. However, the first among the crises of the 1990s was the Western European Exchange Rate Mechanism (ERM) crisis of 1992. It was followed by the Mexican peso crisis (1994–5), the Asian crisis (1997–8), the Russian Ruble crisis and debt moratorium (1998) and the Brazilian crisis (1998–9). Turkey (early 2001) and Argentina (late 2001) were the last to suffer financial crises during this period. This litany could be regarded as an aide memoire of the plausibility that a financially globalized economy could be an unstable economy and that crises are capable of reversing financial globalization. These financial crises demonstrated that small errors in macroeconomic policy could draw swift punishment from the global financial markets. They also showed that severe crises could occur even without any visible signs of weakness in the macroeconomic policy. Despite some similarities, these crises featured substantial differences.

Once this crisis-filled period was over, EMEs again began turning in a stellar economic performance in 2002 and continued thereafter. A period of crisis-free uninterrupted growth followed. Global private market capital flows to EMEs through FDI, portfolio and international bonds were strong. The role of equity financing was greatly expanded. Net financial flows soared at a rapid rate reaching a peak of $617.5 billion in 2007. When they peaked, they were 8.3 percent of the GDP of the EMEs. Judged by historical standards, sovereign spreads remained low for several years. For the majority of EMEs, their external accounts swung sharply toward surpluses. After the crisis-filled 1990s, their foreign exchange reserves accumulation further enlarged. This was particularly true for the Asian EMEs. The accumulation of large reserves could be taken as their self-insurance measure, although many EMEs went well beyond self-insuring their economies (Obstfeld et al., 2008). Net external liabilities of EMEs were much lower. EMEs learned precious lessons from the crises and addressed their financial vulnerabilities by correcting the currency and maturity mismatches in their national balance sheets. Some EMEs abandoned their firm exchange rate pegs, which had proved to be problematic in the past, and moved toward flexible inflation targeting. All these policy moves coalesced to create a superior fiscal and financial policy domain. This scenario suggests that the capacity of EMEs to withstand external financial shocks was markedly enhanced.

A single rationalization is not enough to vindicate this qualitative improvement in EMEs' economic policy and performance. Low real interest rates in the global economy due to high savings during this period reduced the potential for a crisis. Besides, strong net external positions, along with large foreign exchange reserves, were helpful. EMEs spawned greater confidence among the global investing community, both retail and institutional. They began looking for higher potential returns in EMEs. There were two additional factors rationalizing the improvements in economic performance in EMEs. First, their real economic performance was *inter alia* driven to a higher level by a strong export demand from advanced industrial economies, in particular the US. Second, extraordinary firmness in commodity prices had created boom conditions in many EMEs during this period (Devereux and Sutherland, 2009).

Global investors had begun discriminating among the EMEs. They remained invested in those EMEs that had better fundamentals, while shunning those that did not. This proclivity on the part of the global investing community demonstrated the 'sophistication of this asset class' (Lane, 2009, p. 28). A larger pool of investment analysts were able to differentiate across EMEs with different fundamentals. Their expectations were that any future crises need not unleash contagion across all EMEs and that the ones with strong fundamentals would continue to yield healthy returns even in a crisis situation. Other than this pull factor, a reinforcing push factor was also operating. Low interest rates in the large global financial centers during 2001–06 and the compression of spreads between low-risk and high-risk domestic securities increased the perceived attractiveness of EMEs as financial markets that could provide high yields.

One thing that stood out from any previous episodes of high capital inflows into the EMEs and rapid growth was their extraordinary level of participation in financial globalization in this period. During this phase, their participation in the global financial markets had attained unforeseen heights. Their role was no longer confined to being recipients of large amounts of global capital, or the originator of outflows. Many EMEs recorded immense growth in gross external financial assets and liabilities, much larger than their net positions. This trend was identical to the past experiences of many advanced industrial economies documented in the influential publications by Lane and Milsi-Ferretti (2005, 2007).

As set out earlier (Section 2.1), the contemporary period is known for the significant net external surplus of EMEs as well as perverse flows of global capital from EMEs to high-income industrial economies. However, this capital flow was not unilateral. While EMEs were investing in US treasury bills, they were concurrently recipients of large portfolio investments in the form of FDI and equity investment as well as international bond market investment. The majority of EMEs were substantial net debtors in the mid-1990s. Their borrowing from the banks and their US dollar bonds was sizable (Table 4.1). They turned into net creditors in fixed income assets, while net debtors in portfolio equity investments. This is an efficient form of financial globalization in terms of sharing international risk (Devereux and Sutherland, 2009). Based on an analysis built around a dynamic stochastic general equilibrium model of the interaction between an EME and the rest of the world economy, Devereux and Sutherland (2009, p. 182) concluded that an EME may build up 'positive gross positions in non-contingent international bond assets, and negative positions in FDI and portfolio equity, and may offer a considerable enhancement of international risk-sharing'.

The turning point was 2003. At this juncture, private capital flows had recovered and capital flows to EMEs had resumed following the

Table 4.2   Net private capital flows to emerging-market economies (2003–08) (in billions of dollars)

	2003	2004	2005	2006	2007	2008
Total net capital flows	154.21	222.0	226.8	202.8	617.5	109.3
Net foreign direct investment	161.3	183.9	243.7	241.4	359.0	459.3
Net equity investment	−3.8	10.0	−5.6	−100.7	39.5	−155.2
Other net private capital flows	−3.3	28.0	−11.3	62.2	219.2	−194.6
Total net capital flows to						
Africa	4.9	13.0	26.0	35.2	33.4	24.2
Asia	66.9	145.6	85.3	31.8	164.8	127.9
Commonwealth of						
Independent States	19.0	2.6	30.4	55.1	127.2	−127.4
Middle East	1.4	−17.7	−53.7	−50.0	11.0	−120.9
Western Hemisphere	19.7	17.1	39.0	10.8	107.4	58.5

Source: Statistics gleaned from *World Economic Outlook 2009*. April 2009. International Monetary Fund. Washington. DC. Table A13. p. 212.

decline in interest rates in the advanced industrial economies in 2003. The Fed reduced its interest rates to 1 percent. Low interest rates logically attracted investors to the high yields offered by the EMEs, particularly those in Asia and Latin America. Private capital flows from the global financial markets increased almost steadily (Table 4.2). As stated in the introduction, 2007 was the peak performance year for capital flows to EMEs. This was the fifth year of strong gains. Financial integration between EMEs and advanced industrial economies had deepened over this period and the emerging-market asset class had moved into the mainstream. Macroeconomic and financial management in the EMEs and large developing economies had considerably improved. The standing of EMEs in the global economic and financial order had changed.

Banking systems in the EMEs were increasingly perceived as healthy and well-capitalized. They had diverse earning sources and sound asset quality. Improved economic fundamentals, abundant reserves and strong GDP growth all helped attract global private capital glows to EMEs. Banks and firms in EMEs raised $1.2 trillion during 2003–07 at a reasonable interest rate, in the neighborhood of 6.4 percent (WB, 2009a). The EMEs of Asia continued to be the largest attraction for global private investors, even in 2007 (Table 4.2). Spreads on foreign-currency denominated bonds issued by EMEs declined between 2003 and 2007, reaching their lowest level since the onset of Asian crisis in 1997. There were two causal factors for this decline. Benign conditions in the global financial markets, or the pull factor, was the first factor. Second, the steady improvements in EMEs' macroeconomic fundamentals, or the push factor, had a decisive influence (Ciarlone et al., 2009). The sub-prime mortgage crisis erupted in the UK and US in the fall of 2007. The financial markets in EMEs were initially expected to remain impervious to financial shocks from the matured financial markets. However, as analyzed below, these hopes for the decoupling of EMEs did not last for long (Section 6).

Private capital flows to EMEs slumped precipitously in 2008 to $109.3 billion (Table 4.2). Deleveraging by global financial institutions raised the cost and reduced the availability of finance from global capital markets. In addition, investor risk appetite had declined, sharply reducing the demand for EME assets. Bank assets fell at their most rapid rate in 2008 (Table 4.2). The two factors driving cross-border deleveraging were: First, credit risk concerns by banks that induced them to withdraw funds because they perceived themselves as less able to manage credit risk from a distance. Second, cross-border exposures typically involved a higher regulatory capital charge due to currency or country risk. Therefore, shedding these assets was a quick route to improving capital ratios. These factors and risks were particularly strong in case of lending to EMEs. In addition, EMEs experienced large outflows of portfolio capital in 2008. They accelerated in the last quarter. Given continued pressure on leveraged investors to shed assets, there was a risk of further redemption from EMEs. Similarly, FDI flows slowed. Due to the lack of credit available to finance acquisitions FDI flows were set to slow further. According to the projections of the latest *Global Financial Stability Report*, on balance, EMEs should see net private capital outflows in 2009 and a weak recovery in 2010 (IMF, 2009c).

6. Transforming debt structure of firms in the EMEs

Matured financial markets are liquid and can offer longer-term financing than ones that are shallow and less liquid. When financial globalization progresses and firms from EMEs gain access to the matured financial markets, their debt structure changes. Financial globalization has had a definite impact on the debt structure of borrowing firms in the EMEs. It has also helped develop domestic financial systems in EMEs and reduce cost of capital for the borrowing firms (Edison and Warnock, 2003).

For the firms that could access international financial markets, their maturity structure of debt, as reported in their balance sheets, was found to have changed. Using firm level data for 686 non-financial firms in seven EMEs of East Asia and Latin America, Schmukler and Vesperoni (2006) constructed a long time series for the 1980s and 1990s. This period characterized both financial repression and financial liberalization. To test the effect of globalization at the macro level, they used country-level data to determine when countries liberalized their financial systems.

Their results show that the effects of financial globalization on debt structure are significant. For average-sized firms, financial globalization is associated with a shorter maturity structure. The effects were not uniform or equal across firms. Firms that relied on domestic financing alone shortened their maturity structure after liberalization measures were adopted by the government. However, firms that had access to international bond and equity markets were found to obtain more long-term debt and extend their maturity structures. These effects of financial globalization were found to be stronger in EMEs that had relatively less-developed domestic financial systems.

7. Case study of China and India

Recent macroeconomic and financial reforms and restructuring leading to rapid growth first in China and then India not only altered the domestic economic structures in these economies but also influenced the regional and global economies. Their contribution to the global GDP has been steadily increasing, consequently their combined global economic profile has been rising. According to 2008 statistics, the size of the Chinese GDP was $3.9 trillion at the market exchange rate and it was the third largest economy in the world, while that of India was $1.2 trillion and it was the 12th largest economy.[13] Due to the large sizes of their economies, huge populations and adoption of increasingly open and outward-orientated economic strategy – particularly in case of China – they have a great deal of impact over other economies, both regionally and globally. As set out in Chapter 4 (Section 8.4), China demonstrated the earliest signs of recovery from the current financial crisis and recession. Japan and the Asian EMEs followed. The recession enhanced China's global status and accelerated China's rise in the pecking order of systemically significant economies.

The influence of rapid growth in these two EMEs over multilateral trade and finance as well as the global economic growth in general has been methodically examined and documented in Das (2006) and Winters and Yusuf (2007). They were and are recipients of global finance through various channels. Of late, they have become its sources as well. Their financial systems are not completely liberalized and capital accounts are not entirely open, but they have made substantial progress in this direction in the recent past. The probability of the global profile of these two EMEs continuing to rise is exceedingly high. As demonstrated in Section 7, in the face of global recession in 2008 and 2009 both of these economies remained resilient and continued to post positive GDP growth figures.

Slowly but surely, their activities and prominence in the global financial markets have been expanding. Both EMEs have been making their presence felt in the international capital markets. China's status as the largest ($2.1 trillion) holder of foreign exchange reserves and a net exporter of capital is particularly noteworthy.[14] Like China, India also holds an unusually high level of reserves and exports relatively small sums. In addition, after 2000 both of them emerged as investors in the private sector of advanced industrial economies. Initially this was carried out in a small way but their standing as foreign investors went on rising from year to year. It was not a coincidence that General Motors sold its Hummer brand to a Sichuan Tengzhhong Heavy Industrial Machinery Co. in June 2009. During 2000–08, Indian companies announced over 1,000 international mergers and acquisitions, worth $72 billion (*The Economist*, 2009e).

In terms of the composition of gross assets and liabilities, the global financial integration of China and India has thus far been highly asymmetric. Lane and Schmukler (2007) pointed out that on the asset side both the countries hold low-return foreign reserves. The benefit that they provide is that these assets are relatively liquid and can protect these economies at the time of adverse external shocks. This benefit has a high opportunity cost. The liability side was represented by FDI, bank loans and portfolio equity, all of which normally yielded high rates of return. Among the developing economies, China established itself as the most successful economy in attracting global FDI. While India failed to draw comparable amounts of FDI – if anything this remained a weak spot for the Indian economy – it succeeded in drawing impressive sums as equity investment. China and India have not crowded out FDI from the other developing economies in a conspicuous manner. The two are also not among the major accumulators of non-reserve foreign assets. An extraordinary feature of their global financial integration is the reduction in their net liability positions. This runs counter to the grain of the neoclassical maxim which suggests that at their stage of economic development they should run large current account deficits.

The exchange rate and capital account liberalization policies of both these economies are in their evolutionary phase. Both of them are sure to undergo further financial development and liberalization. They are well on their way to having an increasing role in the global financial system as well as in private capital markets. According to the projections made by Lane and Schmukler (2007), the future composition of the international financial balance sheet of these two economies will grow less asymmetrical. Both of them are likely to accumulate far more non-reserve foreign assets. They will also have a balanced distribution of external liabilities between FDI, debt and portfolio equities. Both China and India are turning into investor economies, which will work to the benefit of other developing economies.

8. Current global financial crisis and the emerging-market economies

As the financial markets in EMEs were not directly exposed to the sub-prime mortgage crisis that originated in two matured economies, the UK and the US, and did not have much exposure to sub-prime related and other toxic securitized assets, initial expectation in EMEs was that the impact of the financial crisis would be confined to advanced industrial economies (Section 5). In the early phase of the crisis, EMEs did remain resilient and continued on their normal growth trajectories. Their initial position was strong *inter alia* due to the strength of their financial sectors. The capital base of the banking sector was robust in the EMEs and they had a low reliance on external finance. This observation applied *a fortiori* to the Asian EMEs. At this early juncture, the majority of EMEs did not suffer from external vulnerabilities. Many of them, particularly those from Asia, also had large liquidity reserves for self-insurance, continuing current account surpluses and low external debt. Besides, their economic fundamentals had improved markedly over the years, which had helped them in enhancing their policy space as well as their ability to adjust to external shocks. This strong and stable macroeconomic scenario was not an accident. It had resulted from the methodical implementation of reforms over the last two or three decades, adopting and maintaining disciplined macroeconomic policies and strengthening supervision of the financial and banking systems.

There was one more reason why EME policy makers initially thought that they will be able to shrug off the crisis. The decoupling debate was gaining ground since 2007, which questioned whether the EMEs of Asia had decoupled from the global business cycle of the advanced industrial countries (Section 2.2). It was because this line of thinking by EME policy makers squared up with the decoupling theory that had been gaining ground for the last few years, that EMEs thought that they would be able to remain unscathed by the crisis. In the last quarter of 2008, following the bankruptcy of Lehman Brothers, the financial turmoil mutated into a full-blown global financial and economic crisis. EMEs were affected substantially by the contagion. The credit crunch proliferated instantaneously in a financially globalized economy. It became difficult for EMEs to access the global capital market.

As the contagion reached the EMEs, many of them came under financial stress in their foreign exchange, stock and sovereign debt markets. This happened during the last quarter of 2008. Large banks trimmed their cross-border credit to EMEs. During the last quarter of 2008 they declined by $282 billion, or 10 percent of the total. Claims on the EMEs from Asia declined most (Gyntelberg, 2009). Market sentiments turned fragile and financial strains from the global credit crisis continued to weigh on the EMEs' economic prospects. The total value of financial assets in EMEs fell by $5.2 trillion in 2008 alone, a loss of 15 percent. As foreign lending flows reversed, the cost of raising capital in many EMEs skyrocketed (MGI, 2009). The decoupling hypothesis that had been developing over the years, abruptly packed up (Kose and Prasad, 2009). The emerging global circumstances exerted pressure on exchange rates in the EMEs. They caused currency depreciation and depletion of foreign exchange reserves. Although large liquidity reserves provided self-insurance to many EMEs, several of them were affected by the global financial crisis, particularly the EME-6.

As the global banks lending capacity shrank and global investors reduced leverage, capital inflows to EMEs dwindled. Equity investment from the global investing community, particularly large institutional investors began to be swiftly withdrawn from EMEs in the third quarter of 2008 (Dattels and Miyajima, 2009). Institutions like the IMF and IIF reported sharply falling capital inflows into EMEs in 2008 and forecasted further sharp declines in 2009. The IIF forecasted a paltry $170 billion for 2009, with bank lending turning negative (IIF, 2009). Concerns regarding external sustainability drove sovereign spreads up.

Since the fourth quarter of 2008, when the crisis turned into a global recession, the EMEs in Europe and Latin America have been the most adversely affected by rising spreads. However, these EMEs were not the worst affected groups overall. The four newly industrialized economies of Asia, namely, Korea, Hong Kong SAR, Singapore and Taiwan were the worst afflicted group of economies. There were two reasons they experienced such a severe impact: First, these economies were highly export-dependent and second, their manufacturing sectors operated through regional production networks. These two factors rendered them vulnerable to sharp contraction in demand in the European Union (EU) and North America. According to the projections of the IMF (2009a), the four newly industrialized economies of Asia were projected to perform the worst and contract by 5.6 percent in 2009. The EMEs of Europe and Latin America would record a contraction of 4.5 percent and 1.7 percent, respectively. In contrast, China and India remained resilient and well-positioned to continue growing. They were projected to grow at the rate of 6.5 percent and 4.5 percent in 2009, respectively. While astonishingly healthy in this environment, these growth rates are far below the recent performance of these two economies. However, the stock markets in EMEs that had performed steadily and well over the last few years were the hardest hit. Stock indices in many of them went into an abrupt decline, some even nosedived.

High-frequency measures of global private capital flows to EMEs in the issuance data on bonds, equity and bank loans were computed by the IMF (2009a). These statistics substantiated the same trend as indicated in the preceding paragraph. That is, global capital flows to EMEs from these financial channels decelerated in the third quarter of 2008. Capital flows through bonds and equity channels affected the EMEs in Asia and Europe to the maximum degree. Similarly, bank lending was sharply scaled back. For many EMEs, bank liabilities shrank as much as 20 percent of the receiving EME's GDP by September. Currencies in EMEs appreciated vis-à-vis the dollar during the first half of 2008, which was partly responsible for the declining capital inflows.[15]

In first half of 2009, advance industrial economies in North America and Europe were in recession. The only exceptions were Norway, Slovenia and Slovakia, although all the three were on the brink of a downturn. The EU and the US both recorded negative GDP growth rates in the second quarter of 2009. In contrast EMEs were in better economic shape and GDP growth rates in several of them bounced back into the positive quadrant. As discussed in Section 8.4, the EMEs of Asia performed in the most buoyant manner.

The financial crisis and recession adversely affected the four BRIC economies. As a group, they were diminished due to downturns in Brazil and the Russian Federation. However, China and India continued to chug along. China's GDP growth was 7.9 percent during the second quarter of 2009, while that of India 7.6 percent. These growth rates were considered much too high for a period when the global economy was in a state of recession and there were worries that these two economies were overheating. China's economic stimulus package was apparently hugely effective. One important reason behind the faster rebound of the Chinese economy compared to other major economies was that much of the slowdown in the economy was self-inflicted, rather than the result of global recession.[16] When the global recession started, China was already tightening its monetary policy to bring to an end an inflation that had been worrying the authorities for a year. Their restrictive monetary policy succeeded in pricking the bubble in the Shanghai and Shenzhen stock markets and caused a pause in the real estate boom in the large Chinese cities. Indian economy was affected less adversely by the global recession than the other large Asian EMEs because its export sector, measured as a proportion of GDP, is comparatively smaller. In 2008, exports accounted for only 15 percent of India's GDP, compared to 33 percent for China.

The crisis-afflicted global economy was helped by unprecedented macroeconomic and financial policy support. Aggressive and determined policy action in many EMEs began to show results. Timely stimulus packages that many EMEs and advanced industrial economies implemented improved financial conditions, both in individual economies and the global economy. Consequently, the rate of GDP contraction began moderating. During the middle of 2009, high-frequency data pointed to a return to modest growth at the global level. In July 2009, the IMF (2009d) revised the growth projections made earlier, in the *World Economic Outlook* in April (IMF, 2009a). According to the revised projections, global GDP was expected to contract in 2009 by 1.4 percent, with advanced industrial countries contracting by 3.8 percent. Their rate of contraction was not readjusted in the revised projections. Conversely, EMEs were projected to grow by 1.5 percent during 2009, with the Asian EMEs growing by 5.5 percent. The four newly industrialized economies of Asia were to contract by less than projected earlier (in IMF, 2009a), by 5.2 percent. Likewise, China and India, the two resilient economies were projected to grow at a higher rate in 2009 than computed earlier, at 7.5 percent and 5.4 percent, respectively.[17] During the third quarter of 2009, quarterly GDP growth and manufacturing output growth statistics showed that several Asian EMEs that had started the year in deep recession were bouncing back to a strong recovery. This observation applied particularly to Korea, Singapore and Taiwan (*The Economist*, 2009c).

Global private capital flows to EMEs declined due to the credit crunch and the global recession was projected to continue. In 2009 the transborder capital flows will be barely positive (WB, 2009a). This decline in external capital flows will have deleterious macroeconomic consequences in EMEs. A good part of the $1.2 trillion debt raised by the banks and firms in EMEs during 2003–07 was maturing in 2009. This would put borrowers' finances under pressure at a time when the average cost of external borrowing has increased to 11.7 percent, compared to 6.4 percent in the pre-crisis period when the debt was contracted.

8.1 Transmission of financial stress

Abrupt and unexpected slowdown in capital inflows during a crisis period is termed 'sudden stop' in crisis literature. It is known to have dire economic consequences in EMEs. Toward the end of 2008, in many EMEs industrial production either dramatically declined or came to a virtual standstill. The European EMEs recorded a contraction in their industrial output in the early months of 2009. The credit crunch set off by the global financial crisis weakened import demand in advanced industrial economies. This is a common aftereffect of a financial crisis and was observed during the earlier crises as well. In the past crises, global private capital inflows to EMEs dried up for a substantial length of time and industrial output took a fairly long time to recover and reach the level prevailing before the crisis. The Asian crisis (1997–8) testifies to this trend. Thus a financial crisis has a large effect on the real economy.

To analyze the level of financial stress in EMEs as well as to study the transmission of stress from advanced industrial economies to them, a stress index was devised by the International Monetary Fund for 18 EMEs (IMF, 2008d, 2009a). The findings of this index were revealing. Its first deduction was that the present crisis is more severe than any in the last three decades in that it has had a negative economic impact over all segments of the global financial system and all regions of the global economy. For EMEs, the financial stress of the current crisis reached the same level as that reached during the peak of the Asian crisis. Second, a strong link was observed between financial stress in advanced industrial economies and EMEs. Due to the progress made in financial globalization, financial stress transmitted swiftly and directly from the former economies to the latter. Crisis transmitted instantly and strongly to the EMEs that had closer financial associations with the financial markets in advanced industrial economies.

The financial stress index revealed that the present level of financial stress is rooted in the banking system of advanced industrial economies. It can therefore be projected that capital flows to EMEs will suffer a large decline. The recovery to normalcy will be slow. Capital flows through the banking sector will be the slowest to recover. One favorable characteristic that saved the EMEs from more financial stress and dire consequences was that their current account and fiscal deficit were low, reflecting their superior macroeconomic management over the past decades. EMEs had also succeeded in accumulating a sizable level of foreign exchange reserves. These large reserves can help EMEs during their sudden stop periods.

As for the appropriate response to cope with the financial crisis, EMEs need to focus macroeconomic and financial policies 'on averting further escalation of stress in emerging economies. This would not only limit the impact on the real economy in these countries, but also would thwart a second round of global deleveraging in the wake of damage to lenders' balance sheets in mature markets' (IMF, 2009d, p. 141). In a financially integrated global economy cross-country spillover tends to occur promptly. This is a strong reason supporting the need for a coordinated strategy between the EMEs and the advanced industrial economies. The systemic stabilization endeavors in the latter should not only be aimed at their own financial systems but also toward fostering a reduction of stress in the EMEs.

Continuance of progress in global financial integration is an essential element of a prospering global economy. The current financial crisis provides a meaningful perspective for the policy mandarins. As strengthening financial linkages also increase the transmission of financial stress from the crisis economies to others, there is a collective need to multilaterally indemnify against the external financial shocks. The objective is to shield and support the economies that have creatively and ingeniously followed sound macroeconomic and financial sector policies, governed their economies well and promoted global integration.

8.2 Composition of recovery from the crisis

In the mid-2009 review of the global recession, the World Bank warned that global growth in 2009 will be more negative than computed earlier. The new projection for contraction in the global GDP was 2.9 percent (WB, 2009a). The global economy was showing symptoms of entering a period of slow growth, which called for tighter and more effective oversight of the global financial system. In the revised projections, the global contraction has been forecast to turn into a mild recovery. The global economy will grow at the rate of 2 percent in 2010.

Although there are normal caveats about these projections, there were signs in the third quarter of 2009 that the bottom was reached in several large industrial economies, although recovery did begin earlier in several EMEs. It was also evident that the large EMEs, like the BRICs, were driving demand and growth in the global economy. EMEs were projected to perform better in 2010 than the global economy. Their growth was projected at 3.2 percent. The performance of advanced industrial economies is forecast to be markedly different (1.3 percent). Also, growth rates within regions will vary substantially. The EMES of Asia and South Asia are expected to lead with 5.0 and 5.3 percent growth rates, respectively. Once again, China and India will turn in stellar performances, with 7.5 percent and 5.6 percent growth, respectively (WB, 2009a). A global financial crisis and recession of the present dimension tested the EMEs and their economic models. The majority of them, particularly the large ones, were able to withstand the stress. It gave a good account of their economic robustness and buoyancy.

8.3 Challenges pushed to the fore by the crisis

The positive aspect of a crisis is the lessons that public policy professionals can learn that have high relevance and utility for the future. It also brings to light weak spots. Once revealed, these systemic limitations can be addressed. EMEs can individually and collectively learn lessons from the current crisis and benefit from these. They can find pragmatic ways to resolve problematic issues. The first and most imperative lesson regards regulatory and supervisory bodies. A great deal of culpability for the current crisis has been put at their doors (Chapter 3). In view of the transforming global financial scenario, these systems need updating and redesigning. They need to reflect the changing structure, practices and procedures in the global capital markets. They should be more meticulously redesigned than in the past. Most importantly, these regulatory and supervisory institutions need to remain ever more vigilant.

The large foreign reserves accumulated by several EMEs, particularly those from Asia, is another germane issue. They went a long way in cushioning many EMEs from the current global financial crisis. The question that needs to be deliberated upon is whether the cost involved in maintaining such large reserves is worth it. If this cushion could be provided by a lower level of forex reserves, then it needs to be determined what an appropriate lower level is. This would enable EMEs to avoid the high costs of maintaining excessive reserves. A related issue is the role of dollars as the first priority reserve assets in the world. Calls for a new reserve currency that is not the currency of a country have recently been made by large EMEs. According to some EMEs, Special Drawing

Rights (SDR), managed by the IMF, fit the bill and should be made the *de jure* reserve currency for the global economy. In the Group-of-Twenty (G-20) summit in London, in April 2009, China was the first to broach this issue. Subsequently the Russian Federation joined in. Before the G-8 summit in the Italian city of L'Aquila began on 8 July 2009, China, India and the Russian Federation again called for an end to the dollar's dominance in the global monetary system. According to the Chinese proposal, the dollar should no longer be an international reserve currency. It should be replaced with a global reserve currency, the DSR or Special Drawing Rights, created by the IMF in 1969.[18] China also wants the SDR basket to be expanded to include the renminbi yuan. An interesting point is that nothing needs to be done *de jure* in this regard. If China and other EMEs stop accumulating their forex reserves in the dollar, its significance will decline, which in turn is not in the interest of EMEs like China, who have large investments in US treasury securities.

The EMEs of Europe opened their capital account a bit too rapidly. These countries allowed a lot of capital to gush in from the global capital markets. They ran a current account deficit of the order of 10 percent, even more. Their economies suffered serious damage when capital flows reversed and capital fled to safety in 2008. When the recession started, these economies suffered huge disruptions to their exchange rates, asset prices and financial systems. To an extent, the policies pursued in opening their capital account were to be blamed. The IMF needs to provide policy advice to this group of EMEs regarding the adoption of the most pragmatic ways of capital account liberalization.

8.4 How much did the financial crisis impair the EMEs?

While the financial crisis and recession affected EMEs, it failed to cripple them or inflict any kind of permanent damage. In many cases the GDP growth rate decelerated during the crisis and EMEs seemed to respond to the crisis by pausing. The preceding section brought to the fore the initial symptoms of recovery and rebound in EMEs. One convincing indicator leading to this inference is the equity market performance in EMEs. In the first half of 2009, they gained more than 30 percent. The EMEs in Latin America gained more than 40 percent and outperformed those from other parts of the global economy (MGI, 2009). This performance is superior to that of the stock markets in advanced industrial economies and suggested the probability of strong GDP growth in 2010.

Both governments and business corporations in the EMEs did not issue much debt in the latter half of 2008 in the global financial markets, but as their early recovery efforts strengthened in the first half of 2009, their debt issuance grew. The overall impression that EMEs tended to give in the third quarter of 2009 was that these economies not only promised more than mere short-term recovery, but that their long-term drivers of growth were not debilitated. Financial markets and macroeconomic fundamentals had succeeded in maintaining their resilience not only in EMEs but also in many large developing economies. This implies that, notwithstanding the current financial crisis and recession, this group of economies will recover near-normal health in the post-crisis period relatively swiftly.

9. Did the Asian EMEs play an extraordinary role?

In the fall of 2007, when the global financial crisis began, Asia was a bastion of economic stability. The GDP growth rate for the regional economy, particularly the EMEs, was high. Many Asian EMEs enjoyed large trade surpluses and an impressive accumulation of foreign exchange reserves. Large Asian corporations were well capitalized and so were the banks. Asian banks did not have large toxic assets on their books. As the crisis deepened and spread to other parts of the global economy, the Asian economy could not escape its domino effect. Both real economy and the financial markets suffered.

The regional economy of Asia, including the export-dependent Asian EMEs, was initially hit exceedingly hard by the global financial crisis. In the early stages output contraction was greater in Asia and the Asian EMEs than that in the economies that were at the epicenter of the crisis. Four EMEs suffered particularly severe recession. They were Malaysia, Singapore, Taiwan and Thailand. However, in the second quarter of 2009 the EMEs of Asia began showing what became known as 'green shoots'. The four recession-afflicted economies also rebounded from recession during the second quarter. Subsequently, Asia began to be credited with leading the global recovery (Section 9.1).

Two of the principal factors that meaningfully contributed to Asia's early rebound were: First, Asia's forceful and comprehensive policy response and, second, near normalization of international trade and financial flows. Ironically, the export-dependent Asian EMEs rebounded at the fastest pace. Asian EMEs and the NICs did play a proactive and dynamic role in the recovery. This development motivated some analysts once again to express their belief in the old hypothesis of Asia's 'decoupling' from the rest of the global economy.

9.1 Asian EMEs and the green shoots of recovery

According to the forecasts made by the IMF (2009e), real GDP growth in EMEs will be in the vicinity of 5.1 percent in 2010, up from 1.7 in 2009.[19] Performance of EMEs in general, in the second quarter of 2009, was far superior in comparison to other economies (Section 8). This applied *a fortiori* to the export-oriented EMEs of Asia, which were undeniably severely battered by the financial crisis and recession in the initial stages. Recovery, like the earlier decline, was more pronounced in the more open EMEs of Asia, particularly in those that had a high share of high-technology manufactured products in their total exports. However, the downward slide moderated during the first half of 2009 and regional economies began improving. Their domestic demand was showing signs of strengthening. This is not to imply that industrial production in the Asian economies recovered to their pre-crisis level. Even in the fourth quarter of 2009, industrial production levels were at least 10 percent below their pre-crisis peak levels. Besides, there was substantial disparity in the levels of production recovery across the region. China, Korea and Indonesia recorded the most rapid recovery in production.

According to the IMF (2009e, p. 1), Asian EMEs were exerting a 'pulling up' force on the global recovery. During the second quarter, the Asian EMEs grew at an average annualized rate of 10 percent. According to recent forecasts, this sub-group of EMEs may well record a GDP growth rate of 5 percent for the 2009 year (*The Economist*, 2009f). As the Group-of-Seven (G-7) economies were projected to contract by 3.5 percent in 2009, the growth gap between the two groups would thus be at its widest. Interestingly, a small group of outer-oriented EMEs managed to decouple from the advanced industrial economies in this period of dire global recession.

The EMEs of Asia performed better than the rest of the global economy in the second quarter of 2009. During the third quarter, the term 'green shoots' began to be used for symptoms of recovery. Recovery first took hold in China. During the first half of 2009, Chinese economy grew by 7.1 percent in real terms; this growth was entirely driven by domestic demand. In Japan, the turnaround was not comparable to that of China. It was moderate. The other EMEs of Asia followed China and showed distinct signs of stabilization (Chapter 3, Section 7). Industrial production rebounded in Hong Kong SAR, India, Korea, the Philippines, Taiwan and Thailand. Also, financial pressures in these Asian economies had eased and business confidence was largely restored. Thus viewed, Asia had a lush jungle of the so-called green shoots. The emergence and growth of the middle-class in China, India and other Asian EMEs will continue to

drive domestic consumption of the region (Das, 2009e). China in particular was singled out by Robert Zoellick, the president of the World Bank,
for helping to prevent the global financial crisis from getting worse (AFP,
2009). It played a consequential role in leading the region out of difficulties. During the third quarter of 2009 recovery continued unabated
in this group of Asian economies.

Growth forecasts for the Asian regional economy were revised upward
in mid-September 2009 by the Asian Development Bank (ADB). According to the adjusted update, the region was projected to grow by
3.9 percent in 2009 and 6.4 percent in 2010, up from 3.4 percent and
6.0 percent, respectively (ADB, 2009). Performance of some sub-regions,
East Asian and South Asian, recorded remarkable gains, improving
prospects for the region as a whole. During the third quarter, some
glimmers of green shoots were also visible in the EU and US economies
(Chapter 3, Section 7).

Average statistics conceal a great deal of diversity in growth performance in Asia. As noted, three large Asian EMEs, China, India and
Indonesia, as well as Vietnam, had managed to continue to grow
despite the global economic downturn. Although their growth rates
were adversely affected, they did not record even one quarter of GDP
contraction or negative growth. One of the reasons was that their financial markets were among the least open. Besides, these four economies
suffered limited direct exposure to the global financial crisis. To be sure,
some of the relatively smaller Asian EMEs, for instance Hong Kong
SAR, Korea, Malaysia, Singapore, Taiwan and Thailand, were in recession and were hit hard by the global financial crisis. Of these, Korea and
Singapore rebounded vigorously in the second quarter of 2009. Part of
the reason behind the rebounding Asian EMEs was an impressive upturn
in their industrial production during the second quarter of 2009. This
upturn was assisted by an 11 percent growth in imports in China.[20] Thus
viewed, China helped in stabilizing Asian economy and Asia's EMEs in
turn were played a meaningful role in the global recovery. They evidently were leading it. The other factors that underpinned the rebound
of the Asian EMEs were aggressive monetary and fiscal easing by them
as well as the ripple effects of large stimulus programs in many other
economies around the globe.

There was an element of surprise in Asia's export-dependent EMEs
resuming growth before the rest of the global economy, particularly
the G-7 economies. The factors behind this surprising performance are:
First, aggressive domestic fiscal and monetary stimulus packages were
launched throughout the region, which helped strengthen domestic
demand. If a regional comparison is made, no other region launched

stimulus packages as large as the Asian economies. In several Asian EMEs it was as large as 4 percent of the GDP. Asian central banks loosened monetary policy and governments dramatically increased spending. China's massive 4 trillion renminbi yuan ($585 billion) stimulus package was 4.8 percent of Chinese GDP ($3.9 trillion). In terms of sheer size, it was robust and one of the largest of any economy (Chapter, Section 7.2). It was accompanied by a huge surge in government-mandated bank lending; this amounted to 7 trillion renminbi yuan between January and June 2009. This monetary expansion resulted in a huge proportion of new bank lending – almost 20 percent of the GDP. A major part of this was committed to infrastructure projects. The fiscal stimulus and credit expansion are justly credited with offsetting the export downturn, rescuing the domestic economy and propping up the regional economy.

Second, when the global recession began, most Asian economies had fairly strong macroeconomic fundamentals and a healthy budgetary situation. India was the only errant Asian economy. Budget deficit in the other Asian EMEs was low, or non-existent. By and large, inflation rates were low and current account positions were favorable. Consequently, notwithstanding reasonably sized stimulus packages, the public debt in the region would rise to a meager 45 percent of the GDP at the end of 2009. This was an indication of unassailable budgetary health. To put this in perspective, the estimates of public debt of OECD countries at the end of 2009 were double the Asian level. Third, in comparison to the advanced industrial economies, the financial sector in the Asian EMEs was robust. It provided a buffer against the global financial turmoil. Banks in the region were well-capitalized and after 1997–8 they had implemented much-needed banking reforms. Also, improved banking supervision since the crisis of 1997–8 helped limit financial contagion and the transmission of global recession. Fourth, Asian economies have traditionally been high-savers. As Asian households were not debt-ridden, fiscal and monetary stimulus was more likely to be spent by them than saved, rendering it more effective than that in the G-7 economies. That being said, as demand from the advanced industrial economies is weak and likely to continue to be so, it will be difficult for Asian economies to resume their pre-crisis growth trajectories.

9.2 Medium-term ramifications of the financial crisis on the Asian EMEs

History testifies to the fact that it is frequently difficult for economies to return to their pre-crisis growth trajectories after a recession, particularly if the recession is deep. Deep recessions, which are defined to be a 5 percentage points decline in GDP growth, usually undermine medium-term GDP growth. The historical experience of the Asian EMEs confirms this general observation. In around two-thirds of cases they did not return to their pre-crisis growth trajectories following a deep recession in the past. According to an estimate made by the IMF, average output loss in the post-crisis period for an economy was 10 percent; this proportion was a trifle higher for the Asian economies (IMF, 2009f). These estimates were based on 182 episodes of recession, which included 27 episodes of recession in Asian economies. Larger growth loss in the Asian EMEs was largely caused by significant liberalization measures taken by these economies and their rapidly increasing openness.

After the present recession ends, medium-term output losses during the post-crisis period are likely to be high in terms of GDP growth rates and loss of output. The reasons for this are sluggish recovery, weak pick-up in consumer demand in the principal export markets of the Asian EMEs as well as challenges in rebalancing growth from export sectors to domestically oriented industrial sectors. Loss of output in the post-crisis period was estimated at 2–6 percent for China and India and up to approximately 10 percent for the NIEs (IMF, 2009f). No doubt individual country experiences will vary in this regard, although the channels through which reduction in output will occur will necessarily be the same. First, reduction in investment would be the first channel, and this would lead to the erosion of productive capital stock. Second, prolonged unemployment for workers would be the second channel, which also erodes skill levels in the economy. Some of them will never be able to return to work even after the recovery takes hold. Third, profitability is reduced and credit conditions market remain stringent in the early stages of a recovery. These conditions force businesses to cut their research and development outlays, which in turn leads to depressed productivity.

9.3 China's role in propping up the rebound of the regional and global economy

For some time, China's contribution to global GDP growth has been on the rise and has been discussed in economy literature (Das, 2008d). China not only helped regional economies to stabilize and grow but also made its contribution to a nascent global recovery. After slackened growth rate in the early stages of the global financial crisis and recession, fiscal stimulus, inventory restocking and increasing final demand in the domestic economy was responsible for rising industrial production in China as well as across Asia. Both GDP growth rate and output recuperated in a V-shaped recovery. This happened before the advanced industrial economies began to show signs of recovery from the global financial crisis. The Purchasing Managers' Index also rebounded dramatically. This important index reflects business confidence in the expansion of production, sales and employment. The flip side of this argument is that there were limits to what this one economy could do in the face of feeble demand from the EU, Japan and the US. The fact that China's GDP is only a tenth of these three economies combined cannot be ignored.

10. Prospects for the global financial institutions during the credit crunch

The credit crunch that broke out during in the last quarter of 2007 took many twists and continued to worsen in 2008. Notwithstanding the uncertainty and dismal financial and economic global environment, prospects for investment banking and other financial institutions in EMEs were not gloomy. If anything the EMEs managed to remain a relatively lucrative area of financial business. Bohme et al. (2008) computed good and bad case scenarios and inferred that even in the latter case the EMEs of Asia, Latin America and the Middle East would account for absolute growth in revenues for the investing institutions. According to their projections, the collective revenue earnings from investment-banking and other capital market activities in EMEs from these regions would equal those in North America by 2010. In 2006, these EMEs had accounted for a mere half of North American revenue earnings.

There are several factors that suggested the possibility of a better performance by EMEs during the current financial crisis period than by other groups of economies. First, while the decoupling debate now seems a trifle premature, the macroeconomic environment in EMEs has remained comparatively benign. Second, the crisis-driven collapse of global demand was projected to drive multilateral exports down by 9 percent in volume terms in 2009 (WTO, 2009). Therefore, EMEs exports, particularly to the advanced industrial economies, are likely to suffer. However, their regional exports and those to other EMEs are not likely to slacken by much. This includes their exports of manufactures and commodities. In addition, the large infrastructure projects that many EMEs have launched will continue to underpin growth. Third, a new breed of transnational corporations (TNCs) has emerged in large

EMEs like Brazil, China, India, Mexico, South Africa and the United Arab Emirates (UAE). They have become users of the sophisticated banking and financial services that were demanded by the TNCs from the Western world in the past. This new type of TNCs has become an increasingly attractive fee pool for the banks and financial institutions in advanced industrial economies.

Turning to the supply side, domestic financial markets in EMEs have been steadily developing. Their growth endeavors were partly driven by intra-regional competition. An apt example of this is the rush to develop financial centers in the Middle East. Also, global banks and financial institutions have been redeploying their human and capital resources toward EMEs. They logically see EMEs as a new source of revenue. Their strategy is to nurture their EME businesses to provide a contingency for lean periods in their own domestic economies.

In a steady recovery scenario, Bohme et al. (2008) computed that the revenues of investment banks from EMEs will rise at the rate of 16 percent annually over the 2007–10 period. This group of economies will generate 28 percent of global total revenues during this period. Among various regional groups, the Asian EMEs would contribute the largest amount of revenue. They will account for 66 percent of the total revenue from EMEs, which in turn would be of something in the order of $120 billion per annum.

11. Summary and conclusions

The concept of EMEs is somewhat loosely defined, leaving it open to multiple definitions. Therefore, there are many country classifications of EME. Yet it is possible to assign certain common characteristics to EMEs. Integration of EMEs into the global financial markets has been growing, albeit not steadily. Although this group of economies have not become an integral part of the financially globalized economy, they have become active participants. It is logical to focus on the financial globalization of this group because there are important differences across their country groups in this regard, particularly in the relative importance of different types of capital inflows and the pace of financial globalization. That the extent of financial globalization in EMEs is both qualitatively and quantitatively different from other country groups can be established with the help of the *de jure* and *de facto* measures.

This chapter provided details of global private capital flows to the EMEs since the early 1970s, when the so-called oil shock struck the global economy. This had enormous significance for global financial markets. The relevant time period was divided into various sub-periods, which were analyzed independently. The characteristic features and trends for each period have been identified and analyzed. Also, the temporal evolution of capital flows to EMEs has been portrayed for each sub-period. Both qualitative and quantitative details of the financial flows and the emerging trends during each sub-period have been analyzed. The Latin American and Asian financial crises have not been analyzed in-depth but have been alluded to in the discussion of the relevant sub-periods.

The 1973 oil-price hike left many large money center banks in the US, Europe and Japan holding large sums in petro-dollar deposits. They began investing them in the EMEs, particularly those of Latin America. In the early 1980s the global economic climate changed and several factors coalesced to create serious debt-servicing problems for the Latin American EMEs. They found themselves in dire financial straits. Beginning with Mexico in August 1982, several of them declared moratoriums on their sovereign obligations. This developed into a major financial crisis of global proportion, the first in the post-World War II era. For the global financial markets, EMEs suddenly became pariahs and capital flows to them dwindled.

Toward the end of the 1980s, the gloomy relationship between the EMEs and the global capital markets began to transform. They again became a favorite investment destination. This time capital flows to the Asian EMEs surged at a rapid clip. Global private capital flows to this group of EMEs were ten times larger in the late 1980s compared to their average in the early part of the decade. The 1990s were a period of acceleration in the financial integration of EMEs. After peaking in nominal terms in 1996, net capital flows to EMEs did not recover for a while. The Asian financial crisis precipitated in 1997. Considerable tightening in emerging-market financial conditions took place after this juncture. The principal reason was obviously recurring crises in individual EMEs and country groups during 1997–8 (Section 5), which led to an increased perception of risk in them in the global private capital markets. The Asian crisis (1997–8) and the Russian default (1998) in particular had a pronounced effect on the global financial markets and the psychology of investors. At the turn of the twenty-first century global equity markets were volatile. Particularly noteworthy was the sovereign default by Argentina and subsequent deep recession in the EMEs of the western hemisphere during 2001–02.

The financial crises of the 1990s and early 2000s are a reminder of the plausibility of the argument that a financially globalized economy could be an unstable economy and that rises can also reverse financial globalization. Once these crises were over, a period of crisis-free uninterrupted growth followed. Global private market capital flows to EMEs through FDI, portfolio and international bonds were strong. The net financial flows soared at a rapid rate, reaching a peak of $617.5 billion in 2007. When they peaked, they were 5 percent of the GDP of the EMEs. However, judged by historical standards sovereign spreads were low for several years. For the majority of EMEs, external accounts swung sharply toward surpluses and their foreign exchange reserves accumulation further enlarged. EMEs learned precious lessons from the previous crises and addressed their financial vulnerabilities by correcting the currency and maturity mismatches in their national balance sheets. Some EMEs abandoned their firm exchange rate pegs, which had proved to be problematic in the past, and moved toward flexible inflation targeting. All these policy moves coalesced to create a superior fiscal and financial policy domain.

This period was known for the significant net external surplus of EMEs as well as perverse flows of global capital from EMEs to high-income industrial economies. However, this capital flow was not unilateral. While EMEs were investing in US treasury bills, they were concurrently recipients of large portfolio investments in the form of FDI and equity investment as well as international bond market investment. The majority of the EMEs were substantial net debtors in the mid-1990s. Their borrowing from the banks and from US dollar bonds was sizable. They turned into net creditors in fixed income assets, and net debtors in portfolio equity investments. This is an efficient form of financial globalization in terms of sharing international risk.

Two large EMEs, China and India, have been slowly but surely expanding their activities and prominence in the global financial markets. Both EMEs have been making their presence felt in the international capital markets. The exchange rate and capital account liberalization policies of both economies are in their evolutionary phase. Both of them are sure to undergo further financial development and liberalization. They are well on their way to having an increasing role in the global financial system as well as in private capital markets in the future.

During this crisis, the EME-6 suffered from a small foreign currency mismatch, that is, if the term mismatch is used to imply 'net short foreign currency' situation. In the past crises, extensive foreign currency mismatches caused what is known as 'fear of floating', which in turn became one of the principal causes of the crisis. Crises in Brazil, Mexico and the Russian Federation are apt examples. Due to large reserve accumulations, the EME-6 either had absolutely no foreign currency mismatches, or very few (which were therefore manageable). China and India came into the first category, while the other members of the EME-6 fell under the second. Due to large reserves, external liquidity risks were also manageable for all the EME-6. The reserves were much larger than what was needed to cover the external financing requirements for 2009, which was the cumulative sum of the current account deficit, short-term debt and long-term amortization.

Initial expectation in EMEs was that the impact of the current financial crisis would be confined to the advanced industrial economies. In the early phase of the crisis, EMEs did remain resilient and continued on their normal growth trajectory. However, in the last quarter of 2008, following the bankruptcy of Lehman Brothers, the crisis mutated into a full-blown global financial crisis. The credit crunch proliferated instantaneously through financially globalized economies. The specter of the Great Depression seemed to rise from history. EMEs were badly affected by the crisis, although not quite as badly as the advanced industrial economies. Capital flows precipitously declined in 2008. This decline is projected to continue in 2009, setting off financial deglobalization while concerns regarding external sustainability drove the sovereign spreads for EMEs sharply up.

Notes

1. The source of these statistical data is *World Development Indicators Database*, July 2009, published by the World Bank.
2. It is easy to find numerous illustrations of this fact. In February 2007 and September 2009, when the Shanghai and Shenzhen stock markets retreated, a ripple effect was felt in stock markets around the globe. They set off a wave of worldwide sell-off that spread to the EU and US markets. The impact on stock and bond markets and currencies in EMEs was particularly bad. They fell due to concern regarding economic growth in China.
3. The source of these statistical data is *World Development Indicators Database*, 1 July 2009, published by the World Bank.
4. The acronym BRIC stands for Brazil, the Russian Federation, India and China. It came in use in 2001 for the emerging economic powerhouses.
5. Numerous research papers were published in various journals on the theme of decoupling. The *World Economic Outlook*, April 2007, devoted an entire chapter to this theme; see Chapter 4, pp. 121–160.
6. The 23 countries on the IMF list classified as EMEs are: Argentina, Brazil, Chile, China, Colombia, the Czech Republic, Hungary, Hong Kong SAR, India, Indonesia, the Republic of Korea, Malaysia, Mexico, Peru, the Philippines, Poland, the Russian Federation, Singapore, South Africa, Taiwan, Thailand, Turkey and Venezuela.

7. See also Kose et al. (2006).
8. Das (2004) compiled and reported these statistical data from the *World Economic Outlook* for various years.
9. Ibid.
10. The Asian crisis started in Thailand, but the contagion effect soon gripped other Asian economies and subsequently the region. The Thai baht collapsed due to the decision of the Thai government to float it, cutting its peg to the dollar.
11. This group comprised Argentina, Brazil, Chile, China, India, Indonesia, the Republic of Korea, Malaysia, Mexico, the Russian Federation, Thailand and Turkey.
12. Das (2004) compiled and reported these statistical data from the *World Economic Outlook* for various years.
13. The source of these statistical data is *World Development Indicators Database*, July 2009, published by the World Bank.
14. In April 2009, China's stock of foreign exchange reserves crossed the $2 trillion mark. In December 2009 they were $2.3 trillion, which was 23.3 percent of total global reserves.
15. The source of statistics in this section is the IMF (2009a).
16. Concerns about the overheating of the economy had prompted the Chinese government to clamp down restraining policies since early 2007. Credit flows to several large sectors, including construction, were curbed. Credit restraints caused the economy to decelerate sharply even before the global financial crisis started.
17. See Table 1, IMF (2009d), p. 2.
18. The SDR or Special Drawing Rights are based on the weighted average of the dollar, euro, yen and pound. The SDR was designed as a reserve currency, but it never took off. In 2009, SDR added up to less than 1 percent of total global reserves.
19. See Chapter 1, Table 1, p. 2 (IMF, 2009e).
20. This increase took place during one year, between July 2008 and July 2009.

References

Agence France-Presse (AFP). 2009. "World Bank Chief Says China Stimulus Should Continue". 9 September. Available on the Internet at http://www.google.com/hostednews/afp/article/ALeqM5jp2zZO9hHz2SgVQ7g_vptcRXP71g. 10 October 2009.

Asian Development Bank (ADB). 2009. *Asian Development Outlook 2009: Update*. Manila. 17 September.

Bohme, M., D. Chiarella and M. Lemerle. 2008. "The Growing Opportunities for Investment Banks in Emerging Markets". *The McKinsey Quarterly*. August. Available on the Internet at http://www.mckinseyquarterly.com/article_print.aspx?L2=10&l3=51&AR=2183. 15 January 2009.

Bradford, C. and J. Linn. 2009. "Welcome to the New Era of G-20 Global Leadership" in K. Dervis (ed.) *G-20- Summit: Recovering from the Crisis*. Washington. DC. Brookings Institution. pp. 16–18.

Ciarlone, A., P. Piselli and G. Trebeschi. 2009. "Emerging Market' Spread and Global Financial Conditions". *Journal of International Financial markets, Institutions and Money.* Vol. 19. No. 1. pp. 222–239.

Das, Dilip K. 2009a. *The Two Faces of Globalization: Munificent and Malevolent.* Northampton. MA. USA and Cheltenham. Glos. UK. Edward Elgar Publishing, Inc.

Das, Dilip K. 2009c. "Globalization and an Emerging Global Middle Class". *Economic Affairs.* London. Vol. 29. No. 3. pp. 89–99.

Das, Dilip K. 2008d. *The Chinese Economic Renaissance: Apocalypse or Cornucopia.* Palgrave Macmillan Ltd. Houndmills, Hampshire, UK. 2008.

Das, Dilip K. 2008e. "China's Newly Evolving Role in the Global Economy". *CESifo Forum.* Vol. 9. No. 1. Munich. April. pp. 39–46.

Das, Dilip K. 2006. *China and India: A Tale of Two Economies.* London and New York. Routledge.

Das, Dilip K. 2004. *Financial Globalization and the Emerging Market Economies.* London and New York. Routledge.

Das, Dilip K. 2003. "Financial Flows and Global Integration". Coventry. UK. University of Warwick. Center for the Study of Globalization and Regionalization. CSGR. Working Paper No. 132/04. June.

Dattels, P. and K. Miyajima. 2009. "Will Emerging Markets Remain Resilient to Global Stress?" *Global Journal of Emerging Market Economies.* Vol. 1. No. 1. pp. 5–24.

Devereux, M.B. and A. Sutherland. 2009. "A Portfolio Moel of Capital Flows to Emerging Markets". *Journal of Development Economics.* Vol. 89. No. 2. pp. 181–193.

The Economist. 2009c. "From Slump to Jump". 1 August. p. 16.

The Economist. 2009e. "Gone Shopping". 30 May. p. 65.

The Economist. 2009f. "On the Rebound". 15 August. pp. 69–72.

Edison, H.J. and F.E. Warnock. 2003. "A Simple Measure of the Intensity of Capital Controls". *Journal of Empirical Finance.* Vol. 10. No. 1. pp. 81–103.

Gyntelberg, J. 2009. "Highlights of International Banking and Financial Market Activity". *BIS Quarterly Review.* June. pp. 19–34.

Institute of International Finance (IIF). 2009. "Capital Flows to Emerging Market Economies". Washington. DC. 27 January.

The International Monetary Fund (IMF). 2009a. *World Economic Outlook.* Washington. DC. April.

The International Monetary Fund (IMF). 2009b. *World Economic Outlook Database.* Washington. DC. January.

The International Monetary Fund (IMF). 2009c. *Global Financial Stability Report.* Washington. DC. April.

The International Monetary Fund (IMF). 2009d. *World Economic Outlook Update.* Washington. DC. 8 July.

The International Monetary Fund (IMF). 2009e. *World Economic Outlook.* Washington. DC. October.

The International Monetary Fund (IMF). 2009f. "Regional Economic Outlook: Asia and Pacific". Washington. DC. October.

The International Monetary Fund (IMF). 2008d. *World Economic Outlook.* Washington. DC. October.

Joyce, J.P. 2009. "Financial Globalization and Banking Crises in Emerging Markets". Wellesley. MA. Wellesley College. Department of Economics. Working Paper. January.

Kaminsky, G. 2005. "International Capital Flows, Financial Stability and Growth". Washington. DC. George Washington University. The GW Center for the Study of Globalization. Occasional paper Series. December.

Kaminsky, G. and S.L. Schmukler. 2003. "Short-Term Pain, Long-Term Gain: The Effects of Financial Liberalization". Cambridge. MA. National Bureau of Economic Research. NBER Working Paper No. 9787. June.

Kose, M.A. and E.S. Prasad. 2009. "The Decoupling is Back!" Washington. DC. Brookings Institution. Available on the Internet at http://www.foreignpolicy.com/story/cms.php?story_id=5010&print=1. 12 June 2009.

Kose, M.A., E.S. Prasad, K.S. Kogoff and S.J. Wei. 2009. "Financial Globalization and Economic Policies". Washington. DC. The Brookings Institution. Working Paper No. 24. April.

Kose, M.A., C. Otrok and E.S. Prasad. 2008. "Global Business Cycles: Convergence or Decoupling?" Cambridge. MA. National Bureau of Economic Research. Working Paper No. 14292. October.

Lane, P.R. 2009. "The Global Crisis and Capital Flows to Emerging Markets" in M. Dewatripont and X. Freixas (eds) *Macroeconomic Stability and Financial Regulation*. London. Centre for Economic Policy Research. pp. 27–48.

Lane, P.R. and G.M. Milesi-Ferretti. 2007. "The External Wealth of Nations Mark II". *Journal of International Economics*. Vol. 73. No. 2. pp. 223–250.

Lane, P.R. and G.M. Milesi-Ferretti. 2005. "A Global Position on External Positions". Dublin. Institute for International Integration Studies. Trinity College. IIIS Discussion Paper No. 79. December.

Lane, P.R. and S.L. Schmukler 2007. "The Evolving Role of China and India in the Global Financial System". *Open Economies Review*. Vol. 18. No. 4. pp. 499–520.

Leijonhufvud, C. 2007. "Financial Globalization and Emerging Market Volatility". *The World Economy*. Vol. 30. No. 12. pp. 1817–1842.

McKinsey Global Institute (MGI). 2009. *Global Capital Markets: Entering a New Era*. San Francisco. September.

Mizen, P. 2008. "The Credit Crunch of 2007–2008: A Discussion of the Background". *Federal Reserve Bank of St. Louis Review*. Vol. 50. No. 5. pp. 531–567.

Obstfeld, M., J. Shambaugh and A. Taylor. 2008. "Financial Stability, the Trilemma and International Reserves". Cambridge. MA. National Bureau of Economic Research. Working Paper No. 14217. June.

Prahalad, C.K. 2004. *Fortune at the Bottom of the Pyramid*. Philadelphia. PA. Wharton School Publishing.

Prasad, E.S. and M.A. Kose. 2009. "The Financial Crisis and Emerging Markets". Washington. DC. Brookings Institution. Available on the Internet at http://www.brookings.edu/opinions/2008/0924_emerging_markets_prasad.aspx?p=1. 13 July 2009.

Pula, G. and T.A. Pultonen. 2009. "Has Emerging Asia Decoupled?" Frankfurt. Germany. European Central Bank. Working Paper Series 993. January 2009.

Schmukler, S.L. and E. Vesperoni. 2006. "Financial Globalization and Debt Maturity in Emerging Economies". *The Journal of Development Economics*. Vol. 79. No. 1. pp. 183–218.

Subramanian, A. 2009. "The G-20: An Idea from India". *The Business Standard.* New Delhi. 28 September. p. 12.

Turner, P. 2008. "Financial Globalization and Emerging Market Capital Flows". Bank for International Settlements. Basel. BIS Paper No. 44. December.

Wang, Q., D. Yam and S. Zhang. 2009. "Upgrade on Stronger-Than-Expected Policy Response". *Global Economic Forum.* New York. Morgan Stanley. 24 April. Available on the Internet at http://www.morganstanley.com/views/gef/archive/2009/20090424-Fri.html#anchor682cdf04-419f-11de-a1b3-c771ef8db296.

Winters, L.A. and S. Yusuf. 2007. *Dancing with Giants.* Washington. DC. The World Bank.

The World Bank (WB). 2009a. *Global Development Finance 2009: Charting a Global Recovery.* Washington. DC. 22 June.

The World Bank (WB). 2009b. *World Development Indicator.* Washington. DC. July 2009.

World Trade Organization (WTO). 2009. "World Trade 2008, Prospects for 2009". Geneva. 23 March. PRESS/554.

5
Macroeconomic Ramifications of Financial Globalization

1. Stylized theoretical perspective

This chapter essentially concentrates on the macroeconomics of financial globalization. It examines the role played by macroeconomic policy measures and establishes the leaders and followers of financial globalization. It provides a macroeconomic assessment of the impact of global financial integration over economies that are undergoing financial integration. The principal issues it focuses on are as follows: It begins with examining the evidence of whether financial globalization elevates growth performance of the integrating economy and supports it macroeconomic stability. It takes a nuanced view and divides the impact of financial integration into direct and indirect benefits. Second, it scrutinizes whether there are some threshold conditions, that is, in their presence and with their support financial globalization underpins growth and stability of the capital importing economy and in their absence it cannot. Third, it delves into the oft-cited allegation of financial globalization being a source of macroeconomic volatility and eventually financial crises. Fourth, as the evidence that emerged regarding the ability of financial globalization to underpin growth was unambiguous, it examines the policy mandarins' options. Lastly, the macro-financial dynamics of global surpluses and deficits has evolved as a problematic issue, which has also been addressed in this chapter.

As global financial integration progressed during the contemporary period, financial globalization became the principal driving mechanism for the global allocation of productive resources. During the contemporary phase of financial globalization, the following queries became progressively prominent and meaningful: Does integrating into the global financial market spur growth and stability in an economy that is endeavoring to do so? Is financial globalization, or the integration of global financial markets, beneficial and growth-promoting for the globalizing economy in particular and for the global economy in general? From a theoretical perspective, one can state that financial globalization implies access to a large reservoir of capital, which if invested prudently and pragmatically increases growth. A second equally plausible answer could be that the integration of financial markets can potentially foster efficient global resource allocation, provide opportunities for risk diversion and underpin financial sector development, which in turn can potentially underpin growth endeavors. The emphasis here is on a 'theoretical' perspective. Theoretical, and for the most part, empirical researches have found that while financial globalization can be growth-promoting and welfare-enhancing, it may not necessarily be so.

Theoretical literature in this regard is ambiguous. Whether growth benefits outweigh the costs and risks is an unsettled issue. No doubt several major channels can be identified through which financial globalization can raise output and productivity in the globalizing economy. While it can be growth-promoting in an ideal or highly disciplined macroeconomic policy environment, in a real life policy environment which may include macroeconomic distortions, its impact may well be negative and result in costly crises (Stiglitz, 2004). Negative side effects frequently spin off from financial globalization in economies that suffer from macroeconomic distortions. The principal question for policy mandarins is why does financial globalization work favorably in some cases and counterproductively in others.

1.1 Macroeconomic policy relevance

Financial globalization or global integration is a subject that has compelling macroeconomic and policy relevance for both the economy that is undertaking these policy measures as well as for the global economy. The driving forces of financial globalization have varied from changes in the economic philosophy of the policy making community to apt domestic political circumstances in the economy adopting global financial integration. This is an intriguing and engrossing area of academic research because of the large array of approaches taken by economies in integrating with global financial markets. These differing approaches resulted in a wide range of experiences and outcomes across countries and country groups. As the present phase of financial globalization is of recent vintage, the academic research in this area is for the most part relatively new. That said, the accepted wisdom on financial globalization has rapidly evolved and the output of scholarly research during the last two decades is nothing short of massive. A large empirical literature analyzes the impact of financial globalization on output and volatility, although it dwells less on productivity growth.

There is little unanimity in the views in the economic profession regarding the macroeconomic implications of financial globalization. Positions have ranged from decidedly favorable to entirely unfavorable. There are many who reached mixed conclusions. The debate on this imperious subject is yet to end on any side of the divide. The failure of empirical studies to come to an agreement has made those who oppose financial globalization and regard it as a source of macroeconomic and financial instability more certain of their negative perspective. One group of noted economists considers swift liberalization of capital account and unrestrained inflows of capital from the global private capital markets serious impediments to growth and macroeconomic and financial stability. Jagdish Bhagwati, a proponent of economic globalization, is thoroughly skeptical about the benefits of financial globalization. Distinguished scholars like Dani Rodrik and Joseph Stiglitz have written at length on this theme and have both advocated caution in the opening up of the capital account and drawn attention to the macroeconomic benefits of maintaining capital controls. The string of crises that occurred in individual and regional economies made their case rationally strong, as did the current global recession, which was christened by the financial media 'the crash of 2008'.

Contrary to this opinion, there are equally eminent economists who regard financial integration as growth-promoting and welfare-enhancing. They hold the view that free trans-border flows of global capital can make a decisive contribution to economic growth and strongly support economies' upgrade from low- to middle- and then eventually to high-income status. This group subscribes to the allocative efficiency logic and is convinced that financial integration supports macroeconomic stabilization of global, regional and individual economies. Kenneth Rogoff, Stanley Fischer, Frederic Mishkin and Larry Summers are prominent among this group of thinkers.

1.2 Leaders and followers in financial integration

The advanced industrial economies, or majority of the 30 members of the Organization for Economic Cooperation and Development (OECD), were the leaders in liberalizing capital account over the preceding three decades. Consequently, they globalized their economies, including their financial markets before other economies. Many attribute efficiency gains in advanced industrial economies, increased diversification and robust development of the financial sector to the liberalization of capital accounts and markets (Edison et al., 2002). This group of economies is presently financially well-integrated into the global economy. However, the exceptions in this regard are the following OECD members: the Czech Republic, Hungary, Mexico, Poland, Slovakia and Turkey. All of these economies fall under the category of the emerging-market economies (EMEs). Although these and other EMEs cannot be regarded as well-integrated into the global economy, they have been taking definitive policy measures to liberalize their capital accounts and financially globalize.

The European EMEs accelerated their move toward financial globalization in the present decade. Some of them are considered to be impetuous in decision-making in this regard. They liberalized their capital accounts somewhat hastily and therefore were open to the accusation that they had made themselves macroeconomically vulnerable. Conversely, China and India have also been taking steps toward capital account liberalization, but cautiously and in a calibrated manner. Some regard them as overly cautious. Essentially, due to persisting weaknesses in their financial markets, these two economies did not plunge headlong into the capital account liberalization process (Das, 2008d; Prasad, 2009). Many other EMEs and middle-income developing economies are following suit and are in the initial stages of capital account liberalization and financial globalization. All these economies are coming to grips with policy decisions regarding the timing and pace of financial globalization.

There is an imperious need for clear thinking and meticulous policy moves regarding these issues. Experience shows that global financial integration is a contentious and error prone policy area. When errors do occur, they have high economic and social costs. Unregulated capital inflows, regardless of the liberalization process, did facilitate precipitations of crises. A survey of empirical cross-country studies on the effect of capital account liberalization on growth reported mixed results from various country exercises (Edison et al., 2002). One reason for ambiguity in the conclusions of various empirical studies is the difficulty in identifying and quantifying capital account liberalization in a consistent manner across a sprawling range of countries. Appropriate and sequential macroeconomic and financial policies are essential for effectively managing capital account liberalization and financial globalization. These measures are warranted to ensure growth and stability benefits in economies that are endeavoring to financially globalize as well as to minimize the potential costs. This chapter delves into and explores such a policy structure.

1.3 Neoclassical logic versus the recent nuanced ideas

As regards the effect of financial globalization, the well-trodden neoclassical economic line of logic is simple and direct. Trans-border capital flows from countries that have surplus savings and are capital rich to those where capital is scarce and is badly needed. In fragmented financial markets such financial flows are not possible. The neoclassical economic argument is that the liberalization of capital account allows global capital to flow into the capital-scarce economies, which lowers the cost of capital for them; it increases domestic investment, growth and welfare-gains. As capital is regarded as a necessary, albeit not solely sufficient, ingredient for growth, external capital from global private capital markets is indeed valuable and contributes to the growth endeavors of the recipient developing economy by augmenting their rate of investment.

This neoclassical view draws heavily on the predictions of the standard neoclassical growth model pioneered by Robert Solow (1956). Capital-rich economies that are the source of trans-border capital flows, also register welfare gains from higher rates of returns on their investment. This is because the marginal product of capital is higher in the capital-scarce less-developed economies. The source economies also enjoy the benefits of reduced risk through international portfolio diversification. One basic point regarding this is that the state of development and efficiency of legal and market institutions differ from country to country. As these differences affect the rate of return on foreign investments, they determine the *ex ante* behavior of the global investing community.

Newer ideas on this vital issue are fairly different from the simple neoclassical thinking set out in the preceding paragraph. Recent literature takes issue with this seemingly simplistic line of logic in a fundamental manner. It takes a more subtle line than the one-channel impact of financial globalization and posits that the link between financial globalization and economic growth and stability is not so direct. Although there is a link, it is indirect (Section 2). In its indirect role, financial globalization plays a catalytic role and thereby underpins economic growth. Benefits of global financial integration do not primarily flow through access to global financial markets, as the neoclassical economies hypothesized. The newer view is that there are myriad plausible channels through which indirect benefits can materialize.

2. Direct and indirect channels of macroeconomic impact: Empirical evidence

Numerous cross-sectional, panel and event studies were conducted in the recent past to examine whether financially integrated economies perform better economically, and whether financial sector liberalization and integration into the global financial markets have a definitive and convincing positive impact on the economic performance of developing and emerging-market economies. These researches add up to a considerable empirical effort. Explorations of a macroeconomic link between financial liberalization and economic growth have resulted in a large research harvest. As a representative study, Gourinchas and Jeanne (2006, p. 716) can be cited. They used a calibrated neoclassical model that conventionally measured gains from this type of convergence. They found that the gains from international financial integration were 'elusive'. These empirical studies failed to clinch the case for capital account liberalization. For the most part their conclusions were mixed, occasionally even paradoxical. An exhaustive and meticulous literature review by Kose et al. (2009a) concluded that the evidence regarding a link between global financial integration and growth is inconclusive. When it is there, it lacks robustness.

The end result is that at the macroeconomic level, it has been difficult to find 'unambiguous evidence that financial opening yields a net improvement in economic performance' Obstfeld (2009, p. 103). Econometric difficulties in studying this relationship are of the same kind that beleaguered the study of trade-growth link for decades, only they are more severe in case of international finance-growth link. Empirical evaluation is rendered more difficult by the lumping together of financial reforms and liberalization with a host of other growth-supporting macroeconomic reforms as well as the endogeneity of the financial liberalization process itself. One way of squaring this circle was to study the direct and indirect impact of global capital flows, independently, on financially integrating economies.

At the outset the direct macroeconomic impact of capital inflows was regarded as favorable and substantive. This view was essentially premised on the neoclassical economic logic. However, it subsequently underwent a dramatic transformation. In the following section we shall analyze the direct and indirect macroeconomic impact of capital flows.

2.1 Direct benefit

As regards the direct, or single-channel, benefit of financial globalization, *prima facie* evidence is available to show that financial globalization did lead to rapid GDP growth. Theoretically, it is the financial channel through which the direct benefit of global capital inflows can be reaped. That is to say, that the global capital inflows and GDP growth do seem to have a positive association. As alluded to in Chapter 3, Section 2.2, the very fact that since 1970 EMEs have achieved much higher cumulative growth than the other two country groups and have made an economic niche for themselves in the global economy, agrees with the fact that liberalizing an economy, particularly through capital account and the financial sector, does lead to rapid GDP growth.

Notwithstanding such broad evidence, numerous scatter diagrams plotting long-term average growth rates and *de facto* financial sector openness show little systematic relationship between the two variables. As stated above (Section 2), macroeconomic evidence of financial integration leading to systematic higher GDP growth in developing economies is weak, particularly when one controls for other variables for growth. Empirical cross-country studies failed to establish a clear link between economic growth and financial opening. An early influential empirical study by Rodrik (1998a) has been extensively cited in the literature to demonstrate the insignificant impact of capital account liberalization and financial integration on economic growth. His conclusion was that 'capital controls are essentially uncorrelated with long-term economic performance' (Rodrik, 1998a, p. 9).

In addition, empirical researches by several other analysts failed to confirm any robust impact of financial liberalization on growth.[1] They concurred with Rodick's well-known conclusions. Little discernible growth effect of financial globalization was found by Edwards (2001). Other scholars went a step further and argued that the record of financial globalization on growth is disappointing and that recipient developing countries failed to show noteworthy growth benefits (Aizenman and Pinto, 2004; Gourinchas and Jeanne, 2006; Tobin, 2000). When an association is found between the two variables, it is usually exceedingly weak. Several computations of cross-country growth regressions in economic literature remained either inconclusive or produced weak results toward confirming that economies that integrate into global financial markets grew faster.

The research department of the International Monetary Fund (IMF), which used to be a compelling proponent of capital account liberalization, spent a good deal of time and resources on this intricate policy issue. They also concluded that a large number of empirical studies provided little robust evidence of a causal relationship between financial integration and financial openness on one side and economic growth on the other (Kose et al., 2009a). Due to differences in approach and econometric techniques, it is difficult to synthesize the conclusions of these studies. Although they started with cross-country growth models, their sample countries differed and so did their time periods.

In contrast to the above-cited empirical literature, Quinn (1997) and Henry (2000) supported the relationship between liberalization to the global capital markets and economic growth and argued in favor of a direct link. Among the empirical studies that focused on the direct channel of impact of financial globalization, those that selected finer *de jure* measures of financial openness as the independent variable came up with relatively more positive results of financial globalization on economic growth. For instance, Quinn and Toyoda (2008) selected refined *de jure* measures of capital account openness for 94 countries between 1950–2004; they did come up with a positive link between the two variables, that is, capital account liberalization and financial openness and growth. They asserted that measurement errors, differing time periods used, and collinearity among independent variables accounted for conflicting conclusions in earlier empirical studies. They also confirmed that equity market liberalization has had an independently positive effect on economic growth. In addition, the empirical studies that utilized both *de jure* and *de facto* measures as independent variables found greater support for the direct effect of financial integration on growth. However, the conclusions of these empirical exercises also varied due to differences in methodology, time periods, sample countries, the data sets and collinearity among independent variables.[2]

Growth benefits from financial globalization also depend on the composition of financial flows. Global capital inflows of equity such as foreign direct investment (FDI) and portfolio equity investments, were known for the following two characteristics. First, they are more stable and second, they are less prone to reversals. In addition, as stated in the following section, additional benefits accompanied this type of financial flows. Conversely, debt flows, particularly those that come in the form of short-term bank loans, tended to be volatile and enlarge the negative impact of external shocks on GDP growth.

Turning to FDI, transnational corporations (TNCs) as major FDI investors bring in knowledge and expertise, which in turn spills over into the domestic industrial firms, and increases their productivity. This intra-industry spillover is known as horizontal spillover and is the micro channel of positive productivity impact. It can also occur through contacts between the foreign affiliate and their local suppliers and customers, which is called the vertical linkage. Although evidence of horizontal spillover in the transmission of productivity benefits was found to be inconclusive, Javorcik (2004) found evidence of productivity spillover through vertical linkages.

Several empirical studies found productivity enhancing effects of FDI using microeconomic – both firm- and sector-level – statistical data (Haskell et al., 2007). FDI was found to favorably affect an economy's productive efficiency (Xu, 2000). Using an annual panel dataset of 83 developing and advanced industrial economies, Noy and Vu (2007) found that liberalizing capital account was not a sufficient condition to generate increases in FDI inflows. It was the domestic economic environment in the host economy which influenced the quantity of FDI far more. In particular, variables like a low level of corruption in the government systems and political stability were important.

Equity markets witnessed a general liberalizing trend across a number of economies. Consequently, the portfolio equity component of global financial flows has expanded rapidly, particularly into EMEs. These equity flows were found to favorably impact GDP growth rate and other macroeconomic variables like consumption, investment, exports and imports. Henry and Sasson (2008) also provided evidence of the favorable impact of global capital inflows through equity markets. Using a sample of 18 developing countries that opened their equity markets to global capital inflows, they reported an increase in both the growth rate of labor productivity and real wages. Bekaert and Lundblad (2005) found that global capital flows by way of portfolio equity increased growth rate by approximately 1 percent in the recipient economy. For the most part, empirical research in this area reported notable positive effects from equity market liberalization. When global capital flows through stock markets, the cost of capital in the recipient economy declines, boosting domestic investment and eventually spurring growth (Alfaro and Hammel, 2007). However, these estimates of growth effect are not beyond doubt. Positive growth effect could well emanate from the general macroeconomic reforms that go with equity market liberalization.

Some studies related global financial flows through equity markets to microeconomic benefits and improvements in total factor productivity (TFP) (Chari and Henry, 2008; Mitton, 2006).

There is a general agreement among the empirical studies regarding the deleterious effect of debt flows. Substantive empirical literature on this issue has been studied by Berg et al. (2004). These empirical studies are by and large unanimous in their conclusion that global capital inflows in the form of short-term debt caused a categorical deterioration of the benefit-risk tradeoff. Many found a direct and systemic relationship between exposure to short-term debt and increased odds of a crisis. In addition, some of them inferred that the larger the short-tem debt the more severe the crisis caused by it. A point to note here is that countries with low credit ratings are often left with few options and have to rely on short-term debt (Eichengreen et al., 2006).

Thus viewed, the overall empirical evidence regarding the direct, single-channel impact of financial globalization on growth is weak, tentative and inconclusive. The neoclassical theory is not buttressed by empirical evidence. Financial integration does not robustly support GDP growth and stability in the globally integrating economy.

2.2 Uphill capital flows: A question mark on the neoclassical proposition

There is a twenty-first century phenomenon, which puts a question mark on the neoclassical proposition. It is the recent change in the direction of capital flows. Financial globalization has taken an unusual turn over the past several years. Since 2002, sizable sums of capital have been flowing from non-industrial countries to advanced industrial countries. Capital flows from economies with a low capital-labor ratio to those with a high capital-labor ratio is an apparent perversion from the perspective of neoclassical economic thought. From the neoclassical perspective, the normal flow of capital is from the rich high capital-labor ratio economies to poor, low capital-labor ratio economies.

In a seminal paper, Lucas (1990) was the first to focus on the capital flows between countries with different capital-labor ratios. He posited that due to low levels of human capital and factor productivity, return on capital invested in low-income developing countries may well be low. In addition, legal and institutional obstacles and market failure frequently impede capital from flowing toward developing economies. These impeding factors rendered them unattractive destinations for global capital.[3] In contrast, the productivity of capital in high-income industrial economies is high therefore capital from the international financial markets would logically flow toward them. This perverse capital flow was termed the Lucas paradox.

This paradox portends to an apparent 'wealth bias' in global capital flows and international investment pattern. That is, a low-income country is less likely to receive and benefit from international investment (Clemens and Williamson, 2004). The results of regression analysis show that higher initial GDP per capita was statistically positively associated with higher capital inflows. This observation applies to financial integration during the earlier pre-World War I era as well as to the contemporary period. High-income countries tend to attract more global capital inflows. Inter-temporally, capital inflows from the global markets and per capita income were more closely co-related during the contemporary period of financial integration than they were in the pre-World War I era. Per capita GDP accounted for 15 percent of the variation of capital inflows per head during the classical period. However, this relationship is much stronger in the contemporary period, as 70 percent of the variation is accounted for by per capita income (Schularick, 2006).

This wealth bias took another turn during the contemporary period of global integration and grew more relevant. There was a rapid rise in the foreign exchange reserves held by developing economies, particularly EMEs, during the 1990s. The myriad crises that precipitated during this period convinced the policy mandarins in developing countries that they could neither rely on the IMF nor wait for reforms in the global financial architecture. Also, it was not enough to count on sound macroeconomic policies because even well-managed economies could be damaged by contagions in other parts of the global economy. Therefore, their best option was to accumulate large reservoirs of forex to ward off future crises. This was a defensive strategy of self-protection through liquidity. It was believed that large accumulations of liquidity would enable economies to withstand any future financial market turmoil better. It was believed that large forex reserves would also prepare economies against the risk of sudden stops and reversals in global capital flows.

The direct consequence of this line of logic was that the forex reserves held by developing economies and EMEs began to increase. In 2009 they were at an all-time high level. If measured as a proportion of GDP or trade the reserves of developing economies and EMEs are several multiples higher than those held by advanced industrial economies. In absolute terms, according to the IMF statistics of March 2009, of the total $6.5 trillion global reserves, $2.4 trillion were held by advanced industrial economies, while $4.1 trillion by developing economies and EMEs.[4] This needs to be compared to the level of forex reserves of developing countries and EMEs in 2000. At $689 billion, these reserves were three-fifths of the amount held by advanced industrial economies.

There is a high social cost to maintaining such high levels of forex reserves. Rodrik (2006) calculated that the cost amounted to more than 1 percentage point of GDP annually for the two groups of economies that maintained them. There was another disadvantage. Some believe that high levels of reserves held by a group of developing and emerging-market economies created global financial and payments imbalances. This group of economies was blamed for the creation of excess liquidity that subsequently swept through global financial markets (Wolf, 2008a). This subsidized interest rates and consumption in the US and created the macroeconomic backdrop for the current global financial crisis.

During the recent period, capital flows from EMEs, particularly those from Asia, and the members of the Gulf Cooperation Council to advanced industrial economies, particularly the US, went on increasing. Owing to the capital account surpluses of these two groups of developing economies the 'world was awash in cheap money, looking for somewhere to go' (Krugman, 2009, p. 16). This so-called 'uphill' flow of finance was largely between governments (Wolf, 2008b). The US went on a borrowing and consumption binge while the saving glut in the global economy, particularly by the EMEs, stoked asset prices (Rodrik, 2008). This uphill flow of capital weakened and obscured the logic of direct impact.

A good part of this uphill capital flow from non-industrial to advanced industrial economies was the official international reserves of these capital-exporting developing countries, particularly the EMEs. However, from a solely financial perspective the net effect is that of reducing the availability of capital for investment in a capital-exporting developing economy or an EME. Flow of capital is in the direction of the richer economies where, given the relative abundance of capital, its marginal productivity will necessarily be lower. An appropriate question is whether this perverse flow of capital is adversely affecting the growth performance in the capital exporting economies. In the preceding section, I have noted that the EMEs have achieved a much higher cumulative growth than the other two country groups (Prasad, 2007). This demonstrates that the perverse capital flows did not deteriorate the growth performance in the capital exporting EMEs (See Chapter 5, Section 2.5).

2.3 Indirect benefit

The indirect channels work as follows. First, by liberalizing the domestic financial sector the economies facilitate proper and methodological development of their domestic financial sector. Financial integration enables a developing economy to develop 'a more complete, deeper, more stable and better regulated financial market' (Schmukler, 2008, p. 49). In many developing economies this development of the financial sector generally begins from a rather low level. Financial sector development makes a decisive contribution to economic growth (Levine, 2005; Levine and Zervos, 1998; Mishkin, 2009). A well-functioning financial system mobilizes credit and promotes economic growth. There is nothing novel about this proposition. For over a century, the relationship between financial sector development and economic growth has been emphasized in the writings of prominent economists. Bagehot (1873) and Schumpeter (1912) rationalized and underscored the role of the banking sector in underpinning the growth process.

Second, to liberalize and financially globalize, economies launch into macroeconomic reforms and restructuring. These measures render macroeconomic policies more disciplined than before and thus are conducive to rapid economic growth. Macroeconomic distortions and their pernicious effect become more obvious in an open liberalized economy, making it easy to identify and eliminate them (Gourinchas and Jeanne, 2005). By liberalizing economically and financially, economies commit to well-ordered and disciplined macroeconomic policies. This is their signal to the world that they are changing tack and that their economic future is more than likely to be different from their past, when they followed sub-optimal macroeconomic strategies and paid a high cost in terms of tepid growth and decrepitude (Bartolini and Drazen, 1997). Third, opening up the economy creates efficiency gains in the domestic corporate sector. As business and financial firms are exposed to competition from the more efficient businesses in advanced industrial economies they are forced to become more efficient themselves. Fourth, studies based on different methodologies demonstrate that as more foreign banks enter the domestic banking sector, competing with them made the domestic banks more efficient, reduced overhead costs and improved profits (Claessens and Laeven, 2004; Schmukler, 2004). Fifth, Likewise stock markets become larger and more liquid after they are liberalized for the entry of global investors (Levine and Zervos, 1998). Liberalization also catalyzes legal and institutional developments in the equity markets (Chinn and Ito, 2006). Lastly, an environment of better public and corporate governance gradually evolves which works toward underpinning growth rate in the liberalizing and globalizing economy (Stulz, 2005).

Thus, financial globalization can indirectly impact through catalyzing different growth-supporting areas of macroeconomic policy and institutions. The principal channels of indirect impact are the domestic financial sector, efficiency gains in public and corporate governance and macroeconomic policy discipline. This indirect effect, or multiple-channel benefits, may well be more important than the tradition financing-channel effect emphasized in neoclassical economics.[5]

Together these indirect effects add up to a significant range of benefits that begin to transform the financially globalizing economy. Kose et al. (2009b, p. 3) designated them as 'collateral' benefits and regarded them as quantitatively the 'most important sources of enhanced growth and stability for a country engaged in financial globalization'. In addition, the single-channel impact, that works by way of augmentation of finance and investment, could have a mere short-term economic impact. Conversely, the multiple-channel or indirect effect of financial globalization can have a long-term impact on the economy (Henry, 2007). Furthermore, certain kinds of global financial flows are accompanied by advance technology, managerial skills and marketing proficiency, all of which are sorely needed in a developing economy. These also have a healthy growth-promoting effect over the financially globalizing economy. Once technological and other know-how reach the recipient economies, they begin to develop the capacity to absorb and adapt them. With the passage of time, they develop capabilities to generate their own technological competencies and managerial skills, indispensable for a modern economy.

Although not many empirical studies addressed the issue of the impact on financial institutions, some indications of improvements in them is available. For instance, countries were found to have made adjustments in their corporate governance in response to demands from international investors (Cornelius and Kogut, 2003). Economies open to financial integration do need to prepare macroeconomically by designing and implementing reforms and restructuring. They generally pay a lot of attention to monetary policy and keep inflation low (Gupta and Yuan, 2009; Spiegel, 2008). No relationship was found between financial integration and fiscal discipline. One cannot assume a positive or a negative link here, although there is always a possibility of running higher fiscal deficits for a longer period with global capital inflows.

The indirect channels of macroeconomic impact can coalesce to 'enhance the growth outcome through their impact on TFP. If financial integration is to have a lasting effect on growth, it must be by moving economies closer to their production possibilities frontiers by eliminating various distortions and creating efficiency gains, for example, in financial intermediation, technological adoption, etc' (Kose et al., 2009b, p. 18). There are empirical studies that have established a link between financial integration and TFP growth (Bonfiglioli, 2008; Kose et al., 2009c). Economies with more open capital accounts were found to have higher TFP growth. However, overall *de facto* financial integration did not seem to have an impact on TFP growth.

By using a wide array of *de jure* and *de facto* measures of financial openness and by disaggregating financial integration into stocks and liabilities of different kinds of financial flows, Kose et al. (2009c) reached an interesting and valuable conclusion. They discerned strong evidence of FDI and portfolio equity on TFP growth. In contrast, debt flows were negatively correlated with GDP growth. The negative relationship between stocks of debt liabilities from global capital markets and TFP was found to be weak in economies with better-developed financial markets due to financial liberalization and better institutional quality. The impact of financial integration on factor productivity is more important than its effect on capital growth, which in turn be achieved through improvements in the banking sector and stock markets. Higher investment efficiency can logically be a source of higher GDP growth (Bekaert et al., 2009). A note of caution is essential here. That financial globalization affects growth largely through indirect channels is a substantive and meaningful proposition. Yet it is not a consensus view and has not gone unchallenged (Rodrik and Subramanian, 2009).

2.4 Differing characteristics of financial flows

The pre-World War I era of financial globalization is well known for a positive relationship between global financial integration and economic growth. Using real-world data, economic historians have pointed out that in the late nineteenth and early twentieth centuries, global financial integration contributed to higher GDP growth in the so-called periphery economies (Feis, 1930; Woodruff, 1966). Britain, with a huge surplus of savings, was the core of this erstwhile financial system and the principal source country. It exported the majority of capital, while France, Germany and Holland provided smaller amounts. Britain persistently maintained current account surpluses during this period, which hovered around 4 percent of the GDP (Bordo and Meissner, 2007). This raises a valid query regarding why financial openness helped advance

growth in the earlier period. Why is the evidence of growth resulting from financial integration so emaciated during the contemporary
period? Are the global capital flows now characteristically different from
those during the earlier era of globalization?

Comparison of the pre-World War I era of financial globalization to
that of the contemporary period of financial globalization provides an
alternative perspective. Using a new *de facto* measure of financial integration and the same estimation technique – a system of generalized
methods of moment (GMM) panel estimation – for the two periods,
Schularick and Steger (2008) compared the impact of financial integration for the 1880–1913 period, covering the 24 countries that accounted
for 80 percent of the global GDP, with that for the 1980–2002 period,
covering the 56 countries that accounted for 80 percent of the global
output. They concluded that during the former period financial opening up led to higher investment in the domestic economy. In stark
contrast to the ambiguous findings for the contemporary period, international financial integration had a statistically significant and robust
effect on economic growth in the pre-World War I era of financial
globalization. Schularick and Steger (2008) found that on an average
a 1 percentage point increase in the capital inflows, measured as as proportion of the GDP, resulted in an increase in the GDP of 0.1 percent.
Correlation between growth and financial integration remained statistically significant over the entire 1880–1913 period. This effect remained
robust despite a number of alternative specifications. In contrast, during the contemporary period global financial integration was found to
be uncorrelated with changes in domestic investment. Also, financial
integration was not associated with higher growth rates. Correlation
coefficients showed insignificant effect from financial integration on
aggregate domestic investment in the contemporary period, while for
the pre-1914 period these correlations were strong.

The two periods of financial globalization are obviously different in
the following manner. The pre-World War I era is characterized by a
massive net capital transfer from rich to poor economies. This was essentially one-way long-term net flow of capital from the haves to have-not
economies, which was in accordance with neoclassical economic principles. In contrast, the contemporary period of financial integration is
characterized by high cross-border flows of finance and limited net capital transfer (Obstfeld and Taylor, 2004; Schularick, 2006). The inflow
of capital may be solely used to augment international reserves. Capital flight is another realistic possibility. This underlying distinction
in the character of financial flows during the two periods of financial

globalization explains why financial globalization was markedly growth-promoting in the pre-1914 era, while not so in the contemporary period.

3. Prerequisite threshold conditions

The indirect benefits of global financial integration, while more significant than the direct benefits, cannot be taken for granted. They do not arrive in a mandatory manner. Until complementary domestic policies and reforms are in place to sustain stability and growth, merely opening up the capital accounts and integrating globally does little good. Complementary policies essentially cover principal macroeconomic policy areas, institutional development and the domestic financial system. Until the prerequisite of certain threshold conditions of financial system and institutional development in the economy are attained, the globally integrating economies cannot profit fully from the indirect benefits of global financial integration (Kose et al., 2009d). One reason why advanced industrial economies have continued to be the principal beneficiaries of financial globalization is that they have more matured institutions and a more stable macroeconomic policy structure as well as deeper and more developed financial markets than EMEs or developing economies. If these preconditions are met, the financially integrating economy would have a far better prospect of enjoying these indirect benefits. Therefore, it seems logical for EMEs and developing economies to first pay attention to policy and devote resources to strengthening their financial sector as well as their institutional development before considering liberalization of capital accounts.

The financial sector in EMEs and developing economies is typically not deep, which becomes a serious hurdle in their attempt to derive benefits from financial globalization. A deep, adequately supervised and well-regulated financial sector is essential for effectively channeling the incoming global capital into productive sectors of the economy. A well-developed financial sector enables an economy to benefit from capital inflows and reduce its vulnerability to crises. Thus, the development, dexterity and refinement of the financial sector in an economy are the *sine qua non* for gaining from financial globalization. Likewise, the stage of institutional development is a second important threshold condition for benefiting from financial integration. Capital account liberalization needs to be accompanied by the development of domestic institutions (Mendoza et al., 2007). Countries which have developed their institutions to a near-maturity level and therefore have no or little corruption and red tape in their public administration and professionalized level of corporate governance, tend to attract more FDI and portfolio investment from global capital markets. Such economies are far more likely to benefit from the indirect channels of benefit discussed in the preceding section.

The insightfulness of the domestic macroeconomic policy is the third threshold condition. The quality of macroeconomic policy designed and pursued by policy mandarins in a country influences both its level and composition of capital inflows from the global capital markets. It also determines its vulnerability to a macroeconomic, financial or currency crisis. The importance of fiscal and monetary policies followed is exceedingly high in this context. A soundly and pragmatically devised macroeconomic policy structure increases the growth benefits of capital account liberalization. It also diminishes the possibility of the precipitation of a crisis in an environment of liberalized capital account. These are the three necessary threshold conditions. In their absence, an economy can derive little economic benefit – direct or indirect – from financial globalization.

4. Macroeconomic volatility

At an early stage of development, financial integration helps a developing economy by augmenting its investment and diversifying its economic base away from the primary sector, which in turn expands its real economy as well as reduces its macroeconomic volatility. When a certain amount of development has taken place, and the economy has grown to a higher stage of economic development, liberalizing the economy for globalization and financial integration spurs specialization. This expands the external sector and trade. This can make a middle-income economy vulnerable to external shocks in the industrial and services sectors in which it develops its specialization and trade. Thus, financial globalization may or may not lead to output volatility. Whether it will be a cause for output volatility will necessarily be economy-specific. As economic growth progresses, the opening up of the financial sector certainly increases the probability of sudden stops. Also, financial liberalization before liberalization of trade makes the economy especially vulnerable to financial crisis, showing the importance of the sequencing of reforms and liberalization (Edwards, 2009). Volatility increases if financial globalization is pursued with a fixed exchange rate.

As set out in Chapter 1 (Section 2.8), most of the advanced industrial world enjoyed an era of unprecedented economic stability in post-1983 period. Although the causal factors are open to debate, improvements in monetary policy have probably been one of the important sources of the Great Moderation. The era of Great Moderation in macroeconomic volatility provided a favorable and nurturing ambiance for the deepening of financial globalization. Output volatility declined in EMEs and in developing economies as well. However, intriguingly empirical literature failed to provide statistically significant evidence on the relationship between financial globalization and macroeconomic volatility.

Using panel data for the 30 OECD countries, Buch et al. (2005) concluded that the impact of financial openness and integration on the volatility of the business cycle depended on, first, the nature of external shock and, second, the links between macroeconomic policy. The absence of a link between financial globalization and output volatility is not without reason. There is no clear theoretical explanation regarding how financial globalization should affect output volatility. However, developing economies were more vulnerable to output volatility, due to structural weaknesses in their economies, than advanced industrial economies. Another more comprehensive empirical study by Kose et al. (2003) worked with data for a much larger group of advanced industrial and developing economies between 1960 and 1999. They found that financial globalization had a non-linear relationship with the volatility of consumption, not output volatility.

In a more recent study, van Hagen and Zhang (2006) developed a dynamic general equilibrium model of a small open economy and explained the lack of empirical evidence on the linkage between financial openness and macroeconomic volatility. As financial integration increased, they found non-monotonic patterns with respect to the three shocks, namely, the foreign interest rate shock, the productivity shock and the terms-of-trade shock. In the absence of any direct or indirect effect, they concluded that financial openness has non-monotonic implications for macroeconomic volatility. This non-monotonic link could either be U-shaped or reverse U-shaped.

The configuration of the financial globalization process determines whether there could be volatility of output in the economy. If the economy relies excessively on debt in its financial integration process, it makes itself vulnerable to variations in global interest rates, which could cause serious output volatility. Rodrik and Velasco (2000) established that the ratio of short-term debt to foreign exchange reserves or GDP can provide a reliable indication of output volatility and the crisis-proneness of an economy. Short-term maturity of debt was found to be a helpful gauge of vulnerability of the Tequila effect in the 1994–5 in Mexican crisis. Short-term maturity of debt also proved highly risk-laden in Asia in 1997. Economies with large short-maturity debt in comparison to GDP quickly suffer from debt crises. If the stock of short-maturity debt is larger than the forex reserves, the economy is three times more likely to suffer a sudden reversal of financial flows. Also, in several crises an empirical link was found between domestic lending booms and financial crises. The former preceded the latter in many instances of output volatility.

4.1 Volatility leading to crisis

One extraordinary development of the 1990s was a surge of private capital flows to the developing economies and widespread borrowings by economies. Both developing and advanced industrial economies had participated in large borrowing from the global capital markets. Central banks and governments were also an important part of this game. The US treasury and household sector was a large borrower in the US, while the corporate and financial sector was a large borrower in Japan. Not all of these borrowings went into productive high-return investments. The European and Monetary Union (EMU) was an exception in this regard as its borrowings remained low.

Likewise, in the developing world, there was a surge of private capital flows to developing economies in the early and mid-1990s. Particularly noteworthy were the flows to East Asian economies. Indonesia, Malaysia, the Philippines, the Republic of Korea and Thailand were large borrowers. The business corporations and banks in these countries were the principal borrowers in the short-term debt market, although their governments were not. Unlike them, in Argentina, Brazil, the Russian Federation and Turkey governments accumulated large foreign currency debts. They did so without regard to their repayment capabilities. This sub-group of economies also made itself vulnerable by prematurely liberalizing its capital markets to free entry of short-term capital. They hastily, and somewhat imprudently, liberalized their financial and capital account transactions.

The crises of the 1990s and early 2000s were dramatic episodes of volatility. They originated from the borrowing behavior described above. The Asian crisis was a severe one and mauled a region that had earned a favorable opinion of being home to several dynamic economies. Following the crisis a professional opinion emerged that financial globalization pushes a stable and well-functioning economy toward macroeconomic volatility and increases vulnerability to sudden stops. In addition, there was the major crisis that was ignited by the sub-prime mortgage debacle in the fall of 2007 and that became global in late 2008. The global economic recession it caused was continuing in 2009, at the time of writing. It further buttressed the harmful image of financial globalization which is routinely blamed for the crises of the recent past.

The question is frequently asked whether such crises are an inevitable element of financial globalization. The antagonists of financial globalization go so far as regarding proliferation of financial crises as a defining characteristic of financial globalization. Crises validated their different negative positions, that financial and capital account transaction should not be liberalized – or that their liberalization should be delayed – and that financial globalization is a villainous economic force that must be contained, if not completely scotched, at the first opportunity.

However, academic literature came up with inconclusive results on this issue as well. Empirical evidence suggested that the relationship between financial integration and volatility, measured by consumption volatility, depends more on an economy's domestic financial development and other so-called threshold conditions alluded to above. In the panel regression results, the estimated slope coefficient on *de facto* financial integration was positive and significant for economies that had relatively weak institutional quality and a low degree of domestic financial sector development. However, the impact was not found to be significantly different from zero for economies with stronger institutions and better-developed domestic financial systems (IMF, 2008a).

It was possible to estimate thresholds for institutional quality and domestic financial sector development from the regression results. Given the uncertainty regarding the estimates, the values of these thresholds needed to be interpreted with caution. Based on the average data for the period 2000–04, virtually all advanced industrial countries and many, almost a third, of EMEs met the threshold levels beyond which the estimated effect of financial integration on consumption volatility was insignificant. All the other countries were found to be below the threshold levels (IMF, 2008a). This valuable empirical exercise reveals which economies can be vulnerable to volatility and crisis caused by financial globalization, and which are relatively safe from it. It takes the wind out of the generalized assertion that financial globalization should cause macroeconomic volatility and crisis.

If crises are an inevitable component of financial globalization, not liberalizing financial and capital accounts should be the apt strategy to ward them off. However, to all appearances capital controls are not the answer. Recent analysis has revealed that countries that maintain stringent capital controls are more susceptible to crises than those who liberalize them. This result needs to be considered with a degree of skepticism because countries that place capital controls are usually the ones whose macroeconomic fundamentals are weak. Their essential objective in clamping capital controls is to try to insulate themselves from the possibility of a crisis. There is empirical evidence to show that opening up capital accounts reduces an economy's vulnerability to a crisis (Glick et al., 2006). In addition, there is little empirical evidence to 'support the oft-cited claim that financial globalization in and of itself is responsible for the spate of financial crises that the world has seen over the last three decades' (Kose et al., 2009a, p. 24). In short, not liberalizing the capital account may not necessarily work as a defensive strategy for warding off a financial crisis while financially globalizing may not be a cause for one.

4.2 Risk-sharing implications

As regards the risk-sharing implications of financial globalization, empirical studies found little supportive evidence. Kose et al. (2009c) focused on cross-country correlations of output and consumption while calibrating the impact of financial integration. They reported that, contrary to the theoretical predictions, there was limited evidence of improvement in risk-sharing across countries due to financial globalization. Only advanced industrial economies were able to clearly benefit from financial integration in terms of improved risk sharing. Astonishingly, even EMEs were not found to have reaped beneficial results in this dimension, notwithstanding the fact that many of them took the initiative in liberalizing their capital accounts and were able to attain a much higher degree of financial integration with the global economy than other developing economies. These are sobering conclusions. A caveat is necessary here. These results depend on county-specific conditions and the level and composition of capital flows from global capital markets.

As regards why no risk-sharing benefit was reported in the EMEs by empirical studies, there can be several theoretical explanations. One possible explanation is that different types of global capital flows are conducive to differing degrees of risk sharing. It is possible that EMEs had not been getting the appropriate types of capital flows to be able to achieve the objective of risk sharing. Other theoretical explanations for a low degree of risk sharing include the importance of non-traded goods in this group of economies, the scarcity of financial instruments for efficiently sharing macroeconomic risk and typically large transaction costs associated with international trade in goods and assets. These are all realistic possibilities that exist in EMEs.

5. Policy options in the backdrop of unambiguous evidence

In the preceding decades, public policy professionals in the developing economies and EMEs were in general convinced about the benefits of financial sector reforms. They demonstrated an increasing penchant for the financial sector's liberalization. These policy mandarins could have been justly impressed by the efficient financial sectors of advanced industrial economies, run with a high degree of proficiency and corporate governance. Consequently, on the whole the financial sector in advanced industrial economies made an enormous contribution to the growth and stability of the economy. There is a likelihood that this policy preference for financial sector reforms will persist in many developing economies and EMEs, and even grow stronger. Periods of global or regional economic turmoil could be exceptions in this regard. There are obvious benefits in implementing reforms and adopting liberalization of the domestic financial sector. The most direct benefit of having a strong and well-regulated financial sector is its ability to underpin growth, which in turn is poverty-alleviating and welfare-enhancing (Levine, 2005; Mishkin, 2009).

A well-developed financial sector smoothes the progress of public and private sector borrowings. As it grows and become deeper, management of domestic monetary policy becomes easier. The costs of maintaining and enforcing capital controls in a deep financial sector are high, particularly when merchandise trade is expanding in an economy. Finally, growth in domestic financial sector reforms assists in its external liberalization, which in turn results in collateral benefits (Section 1.3) and institutional growth in the economy. These channels of benefits are essential for making an open financial and capital account less crisis-prone (Section 3).

The experiences of the last two decades have convincingly demonstrated that embracing globalization and financial integration entails both high costs and sumptuous benefits. Obstfeld (2009, p. 104) prudently observed that, 'Taken all alone, financial openness is not a panacea – it can be poison.' Notwithstanding the weak evidence of direct contribution to growth, stability and welfare gains from the liberalization and globalization of the financial sector, its cautious and well-planned adoption under appropriate domestic economic and financial conditions can certainly be a productive, growth-supporting proposition. When financial globalization is adopted incrementally and sequentially as well as in association with the complementary range of domestic policies and institutional reforms – during a period when the reserve position of the financially globalizing economy is sound – it can be a legitimate instrument of enhancing stability and growth.

In addition, enormous long-term benefits can accrue from financial globalization. It renders the domestic financial system more competitive, transparent and efficient than one that develops in a controlled and restriction-ridden environment. The other side of this assertion is that capital account liberalization and financial integration with the global capital markets need *never* be a priority policy objective for all the countries. Low-income developing economies, having a poorly developed domestic financial sector, pursuing macroeconomic policies of questionable soundness and having small foreign exchange reserves, need not consider it until their macroeconomic and financial circumstances change dramatically.

6. Evolving global macro-financial dynamics of surpluses and deficits

There is an entirely different premise for uphill capital flows (Section 2.2). Since 1999, developing economies as a whole stopped running current account deficits. It is likely that the Asian financial crisis of 1997–8 had inspired this trend. Since the early 2000s, an international monetary system spontaneously evolved in which surplus and deficit economies were tied together in a relationship of co-dependence. China, Germany and Japan were, and continue to be, three large surplus economies. Center-periphery groups of countries of a new and different kind emerged during this period. In the new system a group of Asian economies, which had benefited from rapid export-led growth, had applied capital controls domestically and had intervened in the domestic foreign exchange markets by sterilizing inflows of external capital, succeeded in accumulating large official reserve assets. Dooley et al. (2003) contended that these economies supported undervaluation of their currencies.

This group of Asian economies was the new periphery. They exported their official capital to advanced industrial economies, the center countries. This began the unplanned and unstructured emergence of a new international system, billed the Bretton Woods II, in which economies with high saving rates and current account surpluses on the one hand and those characterized by high consumption and spending and current account deficits on the other became co-dependent on each other. China and the US were two representative economies of each group, respectively. Massive payments imbalances developed in the global economies, which could only be sustainable in the short-run. In the long-run, this was an unsustainable equilibrium and needed to be corrected (Dooley et al., 2007, 2009). Thus, the Bretton Woods II was hardly a system. It had little semblance of an enduring type of global financial architecture. If anything it was an instance of global economic and financial bedlam.

One theory explaining large capital flows from EMEs to advanced industrial economies is that financial markets in many EMEs are still not highly developed and they suffer from so-called 'market imperfections'. These market imperfections include overregulation, slow and inefficient legal systems, poorly enforced financial contracts and shallow capital markets (Valderrama, 2008). A shallow capital market implies *inter alia* small and inactive domestic bond and equity markets. They offer only a limited amount of liquidity, and only large firms raise capital from these shallow markets. In an illiquid and immature capital market, the fundamental task of channeling savings to productive investment opportunities is handled poorly. Also, the cost of raising capital in a shallow capital market is high.

The flow of liquidity under the Bretton Woods II period reduced global interest rates and underpinned consumption and investment. A buoyant period of global growth followed. It reinforced investor confidence and encouraged financial innovation and the development of financial products that rewarded risk-seeking behavior. As the housing market correction began in the US, this period of financial innovation and high-risk appetite abruptly came to an end. As a result of exposure to risky financial instruments, a large number of financial institutions came under severe balance-sheet pressure. Prices for risky assets fell sharply. Excessive market volatility caused spreads on all kinds of assets – risky and non-risky – to rise precipitously. Although structured investment vehicles were blamed, the fundamental reason for the financial turmoil was the unsustainable pace of the credit expansion and liquidity-driven global boom during the so-called Bretton Woods II period. Also, there was widespread recognition of the fact that regulation of financial markets has been much too weak during recent years. While authorities were aware of excesses building up in the financial markets, like mortgage-backed securities, they failed to increase regulation.

7. Summary and conclusions

This chapter addresses the question whether integration with global financial markets spurs growth and stability in an economy. It also addresses related quandaries like the close association between financial globalization and macroeconomic volatility. From a theoretical perspective, it is easy to state that the integration of financial markets can potentially foster growth. Whether it happens in reality is a different matter. There is little agreement in the economic profession on the implications of financial globalization. Positions have ranged from decidedly favorable to entirely unfavorable. There are many who reached mixed conclusions. Financial globalization is an important policy area and there is an imperious need for clear thinking and meticulous policy moves regarding these issues.

The neoclassical line of logic is simple, direct and positive: transborder capital flows from countries that have surplus savings and are capital rich to those where capital is scarce and is badly needed has nothing but favorable ramifications. However, the present thinking on this issue is fairly different. It takes a more subtle line than the direct one-channel impact of financial globalization and posits that the link between financial globalization and economic growth and stability is not so direct. Although there is a link, it is indirect. The cross-sectional, panel and event studies conducted in the recent past found that the gains from international financial integration were 'elusive'. For the most part, the results of these studies were mixed and inconclusive, at times even paradoxical. At the macroeconomic level, it has been difficult to find unambiguous evidence that financial opening yields a net improvement in economic performance.

The study of the indirect and multi-channel impact of financial globalization presented several possibilities of favorable growth impact and economic stabilization. The indirect impact can deliver favorable results through catalyzing different growth-supporting areas of macroeconomic policy and institutions. The principal channels of indirect impact are the domestic financial sector, efficiency gains in public and corporate governance and macroeconomic policy discipline. This indirect effect, or multiple-channel benefits, may well be more important than the traditional financing-channel effect emphasized in neoclassical economics.

Although the indirect benefits of global financial integration are more significant than the direct benefits, they cannot be taken for granted. They would not have much impact unless certain complementary policies were in place. They essentially cover principal macroeconomic policy areas, institutional development and the financial system. Unless these threshold conditions are achieved, globally integrating economies cannot profit fully from the indirect benefits of global financial integration.

Global financial integration is often blamed for causing macroeconomic volatility. However, no clear empirical link has been established between financial globalization and output volatility. There is no clear theoretical explanation regarding how financial globalization should affect output volatility. However, developing economies were more vulnerable to output volatility, due to structural weaknesses in their economies, than advanced industrial economies. Nonetheless, financial globalization was found to have a non-linear relationship with volatility of consumption, not output volatility. The configuration of the financial globalization process determines whether there could be volatility of output in the economy. If an economy relies excessively on debt in its financial integration process, it makes itself vulnerable to variations in global interest rates, which could cause serious output volatility.

The crises of the 1990s and early 2000s were dramatic episodes of volatility. After these crises, a professional opinion emerged that financial globalization pushes a stable and well-functioning economy toward macroeconomic volatility and increases vulnerability to sudden stops. Crises began to be treated as an inevitable element of financial globalization. However, in this area also, academic researchers came to inconclusive results. Empirical evidence suggested that that the relationship between financial integration and volatility, measured by consumption volatility, depends more on an economy's domestic financial development and other so-called threshold conditions.

As regards the risk-sharing implications of financial globalization, empirical studies found little supportive evidence. Cross-country correlations of output and consumption showed that, contrary to the theoretical predictions, there was limited evidence of improvement in risk-sharing across countries due to financial globalization. Only advanced industrial economies were able to clearly benefit from financial integration in terms of improved risk sharing. Astonishingly, even EMEs were not found to have reaped beneficial results in this dimension.

Embracing globalization and financial integration entails both high costs and sumptuous benefits. That being said, notwithstanding the weak evidence of direct contribution to growth, stability and welfare gains from the liberalization, its cautious and well-planned adoption under appropriate domestic economic and financial conditions, can certainly be a productive, growth-supporting, proposition. When financial globalization is adopted incrementally and sequentially as well as in association with a complementary range of domestic policies and institutional reforms – during a period when the reserve position of the financially globalizing economy is sound – it can be a legitimate instrument in enhancing stability and growth.

Notes

1. For instance, see Grilli and Milesi-Ferretti (1995), Kraay (1998), Edison et al. (2002), Fratzscher and Bussiere (2004).
2. For a detailed literature survey, see Henry (2007).
3. Gottschalk (2003) provides an inventory of factors that prevent capital from flowing toward developing countries.
4. See *International Finance Statistics* (IFS), 2009, published regularly by the International Monetary Fund.
5. See, for instance, Aizenman et al. (2007) and Gourinchas and Jeanne (2007).

References

Aizenman, J., B. Pinto and A. Radziwill. 2007. "Sources for Financing Domestic Capital: Is Foreign saving a Viable Option for Developing Countries?" *Journal of International Money and Finance.* Vol. 26. No. 5. pp. 682–702.

Aizenman, J. and B. Pinto. 2004. "Sources of Financing Domestic Capital: Is Foreign Saving a Viable Option?" Santa Cruz. CA. University of Califirnia. Department of Economics. Working Paper No. 576.

Alfaro, L. and E. Hammel. 2007. "Capital Flows and Capital Goods". *Journal of International Economics.* Vol. 72. No. 1. pp. 128–150.

Bagehot, W. 1873. *Lombard Street.* Homewood. Illinois. Richard D. Irwin. 1962 edition.

Bartolini, L. and A. Drazen. 1997. "Capital Account Liberalization as a Signal". *American Economic Review.* Vol. 87. No. 1. pp. 138–154.

Bekaert, G., C.R. Harvey and C. Lundblad. 2009. "Financial Openness and Productivity". Cambridge. MA. National Bureau of Economic Research. Working Paper No. 14843. April.

Bekaert, G. and C. Lundblad. 2005. "Does Financial Liberalization Spur Growth?" *Journal of Financial Economics.* Vol. 77. No. 1. pp. 3–55.

Berg, A., E. Borensztein and C. Pattillo. 2004. "Assessing Early Warning systems: How Have They Worked in Practice?" Washington. DC. International Monetary Fund. Working Paper No. WP/04/52.

Bonfiglioli, A. 2008. "Financial Integration and Capital Accumulation". *Journal of International Economics.* Vol. 76. No. 2. pp. 337–355.

Bordo, M.D. and C.M. Meissner. 2007. "Foreign Capital and Economic Growth in the First Era of Globalization". Cambridge. MA. National Bureau of Economic Research. NBER Working Paper No. 13577. November.

Buch, C.M., J. Doepke and C. Pierdzioch. 2005. "Financial Openness and Business Cycle Volatility". *Journal of International Money and Finance.* Vol. 24. No. 5. pp. 744–765.

Chari, A. and P.B. Henry. 2008. "Firm-Specific Information and the Efficiency of Investment". *Journal of Financial Economics.* Vol. 87. No. 3. pp. 636–655.

Chinn, M. and H. Ito. 2006. "What Matters for Financial Developments?" *Journal of Development Economics.* Vol. 8. No. 1. pp. 163–192.

Claessens, S. and L. Laeven. 2004. "What Drives Bank Competition? Some International Evidence". *Journal of Money, Credit and Banking.* Vol. 36. No. 3. pp. 563–583.

Clemens, M.A. and J.G. Williamson. 2004. "Wealth Bias in the First Global Capital Market Boom, 1870–1913". *The Economic Journal.* Vol. 114. No. 495. pp. 304–337.

Cornelius, P.K. and B. Kogut. 2003. *Corporate Governance and Capital Flows in a Global Economy.* New York. Oxford University Press.

Das, Dilip K. 2008d. *The Chinese Economic Renaissance: Apocalypse or Cornucopia.* Houndmills. Hampshire. UK. Palgrave Macmillan Ltd.

Dooley, M.P., P.M. Garber and D. Folkerts-Landau. 2009. "Bretton Woods II Still Defines the International Monetary System". Cambridge. MA. National Bureau of Economic Research. Working Paper No.14731. February.

Dooley, M.P., P.M. Garber and D. Folkerts-Landau. 2007. "The Crisis of International Economics". Cambridge. MA. National Bureau of Economic Research. Working Paper No. 13197. June.

Dooley, M.P., P.M. Garber and D. Folkerts-Landau. 2003. "An Essay on the Revised Bretton Woods System". Cambridge. MA. National Bureau of Economic Research. Working Paper No. 9971. September.

Edison, H.J., R. Levine, L. Ricci and T. Slok. 2002. "Capital Account Liberalization and Economic Performance: Survey and Synthesis". Washington. DC. International Monetary Fund. Working Paper No. WP/02/120.

Edwards, S. 2001. "Capital Mobility and Economic Performance: Are Emerging Economies Different?" Cambridge. MA. National Bureau of Economic Research. NBER Working Paper No. 8076. January.

Eichengreen, B.J., R. Hausmann and U. Panizza. 2006. "The Pain of Original Sin" in B.J. Eichengreen and R. Hausmann (eds) *Other People's Money.* Chicago. University of Chicago Press. pp. 130–152.

Feis, H. 1930. *Europe the World's Banker, 1870–1914.* New Haven. CT. Yale University Press.

Fratzscher, M. and M. Bussiere. 2004. "Financial Openness and Growth: Short-Run Gain, Lon-Run Gain?" Frankfurt. European Central Bank. Working Paper No. 348.

Glick, R., X. Guo and M. Hutchison. 2006. "Currency Crises, Capital Account Liberalization and Selection Bias". *Review of Economics and Statistics.* Vol. 88. No. 4. pp. 698–714.

Gottschalk, R. 2003. "International Lenders' and Investors' Behavior: What the Markets Tell Us?" Brighton. Institute of Development Studies. University of Sussex. *IDS Working Paper.* No. 193. July.

Gourinchas, P.O. and O. Jeanne. 2007. "Capital Flows to Developing Countries: The Allocation Puzzle". Cambridge. MA. National Bureau of Economic Research. Working Paper No. 13602. June.

Gourinchas, P.O. and O. Jeanne. 2006. "The Elusive Gains from International Financial Integration". *Review of Economic Studies*. Vol. 73. No. 3. pp. 715–741.

Gourinchas, P.O. and O. Jeanne. 2005. "Capital Mobility and Reform". Berkeley. University of California. (mimeo).

Grilli, V. and G.M. Milesi-Ferretti. 1995. "Economic Effects and Structural Determinants of Capital Controls". *IMF Staff Papers*. Vol. 42. No. 3. pp. 517–551.

Gupta, N. and K. Yuan. 2009. "On the Growth Effects of Liberalization". *Review of Financial Studies*.(forthcoming)

Haskell, J.E., S.C. Pereira and M.J. Slaughter. 2007. "Does Inward Foreign Direct Investment Boost the Productivity of Domestic Fitms?" *Review of Economics and Statistics*. Vol. 89. No. 3. pp. 482–496.

Henry, P.B. 2007. "Capital Account Liberalization, Theory, Evidence and Speculation". *Journal of Economic Literature*. Vol. 45. No. 4. pp. 887–935.

Henry, P.B. 2000. "Do Stock Market Liberalizations Cause Investment Boom". *Journal of Financial Economics*. Vol. 58. No. 2. pp. 301–334.

Henry, P.B. and D. Sasson. 2008. "Capital Account Liberalization, Real Wages and Productivity". Washington. DC. The Brookings Institution. Working Paper No. 20. March.

International Monetary Fund (IMF). 2008a. "Reaping the Benefits of Financial Globalization". Washington. DC. Occasional Paper No. 264. December.

Javorcik, B.S. 2004. "Does Foreign Direct Investment Increase Productivity of Domestic Firms?" *American Economic Review*. Vol. 94. No. 3. pp. 605–627.

Kose, M.A., E.S. Prasad, K.S. Kogoff and S.J. Wei. 2009a. "Financial Globalization: A Reappraisal". *IMF Staff Papers*. Vol. 56. No. 1. pp. 8–62.

Kose, M.A., E.S. Prasad, K.S. Kogoff and S.J. Wei. 2009b. "Financial Globalization and Economic Policies". Washington. DC. The Brookings Institution. Working Paper No. 24. April.

Kose, M.A., E.S. Prasad and M.E. Terrones. 2009c. Does Openness to International Financial Flows Raise Productivity Growth? *Journal of International Money and Finance*. (forthcoming)

Kose, M.A., E.S. Prasad and A.D. Taylor. 2009d. "Thresholds in the Process of International Financial Integration". Ithaca. New York. Cornell University. June. (Unpublished Manuscript).

Kose, M.A., E.S. Prasad and M.E. Terrones. 2003. "Financial Integration and Macroeconomic Volatility." *IMF Staff Papers*. Vol. 50. No. 1. pp. 119–142.

Kraay, A. 1998. "In Search of Macroeconomic Effects of Capital Account Liberalization". Washington. DC. The World Bank. (unpublished manuscript).

Krugman, P.R. 2009. "Revenge of the Glut". *The New York Times*. 2 March. p. 16.

Levine, R. 2005. "Finance and Growth: Theory and Evidence" in P. Aghion and S. Durlauf (eds) *Handbook of Economic Growth*. Vol. 1A. pp. 865–934. Amsterdam. Elsevier.

Levine, R. and S. Zervos. 1998. "Capital Control Liberalization and Stock Market Development". *World Development*. Vol. 26. No. 7. pp. 1169–1183.

Lucas, R.E. 1990. "Why Doesn't Capital Flow from Rich to Poor Countries?" *American Economic Review*. Vol. 80. No. 2. pp. 92–96.

Mendoza, E.G., V. Quadrini and J.V. Rios-Rull. 2007. "On the Welfare Implications of Financial Globalization without Financial Development". Cambridge. MA. National Bureau of Economic Research. Working Paper No. 13412. September.

Mishkin, F.S. 2009. "Why We Shouldn't Turn Our Backs on Financial Globalization". *IMF Staff Papers*. Vol. 56. No. 1. pp. 140–170.

Mitton, T. 2006. "Stock Market Liberalization and Operating Performances at the Firm Level". *Journal of Financial Economics*. Vol. 81. No. 3. pp. 625–647.

Noy, I. and T.B. Vu. 2007. "Capital Account Liberalization and Foreign Direct Investment". Honolulu. Hawaii. Department of Economics. University of Hawaii. Working Paper No. 07–8. March.

Obstfeld, M. 2009. "International Finance and Growth in Developing Countries: What Have We Learned?" *IMF Staff Papers*. Vol. 56. No. 1. pp. 63–111.

Obstfeld, M and A.M. Taylor. 2004. *Global Capital Markets: Integration, Crisis and Growth*. Cambridge. Cambridge University Press.

Prasad, E.S. 2009. "India's Approach to Capital Account Liberalization". Bonn. Forschungsinstitut zur Zukunft der Arbeit. The Institute for the Study of Labor (IZA). IZA Discussion Paper No. 3927. January.

Prasad, E.S. 2007. "The Welfare Implications of global Financial Flows". *The Cato Journal*. Vol. 27. No. 2. pp. 185–192.

Quinn, D. 1997. "The Correlates of Change in International Financial Regulation". *American Political Science Review*. Vol. 91. No. 3. pp. 531–551.

Quinn, D. and A.M. Toyoda. 2008. "Does Capital Account Liberalization Lead to Growth?" *The Review of Financial Studies*. Vol. 21. No. 3. pp. 1403–1449.

Rodrik, D. 2008. "We Must Curb International Flow of Capital". London. The Financial Times. 25 February.

Rodrik, D. 2006. "The Social Costs of Foreign Exchange Reserves". *International Economic Journal*. Vol. 20. No. 3. pp. 253–266.

Rodrik, D. 1998a. "Who Needs Capital Account Convertibility?" in *Should the IMF Pursue Capital Account Convertibility?* Princeton. NJ. Princeton University. Princeton Essays in International Finance. pp. 55–65.

Rodrik, D. and A. Subramanian. 2009. "Why Did Financial Globalization Disappoint?" *IMF Staff Papers*. Vol. 56. No. 1. pp. 112–139.

Rodrik, D. and A. Velasco. 2000. "Short-Term Capital Flows" in B. Plescovic and J.E. Stiglitz (eds) *Annual World Bank Conference on Development Economics*. Washington. DC. The World Bank. pp. 59–70.

Schmukler, S.L. 2008. "Benefits and Risks of Financial Globalization" in J. Ocampro and J.E. Stiglitz (eds) *Capital Market Liberalization*. Oxford. UK. Oxford University Press. pp. 48–73.

Schmukler, S.L. 2004. "Financial Globalization: Gain and Pain from Developing Countries". *Economic Review*. Federal Reserve Bank of Atlanta. Quarter 2. pp. 39–66.

Schularick, M. 2006. "A Tale of Two Globalizations". *International Journal of Finance and Economics*. Vol. 11. No. 4. pp. 339–354.

Schularick, M. and T.M. Steger. 2008. "Financial Integration, Investment and Economic Growth". Leipzig. University of Leipzig. Faculty of Economics and Business Administration. Working Paper No. 75. December.

Schumpeter, J.A. 1912. *Theorie der Wirtschaftlichen Entwicklung*. Leipzig. Germany. Dunker & Humblot. (*The Theory of Economic Development*. Translated from

German by Redvers Opie. Published in English by Harvard University Press. Cambridge. MA. 1934).

Solow, R.M. 1956. "A Contribution to the Theory of Economic Growth". *Quarterly Journal of Economics*. Vol. 70. No. 1. pp. 65–94.

Spiegel, M.M. 2008. "Financial Globalization and Monetary Policy Discipline". (unpublished mimeo).

Stiglitz, J.E. 2004. "Capital-Market Liberalization, Globalization and the IMF". *Oxford Review of Economic Policy*. Vol. 20. No. 1. pp. 57–71.

Stulz, R. 2005. "The Limits of Financial Globalization". *Journal of Finance*. Vol. 60. No. 4. pp. 1595–1637.

Tobin, J. 2000. "Financial Globalization". *World Development*. Vol. 28. No. 6. pp. 1101–1114.

Valderrama, D. 2008. "Are Global Imbalances Due to Financial Imbalances in the Emerging-Markets". San Francisco. Federal Reserve Bank of San Francisco. *Economic Letter No. 12*. 11 April.

van Hagen, J. and H. Zhang. 2006. "Financial Openness and Macroeconomic Volatility". Bonn. Center for European Integration Studies. Paper No. B-02.

Wolf, M. 2008a. "Global Imbalances Threaten the Survival of Liberal Trade". *The Financial Times*. London. 2 December.

Wolf, M. 2008b. *Fixing Global Finance*. Baltimore. Maryland. The Johns Hopkins University Press.

Woodruff, W. 1966. *The Impact of Western Man*. London. The Macmillan Press Ltd.

Xu, B. 2000. "Multinational Enterprises, Technology Diffusion and Host Country Productivity Growth". *Journal of Development Economics*. Vol. 62. No. 2. pp. 477–493.

6

Sovereign-Wealth Funds: A Paradigm Shift in Capital Flows in the Global Economy

1. Introduction

Sovereign-wealth funds (SWFs) have emerged as active players with enormous financial influence and weight in the global financial markets. The essential theme of this chapter is to provide readers with the basic conceptual strands of SWFs: their genesis, their coming into prime and the recent spurt in their operations. The structure of this chapter is as follows: Section 2 of this chapter focuses on definition, and tracks the origin and growth of SWFs. Whether they are an aberration of the international financial world is also analyzed in Section 2. The size and quantitative details of SWFs are provided in Section 3. There are different kinds of SWFs, fulfilling different objectives. Section 4 delves into categorization related issues. Also there are diverse management styles, which are discussed in Section 5. Section 6 explores the present and future market size of SWFs and Section 7 examines the ramifications of this group of large institutional investors. It also answers the query concerning whether anxieties about their operations are exaggerated. Section 8 attempts to provide answers regarding some prickly policy questions. Section 9 briefly sums up the chapter.

The recent acceleration in financial globalization has been comprehensively analyzed in Chapters 2 and 3. Over the last two decades the rate of increase of global cross-border investment was twice that of the rate of growth of multilateral trade in goods and services, which in turn exceeded the rate of global GDP growth (Lane and Milesi-Ferretti, 2007). Over this period state-owned and managed SWFs started playing an active and decisive role in underpinning, sustaining and expanding financial globalization. Their present size and rapid growth made them into an important class of global investors. In future, they are certain to play a more significant and weighty role in the global capital markets.

Systemically important countries like China, the Russian Federation and Saudi Arabia have established SWFs, which raised concerns regarding the role of these state actors in the global marketplace. They are becoming increasingly important in the international monetary and financial system and are presently active in all the capital markets. Their prominence has recently increased. Over the last five years their activities were reported daily in the financial media and their importance and relevance rose progressively in the international capital markets and in policy circles. SWF operations have emerged as the hottest theme of intellectual curiosity in the discipline of international finance. Their enlarged operations over the 2007–09 crisis period raised some genuine question marks.

Owing to the sheer amount of liquid resources accumulated by SWFs, they are presently regarded as the financial institutions with the largest concentration of capital in the world. Both their number and size have grown and they are among the largest class of investors in global capital markets. In terms of volume of operations, SWFs only lag behind large institutional asset managers like Fidelity and Barclays. Their ownership of such large resources has made them globally consequential financial institutions in their own right, which could have far-reaching implications for financial markets, institutions and business corporations.

Sovereign governments create SWFs for a range of macroeconomic and financial purposes. They are usually funded by the transfer of foreign exchange assets from the foreign exchange reserves of an economy. As a generalization it can be stated that SWFs are large, liquidity-rich and systemically significant funds that make long-tem investments in corporate and financial enterprises worldwide. Their investments are of a sizeable quantum. They support financial globalization and diversification. They are not a new group of institutional investors. As a well-established group, they have been undertaking cross-border investing for many years. The older ones among them are those established by the governments of Abu Dhabi, Kuwait and Singapore, which have existed for decades.

Notwithstanding the fact that they have operated for a while, the term SWF did not come into vogue until 2005. These behemoths of the global financial world have been investing in a wide range of asset classes. In the recent past, owing to oil price hikes, on-going financial globalization and large global payments imbalances rapid accumulation of foreign assets took place in several Asian economies and in the large oil exporters. Consequently, both the number of SWFs and the volume of their operations in the global capital markets became increasingly prominent (IMF, 2008).

2. Definition and concept

A universally accepted definition of a SWF does not exist because these institutions are hard to define precisely. The International Monetary Fund defines a SWF as a government-owned investment fund, while the US Department of Treasury calls it a government investment vehicle. The International Working Group of SWFs defines it as a special-purpose investment fund that is owned by a government. All three are broad and parallel definitions, stressing government ownership of a SWF and investment as its principal function.

A SWF can be functionally defined as a fund owned and run by the government of a sovereign nation that manages national savings, fiscal surpluses, balance-of-payments surpluses, the proceeds of privatization, excess foreign exchange reserves and receipts resulting from commodity exports in a commercial manner, with an explicit objective to maximize long-term returns on investment. The SWFs invest these financial assets globally into corporate stocks and bonds and other financial instruments.

A SWF is composed of financial assets (such as stocks, bonds and real estate) or other financial instruments funded by foreign exchange assets. SWFs can be structured as a fund, a pool or a corporation. They are a heterogeneous group, having diverse legal, institutional and governance structures. Thus viewed, an SWF is a saving and investment management vehicle of a sovereign government that holds foreign assets for long-term purposes. The foreign currency assets managed by a SWF are separate from the official reserves of the monetary authorities of the country. However, whether these foreign assets are a part of the reserve assets of a country was hitherto ambiguous. As their evident preference is higher returns on investment over liquidity, they have a higher risk tolerance than that of the central bank that manages foreign exchange reserves. Some SWFs also invest directly in state-owned enterprises at home.

Several export-oriented Asian economies steadily build up trade surpluses. On the one hand, the Asian emerging-market economies (EMEs),[1] in particular China, have been increasing their trade surpluses.

Progressively rising oil and gas prices, on the other hand, have increased the revenues of the Gulf Cooperation Council (GCC)[2] and the Russian Federation and turned them into globally significant net investors. In this sub-group of economies, China has been the largest global investor, with almost twice as much foreign investment as the next largest EME, the Russian Federation, and three times as much as the Republic of Korea (hereafter Korea), the third largest investing EME. Economies that make up Asia's financial hub, namely, Hong Kong SAR, Singapore and Taiwan, have strengthened their bond with the EMEs of the region and are expanding global investment rapidly. This wave of Asian financial integration excluded Japan (MGI, 2008).

The source of the accumulated pool of resources of an SWF can be foreign currency deposits earned through the recurrent balance of payment surpluses, or revenues earned from the exports of non-renewable natural resources like petroleum and gas, or the exports of commodities. Gross official international reserves more than doubled between 2002 and 2006, reaching $5 trillion. This led to an unprecedented concentration of liquid forex resources in the official sector. Excess liquidity in the public sector can also be derived from the fiscal surpluses of governments. Besides, a SWF can be a domestic pension fund, funded in domestic currency, but able to diversify into making global investments. The two kinds of SWFs share many common characteristics and are frequently not distinguished from each other.

2.1 Principal objectives

The rationale, objectives and investment behavior of SWFs are identical to other funds like trust, hedge, or private-equity funds. However, as the assets of SWFs belong to a sovereign nation, managed through an ad hoc fund, these funds are aptly christened sovereign-wealth funds. As regards the underlying objectives, in the existing corps of SWFs, five basic objectives stand out. They are macroeconomic economic stabilization; saving financial resources for future generations and, with that, mitigating the effects of Dutch disease; investment of reserves to increase return on them; development funds to promote socio-economic and industrial growth; and contingent pension reserve funds (IMF, 2008). Usually SWFs are multiple purpose funds and therefore have more than one of the above-stated objectives. For instance, some SWFs that were originally launched as stabilization funds soon evolved into saving funds because the liquid resources went on accumulating and became much larger than was need for short-term fiscal stabilization.

The SWFs launched by Botswana and the Russian Federation come under this category.

Although little is known about the nature and degree of government intervention in the operations of individual SWFs, the majority are largely semi-autonomous, self-directed entities, dedicated to professional portfolio management. Enhancing risk-adjusted returns on investment is their overarching objective. They have slowly, steadily and silently (albeit not stealthily) grown into consequential financial players in the global markets.

Foreign exchange reserves of an economy, typically held in euros, dollars and yen, are assets of the official sector and are traditionally managed by the central banks with an explicit short-term objective of protecting and stabilizing the domestic currency and protecting banks during periods of crises. They are also held for liquidity management purposes. These reserves are held in lower-risk and lower-yielding financial vehicles. Evidently, these holdings of reserves have high opportunity costs for the economy. However, the justification of holding large reserves by central banks is, *inter alia*, to defend the economy from crises. Several EMEs suffered from currency and banking crises during the 1990s and early 2000s. Since these reserves are intended for use during such exchange rate or financial emergencies, they were conventionally invested in assets that could be liquidated easily and quickly at the time of need. In managing reserves, the preference of the central banks has been for liquidity for the balance of payment needs. The rate of return on investment was not an important consideration for them. Therefore, low-return investments in US treasury securities and their equivalents were regarded as an acceptable mode of investment. Unlike these investments by central banks, for the most part foreign assets held in SWFs are for the long-term. They are illiquid and not readily available to monetary authorities for balance of payment purposes.

As a generalization, a large number of SWFs are an outgrowth of the expanding foreign exchange reserves of the official sector. When the foreign exchange reserves grew substantially larger than what was regarded as necessary for serving the short-term objectives enumerated above, the mind-set of investing governments began to change. The new line of thinking was that as this was the surplus public wealth of the country, possibilities of higher-returns on it should be explored. The managing governments concluded that at least part of the growing foreign exchange reserves should be placed in high-yielding, high-risk (if less liquid) investments. With this new mandate in mind, some sovereign governments launched SWFs so that they could maximize risk-adjusted long-term returns on their accumulated liquid financial resources. Consequently, large amounts of state-controlled liquidity began flowing into private assets globally. Continual growth in sovereign assets had turned the official sector into an active and prominent investment group.

2.2 Genesis of SWFs

Although SWFs are not a new class of institutional investors, professional and academic interest in them had in general remained subdued for a long time. SWFs had operated in the international capital markets since the early 1950s. Although the term SWF is of recent vintage (Section 1), the first fund-making international investments on behalf of sovereign governments had operated since 1953, when the Kuwait Investment Authority (KIA) was launched. It invested the substantial petroleum revenues of the state of Kuwait. The second such venture was the Kiribati Revenue Equalization Reserve Fund, which was created by the British administration of the Gilbert Islands in 1956. A levy on the export of phosphates from Kiribati resulted in rich revenues, creating an investment pool of over half a billion dollars. Some of the other older state investment funds include the Temasek Holdings of Singapore and the Alaska Permanent Fund, which both began operating in 1974 and the Mubadala Development Company of Abu Dhabi and Alberta Heritage Fund of Canada, which both began operating in 1976.

An age-old adage is that necessity is the mother of invention. It applies flawlessly to the birth of SWFs. No matter what the source, when countries have excess liquidity it is neither desirable nor possible to channel it to present consumption by increasing the level of imports. Exploring the pragmatic possibilities of its inter-temporal utilization is indeed the first and most prudent mode of its utilization. This applies *a fortiori* if the sources of excess liquidity are exports of mineral wealth, precious stone, commodities or strategic raw material like petroleum because these natural resources are non-renewable and exhaustible. Perhaps, though not in the short-term, there can come a day when they can no longer be exploited. Under these circumstances, SWFs can act as a pragmatic saving instrument for future generations. They facilitate the inter-general transfer of proceeds from non-renewable resources. They can also successfully dampen boom and burst cycles created by a simple variation in export prices.

Utilizing present financial assets to generate future resources by thoughtfully investing them is another objective of these financial entities. Third, even while the supply of mineral wealth or commodities continues, the economy can face price and supply volatility, leading to an unsteady revenue stream. In such cases, SWFs can help stabilize revenue stream and eliminate volatility. Fourth, the diversity in the investments made by SWFs is not limited to geographical diversity. SWFs have greater portfolio diversity, which enables them to earn higher returns on their investments. The reserve assets managed by the central banks are devoid of such diversity in their investments, which increases the opportunity cost of holding reserves. When economies come to hold plentiful reserve assets, greater and prudent diversification of investment is essential. Without this assets cannot be managed in a responsible and beneficial manner.

Furthermore, another, although rare, motive to create SWFs is to prepare domestic financial markets for creating an active international financial center. The governments of Korea and Singapore had this motive when they created the Korean Investment Corporation and the GIC, respectively. Presently, SWF industry comprises over 40 of these institutions, run largely by Asian and Middle Eastern governments. Half a dozen more are in the planning stage.

To the extent SWFs are an instrument of the accumulation of savings which cannot be invested domestically or spent on imports in the short-term, they become lucrative sources of global investible resources. In a globalizing world economy the owner governments either channel or recycle this surplus capital to matured industrial economies (MIEs) where profitable investment opportunities in the real or financial markets are available in abundance. Some of MIEs, like the US, need capital for meeting their current account deficits. These capital resources are also channeled to EMEs where they are used for lucrative investment opportunities, or are needed to meet the saving gap. These SWFs can take the form of stabilization funds, non-renewable resource funds, government-owned pension funds, investment companies and the like.

2.3 Maturing of SWFs

In spite of the large volume of their operations, SWFs had managed to remain by and large low-key and obscure for a long while. Only occasionally in the last three or four years, did they became a source of argumentative debate, even of sour controversy, when they tried to make a large and conspicuous acquisition in the industrial economies. Popular and financial media did not begin copious discussions regarding the operations of SWFs until the last quarter of 2007, when they acquired considerable eminence. *The Financial Times* and

The Wall Street Journal have begun covering SWFs extensively and a new class of SWF experts has emerged. Esteemed institutions like Deutsche Bank, Morgan Stanley and Standard Chartered began publishing well-researched pieces on SWFs. In rapidly globalizing financial markets, the growing role and activities of SWFs also began attracting a great deal of attention from the central bankers and finance ministers in industrial economies. In the Group-of-Seven (G-7) meeting, held in October 2007, leaders of industrial economies had expressed concern about the investments made by SWFs; in particular they disapproved of the lack of transparency in their operations.[3] The Senate Banking Committee in the US held lengthy and repeated hearings on SWFs in October and November 2007.[4] In mid-November, the International Monetary Fund convened its first annual roundtable on sovereign assets. For the first time, the US treasury discussed SWF operations in its *Semi-Annual Report on International Economic and Exchange Rate Policies*, published in June 2007.

The sub-prime mortgage crisis of 2007 resulted in daunting losses in the banking industry and a credit crunch ensued. Increase in seriously delinquent sub-prime mortgages, which amounted to an additional $34 billion in troubled loans, disrupted the $57 trillion US financial system (Dodd, 2007). Large US financial institutions sustained heavier losses than previously expected. This, paradoxically, became a window of opportunity for SWFs.[5] In an increasingly globalized economy, SWFs played a notable salvaging role in the aftermath of this crisis. They rose to prominence during the credit crunch. It brought them into public eye and attracted a great deal of market and academic attention to them. Resourceful and enterprising SWFs took the initiative and became active even before the monetary authorities of industrialized countries stunned the global financial markets with a dramatic joint plan to ease the liquidity squeeze. This synchronized central bank policy action was taken on 12 December. The Federal Reserve Board, the European Central Bank (ECB), the Bank of Canada and the Swiss National Bank were its initiators, while the central banks of Japan and Sweden stood by to step in and act as necessary. In an ambiance of severe credit crunch, some of the largest financial institutions like Citicorp, the Union Bank of Switzerland (UBS) and Merrill Lynch needed an infusion of fresh liquidity. SWFs stepped in like chivalrous white knights and came to their rescue. The Abu Dhabi Investment Authority (ADIA) provided an emergency capital injection of $7.5 billion to Citicorp, Singapore's Government Investment Corporation (GIC) provided SFr 11 billion to the UBS and the Temasek Holdings of Singapore helped

Merrill Lynch enhance its capital position by $6.2 billion. By January 2008, SWFs from Kuwait, Korea and Singapore had invested $21 billion in Citicorp and Merrill Lynch, two heavyweight financial institutions, due to their serious losses in the credit crisis (*The Economist*, 2008). High-profile participation in these leading investment activities helped SWFs in emerging as large investors of global significance. They contributed to the stability of international financial markets, presented a matured image and have begun to be regarded as a prominent segment of the global financial system. To an extent, this wave of sizeable investments by SWFs was driven by the boom in petroleum prices.[6]

That being said, the operations of SWFs are unprecedented, even atypical, in several respects. First, they are huge, cash-rich funds, and are presently managing assets almost twice as large as the hedge funds segment of the international financial market. Second, a large majority of them are owned by developing economies, or to be more precise EMEs. Third, states conventionally invested their excess foreign exchange reserves in low-risk, high-grade investment vehicles like US treasury securities, but by investing through SWFs, states moved toward riskier assets like equities and corporate bonds, in the process significantly enhancing liquidity in the global financial markets. Fourth, SWFs changed the character and composition of investments made by states. For the first time, SWFs enabled states to diversify their portfolios. Like any prudent investors, taking advantage of increasing financial globalization, they began to diversify their holdings and look for higher risk-adjusted returns. Fifth, the foreign ownership of SWFs became a source of concern for the host economies, particularly because they are owned by sovereign governments. This exposed them to accusations that their investments were being motivated by strategic and political considerations not economic considerations or profit maximization. The reason behind this indictment is that in the case of SWFs it is the governments that are regarded as the decision-makers of their large investments and governments are not business entities. Therefore, it is believed that the maximization of risk-adjusted return on investment and shareholders' wealth may well be a lower priority for SWFs. Sixth, as more SWFs buy into prestigious firms and business corporations in the MIEs, an uncomfortable scenario of share croppers is conjured up, where foreign-owned firms employ the local high-skill workforce in the MIEs.

One problematical facet of SWFs' investments is the backlash they are provoking from protectionists and nationalists in countries in which they make large investments. They are often perceived as threats and have to face negative attitudes. In the recent past threats of financial protectionism mounted with the rise of global investment by SWFs in private sector corporate assets. Although they are an instrument that enhances liquidity and financial resource allocation in the international capital market, they have also become a source of controversy. Their investments have threatened an escalation in financial protectionism in the host countries.

2.4 Global financial crisis: SWFs as strategic investors

In the initial stage of the global financial crisis of 2008, the role as well as the profile of SWFs in the financial markets increased and they began to be recognized as more important players than ever before. They provided much-needed financial relief to several major banks and financial institutions as well as to eminent business corporations. High-status banks like Citicorp received billions from SWFs in the Middle East.

The current financial crisis and recession turned them into strategic investors. Although these large capital injections were welcome by the capital markets, they were not devoid of controversy. Due their supportive role during the current financial crisis, SWFs are widely acknowledged as rich sources of funds for the future (Fernandes and Bris, 2009). They are regarded not only as potential sources for large global financial investment but also for foreign direct investment (FDI). This can potentially make them inventive growth-supporting institutions in the global economy (Rios-Morales and Brennan, 2009).

2.5 An irony of the global financial system?

Recent theoretical and empirical research focused on the benefits that can be derived from international capital inflows as well as the risks entailed in them.[7] Under appropriate policy environment, external capital inflows can contribute to the smoothing of consumption, or to capital accumulation and thereby to growth and diversification of the domestic economy. They can also be instrumental in institutional improvement that eventually underpins economic performance (Kose et al., 2009). According to standard neoclassical economic theory it is normal for MIEs to invest in developing economies or EMEs because by definition they are the capital rich group of economies. Capital flows should be from rich, high capital-labor ratio economies to poor, low capital-labor ratio economies. The operations of SWFs reverse this relationship. There is a bit of illogicality, even irony, in that EMEs, which should have been attracting global capital, are instead investing in MIEs.

The MIEs are tapping the surplus savings of the EMEs. This uphill flow of capital, known as the Lucas (1990) paradox was alluded to earlier in Chapter 5 (Section 2.2). Prima facie this is capitalism at work, that is, productive capital is flowing from where it is available to where it is needed. However, there has evidently been 'a paradigmatic change from a world in which private investors from wealthy industrialized countries used to invest around the globe to one in which emerging-market governments become major share-holders in Western companies' (DBR, 2007).

In terms of individual economies, China was the largest exporter of net capital, surpassing Germany, Japan, Russia and Saudi Arabia, in that order. On the other side of the equation, since 2001 the US became the largest net consumer of external capital, absorbing 80 percent or more of the global savings. These global capital inflows were needed to meet the capital account deficits of the US. No parallels of this situation – in which the largest global economy turns into a huge capital importer for a sustained period – are available in modern economic history. During 2007, flow of investible capital from the EMEs alone to the MIEs was estimated at well over half a trillion dollars (Summers, 2007). This amount was less than the build-up of foreign exchange reserves in the EMEs.

3. Aggregate assets under management

The seven largest SWFs are known as the 'seven sisters'. The precise amount of aggregate assets under management (AuM) of SWFs is not known because the majority of them keep their operational details shrouded in confidentiality. It can only be estimated imprecisely, based on publicly available market statistics. Numerous reasonable estimates have been attempted. For instance, some of the early estimates made by Morgan Stanley put the value of global corporate asset under the management of SWFs in 2006 at $2.5 trillion (Jen, 2007a). Another source supports this estimate by putting this figure at anything between $2 trillion and $3 trillion (Johnson, 2007). The US Department of Treasury estimated that aggregate assets ranged between $1.5 trillion and $2.5 trillion (The US Department of Treasury, 2007). The IMF's estimated range was between $1.9 trillion and $2.9 trillion (IMF, 2007a). In June 2008, the Federal Reserve System estimated the value of AuM for 2007 at $3.3 trillion (Kotter and Lel, 2008). Deutsche Bank Research (2007, 2009) put this number a tad lower, at $3 trillion.

To put this in perspective, some comparisons need to be made. When compared to the other large institutional investors, AuM of SWFs are larger than those of the much publicized hedge funds. They make highly leveraged investments and have assets in the order of approximately $1 trillion. However, SWFs account for less than one-eighth of the global investment fund industry, which has $22 trillion worth of AuM. The size of the assets of SWFs is less than one-sixth of global pension funds' assets ($19 trillion). Another revealing comparison can be made with the assets held by the global banking sector ($96 trillion). SWFs hold only 3.12 percent of the total assets held by the global banking sector (DBR, 2009). An argument is often put forward that SWFs from EMEs can and should find investment opportunities in their own economies, or at least in their own respective regions.

4. Categorization

SWFs can be categorized according to their sources of wealth and policy objectives. First, the source of foreign wealth of a good number of these funds is exports, or tax on exports, of non-renewable resources or commodities. In the recent past commodity prices, including those of petroleum, had spurted sharply, before settling down at a lower level. Therefore, many SWFs that were originally established for the purpose of fiscal stabilization changed their principal *raison d'être* and were transformed into saving funds. The latter have a different portfolio composition. They invest in a broader range of longer-term assets than those preferred by stabilization funds. Petroleum-producing economies have established funds for both of these objectives. There are 31 petroleum-producing economies, of which 21 have established one kind of SWF or the other; 16 of these were created after 1995. Two of the oil-producing countries (Chad and Ecuador) abolished their funds in 2005–06. In all, ten of these funds have stabilization as their essential objective, while the others are committed to the twin objectives of saving and stabilization (IMF, 2007b). Although the newer oil funds have stabilization as their central policy focus, after oil prices began firming up they began to emphasize the long-term saving objective. Their asset management techniques changed accordingly. Oil producers, like Azerbaijan, that have recently increased oil production, have also established funds to improve the management of additional oil revenue. As the revenues of commodity exports frequently accrue directly to the governments, foreign currency earnings are not converted into domestic currency. In such cases, foreign currency does not enter the domestic economy and therefore need not be sterilized through the issuance of domestic debt by central banks.

Second, non-commodity funds earned foreign exchange through persistent current account surpluses and set up SWFs. Many of the Asian EMEs, particularly China, built up resources for their SWFs in this manner. These EMEs have established themselves as successful exporters of manufactures and other high-value-added products in the global economy. Economies like Korea and Taiwan are major exporters of information technology (IT) products. In many cases their current account surpluses went hand in hand with capital account surpluses. This group of Asian EMEs is marching to a different beat from the MIEs and gives a clear impression of decoupling from them. They are capital-rich while MIEs are short of capital. The resulting expansion of foreign exchange reserves in this country group led to the decision to transfer excess foreign exchange reserves into 'stand-alone funds' (US Department of Treasury, 2007). Third, fiscal surplus or public saving generated through privatization can also be infrequent sources of financial wealth. SWFs created by these financial resources are comparable to SWFs created by non-renewable resources. Fourth, SWFs established with large pension reserve funds are entirely based on domestic financial resources.

Distinction can be made between SWFs on the basis of their policy objectives and *raison d'être*. First in this categorization are the stabilization funds, which are set up by countries exporting commodities and non-renewable natural resources. The basic objective of these funds is to insulate, or at least stabilize, the budget and economy from price volatility. The simple *modus operandi* is to build up assets when revenue inflows are strong and be prepared for lean periods. These funds smooth the net flow of revenue into the budget, while depositing a predetermined part of it into the stabilization fund. Second, as alluded to in Section 2.1, economies exporting non-renewable resources launch saving funds with an objective to store wealth for future generations, when these resources have been exhausted. Financial saving for this purpose has been termed 'intergenerational equity' (IMF, 2007b). These saving funds convert non-renewable resources into a portfolio of diversified financial assets.

A third objective is creating an SWF for the purpose of economic and industrial development. To this end, such a fund accumulates financial wealth for meeting the priority socio-economic objectives of the economy. Infrastructure development, which is a capital-intensive process, takes high priority in this set of objectives. Fourth, pension reserve funds are the last type of SWF. Their principal objective is to achieve high risk-adjusted returns by astutely investing in the global marketplace. These two kinds of SWFs can be regarded as a 'subset of SWFs' that is explicitly or implicitly linked to long-term fiscal commitments (IMF, 2007a). Thus viewed, often SWFs have multiple objectives. Also, many have an ever-changing spectrum of objectives. With changing global economic circumstances and financial conditions, their objectives adjust to the newly emerging situations. The objectives of SWFs influence, and even determine, their asset allocation strategy. For the most part, the investment horizon of SWFs is regarded as long-term, which is a blessing for the recipient corporations. Receiving a large measure of long-term capital from a discreet investing institution that does not demand major management alterations is indeed a providential development.

5. Management

To be sure, each SWF has its own asset allocation and risk management strategy. They need to strike a subtle balance between generating high returns on investments on the one hand and an appropriate level of liquidity, efficiency in fund management and the socio-economic objectives that they have been assigned by their sovereign-owner governments on the other. Their objectives have a strong bearing on this asset allocation strategy. As pointed out earlier in this section, one can assume that in asset allocation, stabilization funds usually adopt a relatively shorter-term approach than the savings-oriented SWFs. The latter obviously prefer investing in long to very long term assets.

Although there are some statutes governing them, which were created at the time of inception, SWFs are given a high degree of autonomy in choosing from a large range of global assets. An additional freedom that SWFs enjoy is that they do not have to work under investment rules binding them to asset classes or norms regarding currency exposure. Private pension and investment funds do need to abide by these rulings. Thus, in choosing their investment options SWFs are more similar to hedge funds than to other regulated fund segments of the industry. However, one clear distinction that SWFs have from hedge funds is that they completely eschew speculative business. Hedge funds have a strong penchant for it.

As SWFs are not bound by the standard mix of assets between equity and fixed income securities, they determine their own asset mix, which is largely based on the potential rate of return. There are exceptions to this. For instance, the Government Pension Fund-Global (GPFG) of Norway does operate like a normal pension fund, following a prescribed mix of equity and fixed income securities in its portfolio. However, other SWFs choose to invest in carefully selected corporate assets. Like private equity funds, SWFs largely play a passive role and do not intervene in the management of the corporate enterprises in which they take stakes. Their active involvement in corporate management has been found to be highly infrequent.

Given their systemic significance, SWFs can potentially create market distortions. If they are inefficiently and imprudently managed or misguidedly take risks, they could cause harmful consequences for global financial markets. SWFs do not have properly set-out liabilities like pension funds. Their objectives are broad. As SWFs are owned by their respective governments, they are only accountable to them. In addition there are few regulations governing SWFs, directly or indirectly. This could create a risk of low accountability leading to an environment of excessive risk-taking for the managers of SWFs. They may even regard their losses as irrelevant (Lowery, 2007). Their incorrect perception of risk could have a larger negative impact over the financial markets than that of other institutional investors. Furthermore, SWFs usually make large investments which are frequently opaque. Therefore, if the SWF suffers from a distorted view of risk, it will potentially influence the financial market. Such an investment may distort (inflate) market prices, in the process misrepresent the true relative market value (Kimmitt, 2008).

5.1 Investment methods and techniques

As alluded to in the discussion about the definition of SWFs (Section 2), their risk tolerance has grown considerably higher than that of central banks that manage the official reserves as they go in search of higher returns. How SWFs will invest their large pools of capital in the foreseeable future is a crucial concern in business, financial and political conclaves. As they are resourceful investors, they invest in all the advanced industrial economies and EMEs. As market players they are a driving force, holding equity positions in a large number of business corporations. Typically they do not take a controlling stake.

Fernandes and Bris (2009) conducted a comprehensive survey of 20,000 SWF holdings across 7,000 business firms in the stock markets of 58 countries. Their study found that, on average, SWFs take 0.74 percent of the shares outstanding in a company. The dollar value of the average position was $46.3 million. Their control reached the 50 percent level only in 1 percent of the total firms in which they have invested. Their investment was heavily biased toward larger and more liquid business and financial firms with a proven record of profitable growth. Like any astute and calculating investor, SWFs are opportunistic. They wait for the appropriate stock prices and enter when they are low. They positively shun investment in countries that do not provide adequate legal protection to investors. Sound corporate governance is another important determinant of SWFs' investment strategy. SWFs are often accused of investing in technology-intensive firms with the objective of gaining corporate intelligence. However, a close scrutiny of the widespread investments made by SWFs fails to show any predilection for high-technology or R&D-oriented companies in their investment strategies.

The business firms that succeed in attracting SWF equity investment benefit in other ways as well. Results of the analysis by Fernandes and Bris (2009) revealed that SWFs have a stabilizing influence over the companies in which they invest and their investment is favorably valued by the market. When a business firm becomes a target of SWF investment its market value is enhanced, which allows the firm to leverage political connections. An SWF connection is equated by the market to a guaranteed long-term and cheap source of capital. This reduces the cost of capital for the firms, in turn increasing its profitability.

SWFs have taken stakes in many high-visibility firms in the recent past. In 2004, China's Lenovo Group took over IBM's personal computer business for $1.7 billion, creating a large splash in world business. Many SWFs recently took significant stakes in important business corporations and banks, in the process provoking the ire of political leaders and public opinion in the host economies. Some of the recent striking examples during 2007 include: The China Investment Corporation (CIC) investing $3 billion in initial public offering (IPO) of Blackstone, a large private equity group, and buying a 9.9 percent stake in it. Qatar Investment Authority (QIA) that owns 25 percent of J. Sainsbury, a large British supermarket chain, unsuccessfully tried to gain total control. Vneshtorgbank, a Russian state-owned bank took a 6 percent stake in EADS, maker of Airbus. Dubai International Capital (DIC), one of the smallest SWFs, bought a stake in EADS as well as making a large acquisition of HSBC stocks. SWFs from the Middle East have invested in prominent auto manufacturers like Porsche and Volkswagen, taking minority stakes. SWFs from China and Singapore succeeded in acquiring a 5.2 percent stake in Barclays Bank. Gazprom, the Russian gas monopoly, tried to buy the gas pipelines and storage facilities in the EU, a move which was trenchantly opposed.

Some observers of this intriguing spectacle have begun uneasily questioning whether this could lead to cash-rich EME governments investing in politically sensitive sectors (like the media), economically sensitive sectors (like energy), or even owning large corporations in MIEs. This appears paradoxical. In a capitalist system, the common objective of shareholders is to see a maximization in shareholders' wealth, or in the value of their shares. It is far from obvious that when the shareholders in large business corporations are sovereign governments, they would act to see the maximization of their share values, or pursue myriad other non-economic objectives. These observers of SWFs do not entirely rule out the probability of SWFs following nationalistic, political and non-profit-maximizing objectives, which in turn creates uneasiness – to put it mildly – about the expanding operations of SWFs. There is considerable scope for corporate governance and strategies being unconventionally influenced by SWFs.

6. Market size and growth dynamics

SWFs proliferated after 2000, as has their global investment. The banking and financial sector has been one of their favored areas of interest. By January 2008, they invested close to $69 billion on recapitalizing some of the largest financial institutions in the MIEs. As alluded to above (Section 3), the majority of SWFs publish little operational details so the market has scanty knowledge about them. Going by what is available, the Sovereign-Wealth Fund Institute compiled basic statistical data on SWFs. According to this compilation, the assets of the ten largest SWF are as follows:

Table 6.1 Largest SWFs by assets under management (as of June 2009) (in billions of dollars)

Country	Name of the SWF	Assets (in billions of dollars)	Source of Funds
UAE	Abu Dhabi Investment Authority	700	Oil
Saudi Arabia	Saudi Arabian Funds (various)	400	Oil
Norway	Government Pension Fund	350	Oil
Singapore	Government Investment Corporation	330	Non-commodity
China	China Investment Corporation	200	Non-commodity
Russia	Stabilization Fund	190	Oil
Kuwait	Kuwait Investment Authority	169	Oil
Singapore	Temasek Holdings	160	Non-commodity
Australia	Future Fund	54	Non-commodity
Qatar	Qatar Investment Authority	50	Oil

Source: DBR, 2009.

Present estimates of the total assets under management (AuM) have been provided in Section 3. In 2009, SWFs were much smaller in size than the other large institutional investors. However, their importance and weight in the global financial market is likely to continue to grow steadily. According to the projections made by the IMF (2007a), SWFs will continue to accumulate global assets at the rate of $800 billion–$900 billion annually. This rate of expansion can bring the aggregate foreign assets under SWFs' management to approximately $12 trillion by 2012. By 2015, they are projected to touch the $12 trillion mark (Jen, 2007a). Growth in the international reserves in EMEs would be the principal factor buttressing this growth dynamic.

A note of caution is essential here. The above-mentioned estimates of AuM growth were made before the global financial crisis, which changed the growth dynamics of SWFs. Between the last quarter of 2007 and the second quarter of 2009, a significant decline in the portfolio book-value of the assets of institutional investors, including SWFs, took place. Equity portfolios held by SWFs lost over 45 percent, reducing overall SWF portfolios by over 18 percent (DBR, 2009). In addition, the current account surpluses of parent countries of major SWFs narrowed as their trade surpluses shrank.

During 2008, petroleum revenue growth in the economies of Latin America and the Middle East was aided by a sharp oil price spike. This revenue growth has since subsided. Commodity prices also softened. Therefore, the pre-crisis projections regarding the growth of AuM may well prove to be overly optimistic. Funds available for SWFs will continue to mount but at a slower pace. New projections made on the basis of the reduced value of AuM show that total AuM are likely to amount to $7 trillion in 2019 (DBR, 2009).

7. Ramifications of a group of large institutional investors

The advent of a group of cash-rich institutional investors, particularly those with a penchant for making large-volume long-term investments in different parts of the global economy, is a wholesome development for equity markets and other segments of the international financial markets. They play a positive role in enhancing market liquidity and financial resource allocation. Therefore, as a purveyor of capital, SWFs should be welcomed, particularly by those business corporations and financial institutions that are in the financial market for long-term capital gains. As long-term investors SWFs can play a stabilizing role in financial markets by supplying liquidity and reducing market volatility. They have contributed to macroeconomic stability by allowing economies to manage their capital inflows and have thus provided an opportunity for sustained economic growth (Gomes, 2008).

The accumulation and channeling of financial capital to productive firms are indeed constructive and welfare-enhancing functions of SWFs that benefit the global economy. Large amounts of capital flows will have a bearing on global asset allocation and prices. According to estimates made by Jen (2007b), capital flows from SWFs should have a far-reaching impact. They should raise the 'safe' bond yields by 30–40 basis points over the next ten years. They should also drive down the average return on equities by 50–70 basis points and reduce the equity premium by 80–110 basis points. Warnock and Warnock (2006) estimated that foreign purchases of US government bonds lowered the US 10-year treasury yield by 90 basis points. They found that two-thirds of this impact was due to Asia.

7.1 So why the anxiety?

If so, why have SWFs generated so much anxiety, essentially in political and legislative circles and among business leaders? Some regard SWFs as a threat to the sovereignty of the countries where they make investments. SWFs are being viewed as turning from creditors to owners. One accusation that is made against SWFs is that by making large investments in the business and financial corporations of advanced industrial economies and EMEs they are converting the host countries status into that of share croppers. The logic is that the ownership of these assets lies with the investing countries, not with the producing countries.

The same accusation is extended to the decision-making process of the SWFs. That is, their investment decisions are based on political considerations rather than commercial ones. SWFs are also accused of making investments in high-technology-oriented businesses so that they can clandestinely access proprietary technological know-how (Section 3.1). The public debate on SWFs in many host countries has unmistakable negative overtones. In some countries there has been an outcry in favour of regulating SWF investments. Financial protectionism has raised its head from time to time. For Truman (2007, p. 2) the very fact that EMEs accumulated 'a vast amount of international assets' raised 'profound questions about the structure and stability of international financial system in the first decade of the 21st century', which seems a tad unconvincing.

However, when SWFs try to acquire substantive stakes in large business corporations and banks that are at the forefront of a country's commercial life, strong protectionist backlash can justifiably arise. The key trigger for concern was SWFs taking stakes in high-profile US and European corporations, some of which are listed in Section 3. With escalating financial wherewithal, the global investments of SWFs are bound to record an upsurge. What the macroeconomic and strategic implications of SWFs' increasing investment in global corporate assets and occasional takeover in the medium- and long-term would be is a question perplexing the professional and policy-making communities.

As the majority of SWFs make little information about their size, operations and investment strategy available, there is a widespread perception in 'countries with liquid and efficient capital markets that SWFs are intransparent if not incalculable participants in global financial markets' (DBR, 2007). This lack of transparency has caused concern. In terms of secretiveness, SWFs rank even below the most secretive hedge funds. The majority of them reveal little regarding their basic philosophy, investment strategy, portfolio composition, operations and return on investments. This opacity has created misgivings regarding their motives and mistrust in their operations. A multivariate analysis shows that the degree of transparency of SWF activities is an important determinant of the market reaction. The adoption of improved disclosure practices by SWFs benefits both the SWF and the existing shareholders of the target firm (Kotter and Lel, 2008). Since October 2008, many SWFs took steps to allay the transparency and disclosure related concerns by agreeing to the Santiago Principles (Section 7.3). They set out common standards not only regarding transparency but also independence and governance.

Often SWFs are suspected of questionable political objectives behind their investments. They are accused of being instrumental in increasing the role of governments in international financial markets as well as in the global economy. Angst regarding their ability to destabilize financial market was also candidly expressed. The flip side of this coin is that SWFs are concerned about financial protectionism damaging their investment plans, which could effectively obstruct capital flows from the SWFs.

Another obvious and understandable cause of anxiety is the state-ownership of the SWFs. It is commonly observed that governments in developing economies, including EMEs, are more actively involved in international investment decisions than those in the MIEs. Although these controls have been loosening in the recent years, they still exist. While so far SWFs have not given any evidence of any 'mischievous behavior', this legitimately intensifies the apprehension in MIEs of government intervention in resource allocation decisions (*The Economist*, 2008). Besides, large private sector corporate assets in the hands of foreign governments 'are at sharp variance with today's general conception of a market-based global economy and financial system', in which commercial decisions are made by individual entrepreneurs based on profit-maximizing motives (Truman, 2007). State-ownership of SWFs runs counter to the grain of capitalist thought and neoclassical economic philosophy. There is no gainsaying this fact.

7.2 Is the anxiety exaggerated?

However, it cannot be refuted that notwithstanding their state-ownerships, investment operations of SWFs are fairly identical to those of other private sector investment funds in terms of motivation and management. Like them, SWFs look for the highest risk-adjusted returns. Their investment activities and mode of operation do not seem strikingly different from those of large pension funds, both in the private and public sectors. That SWFs essentially have a good deal of autonomy in their operations has been noted in Section 3. Therefore, any apprehension caused by mere state-ownership may well be exaggerated, if not misplaced (Section 7.4).

8. Squaring the policy circle

The scale and scope of SWFs operations has grown large and they can indeed move markets. However, the experience thus far shows that large and diversified portfolio investments by them entail few risks of destabilizing the international financial market. Those who regard investments by SWFs as a risky source of destability need to carefully reassess the accuracy of their stance. As stated above (Section 6.1), there is little evidence of unwarranted, undesirable or offensive conduct by SWFs. If anything, investment flows by SWFs should be supported and welcomed by the host country governments. The fact that the large majority of SWFs have a long-term investment horizon and lack of interest in speculative activity should make them a strong stabilizing force in the international financial market. Arbitrary restrictions from the host economies on their activities would deprive international financial markets of a cash-rich group of market players. Any rise of financial protectionism would work as an effective barricade against expanding globalization. Besides, erecting barriers to foreign investment from EMEs on the premise that SWFs may possibly abuse their position, while demanding open access to their economies is patently hypocritical. That said, participation of the SWF in the international financial system can be decisively improved by policy initiatives at SWF level, the host economy level and by the international institutions like the IMF.

8.1 Prickly policy issue

Arguably the thorniest policy issue is regarding investment by SWFs that sometimes enables them to take on management stakes. The knee-jerk reaction of analysts and public policy professionals in the recipient economies is to limit the stakes that SWFs can have in a certain category of industries and keep it below a prescribed proportion. Both the industries and the limit can be determined by the regulatory authorities of the host country. However, this resolution is not easy to implement. It is prickly as the criteria for identifying an investor or a fund should not be subjected to such restrictions. Besides, some host country corporations and pension funds many well be averse to such limitations on SWFs.

One policy resolution of this thorny issue could be allowing SWFs only non-voting shares in specified sectors of the domestic economy. Care should be taken in specifying the industrial sectors for this purpose. Keeping J. Sainsbury out of the hands of QIA did not seem rational. The grocery business was not so strategic for the British economy that decisions made by a SWF could adversely influence the economic wellbeing of either the population or that line of business. Some SWFs have begun taking lessons from the Dubai Ports World experience and the China National Offshore Oil Corporation (CNOOC) bid for Union Oil Company of California (UNOCAL). They have started taking a pragmatic approach in this regard and have voluntarily begun opting for non-voting shares. The China Investment Corporation (CIC) declared their willingness to take non-voting stakes, although they have not ruled out taking positions on boards.

8.2 Self-Correcting policy measures for the SWFs

One strategic measure that SWFs need to take of their own accord is increasing transparency and accountability. This will certainly result in a reduction of the risk of reflexive financial protectionism, or will at least contain its expansion. Legitimate concerns regarding their motivation will be alleviated if SWFs become more transparent. Transparency is indispensable for supporting smoothly operating international capital markets on the one hand and active participation of SWFs on the other.

As Truman (2007) argues, transparency is needed for advancing horizontal accountability among the participants and stakeholders as well as vertical accountability in the policy-making process.

GPFG of Norway is frequently used as an example of an SWF that has exemplary levels of disclosure and is a paragon of transparency. The Permanent Reserve Fund of Alaska (US) and the Alberta Heritage Savings Trust Fund of Alberta (Canada) are also regarded as highly transparent, followed by the Temasek Holdings. The Khazanah Nasional BHD of Malaysia is also regarded as fairly transparent. In case SWFs do not voluntarily adopt high standards of transparency, they can be internationally coaxed to publish audited information about their balance sheets, annual reports and quarterly reports as well as to provide necessary information regarding their rationale, basic philosophy and objectives, portfolio composition, investment strategy and return on investment. Those SWFs that are averse to complying with calls for high standards of voluntary disclosure and transparency may be restricted to purchasing a pre-specified level of non-voting shares in the recipient economies. In fact, given the scale and scope of SWFs' operations, it seems in order to make higher norms of disclosures mandatory.

8.3 Establishing a code of conduct: The Santiago principles

International financial institutions like the IMF can initiate a third line of policy action. International investment operations of sovereign governments warrant a 'collective effort to establish an internationally agreed standard to guide the management of their cross-border investments' (Truman, 2007). Therefore, recognizing the positive liquidity-enhancing and financial resource allocation roles of SWFs, policy makers at the international level have begun deliberations on how to forestall financial protectionism so that an open global financial system can be promoted and buttressed. What code of conduct SWFs need to follow has become a legitimate issue for the international financial community.

The International Monetary and Financial Committee (IMFC) of the IMF have charged the IMF with analyzing the relevant policy issues from the perspective of both investors and recipients of SWF flows. The IMFC has stressed the imperative need for a candid dialogue on identifying best practices so that rising financial protectionism can be nipped in the bud. In the November 2007 roundtable of the IMF (Section 2.2), which was attended by senior level delegates from central banks, ministers of finance, and sovereign asset managers from 28 countries, it was decided that the IMF will take into consideration the viewpoints of the two sides and identify sound practices to be followed in the management of SWFs. Dominique Strauss-Kahn, the managing director of the IMF, emphasized the imperious need for SWFs to function 'in ways that are consistent with global financial stability' (IMF, 2007c). To be sure, an agreed-upon set of best practices could go a long way in maintaining an open global financial system and in discouraging the host countries from imposing unilateral restrictions on SWF operations.

Under the auspices of the IMF, in mid-2008, the International Working Group (IWG) of SWFs, consisting of representatives of the SWFs, met to agree on a common set of principles and practices. This was done in response to growing calls for transparency and commonality in practices followed by SWFs. The IWG agreed on what became known as the Santiago Principles. They set the framework for clarifying and streamlining the operations of the SWFs. The generally accepted principles and practices (GAPP) is a voluntary set of principles and practices that the members of the IWG support and abide by. The GAPP cover the following fundamental areas: (i) legal framework and coordination with macroeconomic principles, (ii) institutional framework and governance structure and (iii) investment and risk management principles.

8.4 Regulations for guarding against foreign stakes

For some time, MIEs have had legislation and regulatory barriers for keeping out foreign investors whose investments were not welcome. At present, the concept of SWFs taking stakes or ownership in important commercial enterprises against the popular will of the business corporations in the forefront of commercial life is not feasible. Therefore, the specter of unwelcome and objectionable intrusion by cash-rich SWFs is overblown. The US government is the best equipped for prohibiting or suspending any unwelcome foreign investment. Since 1950, it has had the Exon-Florio Amendment in place, which is a part of the Defense Production Act. In addition, the Committee on Foreign Investment (CFI) has also been active in identifying and blocking any foreign takeovers that it regards as injurious to US commercial or strategic interests. It was able to stop UNOOC in its tracks.

Japan, the second largest economy, has had stringent limits on inward foreign investment for a while. In several industrial sectors, Japan can also suspend investments by foreign controlled enterprises. Similarly, the German Foreign Trade and Payments Act, amended in 2006, is capable of restricting the investment transactions of foreigners. Its focus of protection is defense-related German companies. The present regime is extra cautious in allowing SWFs from China and the Russian Federation to take stakes in defense-related German firms. It has proposed a CFI-like body for vetting investment proposals from SWFs. Such a protective law in the UK makes use of 'golden shares'. It is more potent and versatile than the German law. Golden shares are nominal shares that are able to outvote all the other shares under certain specified circumstances. The UK also has a 29.5 percent cap on foreign shareholdings in what it regards as strategic industries. The golden share concept is a practicable and no-nonsense one. The deliberations in the European Commission (EC) seemed to favor it because it can prevent the outright takeover of strategic holdings as well as of politically and economically sensitive commercial assets.

However, there is a downside to it, that is, golden shares may be abused to protect European companies. Among members of the European Union (EU) there is disagreement so far on whether there should be a collective policy on restricting SWFs, or whether individual member economies should devise their own policies. While France and Germany strongly favor an EU-wide stand, enthusiasm in the UK is not so high. Ireland follows an open investment regime and may be wary of an EU-led policy regime, although it might accept a code of conduct for the SWFs. The French and German governments agree on not allowing SWFs uncontrolled access to stakes in their business firms. Although unequivocal in their demand for transparency, they have shown a preference for laying down a code of conduct instead of implementing rigid regulations. Canada has legislation restricting foreign ownership to minority shares in a long list of industries. Without discouraging investments by SWFs, it has recently demanded more transparency in their operations and declared that scrutiny of takeovers by them will be higher. Unlike these Group-of-Seven (G-7) economies, Australia and New Zealand have been far more welcoming to SWFs. Therefore, Asian SWFs and those from oil-exporting economies have large investments in these two economies. SWFs from Singapore have more commercial assets in Australia than the government of Australia. SWFs invest in EMEs as well, whose concern regarding transparency and ownership of stocks in sensitive sectors is no different from that of MIES. If anything, they many be more restrictive than the governments in MIEs. Temacek Holdings was recently asked to reduce its holdings in the Shin Corporation of Thailand.

SWFs are going to be active in the foreseeable future and will not disappear as long as surpluses and deficits in the economies continue. One plausible short-term change in this setting is that as domestic financial sector liberalization in the Asian and Middle-Eastern economies continues, its citizenry will play a more active role in making foreign investment than its bureaucrats. This will reduce, although not eliminate, the stigma of state ownership of foreign investment that SWFs represent.

8.5 Reinforcing and refining the Santiago principles further

Although the Santiago Principles are a step in the right direction and they provide practical guidelines, they need to be treated as only a good start. While they indicate initial principles regarding the structure, governance and management of SWFs, they are not without flaws. They need to be refined and developed to make them into a helpful and meaningful structure statute of mutual benefit for the two sides, namely, the SWFs and the recipient economies. Wong (2009) noted that the GAPP focused almost totally on the institutional dimensions of the SWFs. The important issue of their relationship with the recipient economies was not adequately addressed. Ideally the focus of the Santiago Principles should have been the combined interests of SWFs and the recipient economies. A straightforward attempt should have been made to address the interests of both. However, the Santiago Principles were developed in biased manner in the sense that they exclusively addressed SWFs' responsibilities and their *modus operandi*. Over recent years, the interests of SWFs and the host countries were frequently at loggerheads on several issues, which became a source of tension in the financial and political circles. The Santiago Principles ignored these areas of veritable conflict. First, one such contentious issue was the disclosure requirement for SWFs. What is mandatory for a SWF to disclose is not addressed by the Santiago Principles. Whether they need to publicize the list of the business firms in which they invest and the size of their investments individually is another difficult issue.

Second, absolutely no norms have been established to measure compliance with or deviations from the prescribed Santiago Principles. Measurable criteria are a necessity for monitoring whether the two sides are abiding by whatever guidelines have been provided. In addition, a constructive feedback channel which could improve and refine the Santiago Principles from year to year is also needed but is so far nonexistent. Furthermore, the financial market landscape is ever-changing. To adjust and adapt to these changes, it is necessary that an efficient and constructive feedback mechanism is created and implemented.

Third, the Santiago Principles ignored the asymmetric information problems faced by the recipient countries. Transparency in financial operations is indispensable. Not only do the required financial data and information need to be made public, but they should also be verifiable. If there are no means of ascertaining the veracity of the publicized data, the utility and effectiveness of its disclosure will necessarily be limited.

9. Summary and conclusions

This chapter focuses on the concept of SWFs and the recent spurt in their activities and significance. They played a meaningful role during the initial stage of the current financial crisis as providers of much-needed liquid capital to sustain and support financial institutions and large business corporations that were in dire straits. Although they are an instrument that enhances liquidity and financial resource allocation in the international capital market, they have become a source of controversy and threaten an escalation in financial protectionism. SWFs are state-owned and managed and have started playing a decisive role in underpinning, sustaining and expanding financial globalization. They are a fairly mature group of large, liquidity-rich funds supporting financial globalization and diversification. They manage national savings, budget surplus and excess foreign exchange reserves by investing them into corporate stocks, bonds and other financial instruments.

In spite of large volume of their operations, SWFs had managed to remain by and large obscure. Over the last three or four years they often became a source of controversy. Consequently, they began to attract negative public attention. The popular and financial media did not begin copious discussions regarding the operations of the SWF until the last quarter of 2007, when they acquired considerable eminence as the sub-prime mortgage crisis, and the credit crunch created by it, became a window of opportunity for SWFs.

SWFs are often regarded as ironic entities because it is normal for MIEs to invest in developing economies or in EMEs as they are by definition the capital-rich group of economies. However, through SWFs this relationship has reversed and the developing economies invest in the MIEs. Several categories of SWFs have emerged. They can be categorized according to their sources of wealth as well as their policy objectives.

The total assets under management (AuM) of SWFs have been estimated at around $2.5 trillion at present. Their future rate of expansion is likely to be rapid and by 2015 they have been projected to rise to $12 trillion. Growth in international reserves in EMEs would be the principal factor buttressing this growth dynamic. For the most part, the advent of a group of cash-rich institutional investors, particularly those with a penchant for making large-volume long-term investments, is a wholesome development for the international equity markets and other segments of international financial markets. However, their state-ownership and lack of transparency has created considerable anxiety about their operations. SWFs are being viewed as turning from creditors to owners. When SWFs try to acquire substantive stakes in large business corporations and banks that are at the forefront of a country's commercial life, strong protectionist backlash can justifiably arise.

However, large and diversified portfolio investments by SWFs entail few risks for the international financial market and anxiety about them is exaggerated. Those who regard investments by SWFs as risky need to carefully assess the risks caused by them thus far. Restrictions from host economies on SWF activities would deprive international financial markets of a cash-rich market player. Rise of financial protectionism would work as a barricade against expanding globalization. Participation of SWFs in the international financial system can be improved by policy initiatives at three levels, namely, the SWF level, the host economy level and the international institutions level (such as the IMF), which need to devise a set of best practices for the operations of SWFs. This chapter profiles various policy measures that are necessary at the present stage of operations of the SWFs. That being said, in most MIEs legislation and regulatory barriers for keeping foreign investors out are already in existence. The specter of unwelcome and objectionable intrusion by cash-rich SWFs into a country's economic life is overly puffed up.

Notes

1. Emerging-market economy is a term coined by Antoine W. van Agtmael of the International Finance Corporation in 1981. It is a sub-set of developing economies. See Das (2004), Chapters 1 and 2 for an explanation of what emerging-market economies (EMEs) are and how are they defined.
2. The Gulf Cooperation Council (GCC) was established in 1981. Its members are Bahrain, Kuwait, Oman, Qatar, Saudi Arabia and the United Arab Emirates (UAE).
3. This G-7 meeting was hosted by the US Treasury Secretary Henry Paulson and Federal Reserve Chairman Ben S. Bernanke in Washington DC, on October 22. Aside from the US, members of the G-7 include Japan, Germany, France, Britain, Italy and Canada.
4. Several noted scholars including Kenneth Rogoff, Patrick Mulloy and Edwin Truman participated in these hearings. Christopher Cox, the chairman of the

Securities and Exchange Commission, expressed his concern regarding the operations of SWFs in a speech at Harvard University on 24 October 2007.

5. The sub-prime mortgage financial crisis of 2007 entailed a precipitous increase in home foreclosures. Although it started in the US during the fall of 2006, it began affecting the global economy in 2007. This then became a gloomy year for some of the largest financial institutions in the world.

6. During 2007, the supply-demand fundamentals for crude oil were in clear deficit. Toward the end of September 2007, the average petroleum spot price (APSP) of benchmark West Texas Intermediate (WTI) shot up to $83.90 per barrel and in early November it topped $99. This was a 65 percent increase in petroleum prices in one year. The global consumption of oil has been growing at an average annual rate of 1.9 percent; 2007 was the sixth consecutive year of oil price increases.

7. See, for instance, Edwards (2001), Klein and Olivei (1999) and Rodrik (1998b).

References

Das, Dilip K. 2004. *Financial Globalization and the Emerging Market Economies.* London and New York. Routledge.

Deutsche Bank Research (DBR). 2009. "Sovereign Wealth Funds: State Investments During the Financial Crisis". Frankfurt. Germany. 15 July.

Deutsche Bank Research (DBR). 2007. "Sovereign Wealth Funds: State Investments on the Rise". Frankfurt. Germany. 10 September.

Dodd, R. 2007. "Subprime: Tentacles of a Crisis". *Finance and Development.* Vol. 44. No. 4. pp. 15–19.

The Economist. 2008. "The Invasion of the Sovereign-Wealth Funds". 19 January. p. 11.

Edwards, S. 2001. "Capital Mobility and Economic Performance: Are Emerging Economic Different?" Cambridge. MA. National Bureau of Economic Research. NBER Working Paper No. 8076.

Fernandes, N. and A. Bris. 2009. "Sovereign Wealth Revalued". *The Financial Times.* 12 February. p. 16.

Gomes, T. 2008. "The Impact of Sovereign Wealth Funds on International Financial Stability". Ottawa. Ontario. Bank of Canada. Discussion Paper No. 2008-14. September.

International Working Group of Sovereign-Wealth Funds (IWG). 2008. "Sovereign-Wealth Funds: Generally Accepted Principle and Practices". Abu Dhabi. UAE and Washington. DC. October.

The International Monetary Fund (IMF). 2008. "Sovereign Wealth Funds: A Work Agenda". Washington. DC. 29 February.

The International Monetary Fund (IMF). 2007a. "Global Financial Stability Report". Washington. DC. September.

The International Monetary Fund (IMF). 2007b. "The Role of Fiscal Institutions in Managing the Oil Revenue Boom". Washington. DC. 5 March.

The International Monetary Fund (IMF). 2007c."IMF Convenes First Annual Roundtable of Sovereign Asset and Reserve Managers". Washington. DC. Press Release No. 07/267, 16 November.

Jen, S.L. 2007a. "How Big Could Sovereign Wealth Funds Be?" *Global Economic Forum.* New York. Morgan Stanley Research. 4 May.

Jen, S.L. 2007b. "Sovereign Wealth Funds". New York. Morgan Stanley Research. October.

Johnson, S. 2007. "The Rise of Sovereign Wealth Funds". *Finance and Development.* Vol. 44. No. 3. pp. 56–59.

Kimmitt, R.M. 2008. "Public Footprints in Private Markets: Sovereign Wealth Funds". *Foreign Affairs.* Vol. 87. No. 1. January/February. pp. 119–131.

Klein, M.W. and G. Olivei. 1999. "Capital Account Liberalization, Financial Depth and Economic Growth". Cambridge. MA. National Bureau of Economic Research. NBER Working Paper No. 7384.

Kose, M.A., E.S. Prasad, K.S. Kogoff and S.J. Wei. 2009. "Financial Globalization: A Reappraisal". *IMF Staff Papers.* Vol. 56. No. 1. pp. 8–62.

Kotter, J. and U. Lel. 2008. "Friends or Foes? The Stock Price Impact of Sovereign Wealth Fund Investments and the Price of Keeping Secrets". Washington. DC. Board of Governors of the Federal Reserves System. International Finance Discussion Paper No. 940. August.

Lane, P.R. and G.M. Milesi-Ferretti. 2007. "The External Wealth of Nations Mark II". *Journal of International Economics.* Vol. 73. No. 2. pp. 223–250.

Lowery, C. 2007. "Remarks on Sovereign Wealth Funds and the International Financial System". Washington. DC. The United States Department of the Treasury. 21 June. Available on the Internet at http://www.treas.gov/press/release/hp471.htm. 11 September 2009.

Lucas, R.E. 1990. "Why Doesn't Capital Flow from Rich to Poor Countries?" *American Economic Review.* Vol. 80. No. 2. pp. 92–96.

McKinsey Global Institute (MGI). 2008. "Mapping Global Capital Markets: Fourth Annual Report". San Francisco.

Rios-Morales, R. and L. Brennan. 2009. "The Emergence of SWFs as Contributors of Foreign Direct Investment". Paper Presented at the St. Hugh's College, Oxford University. Oxford. UK, on 24–25 June.

Rodrik, D. 1998b. "Who Needs Capital Account Convertibility? in *Princeton Essays in International Finance.* No. 207. Princeton. NJ. Princeton University Press.

Summers, L. 2007. "Funds that Shake Capitalist Logic". *The Financial Times.* 29 July. p. 9.

Truman, E.M. 2007. "Sovereign Wealth Funds: The Need for Greater Transparency". Washington. DC. Peterson Institute for International Economics. Policy Brief No. 07-06. August.

The United States Department of Treasury. 2007. "Semi-Annual Report on International and Exchange Rate Policies". Washington. DC. June.

Warnock, F.E. and V.C. Warnock. 2006. "International Capital Flows and US Interest rates". Cambridge. MA. National Bureau of Economic Research. Working Paper No. 12560. June.

Wong, A. 2009. "Sovereign Wealth Funds and the Problem of Asymmetric Information". *Brooklyn Journal of International Law.* Vol. 34. No. 3. pp. 1082–1109.

7
Epilogue

In the contemporary global economic and financial environment, financial globalization is as important a policy area as it is intriguing. The global macroeconomic and financial crisis of 2007–09 put an end to three decades of commendable progress in financial globalization. It also put this phenomenon under the spotlight again and gave it additional relevance. It is sure to influence the global economy as well as the systemically important individual economies during the rest of the twenty-first century in a substantive manner. Clear thinking, appropriate comprehension and a nuanced understanding of the principal issues in this crucial policy area are indispensable.

A degree of separation persists between the theoretical percepts and practical realities in the realm of financial globalization. While theorists conclude that the integration of financial markets can potentially foster growth, in reality this may or may not transpire. Although such integration can be a benign force capable of spurring growth and stability, it can also lead to severe macroeconomic and financial volatility. Whether it is a phenomenon to embrace or a malevolent one to be shunned is often unclear. Recent examples of both outcomes of financial globalization abound. There is little agreement in the economic profession on the implications of financial globalization. Positions have ranged from decidedly favorable to entirely unfavorable. Many economists have reached mixed conclusions.

The mainstream neoclassical view on financial globalization is linear, simple and direct and regards it as a favorable phenomenon to be promoted. Numerous cross-sectional, panel and event studies conducted in the recent past found that the gains from international financial integration can be uncertain and indefinable. For the most part, the results of these studies were mixed and inconclusive, at times even paradoxical. It was difficult to unambiguously establish that global financial integration causes net improvement in economic performance. Present experiences and assessments regarding financial globalization are nuanced and subtle. Rejecting the one-channel ramifications of financial globalization, one can pragmatically and prudently believe that economic growth and stability can be one of its many outcomes.

Financial globalization is capable of indirect and multi-channel impact, which in turn presents real possibilities of favorable growth performance and economic stabilization. These results were delivered through catalyzing different growth-supporting areas of macroeconomic policy and institutions. The principal channels of indirect impact are the domestic financial sector, efficiency gains in public and corporate governance and macroeconomic policy discipline. This indirect effect, or multiple-channel benefit, may well be more important than the tradition financing-channel effect emphasized in neoclassical economics. However, while the indirect benefits are significant, they cannot be taken for granted. They are only capable of occurring if complementary policy measures are in place.

The most strident complaint against globalization is that it causes macroeconomic volatility, although no clear or direct empirical link has been established between financial globalization and output volatility. Theoretical research has thus far failed to establish a nexus between financial globalization and output volatility. However, financial globalization was found to have a non-linear relationship with the volatility of consumption.

The macroeconomic and financial crises of the 1990s and early 2000s were dramatic episodes of volatility. After these crises, a strong professional opinion emerged that financial globalization pushes a stable and well-functioning economy toward macroeconomic volatility and increases vulnerability to sudden stops. Crises began to be treated as an inevitable element of financial globalization. In this area academic researchers also came to inconclusive results.

A level-headed perspective in this regard is that embracing globalization and financial integration entails both high costs and sumptuous benefits. That being said, notwithstanding the weak evidence of liberalization's direct contribution to growth, stability and welfare gains, its cautious and well-planned adoption under appropriate domestic economic and financial conditions can certainly be a productive, growth-supporting proposition. When, during a period when the reserve position of the financially globalizing economy is sound, financial globalization is adopted incrementally and sequentially as well as in association with the complementary range of domestic policies and institutional reforms it can be a legitimate instrument for enhancing stability and economic growth.

Timely and coordinated fiscal and monetary stimuli in the advanced industrial economies and emerging-market economies (EMEs) prevented the recent crisis from turning into a second Great Depression. It was christened the Great Recession. The EMEs of Asia spearheaded the recovery. China played the most notable role in supporting the nascent recovery. Toward the end of 2009, the global macroeconomic and financial crisis began to recede, although recovery was moderate and uneven. Central banks in advanced industrial economies gradually began to unwind the emergency liquidity facilities which were introduced at the height of the crisis. Similarly, EMEs began to rein in their monetary policy.

In early 2010, the threat of sovereign default in four Eurozone economies loomed large. European banks were struggling to preclude the most serious financial disaster in the 11-year life span of the euro. Greece was closest to a sovereign default. Ireland, Portugal and Spain were also at the brink, with menacing levels of deficits and alarming rates of unemployment. At this juncture, the global economy looked very different from what it normally had been in the past. The large EMEs were in robust health, with strong domestic demand and little spare capacity. Brazil, China and India were in their post-crisis phase. In contrast, there were few signs of strong demand growth in advanced industrial economies. The annualized GDP growth rate of 5.7 percent in the fourth quarter of 2009 in the US was considered strong but misleading. The reason for this strong showing was that firms were rebuilding their inventories. It is widely agreed that advanced industrial economies will continue to recover from the global financial crisis slowly.

At the end of the first quarter of 2010, global financial markets began to recover faster than expected. Money markets were by and large stabilized. Bank lending standards were moderating. The crisis-period tightening was being abandoned. Yet, bank lending should be expected to remain sluggish due to the need to rebuild capital. At this juncture, global equity markets were rebounding fast and corporate bond issuance reached a high level. However, the surge in corporate bond issuance did not offset the reduction in bank credit growth to the private sector. Portfolio capital flows into the EMEs picked up, which eased financial conditions. In contrast, cross-border lending bank financing was still contracting. Large global banks continued to delevel.

Bibliography

Abu-Lughod, J. 1989. *Before European Hegemony: The World System A.D. 1250–1350*. New York. Oxford University Press.

Agence France-Presse (AFP). 2009. "World Bank Chief Says China Stimulus Should Continue". 9 September. Available on the Internet at http://www.google.com/hostednews/afp/article/ALeqM5jp2zZO9hHz2SgVQ7g_vptcRXP71g. 10 October 2009.

Ahmad, S., A. Levin and A. Wilson. 2002. "Recent US Macroeconomic Stability: Good Policies, Good Practices or Good Luck?" Washington. DC. The Board of Governors of the Federal Reserve System. International Finance Discussion Paper 2002-730. July.

Aizenman, J. and B. Pinto. 2004. "Sources of Financing Domestic Capital: Is Foreign Saving a Viable Option?" Santa Cruz. CA. University of Califirnia. Department of Economics. Working Paper No. 576.

Aizenman, J., J.R. Lothian and B. Pinto. 2007. "Overview of Conference Volume: Financial and Commercial Integrations". *Journal of International Money and Finance*. Vol. 26. No. 7. pp. 657–672.

Alfaro, L. and E. Hammel. 2007. "Capital Flows and Capital Goods". *Journal of International Economics*. Vol. 72. No. 1. pp. 128–150.

Altman, R.C. 2009. "Globalization in Retreat". *Foreign Affairs*. Vol. 88. No. 4. pp. 1–6.

Andersen, T. and F. Tarp. 2003. "Financial Liberalization, Financial Development and Economic Growth in LDCs". *Journal of International Development*. Vol. 15. No. 2. pp. 189–209.

Asian Development Bank (ADB). 2009. *Asian Development Outlook 2009: Update*. Manila. 17 September.

Atkins, R. 2009. "Eurozone Escapes Recession after Five Quarters". *The Financial Times*. 13 November. p. 16.

Bagehot, W. 1873. *Lombard Street*. Homewood. Illinois. Richard D. Irwin. 1962 edition.

Bairoch, P. 1989. "European Trade Policy, 1815–1914" in P. Mathias and S. Pollard (eds) *The Cambridge Economic History of Europe*. Cambridge. UK. Cambridge University Press. Vol. 8. pp. 1–160.

The Bank for International Settlements (BIS). 2009. "BIS Report on Derivatives". Basel. Switzerland. Bank for International Settlements. 19 May.

The Bank for International Settlements (BIS). 2007. *Triennial Central Bank Survey of Foreign Exchange and Derivatives Market Activity*. Basel. Switzerland. December.

The Bank for International Settlements (BIS). 2005. *74th Annual Report, 2004*. Basel. Switzerland. 28 June.

Bartolini, L. and A. Drazen. 1997. "Capital Account Liberalization as a Signal". *American Economic Review*. Vol. 87. No. 1. pp. 138–154.

Bekaert, G. and C. Lundblad. 2005. "Does Financial Liberalization Spur Growth?" *Journal of Financial Economics*. Vol. 77. No. 1. pp. 3–55.

Bekaert,G., C.R. Harvey and C. Lundblad. 2009."Financial Openness and Productivity". Cambridge. MA. National Bureau of Economic Research. Working Paper No. 14843. April.

Berg, A., E. Borensztein and C. Pattillo. 2004. "Assessing Early Warning Systems: How Have They Worked in Practice?" Washington. DC. International Monetary Fund. Working Paper No. WP/04/52.

Bernanke, B.S. 2010. "Monetary Policy and the Housing Bubble". Paper presented at the annual meeting of the American Economic Association held in Atlanta. Georgia, on 3 January.

Bernanke, B.S. 2009. "Reflections on a Year of Crisis". Paper presented at the Federal Reserve Bank of Kansas City's *Annual Economic Symposiumon Financial Stability and Macroeconomic Stability* at Jackson Hole. Wyoming, on 21–22 August.

Bernanke, B.S. 2007. "Globalization and Monetary Policy". Lecture delivered at Stanford Institute for Economic Policy Research, Stanford University, Stanford, California, on 2 March.

Bernanke, B.S. 2006. "Global Economic Integration: What's New and What's Not?" in *The New Economic Geography: Effects and Policy Implications*. Kansas City. KA. The Federal Reserve Bank of Kansas City. pp. 1–14. August.

Bernanke, B.S. 2004. "Remarks by Governor Ben Bernanke" at the meeting of the Eastern Economic Association, in Washington. DC, on 20 February.

Blanchard, O. 2009. "The Perfect Storm". *Finance and Development*. Vol. 46. No. 2. pp. 37–39.

Blanchard, O. and J. Simon. 2001."The Long and Large Decline in US Output Volatility". *The Brookings Papers on Economic Activity*. Vol. 1. pp. 135–164.

Bohme, M., D. Chiarella and M. Lemerle. 2008. "The Growing Opportunities for Investment Banks in Emerging Markets". *The McKinsey Quarterly*. August. Available on the Internet at http://www.mckinseyquarterly.com/article_print. aspx?L2=10&l3=51&AR=2183. 15 January 2009.

Bonfiglioli, A. 2008. "Financial Integration and Capital Accumulation". *Journal of International Economics*. Vol. 76. No. 2. pp. 337–355.

Bordo, M.D. and B.J. Eichengreen. 1999. "Is Our Current International Economic Environment Unusually Crisis Prone?" in D. Gruen and L. Gower (eds) *Capital Flows and International Financial System*. Sydney. The Reserve Bank of Australia. pp. 18–75.

Bordo, M.D. and C.M. Meissner. 2007. "Foreign Capital and Economic Growth in the First Era of Globalization". Cambridge. MA. National Bureau of Economic Research. NBER Working Paper No. 13577. November.

Bordo, M.D., B.S. Eichengreen and D.A. Irwin. 1999a. "Is Globalization Today Really Different than Globalization a Hundred Years Ago?" Cambridge. MA. National Bureau of Economic Research. Working Paper. No. 7185. April.

Bordo, M.D., M. Edelstein and H. Rockoff. 1999b. "Was Adherence to the Gold Standard a 'Good Housekeeping Seal of Approval' During the Interwar Period?" Cambridge. MA. National Bureau of Economic Research. Working Paper No. 7186. June.

Borio, C. 2009. "Ten Propositions about Liquidity Crisis". Basel. Switzerland. Bank for International Settlements. BIS Working Paper No. 293. November.

Bradford, C. and J. Linn. 2009. "Welcome to the New Era of G-20 Global Leadership" in K. Dervis (ed.) *G-20- Summit: Recovering from the Crisis*. Washington. DC. Brookings Institution. pp. 16–18.

Brender, A. and F. Pisani. 2009. *Globalized Finance and its Collapse*. Brussels. Belgium. Dexia Asset Management.

Buch, C.M., J. Doepke and C. Pierdzioch. 2005. "Financial Openness and Business Cycle Volatility". *Journal of International Money and Finance*. Vol. 24. No. 5. pp. 744–765.

Calomiris, C.W. 2008. "The Sub-Prime Turmoil: What's Old, What's New" in *Maintaining Stability in a Changing Financial System*. Kansas City. MO. The Federal Reserve Bank of Kansas City. pp. 19–110.

Cameron, R.E. 1993. *A Concise Economic History of the World*. New York. Oxford University Press.

Carbaugh, R.J. and D.W. Hedrick. 2009. "Will the Dollar be Dethroned as the Main Reserve Currency?" *Global Economy Journal*. Vol. 9. No. 3. Article 1. pp. 1–14.

Chandy, L., G. Gertz and J. Linn. 2009. "Tracking the Global Financial Crisis". Washington. DC. The Brookings Institution. May.

Chari, A. and P.B. Henry. 2008. "Firm-Specific Information and the Efficiency of Investment". *Journal of Financial Economics*. Vol. 87. No. 3. pp. 636–655.

Chinn, M. and H. Ito. 2006. "What Matters for Financial Developments?" *Journal of Development Economics*. Vol. 8. No. 1. pp. 163–192.

Ciarlone, A., P. Piselli and G. Trebeschi. 2009. "Emerging Market' Spread and Global Financial Conditions". *Journal of International Financial Markets, Institutions and Money*. Vol. 19. No. 1. pp. 222–239.

Cipriani, M. and G. Kaminski. 2006. "A New Era of International Financial Integration". Washington. DC. George Washington. DC. The GW Center for the Study of Globalization. Occasional Paper Series.

Claessens, S. and L. Laeven. 2004. "What Drives Bank Competition? Some International Evidence". *Journal of Money, Credit and Banking*. Vol. 36. No. 3. pp. 563–583.

Claessens, S. and S.L. Schmukler. 2007. "International Financial Integration through Equity Markets". *Journal of International Money and Finance*. Vol. 26. No. 3. pp. 788–813.

Claessens, S. and N. van Horen. 2009. "Being a Foreigner among Domestic Banks: Asset or Liability". Available on the Internet at http://mpra.ub.uni-muenchen. de/13467/1/MPRA_paper_13467.pdf. 20 January 2009.

Claessens, S., M.A. Kose and M.E. Terrones. 2008. "What Happens During Recessions, Crunches and Busts?" Washington. DC. International Monetary Fund. Working Paper No. WP/08/274. December.

Clemens, M.A. and J.G. Williamson. 2004. "Wealth Bias in the First Global Capital Market Boom, 1870–1913". *The Economic Journal*. Vol. 114. No. 495. pp. 304–337.

Cline, W. 2006. "The US External Deficits and the Developing Economies". Washington. DC. The Center for Global Development. Working Paper No. 86. March.

Cline, W.R. 2009. "The Global Financial Crisis and Developing Strategy for Emerging Market Economies". Paper presented at the Annual Bank Conference on Development Economics, 23 June, in Seoul, the Republic of Korea.

Cornelius, P.K. and B. Kogut. 2003. *Corporate Governance and Capital Flowsin a Global Economy*. New York. Oxford University Press.

Council of Economic Advisers (CEA). 2009. "First Quarterly Report" Washington. DC. Executive Office of the President of the United States. 10 September.

Crafts, N. 2000. "Globalization and Growth in the Twentieth Century". Washington DC. International Monetary Fund. Working Paper No. WP/00/44. March.

Crockett, A. 2009. "Asia and the Global Financial Crisis". Paper presented at the conference on *Reforming the Global Financial Architecture* sponsored by the Federal Reserve Bank of San Francisco, Santa Barbara. California, 18–20 October.

Das, Dilip K. 2010. "The Renminbi Yuan and its Accelerating Global Clout". *Journal of Asian Business Studies*. San Francisco. Vol. 5. No. 1. Spring. (forthcoming).

Das, Dilip K. 2009a. *The Two Faces of Globalization: Munificent and Malevolent*. Northampton. MA. USA and Cheltenham. Glos. Edward Elgar Publishing, Inc.

Das, Dilip K. 2009b."Short- and Long-Term Prospects of Indian Economic Growth: A Dispassionate Analysis". *International Journal of Trade and Global Markets*. Vol. 20. No. 2. pp. 194–210.

Das, Dilip K. 2009c. "Globalization and an Emerging Global Middle Class". *Economic Affairs*. London. Vol. 29. No. 3. pp. 89–99.

Das, Dilip K. 2008a. "Repositioning the Chinese Economy on the Global Economic Stage". *International Review of Economics*. Vol. 55. No. 4. September 2008. pp. 4–417.

Das, Dilip K. 2008b. "Sovereign-Wealth Funds: A New Role for the Emerging Market Economies in the World of Global Finance". *International Journal of Development Issues*. Sydney. Vol. 7. No. 2. pp. 80–96.

Das, Dilip K. 2008c. *Winners of Globalization*. University of Warwick. UK. Center for the Study of Globalization and Regionalization, CSGR Working Paper No. 249/08. Also available on the Internet at http://www2.warwick.ac.uk/fac/soc/csgr/research/workingpapers/2008/24908.pdf. August 2008.

Das, Dilip K. 2008d. *The Chinese Economic Renaissance: Apocalypse or Cornucopia*. Houndmills. Hampshire. UK. Palgrave Macmillan Ltd.

Das, Dilip K. 2008e. "China's Newly Evolving Role in the Global Economy". *CESifo Forum*. Vol. 9. No. 1. Munich. April. pp. 39–46.

Das, Dilip K. 2007. "The East is Rich: China's Inexorable Climb to Economic Dominance". Sydney. Macquarie University. Center for Japanese Economic Studies. Research Paper No. 2007–4. December.

Das, Dilip K. 2006a. *China and India: A Tale of Two Economies*. London and New York. Routledge.

Das, Dilip K. 2006b. "Globalization in the World of Finance: An Analytical History". *Global Economic Journal*. Vol. 6. No. 1. Article 2. Berkeley. CA. The Berkeley Electronic Press. Available on the Internet at http://www.bepress.com/cgi/viewcontent.cgi?article=1115&contex=gej. 12 January 2009.

Das, Dilip K. 2005. *Asian Economy and Finance: A Post-Crisis Perspective*. Cambridge. and New York. USA. Springer Publications.

Das, Dilip K. 2004. *Financial Globalization and the Emerging-Market Economies*. London and New York. Routledge.

Das, Dilip K. 2003a. "Globalization in the World of Finance" in Dilip K. Das (ed.) *An International Finance Reader*. London and New York. Routledge. pp. 12–26.

Das, Dilip K. 2003b. "Financial Flows and Global Integration". Coventry. UK. University of Warwick. Center for the Study of Globalization and Regionalization. CSGR Working Paper No. 132/04. June.

Das, Dilip K. 2001. *The Global Trading System at Crossroads: A Post-Seattle Perspective*. London and New York. Routledge.

Das, Dilip K. 2000. *Asian Crisis: Distilling Critical Lessons*. United Nations Conference on Trade and Development (UNCTAD). Geneva. Discussion Paper No. 152. December.

Das, Dilip K. 1989. "Brady Plan and the International Banks: A Cautious Reception". *The Business Standard*. Bombay. 24 August. p. 8.

Das, Dilip K. 1986. *Migration of Financial Resources to Developing Countries*. London. The Macmillan Press Ltd. and New York. St. Martin's Press, Inc.

Dattels, P. and K. Miyajima. 2009. "Will Emerging Markets Remain Resilient to Global Stress?" *Global Journal of Emerging Market Economies*. Vol. 1. No. 1. pp. 5–24.

Daudin, G., M. Morys and K.H. O'Kourke. 2008. "Globalization 1870–1914". Dublin. Ireland. Trinity College. IIIS Discussion Paper No. 250. May.

de la Torre, A. and S.L. Schmukler. 2007. *Emerging Capital Markets and Globalization*. Palo Alto. CA. Stanford University Press.

de la Torre, A. and S.L. Schmukler. 2005. "Small Fish, Big Pond". *Finance and Development*. Vol. 42. No. 2. pp. 47–49.

de la Torre, A., S. Schmukler and L. Serven. 2009. "Back to Global Imbalances?" Washington. DC. The World Bank. 13 July.

Demirguc-Kunt, A. and E. Detragiache. 1998. "The Determinants of Banking Crises in Developing and Developed Countries". *IMF Staff Papers*. Vol. 45. No. 1 pp. 81–109.

Demirguc-Kunt, A. and L. Serven. 2009. "Are All the Sacred Cows Dead?" The World Bank. Policy Research Working Paper No. 4807. January.

Dervis, K. 2009. "The G-20, the Istanbul Decisions and the Way Forward". Washington. DC. The Brookings Institution. 17 November. Available on the Internet at http://www.brookings.edu/opinions/2009/1008_g20_istanbul_dervis.aspx?p=1. 12 October 2009.

Devereux, M.B. and A. Sutherland. 2009. "A Portfolio Moel of Capital Flows to Emerging Markets". *Journal of Development Economics*. Vol. 89. No. 2. pp. 181–193.

Deutsche Bank Research (DBR). 2009. "Sovereign Wealth Funds: State Investments During the Financial Crisis". Frankfurt. Germany. 15 July.

Deutsche Bank Research (DBR). 2007. "Sovereign Wealth Funds: State Investment on the Rise". Frankfurt. Germany. 10 September.

Dodd, R. 2007. "Subprime: Tentacles of a Crisis". *Finance and Development*. Vol. 44. No. 4. pp. 15–19.

Dooley, M.P., P.M. Garber and D. Folkerts-Landau. 2009. "Bretton Woods II Still Defines the International Monetary System". Cambridge. MA. National Bureau of Economic Research. Working Paper No.14731. February.

Dooley, M.P., P.M. Garber and D. Folkerts-Landau. 2007. "The Crisis of International Economics". Cambridge. MA. National Bureau of Economic Research. Working Paper No. 13197. June.

Dooley, M.P., P.M. Garber and D. Folkerts-Landau. 2003. "An Essay on the Revised Bretton Woods System". Cambridge. MA. National Bureau of Economic Research. Working Paper No. 9971. September.

Dowrick, S. and J.B. DeLong. 2005. "Globalization and Convergence" in M.D. Bordo, A.M. Taylor and J.G. Williamson (eds) *Globalization in Historical Perspective*. Chicago. The University of Chicago Press. pp. 191–205.

The Economist. 2009a. "Two Billion More Bourgeois". 14 February. p. 18.

The Economist. 2009b. "Whom Can They Rely on?" 6 May. p. 61.

The Economist. 2009c. "From Slump to Jump". 1 August. p. 16.

The Economist. 2009d. "Rearranging the Towers of Gold". 12 September. pp. 75–77.

The Economist. 2009e. "Gone Shopping". 30 May. p. 65.

The Economist. 2008. "The Invasion of the Sovereign-Wealth Funds". 19 January. p. 11.

The Economic Intelligence Unit (EIU). 2009. "World Economy: BRIC, but No Bloc". Available on the Internet at http://viewswire.eiu.com/index.asp?layout=VWPrintVW3&article_id=734586458&printer=. Posted on 16 June.

The Economic Intelligence Unit (EIU). 2009a. "The Risk of Trade protectionism". Available on the Internet at http://viewswire.eiu.com/index.asp?layout=VWPrintVW3&article_id=1714520356&printer=printer&rf=0. Posted on 19 May.

The Economic Intelligence Unit (EIU). 2009b. "World Economy: Balancing Act". London. 31 August.

Edelstein, M. 2004. "Foreign Investment, Accumulation and Empire 1860–1940" in R. Floud and P. Johnson (eds) *The Cambridge Economic History of Modern Britain*. Cambridge. Cambridge University Press.

Edison, H.J. 2000. "Do Indicators of Financial Crises Work? An Evaluation". Washington. DC. The Board of Governors of the Federal Reserve Board. International Finance Discussion Paper No. 675. November.

Edison, H. and F.E. Warnock. 2003. "A Simple Measure of the Intensity of Capital Controls". *Journal of Empirical Finance*. Vol. 10. No. 1. pp. 81–103.

Edison, H.J., R. Levine, L. Ricci and T. Slok. 2002. "Capital Account Liberalization and Economic Performance: Survey and Synthesis". Washington. DC. International Monetary Fund. Working Paper No. WP/02/120.

Edwards, S. 2009. "Sequencing of Reforms, Financial Globalization and Macroeconomic Vulnerability". *Journal of Japanese and International Economy*. Vol. 23. No. 2. pp. 131–148.

Edwards, S. 2001. "Capital Mobility and Economic Performance: Are Emerging Economic Different?" Cambridge. MA. National Bureau of Economic Research. NBER Working Paper No. 8076. January.

Edwards, S. 1999. "How Effective are Capital Controls?" *The Journal of Economic Perspectives*. Vol. 13. No. 4. (Autumn) pp. 65–84.

Eichengreen, B.J. 2008. "The Global Credit Crisis as History". Paper presented at Bank of Thailand International Symposium on *Financial Globalization and Emerging Market Economies* at Dusit Thani Hotel. Bangkok, during 7–8 November.

Eichengreen, B.J. 2001. "Capital Account Liberalization: What Do Cross-Country Studies Tell Us?" *World Bank Economic Review*. Vol. 15. No. 2. pp. 341–365.

Eichengreen, B.J. 1999. *Globalizing Capital: A History of the International Monetary System*. Princeton. NJ. Princeton University Press.

Eichengreen, B.J. and M.D. Bordo. 2002. "Cries Then and Now: What Lessons from the Last Era of Globalization". Cambridge. MA. National Bureau of Economic Research. NBER Working Paper 8716. January.

Eichengreen, B.J. and H. James. 2005. "Monetary and Financial Reforms in Two Eras of Globalization" in M.D. Bordo, A.M. Taylor and J.G. Williamson (eds) *Globalization in Historical Perspective*. Chicago. The University of Chicago Press. pp. 515–548.

Eichengreen, B.J. and K. O'Rourke. 2009. "A Tale of Two Depressions". Available on the Internet at http://www.voxeu.org/index.php?q=node/3421. 12 October 2009.

Eichengreen, B.J. and A. Rose. 1998. "Staying Afloat When the Wind Shifts. External Factors and Emerging-Market Banking Crisis". Cambridge. MA. National Bureau of Economic Research. Working Paper No. 6370.

Eichengreen, B.J. and N. Sussman. 2000. "The International Monetary System in the Very Long Run" in *World Economic Outlook Supporting Studies*. Washington. DC. International Monetary Fund. pp. 52–85.

Eichengreen, B.J., R. Hausmann and U. Panizza. 2006. "The Pain of Original Sin" in B.J. Eichengreen and R. Hausmann (eds) *Other People's Money*. Chicago. University of Chicago Press. pp. 130–152.

Elliott, A. and C. Lemert. 2009. *Globalization*. London and New York. Routledge.

Farrell, D., C.S. Folster and S. Lund. 2008. "Long-Term Trends in the Global Capital Markets". *The McKinsey Quarterly*. February. Available on the Internet at http://www.stern.nyu.edu/eco/B012303/Backus/Writing_samples/ McKinsey%20Quarterly%2008.PDF. 22 January 2009.

Feis, H. 1930. *Europe the World's Banker, 1870–1914*. New Haven. CT. Yale University Press.

Feldstein, M. and C. Horioka. 1980. "Domestic Savings and International Capital Flows". *The Economic Journal*. Vol. 90. No. 2. pp. 314–329.

Felton, F. and C. Reinhart. 2008. *The First Financial Crisis of the 21st Century*. London. Center for Economic Policy Research.

Ferguson, N. 2008. *The Ascent of Money*. New York. The Penguin Press.

Fernandes, N. and A. Bris. 2009. "Sovereign Wealth Revalued". *Financial Times*. 12 February. p. 16.

Findlay, R. and K.H. O'Rourke. 2007. *Power and Plenty*. Princeton. Princeton University Press.

Fischer, S. 2003. "Globalization and its Challenges". *American Economic Review*. Vol. 93. No. 2. pp. 1–30.

Fischer, S. 1997. "Capital Account Liberalization and the Role of the IMF". Lecture at the annual Meeting of the International Monetary Fund, 19 September. Available on the Internet at http://www.imf.org/external/np/speeches.199/ 091997.htm. 29 January 2009.

Fratzscher, M. and M. Bussiere. 2004. "Financial Openness and Growth: Short-Run Gain, Lon-Run Gain?" Frankfurt. European Central Bank. Working Paper No. 348.

Freund, C. 2009. "The Trade Response to Global Downturns: Historic Evidence". Washington. DC. The World Bank. Research Working Paper No. 5015. November.

Frieden, J.A. 2007. *Global Capitalism, Its Fall and Rise in the Twentieth Century*. New York. W.W. Norton & Co.

Fry, M.J. 1997. "In Favor of Financial Liberalization". *Economic Journal*. Vol. 107. pp. 754–770.

Fry, M.J. 1995. *Money, Interest and Banking in Economic Development*. Baltimore. MD. The Johns Hopkins University Press.

Gallegati, M., B. Greenwald, M.G. Richiardi and J.E. Stiglitz. 2008. "The Asymmetric Effect of Diffusion Process: Risk Sharing and Contagion". *Global Economy Journal*. Vol. 8. No. 2. pp. 30–58.

Glick, R., X. Guo and M. Hutchison. 2006. "Currency Crises, Capital Account Liberalization and Selection Bias". *Review of Economics and Statistics*. Vol. 88. No. 4. pp. 698–714.

Global Economic Prospects (GEP). 2010. Washington. DC. The World Bank. 16 January.

Goldman Sachs. 2005. "How Solid are the BRICs?" New York. Global Economics Paper No: 134. December.

Goldman Sachs. 2003. "Dreaming With BRICs: The Path to 2050". New York. Global Economics Paper No. 99. October.

Gomes, T. 2008. "The Impact of Sovereign Wealth Funds on International Financial Stability". Ottawa. Ontario. Bank of Canada. Discussion Paper No. 2008-14. September.

Gottschalk, R. 2003. "International Lenders' and Investors' Behavior: What the Markets Tell Us?" Brighton. Institute of Development Studies. University of Sussex. *IDS Working Paper*. No. 193. July.

Gourinchas, P.O. and O. Jeanne. 2007. "Capital Flows to Developing Countries: The Allocation Puzzle". Cambridge. MA. National Bureau of Economic Research. Working Paper No. 13602. June.

Gourinchas, P.O. and O. Jeanne. 2006. "The Elusive Gains from International Financial Integration". *Review of Economic Studies*. Vol. 73. No. 3. pp. 715–741.

Gourinchas, P.O. and O. Jeanne. 2005. "Capital Mobility and Reform". Berkeley. University of California. (mimeo).

Gozzi, J.C., R. Levine and S.L. Schmukler. 2008. "Patterns of International Capital Ratings". Washington. DC. The World Bank. Policy Research Working Paper No. 4687. August.

Greenlaw, D., J. Hatzius, A.K. Kashyap and H.S. Shin. 2008. "Leveraged Losses: Lessons from the Mortgage Market Meltdown". Chicago. University of Chicago. Graduate School of Business. Monetary Policy Forum Report No. 2.

Greenspan, A. 2007. *The Age of Turbulence: Adventures in a New World*. New York. Penguin Press.

Greenspan, A. 2005. "International Imbalances". Speech given to the Advancing Enterprise Conference. London. UK. on 2 December.

Griffith-Jones, S. and J.A. Ocampo. 2008. "Sovereign Wealth Funds: A Developing Country Perspective". Paper presented at a conference on sovereign wealth funds organized by the Andean Development Corporation. London, on 18 February.

Grilli. V. and G.M. Milesi-Ferretti. 1995. "Economic Effects and Structural Determinants of Capital Controls". *IMF Staff Papers*. Vol. 42. No. 3. pp. 517–551.

Grinblatt, M. and M. Keloharju. 2001. "How Distance, Language and Culture Influence Stockholdings and Trades". *Journal of Finance*. Vol. 56. No. 3. pp. 1053–1074.

Guttmann, R. 2009. "The Collapse of Securitization: From Subprime to Global Credit Crunch". International Economic Policy Institute. Laurentian University. Ontario. Canada. Working Paper 2009-05. June.

Gupta, N. and K. Yuan. 2009. "On the Growth Effects of Liberalization". *Review of Financial Studies*. Vol. 22. No. 11. pp. 4715–4752.

Gyntelberg, J. 2009. "Highlights of International Banking and Financial Market Activity". *BIS Quarterly Review*. June. pp. 19–34.

Haskell, J.E., S.C. Pereira and M.J. Slaughter. 2007. "Does Inward Foreign Direct Investment Boost the Productivity of Domestic Fitms?" *Review of Economics and Statistics*. Vol. 89. No. 3. pp. 482–496.

Helleiner, E. and J. Kirshner. 2009. *The Future of the Dollar*. Ithaca. New York. Cornell University Press.

Henning, C.R. 2009. "The Future of Chiang Mai Initiative: An Asian Monetary Fund". Washington. DC. Peterson Institute of International Economics. Policy Brief no. PB09-5. February.

Henry, P.B. 2007. "Capital Account Liberalization, Theory, Evidence and Speculation". *Journal of Economic Literature*. Vol. 45. No. 4. pp. 887–935.

Henry, P.B. 2000. "Do Stock Market Liberalizations Cause Investment Boom". *Journal of Financial Economics*. Vol. 58. No. 2. pp. 301–334.

Henry, P.B. and D. Sasson. 2008. "Capital Account Liberalization, Real Wages and Productivity". Washington. DC. The Brookings Institution. Working Paper No. 20. March.

Highfill, J. 2009. "The Economic Crisis as of December 2008". *Global Economy Journal*. Vol. 8. No. 4. pp. 1–5.

Institute of International Finance (IIF). 2009. "Capital Flows to Emerging Market Economies". Washington. DC. 27 January.

The International Monetary Fund (IMF). 2009a. *World Economic Outlook*. Washington. DC. April.

The International Monetary Fund (IMF). 2009b. *World Economic Outlook Database*. Washington. DC. January.

The International Monetary Fund (IMF). 2009c. *Global Financial Stability Report*. Washington. DC. April.

The International Monetary Fund (IMF). 2009d. *World Economic Outlook Update*. Washington. DC. 8 July.

The International Monetary Fund (IMF). 2009e. *World Economic Outlook*. Washington. DC. October.

The International Monetary Fund (IMF). 2009f. "Regional Economic Outlook: Asia and Pacific". Washington. DC. October.

The International Monetary Fund (IMF). 2008. "Sovereign Wealth Funds: A Work Agenda". Washington. DC. 29 February.

The International Monetary Fund (IMF). 2008a. "Reaping Benefits of Financial Globalization". Washington. DC. Occasional Paper 264. December.

The International Monetary Fund (IMF). 2008b. *World Economic Outlook*. Washington. DC. April.

The International Monetary Fund (IMF). 2008c. "Globalization: A Brief Overview". *Issues Brief*. No. 02/08. Washington. DC. May.

The International Monetary Fund (IMF). 2008d. *World Economic Outlook*. Washington. DC. October.

The International Monetary Fund (IMF). 2007a. "Global Financial Stability Report". Washington. DC. September.

The International Monetary Fund (IMF). 2007b. "The Role of Fiscal Institutions in Managing the Oil Revenue Boom". Washington. DC. 5 March.

The International Monetary Fund (IMF). 2007c. "IMF Convenes First Annual Roundtable of Sovereign Asset and Reserve Managers". Washington. DC. Press Release No. 07/267, 16 November.

The International Monetary Fund (IMF). 1997. "Communiqué of the Interim Committee of the Board of Governors: The Liberalization of Capital Movements under an Amendment of the IMF's Articles". Washington. DC. Press Release No. 97/44.

International Working Group of Sovereign-Wealth Funds (IWG). 2008. "Sovereign-Wealth Funds: Generally Accepted Principle and Practices". Abu Dhabi. UAE and Washington. DC. October.

James, H. 2009. "The Making of a Mess". *Foreign Affairs*. January/February. Vol. 80. No. 1. pp. 48–59.

James, H. 2001. *The End of Globalization: Lessons from the Great Depression*. Cambridge. MA. Harvard University Press.

Javorcik, B.S. 2004. "Does Foreign Direct Investment Increase Productivity of Domestic Firms?" *American Economic Review*. Vol. 94. No. 3. pp. 605–627.

Jen, S.L. 2007a. "How Big Could Sovereign Wealth Funds Be?" *Global Economic Forum*. New York. Morgan Stanley Research. 4 May.

Jen, S.L. 2007b. "Sovereign Wealth Funds". New York. Morgan Stanley Research. October.

Johnson, S. 2007a. "The Rise of Sovereign Wealth Funds". *Finance and Development*. Vol. 44. No. 3. pp. 56–59.

Joyce, J.P. 2009. "Financial Globalization and Banking Crises in Emerging Markets". Wellesley. MA. Wellesley College. Department of Economics. Working Paper. January.

Kaminsky, G. 2005. "International Capital Flows, Financial Stability and Growth". Washington. DC. George Washington University. The GW Center for the Study of Globalization. Occasional paper Series. December.

Kaminsky, G. and C. Reinhart. 1999. "The Twin Crises: The Causes of Banking and Balance-of-Payments Problems". *American Economic Review*. Vol. 89. No. 2. pp. 473–500.

Kaminsky, G. and S. Schmukler. 2008. "Short-Run Pain, Long-Run Gain: The Effects of Financial Liberalization". *Review of Finance*. Vol. 12. No. 2. pp. 253–292.

Kaminsky, G. and S. L. Schmukler. 2003. "Short-Term Pain, Long-Term Gain: The Effects of Financial Liberalization". Cambridge. MA. National Bureau of Economic Research. NBER Working Paper No. 9787. June.

Kaminsky, G., C. Reinhart and C.A. Vegh. 2004. "When it Rains, It Pours: Procyclical Capital Flows and Macroeconomic Development". Cambridge. MA. National Bureau of Economic Research. Working Paper. No. 10780. September.

Kane, E.J. 2009. "Incentive Roots of the Securitization Crisis and Its Early Mismanagement". *The Yale Journal on Regulation*. Vol. 26. No. 2. pp. 405–416.
Kenen, P.B. 2007. "The Benefits and Risks of Financial Globalization". *The Cato Journal*. Vol. 27. No. 2. pp. 179–183.
Keynes, J.M. 1936. *The General Theory of Employment, Interest and Money*. Cambridge. UK. Cambridge University Press for Royal Economic Society.
Kindleberger, C.P. 2000. *Manias, Panics and Crashes*. New York. Wiley & Sons.
Kimmitt, R.M. 2008. "Public Footprints in Private Markets: Sovereign Wealth Funds". *Foreign Affairs*. Vol. 87. No. 1. January/February. pp. 119–131.
King, R.G. and R. Levine. 1993. "Finance and Growth: Schumpeter Might Be Right". *Quarterly Journal of Economics*. Vol. 108. No. 3. pp. 717–738.
Klein, M.W. and G. Olivei. 1999. "Capital Account Liberalization, Financial Depth and Economic Growth". Cambridge. MA. National Bureau of Economic Research. NBER Working Paper No. 7384.
Kohler, H. 2002. "Strengthening the Framework for the Global Economy", A speech given on the occasion of the Award Ceremony of the Konrad Adenauer Foundation, Berlin, Germany. 15 November 2002. Available on the Internet at http://www.imf.org/external/np/speeches/2002/111502.htm. 15 October 2009.
Kose, M.A. and E.S. Prasad. 2009. "The Decoupling is Back!" Washington. DC. Brookings Institution. Available on the Internet at http://www.foreignpolicy.com/story/cms.php?story_id=5010&print=1. 12 June 2009.
Kose, M.A., C. Otrok and E.S. Prasad. 2008. "Global Business Cycles: Convergence or Decoupling?" Cambridge. MA. National Bureau of Economic Research. Working Paper No. 14292. October.
Kose, M.A., E.S. Prasad and A.D. Taylor. 2009. "Thresholds in the Process of International Financial Integration". Ithaca. New York. Cornell University. June. (Unpublished Manuscript).
Kose, M.A., E.S. Prasad and M.E. Terrones. 2009. Does Openness to International Financial Flows Raise Productivity Growth? *Journal of International Money and Finance*. Vol. 28. No. 4. pp. 554–580.
Kose, M.A., E.S. Prasad and M.E. Terrones. 2006. "How Do Trade and Financial Integration Affect the Relationship between Growth and Volatility?" *Journal of International Economics*. Vol. 69. No. 1. pp. 176–202.
Kose, M.A., E.S. Prasad and M.E. Terrones. 2003. "Financial Integration and Macroeconomic Volatility". *IMF Staff Papers*. Vol. 50. No. 1. pp. 119–142.
Kose, M.A., E.S. Prasad, K.S. Kogoff and S.J. Wei. 2009. "Financial Globalization and Economic Policies". Washington. DC. The Brookings Institution. Working Paper No. 24. April.
Kose, M.A., E.S. Prasad, K. S. Kogoff and S.J. Wei. 2009b. "Financial Globalization: A Reappraisal". *IMF Staff Papers*. Vol. 56. No. 1. pp. 8–62.
Kotter, J. and U. Lel. 2008. "Friends or Foes? The Stock Price Impact of Sovereign Wealth Fund Investments and the Price of Keeping Secrets". Washington. DC. Board of Governors of the Federal Reserves System. International Finance Discussion Paper No. 940. August.
Kraay, A. 1998. "In Search of Macroeconomic Effects of Capital Account Liberalization". Washington. DC. The World Bank. (unpublished manuscript).
Kramer, A.E. 2009. "Emerging Economies Meet in Russia". *New York Times*. 17 June. p. 3.

Krugman, P.R. 2009. "Revenge of the Glut". *The New York Times*. 2 March. p. 16.

Krugman, P. 2009a. "The Dark Age of Macroeconomics" *The New York Times*. 27 January. Available on the Internet at http://krugman.blogs.nytimes.com/2009/01/27/a-dark-age-of-macroeconomics-wonkish/.

Krugman, P. 2009b. "How Did Economists Get it So Wrong?" *The New York Times*. 6 September. p. 14.

Krugman, P. 2009c. "Averting the Worst". *The New York Times*. 9 August. p. 12.

Krugman, P. 1998. "What Happened to Asia?" Available on his website at http://www.hartford-hwp.com/archives/50/010.html. 24 January 2009.

Krugman, P.R. 2000. "Crises: A Price of Globalization?" in *Global Economic Integration: Opportunities and Challenges*. Kansas City. KA. The Federal Reserve Bank of Kansas City. pp.75–109. August.

Krugman, P.R. and M. Obstfeld. 2008. *International Economics: Theory and Policy*. 8th edition. Boston. Pearson Addison Wesley.

Lane, P.R. 2009. "The Global Crisis and Capital Flows to Emerging Markets" in M. Dewatripont and X. Freixas (eds) *Macroeconomic Stability and Financial Regulation*. London. Centre for Economic Policy Research. pp. 27–48.

Lane, P.R. and G.M. Milesi-Ferretti. 2008a. "The Drivers of Financial Globalization". *American Economic Review*. Vol. 98. No. 2. pp. 327–332.

Lane, P.R. and G.M. Milesi-Ferretti. 2008b. "International Investment Patterns". *The Review of Economics and Statistics*. Vol. 90. No. 3. pp. 538–549.

Lane, P.R. and G.M. Milesi-Ferretti. 2007. "The External Wealth of Nations Mark II". *Journal of International Economics*. Vol. 73. No. 2. pp. 223–250.

Lane, P.R. and G.M. Milesi-Ferretti. 2005. "A Global Position on External Positions". Dublin. Institute for International Integration Studies. Trinity College. IIIS Discussion Paper No. 79. December.

Lane, P. R. and G.M. Milesi-Ferrtti. 2003. "International Financial Integration". *IMF Staff Papers*. Vol. 50. Special Issue. pp. 82–113.

Lane, P.R. and S.L. Schmukler. 2007. "The Evolving Role of China and India in the Global Financial System". *Open Economies Review*. Vol. 18. No. 4. pp. 499–520.

Lardy, N.R. 2006. "China's Interaction with the Global Economy" in R. Garnaut and L. Song (eds)*The Turning Point in China's Economic Development*. Canberra. Australia. The Asia Pacific Press. Australian National University. pp. 76–86.

Lardy, N.R. 2002. *Integrating China into the Global Economy*. Washington. DC. The Brookings Institutions.

Leijonhufvud, C. 2007. "Financial Globalization and Emerging Market Volatility". *The World Economy*. Vol. 30. No. 12. pp. 1817–1842.

Levine, R. 2005. "Finance and Growth: Theory and Evidence" in P. Aghion and S. Durlauf (eds) *Handbook of Economic Growth*. Vol. 1A. pp. 865–934. Amsterdam. Elsevier.

Levine, R. and S.L. Schmukler. 2006. "Internationalization and Stock Market Liquidity". *Review of Finance*. Vol. 10. No. 1. pp. 153–187.

Levine, R. and S. Zervos. 1998. "Capital Control Liberalization and Stock Market Development". *World Development*. Vol. 26. No. 7. pp. 1169–1183.

Lin, J.Y. 2009. "Learning from the Past to Reinvent the Future". Opening remarks at the Annual Bank Conference on Development Economics, 23 June. Seoul. Republic of Korea.

Lin, Justin Yifu. 2008. "Foreword". *Global Development Finance*. The World Bank. Washington. DC.

Lipsky, J. 2009. "Preparing for a Post-Crisis World". *Finance and Development*. Vol. 46. No. 2. pp. 29–31.

Lipsky, J. 2007. "The Global Economy and Financial Markets: Where Next?" Speech given at the Lowy Institute. Sydney. Australia, on 31 July.

Litan, R., P. Masson and M. Pomerleano. 2001. *Open Doors: Foreign Participation in Financial Systems in Developing Countries*. Washington. DC. The Brookings Institution.

Lombardi, D. 2009. "Washington Roundtable on the Global Economic Agenda". Washington. DC. The Brookings Institution. Issues Paper. October.

Lowery, C. 2007. "Remarks on Sovereign Wealth Funds and the International Financial System". Washington. DC. The United States Department of the Treasury. 21 June. Available on the Internet at http://www.treas.gov/press/release/hp471.htm. 11 September 2009.

Lucas, R.E. 2000. "Some Macroeconomics for the 21st Century". *Journal of Economic Perspectives*. Vol. 14. No. 1. pp. 159–168.

Lucas, R.E. 1990. "Why Doesn't Capital Flow from Rich to Poor Countries?" *American Economic Review*. Vol. 80. No. 2. pp. 92–96.

Lucchetti, A. and S. Ng. 2007. "Credit and Blame: How Rating Firms' Calls Fueled Subprime Mess". *Wall Street Journal*. 15 August. p. A1.

Maddison, A. 2003. *The World Economy: Historical Statistics*. Paris. The Development Center. Organization for Economic Cooperation and Development.

Maddison, A. 1995. *Monitoring the World Economy 1920–1992*. Paris. Organization for Economic Cooperation and Development.

Martin, P. and H. Rey. 2004. "Financial Super-Markets: Size Matters for Asset Trade". *Journal of International Economics*. Vol. 64. No. 2. pp. 335–361.

Masson, P. 2001. "Globalization: Facts and Figures". Washington. DC. International Monetary Fund. Policy Discussion Working Paper. October.

Mauro, P., N. Sussman and Y. Yafeh. 2006. *Emerging Markets, Sovereign Debts and International Financial Integration*. New York. Oxford University Press.

McCauley, R.N. 2008. "Fuller Capital Account Opening in China and India". Paper presented at the third research meeting of NIPFP-DEA Program on Capital Flows, held in New Delhi, on 30 September.

McKinnon, R.I. 1973. *Money and Capital in Economic Development*. Washington. DC. The Brookings Institution Press.

McDonald, L.G. and P. Robinson. 2009. *A Colossal Failure of Commonsense: The Inside Story of the Collapse of Lehman Brothers*. New York. Crown Business.

McKinsey Global Institute (MGI). 2009a. "The New Power Brokers". San Francisco. July.

McKinsey Global Institute (MGI). 2009b. *Global Capital Markets: Entering a New Era*. San Francisco. September.

McKinsey Global Institute (MGI). 2008. "The New Power Brokers: Gaining Clout in Turbulent Markets". San Francisco. July.

Mendoza, E.G., V. Quadrini and J.V. Rios-Rull. 2009. "Financial Integration, Financial Development and Global Imbalances". *Journal of Political Economy*. Vol. 117. No. 2. pp. 60–89.

Mendoza, E.G., V. Quadrini and J.V. Rios-Rull. 2007. "On the Welfare Implications of Financial Globalization without Financial Development". Cambridge. MA. National Bureau of Economic Research. Working Paper No. 13412. September.

Mihn, S. 2008. "Dr. Doom". *The New York Times*. 15 August. p. 3.

Mishkin, F.S. 2009. "Why We Shouldn't Turn Our Backs on Financial Globalization". *IMF Staff Papers*. Vol. 56. No. 1. pp. 140–170.

Mishkin, F.S. 2006. *The Next Great Globalization*. Princeton and Oxford. Princeton University Press.

Mishkin, F.S. 2003. "Financial Policies and the Prevention of Financial Crises in Emerging Markets" in M. Feldstein (ed.) *Economic and Financial Crisis in Emerging Markets*. Chicago. University of Chicago Press. pp. 130–147.

Mishkin, F.S. 2001. "Financial Policies and Prevention of Financial Crises in Emerging Market Economies". Cambridge. MA. National Bureau of Economic Research. Working Paper. No. 8087. April.

Mitton, T. 2006. "Stock Market Liberalization and Operating Performances at the Firm Level". *Journal of Financial Economics*. Vol. 81. No. 3. pp. 625–647.

Mizen, P. 2008. "The Credit Crunch of 2007–2008: A Discussion of the Background". *Federal Reserve Bank of St. Louis Review*. Vol. 50. No. 5. pp. 531–567.

Mundell, R.A. 2000. "A Reconsideration of the Twentieth Century". *American Economic Review*. Vol. 90. No. 3. pp. 327–340.

Mundell, R.A. 1960. "The Monetary Dynamics of International Adjustment under Fixed and Flexible Exchange Rates". *Quarterly Journal of Economics*. Vol. 84. No. 2. pp. 227–257.

Mussa, M. 2009. "Global Economic Prospects as of September 2009". Paper presented at the sixteenth semiannual meeting on Global Economic Prospects, organized by the Peterson Institute of International Economics in Washington. DC, on 17 September.

Mussa, M. 2000. "Factors Driving Global Economic Integration" in *Global Economic Integration: Opportunities and Challenges*. Kansas City. Missouri. The Federal Reserve Bank of Kansas City. pp. 8–56. August.

Mussa, M. and M. Goldstein. 1993. "The Integration of World Capital Markets" in *Changing Capital Markets: Implications for Monetary Policy*. Kansas City. Missouri. The Federal Reserve Bank of Kansas City. pp. 55–93. August.

National Bureau of Economic Research (NBER). (2008). "Determination of December 2007 Peak in Economic Activity". Business Cycle dating Committee. Cambridge. MA. Available on the Internet at http://www.nber.org/dec2008.pdf. Posted on 11 December.

Neal, L. 1990. *The Rise of Financial Capitalism: International Capital Markets in the Age of Reason*. Cambridge. Cambridge University Press.

Neal, L. and M. Weidenmier. 2005. "Crises in the Global Economy from Tulip to Today" in M.D. Bordo, A.M. Taylor and J.G. Williamson (eds) *Globalization in Historical Perspective*. Chicago. The University of Chicago Press. pp. 473–513.

Nellor, D.C. 2008. "The Rise of Africa's Frontier Markets". *Finance and Development*. Vol. 45. No. 3. pp. 28–32.

Newbery, D.M. and J.E. Stiglitz. 1984. "Pareto Inferior Trade". *Review of Economic Studies*. Vol. 51. No. 1. pp. 1–12.

Norris, F. 2009. "A Retreat from Global Banking". *The New York Times*. 24 July. p. 2.

Noy, I. and T.B. Vu. 2007. "Capital Account Liberalization and Foreign Direct Investment". Honolulu. Hawaii. Department of Economics. University of Hawaii. Working Paper No. 07-8. March.

Obstfeld, M. 2009. "International Finance and Growth in Developing Countries: What Have We Learned?" *IMF Staff Papers*. Vol. 56. No. 1. pp. 63–111.

Obstfeld, M. 2007. "International Risk Sharing and the Cost of Trade". Ohlin lectures delivered at the Stockholm School of Economics, in May.

Obstfeld, M. and A.M. Taylor. 2005. "Globalization and Capital Markets" in M.D. Bordo, A.M. Taylor and J.G. Williamson (eds) *Globalization in Historical Perspective*. Chicago. The University of Chicago Press. pp. 121–183.

Obstfeld, M. and A.M. Taylor. 2004. *Global Capital Markets: Integration, Crisis and Growth*. Cambridge. Cambridge University Press.

Obstfeld, M. and A.M. Taylor. 2003. "Sovereign Risk, Credibility and the Gold Standard: 1870–1913 Versus 1925–31". *The Economic Journal*. Vol. 113. April. pp. 241–275.

Obstfeld, M. and A.M. Taylor. 1998. "The Great Depression as a Watershed: International Capital Mobility over the Long Run" in M.D. Bordo, D.G. Claudia and E.N. Eugene (eds) *The Defining Moment: The Great Depression and the American Economy*. Chicago. The University of Chicago Press. pp. 353–402.

Obstfeld, M., J. Shambaugh and A. Taylor. 2008. "Financial Stability, the Trilemma and International Reserves". Cambridge. MA. National Bureau of Economic Research. Working Paper No. 14217. June.

O'Neill, J. 2008. "Boom Time for the Global Bourgeoisie". *The Financial Times*. 15 July. p. 16.

Organization for Economic Cooperation and Development (OECD). 2009a. *OECD Employment Outlook 2009*. Paris. September.

Organization for Economic Cooperation and Development (OECD). 2009b. *OECD Economic Outlook*. No. 86. Paris. 19 November.

O'Rourke, K. and J.G. Williamson. 2002. "When Did Globalization Really Begin?" Cambridge. MA. National Bureau of Economic Research. Working Paper. No. 7632. April.

Peters, R.T. 2004. *The Ethics of Globalization*. New York. Continuum International Publishing.

Prahalad, C.K. 2004. *Fortune at the Bottom of the Pyramid*. Philadelphia. PA. Wharton School Publishing.

Prasad, E.S. 2009. "India's Approach to Capital Account Liberalization". Bonn. Forschungsinstitut zur Zukunft der Arbeit. The Institute for the Study of Labor (IZA). IZA Discussion Paper No. 3927. January.

Prasad, E.S. 2007. "The Welfare Implications of global Financial Flows". *The Cato Journal*. Vol. 27. No. 2. pp. 185–192.

Prasad, E.S. and M.A. Kose. 2009. "The Financial Crisis and Emerging Markets". Washington. DC. Brookings Institution. Available on the Internet at http://www.brookings.edu/opinions/2008/0924_emerging_markets_prasad.aspx?p=1. 13 July 2009.

Prasad, E.S., K. Rogoff, S.J. Wei and M.A. Kose. 2003. "Effects of Financial Globalization on Developing Countries: Some Empirical Evidence". Washington. DC. International Monetary Fund. Occasional Paper No. 220.

Pula, G. and T.A. Pultonen. 2009. "Has Emerging Asia Decoupled?" Frankfurt. Germany. European Central Bank. Working Paper Series 993. January 2009.

Quinn, D. "The Correlates of Change in International Financial Regulation". *American Political Science Review*. Vol. 91. No. 3. pp. 531–551.

Quinn, D. and A.M. Toyoda. 2008. "Does Capital Account Liberalization Lead to Growth?" *The Review of Financial Studies*. Vol. 21. No. 3. pp. 1403–1449.

Rajan, R.G. and L. Zingales. 2003. *Saving Capitalism from the Capitalists*. New York. Crown Business Division of Random House.

Ravallion, M. 2009. "The Developing World's Bulging (but Vulnerable) Middle Class". Washington. DC. The World Bank. Policy Research Working Paper 4816. January.

Reinhart, C.M. and V.R. Reinhart. 2008. "Capital Flow Bonanzas: An Encompassing View of the Past and Present" in J. Frankel and F. Giavazzi (eds) *NBER International Seminar in International Economics*. Chicago. University of Chicago Press. pp. 188–207.

Reinhart, C.M. and K.S. Rogoff. 2009a. *This Time is Different: Eight Centuries of Financial Folly*. Princeton. NJ. Princeton University Press.

Reinhart, C.M. and K.S. Rogoff. 2009b. "The Aftermath of Financial Crises". *American Economic Review*. Vol. 99. No. 2. pp. 466–472.

Reinhart, C.M. and K.S. Rogoff. 2004a. "The Modern History of Exchange Rate Arrangements: A Reinterpretation". *The Quarterly Journal of Economics*. Vol. CXIX. No. 1. pp. 1–40.

Reinhart, C.M. and K.S. Rogoff. 2004b. "Serial Default and the 'Paradox' of Rich to Poor Capital Flows". *American Economic Review*. Vol. 94. No. 3. pp. 73–95.

Reinhart, C.M., K.S. Rogoff and M.A. Savastano. 2003. "Debt Intolerance" in W. Brainard and G. Perry (eds) *Brookings Papers on Economic Activity*. Vol. 1. Spring. pp. 1–73.

Rios-Morales, R. and L. Brennan. 2009. "The Emergence of SWFs as Contributors of Foreign Direct Investment". Paper Presented at the St. Hugh's College. Oxford University. Oxford. UK, on 24–25 June.

Rodrik, D. and A. Subramanian. 2009. "Why Did Financial Globalization Disappoint?" *IMF Staff Papers*. Vol. 56. No. 1. pp.112–139.

Rodrik, D. 2008. "We Must Curb International Flow of Capital". *The Financial Times*. London. 25 February.

Rodrik, D. 2006. "The Social Costs of Foreign Exchange Reserves". *International Economic Journal*. Vol. 20. No. 3. pp. 253–266.

Rodrik, D. 1998a. "Who Needs Capital Account Convertibility?" in *Should the IMF Pursue Capital Account Convertibility?* Princeton. NJ. Princeton University. Princeton Essays in International Finance. pp. 55–65.

Rodrik, D. 1998b. "Who Needs Capital Account Convertibility?" in *Princeton Essays in International Finance*. No. 207. Princeton. NJ. Princeton University Press.

Rodrik, D. and A. Velasco. 2000. "Short-Term Capital Flows" in B. Plescovic and J.E. Stiglitz (eds) *Annual World Bank Conference on Development Economics*. Washington. DC. The World Bank. pp. 59–70.

Roubini, N. 2009. "The Great Preventer". *The New York Times*. 26 July. p. 18.

SaKong, I. 2009. "The Global Financial Crisis: Causes and Policy". Paper presented at the Annual Bank Conference on Development Economics, on 23 June. Seoul. Republic of Korea.

Schmukler, S.L. 2008. "Benefits and Risks of Financial Globalization" in J. Ocampro and J.E. Stiglitz (eds) *Capital Market Liberalization*. Oxford. Oxford University Press. pp. 48–73.

Schmukler, S.L. 2004. "Financial Globalization: Gain and Pain from Developing Countries". *Economic Review*. Federal Reserve Bank of Atlanta. Quarter 2.
pp. 39–66.

Schmukler, S.L. and E. Vesperoni. 2006. "Financial Globalization and Debt Maturity in Emerging Economies". *The Journal of Development Economics*. Vol. 79.
No. 1. pp. 183–218.

Schularick, M. 2006. "A Tale of Two Globalizations". *International Journal of
Finance and Economics*. Vol. 11. No. 4. pp. 339–354.

Schularick, M. and T.M. Steger. 2008. "Financial Integration, Investment and
Economic Growth". Leipzig. University of Leipzig. Faculty of Economics and
Business Administration. Working Paper No. 75. December.

Schumpeter, J.A. 1912. *Theorie der Wirtschaftlichen Entwicklung*. Leipzig. Germany.
Dunker & Humblot. (*The Theory of Economic Development*. Translated from
German by Redvers Opie. Published in English by Harvard University Press.
Cambridge. MA. 1934).

Shaw, E. 1973. *Financial Deepening in Economic Development*. New York. Oxford
University Press.

Shin, H.S. 2009a. "Securitization and Financial Stability". *The Economic Journal*.
Vol. 119. pp. 309–332. March.

Shin, H.S. 2009b. "Financial Intermediation and Post-Crisis Financial System".
Paper presented at the Eight BIS Annual Conference held at Basel. Switzerland,
during 25–26 June.

Shirakawa, M. 2009. "International Policy Response to Financial Crisis". Paper
presented at the Federal Reserve Bank of Kansas City's *Annual Economic
Symposium on Financial Stability and Macroeconomic Stability* at Jackson Hole.
Wyoming, on 21–22 August.

Solow, R.M. 1956. "A Contribution to the Theory of Economic Growth". *Quarterly
Journal of Economics*. Vol. 70. No. 1. pp. 65–94.

Spehar, A.O. 2009. "The Great Moderation and the New Business Cycle". Munich.
Munich Personal RePEc Archive. MPRA Paper No. 12274. February. Available
on line at http://mpra.ub.uni-muenchen.de/12274/.

Spiegel, M.M. 2008. "Financial Globalization and Monetary Policy Discipline".
(unpublished mimeo).

Steil, B. 2006. "The Developing World Should Abandon Parochial Currencies".
The Financial Times. 16 January. p. 16.

Stiglitz, J.E. 2009. "Explaining the Financial Crisis". Lecture given under
the Emerging Thinking on Global Issues Lecture Series at the United
Nations University, the UN Headquarters. New York, on 24 February. Available on the Internet at http://www.google.ca/search?hl=en&source=hp&q=
joseph+stiglitz+UNU+lecture+february+2009&meta=&aq=f&oq=. 13 April
2009.

Stiglitz, J.E. 2008. "Capital Account Liberalization" in J.E. Stiglitz and J.A.
Ocampo (eds) *Capital Market Liberalization and Development*. New York. Oxford
University Press. pp. 76–100.

Stiglitz, J.E. 2004. "Capital-Market Liberalization, Globalization and the IMF".
Oxford Review of Economic Policy. Vol. 20. No. 1. pp. 57–71.

Stiglitz, J.E. and J.A. Ocampo. 2008. *Capital Market Liberalization and Development*.
New York. Oxford University Press.

Stulz, R. 2005. "The Limits of Financial Globalization". *Journal of Finance*. Vol. 60. No. 4. pp. 1595–1637.

Subramanian, A. 2009. "The G-20: An Idea from India". *The Business Standard*. New Delhi. 28 September. p. 12.

Summers, L. 2007. "Funds that Shake Capitalist Logic". *The Financial Times*. 29 July. p. 9.

Summers, L.H. 2008. "The Future of Market Capitalism". Keynote address at the Global Business Summit, held at the Harvard Business School. Cambridge. MA, on 14 October.

Summers, P.M. 2005. "What Caused the Great Moderation? Some Cross-Country Evidence". Available on the Internet at http://www.kc. Frb.org/Publicat/Econrev/PDF/3q05summ.pdf. 5 November 2009.

Tobin, J. 2000. "Financial Globalization". *World Development*. Vol. 28. No. 6. pp. 1101–1114.

Truman, E.M. 2007. "Sovereign Wealth Funds: The Need for Greater Transparency". Washington. DC. Peterson Institute for International Economics. Policy Brief No. 07-06. August.

Turner, P. 2008. "Financial Globalization and Emerging Market Capital Flows". Bank for International Settlements. Basel. BIS Paper No. 44. December.

Union Bank of Switzerland (UBS). 2009. *Financial Crisis and Its Aftermath*. Zurich. Switzerland.

United Nations Conference on Trade and Development (UNCTAD). 2009. *Trade and Development Report 2009*. Geneva and New York. 7 September.

United Nations-World Institute of Development Economics Research. (UN-WIDER). 1990. *Foreign Portfolio Investment in Emerging Equity Markets*. Helsinki. Finland. Study Group Report No. 5.

United States Department of Commerce (USDC). 2009. "US Current Account Deficit Decreases in Second Quarter 2009". Washington. DC. 16 September. Available on the Internet at http://www.bea.gov/newsreleases/international/transactions/trans_highlights.pdf.

The United States Department of Treasury. 2007. "Semi-Annual Report on International and Exchange Rate Policies". Washington. DC. June.

Valderrama, D. 2008. "Are Global Imbalances Due to Financial Imbalances in the Emerging-Markets". San Francisco. Federal Reserve Bank of San Francisco. *Economic Letter No. 12*. 11 April.

van Hagen, J. and H. Zhang. 2006. "Financial Openness and Macroeconomic Volatility". Bonn. Center for European Integration Studies. Paper No. B-02.

Wang, Q., D. Yam and S. Zhang. 2009. "Upgrade on Stronger-Than-Expected Policy Response". *Global Economic Forum*. New York. Morgan Stanley. 24 April. Available on the Internet at http://www.morganstanley.com/views/gef/archive/2009/20090424-Fri.html#anchor682cdf04-419f-11de-a1b3-c771ef8db296. 14 June 2009.

Warnock, F.E. and V.C. Warnock. 2006. "International Capital Flows and US Interest Rates". Cambridge. MA. National Bureau of Economic Research. Working Paper No. 12560. June.

Wellink, N. 2008. "Financial Globalization, Growth and Asset Prices". Paper presented at a conference on *Globalization, Inflation and Monetary Policy* organized by the Bank of France, in Paris, on 7 March.

Williamson, J.G. 2002. "Winners and Losers over Two Centuries of Globalization". Cambridge. MA. National Bureau of Economic Research. NBER Working Paper 9161. September.

Williamson, J.G. 1996. "Globalization, Convergence and History". *Journal of Economic History*. Vol. 56. No. 2. pp. 277–310.

Wilson, D. and R. Dragusanu. 2008. "The Expanding Middle: The Exploding World Middle Class". New York. Goldman Sachs. July.

Winters, L.A. and S. Yusuf. 2007. *Dancing with Giants*. Washington. DC. The World Bank.

Wolf, M. 2009. "Why China do More to Rebalance its Economy". *The Financial Times*. 22 September. p. 12.

Wolf, M. 2008a. "Global Imbalances Threaten the Survival of Liberal Trade". *The Financial Times*. London. 2 December.

Wolf, M. 2008b. *Fixing Global Finance*. Baltimore. Maryland. The Johns Hopkins University Press.

Wong, A. 2009. "Sovereign Wealth Funds and the Problem of Asymmetric Information". *Brooklyn Journal of International Law*. Vol. 34. No. 3. pp. 1082–1109.

Woodruff, W. 1966. *The Impact of Western Man*. London. The Macmillan Press Ltd.

The World Bank (WB). 2009a. *Global Development Finance: Charting a Global Recovery*. Washington. DC. 22 June.

The World Bank (WB). 2009b. *World Development Indicator*. Washington. DC. July 2009.

The World Bank (WB). 2009c. *China Quarterly Update*. Beijing. 30 June.

The World Bank (WB). 2008. *Global Development Finance 2008*. Washington. DC.

The World Bank (WB). 2007. *Global Economic Outlook*. Washington. DC.

World Investment Report 2009 (WIR). 2009. Geneva ad New York. United Nations Conference on Trade and Development. 17 September.

World Trade Indicators 2008 (WTI). Washington. DC. The World Bank.

World Trade Organization (WTO). 2009. "World Trade 2008, Prospects for 2009". Geneva. Switzerland. WTO Press Release No. 554. 23 March.

Xu, B. 2000. "Multinational Enterprises, Technology Diffusion and Host Country Productivity Growth". *Journal of Development Economics*. Vol. 62. No. 2. pp. 477–493.

Zoellick, R.B. 2009. "After the Crisis?" Speech delivered at the Paul H. Nitze School of Advanced International Studies of the Johns Hopkins University. Washington. DC, on September.

Index